PERESTROIKA IN ACTION

A Collection
of Press Articles
and Interviews

Edited by *Vladimir Mezhenkov*
and *Eva Skelley*

London and Wellingborough

First published in Great Britain by
Collet's (Publishers) Limited
Denington Estate
Wellingborough
Northants, NN8 2QT

Selection by Collets
and Progress Publishers
Selection and English translation © Copyright Progress Publishers 1988

Printed in the USSR

Contents

FROM THE EDITORS

Optimistically, we thought our editorial difficulties would drastically diminish after our first volume. Rashly, we even said so. But the fierce pace of social and political developments — not to mention the vast quantity of commentary they generate — confronts us with obvious problems of selection and 'up-to-dateness'.

Totally iconoclastic ideas, expressed with breathtaking bravado in what were previously 'establishment', essentially conservative organs, are taken for granted by the public within months, or even weeks. Before the dust can settle, a new onslaught is unleashed against some other hitherto sanctified notion.

The Soviet press has undergone an astonishing metamorphosis, becoming transformed in a manner that can scarcely be credited. The public appetite for the diet it provides is insatiable. And we must try to convey this spirit in *Soviet Scene...*

The stark light cast by *glasnost* into dark corners has changed the Soviet intellectual scene—permanently, we believe. *Glasnost*, cauterising old sores, ventilating current problems, is there to stay.

But can one be as certain about the outcome of *perestroika*, the fundamental restructuring and regeneration of the political and economic basis of Soviet society?

One thing more than anything else needs to be understood about Gorbachev's conception of *perestroika*. It is not seen as a 'spectator sport', with masses of people on the sidelines and a few protagonists in the arena. Neither is it a matter of searching out 'devils' in the leadership, uncovering the 'goodies' and the 'baddies'.

The make or break issue, the unavoidable challenge Gorbachev must meet, is the vital one of winning the hearts and minds of the people and their involvement in the entire process. As Gorbachev puts it, *perestroika* must become the practical business of millions of people. As that begins to happen the bureaucrats and the work-shy will be thrown aside.

A small, but significant example of this process at work will be found on pages 148-161, where we carry forward the story begun in *Soviet Scene 1987* * about the workers of the Riga Bus Factory who, in a situation of declining production, elected a new director. The snags and the successes are frankly discussed by the workers after one year's hectic experience of self-management and the incredibly difficult — and elusive — objective of profitability...

Whilst *Soviet Scene 1988* includes material on general policy, it is the processes set in motion to involve the overwhelming mass of the people, to integrate them into the management of production and government, which we have endeavoured to reveal in the selection of many of the items included.

One reviewer, welcoming the book, nevertheless urges us to avoid 'open propaganda'. Anxious as we are to please, that's quite a difficult one. This is the kind of project for human betterment that provokes partisanship ... and that is our position, it must be said. But please be assured, we welcome readers' comments and suggestions.

Fascinating as it is to observe these Soviet developments, there is plenty of evidence abroad to show that the conviction is widespread that the changes are not simply of domestic importance. We are encouraged by our modest success. The English language edition of *Soviet Scene 1987* sold almost 20,000 copies. We hope the 1988 edition will reach even wider afield.

October 1988   Vladimir MEZHENKOV

                         Eva SKELLEY

---

*   *Soviet Scene 1987*, p. 92.

19th **National Party Conference**

*From June 28 to July 1, 1988, the 19th National Confer-
ence of the Communist Party of the Soviet Union was held in
Moscow, in the Kremlin Palace of Congresses. Its work and
the resolutions adopted aroused avid interest not only in the
USSR, but throughout the world. In our next issue,* Soviet
Scene 1989, *we will tell you about how these resolutions are
being put into practice. Meanwhile, we would like to acquaint
our readers with some of the foreign media's responses to the
conference, and offer an article by* ALEXANDER GUBER.

*Moscow, July 1. — ... Although the concrete effect of the con-
ference on the political system remains to be seen — and will
depend on how the resolutions are put into operation — the
meeting clearly altered the political climate.*

*More than any event since Mr. Gorbachev took office in
March 1985, the conference shattered the stifling political
customs of the Soviet system, making candor, pointed debate,
even public confrontation between party leaders acceptable...*

By Philip Taubman
(Special for The New York Times)

*...East-West relations were now on a better footing than
for many years, Sir Geoffrey Howe, Foreign Secretary, said
when opening a Commons debate on foreign affairs.*

*A great deal depended on the effect of Mr. Gorbachev's at-
tempts to reform the Soviet Union. This week, a drama of
much potential significance was being played out in Moscow.*

Thanks to glasnost *and the television cameras, they could
follow the proceedings of the first party conference since 1941
with a good deal more insight into party workings than usual.*

*They could not yet know the outcome, but the fact that
there was at least the beginning of a genuine debate was im-
mensely encouraging. They all admired the courage and determination of Mr. Gorbachev in tackling the failings of Soviet society.*

The Times, *London*

*...Moscow, July 1. Not since the early days of the Bolshevik
revolution has there been a political debate in the Soviet hie-
rarchy as public and emotional as the one that took place in
the Kremlin today.*

*Boris Yeltsin, the former Moscow party chief who was fi-
red in disgrace from the ruling Politburo, made an emotional — but apparently futile — bid for "political rehabilitation" at the closing session of the Communist Party's special
conference.*

*Soviet viewers were glued to the evening news program,
"Vremya", as they watched Yeltsin's impassioned appeal for
clemency, Ligachev's angry personal rebuttal and Gorbachev's own definitive critique. The affair dominated the final
day of what has been the most dramatic Communist Party
meeting in recent Soviet history.*

By David Remnick, Washington Post

*Today's discussions are interesting, because as opposed to
previous forums, where the reasons for difficulties were
sought in the past, attention is now being directed towards
analyzing and critically assessing mistakes made in the course
of the last three years, i.e. in the period of* perestroika. *Emphasis is being placed on inconsistency in carrying out reforms and on the marked unpreparedness of Party and administrative apparatus to renounce their administrative-
command positions. ★*

Politika, *Yugoslavia*

*Attracting special attention is the proposal to elect repre-
sentatives of Party, trade-union, youth and other social organizations to the Congress of People's Deputies of the USSR.
It would seem that Mikhail Gorbachev is in this way seeking*

★   Retranslated from the Russian.

to create a political force out of those who hold the most re-formist positions. Important in this connection is the question of whether delegates from unofficial organizations will be able to take part in this organ of state power.

Asahi, *Japan*

Despite an overall visible unanimity, the delegates to the conference are voicing criticism in their addresses. Representatives of the various republics understand the perestroika *being proclaimed in the USSR in different ways. In any case, their statements and speeches create a rather heterogeneous picture of the life of Soviet state, since each speaker was talking about what is taking place within their particular republic or factory.* *

Libération, *France*

Fresh impetus to perestroika

Notes on the 19th CPSU Conference

It was a conference that resembled no previous Party forum. What can one say about it, when so much has already been said and written? There are, in my view, two starting points: the comparison with what existed before it, and the comparison with what we expected from it. And we expected a lot, forgetting at times the real possibilities, forgetting that only three years ago our hopes were much more modest; today they have been fulfilled, so we are beginning to take them for granted.

Compared with the past, the present Party conference stands head and shoulders above any of its predecessors for its democracy and the depth of discussion, the pluralism of views, the sincerity of all the speeches, and the boldness of the decisions adopted.

To compare it with our expectations would be the virtual equivalent of comparing a live person with an ideal. Not all the delegates, not all the speeches satisfied us, some liked

* Retranslated from the Russian.

some, while others liked others. It could not have been otherwise. The composition of the delegates reflected the state of Soviet society: the overwhelming majority are in favour, in principle, of continuing *perestroika*, but far from everyone shares the same views as to how this should be done in practice. And when at times from the rostrum of the conference we detected a false note, we forgot that others might perceive it differently.

The conference was held in the spirit encouraged by Lenin: the spirit of great responsibility to the people and the revolution triumphed. Attempts to deviate from the Leninist line were given a strong rebuff.

Time will have to pass before we can fully appreciate the significance of the conference and its decisions. But it is already absolutely clear that it was a major landmark in the course of *perestroika*. The decisions it elaborated are an integral part of *perestroika* and at the same time a catalyst for renewal.

The principal result of the conference, Mikhail Gorbachev pointed out in his concluding speech, is that a programmed political stand has been drawn up on all the basic issues that have been the subject of discussion by the entire Party and the entire people on the basis of the CC CPSU motions.

The first reaction to Gorbachev's speech both in the conference hall and outside it was: how unexpected and how typical of him! The speech contained none of customary unambiguous answers to many of the questions that troubled the Party and the people. We were all used to a different style: Party and state forums open with a report where all the t's are crossed, all the i's dotted, so that further discussions are reduced chiefly to approval of the points made in the report and minimum amendments. This time, and therein lies the new style of the report, plenty of room was left for discussion of the most significant issues. Both from the rostrum and in the conference lobby delegates argued, at times expressing diametrically opposite veiws, and not merely pretending to be looking for the truth which had long been found, but genuinely seeking it. Gradually we came to understand that it was time we got used to such reports and such discussions. But how difficult it is to get used to that and adapt not simply to approving what the leader says with stormy applause, but to taking a real part in drafting decisions, taking a certain public stand, without knowing for certain how it will be received 'at the top'.

The conference showed that most people in the Party were ready for this. About 300 people put down their names to speak in the discussions. About 150 had their say in the commissions editing the resolutions. But the main thing is how the delegates spoke and what they said. They not only supported the proposals made by the CC CPSU, but substantially enriched them with the experience of Party organisations and work collectives. The discussions at the conference carried on and in effect developed the new political atmosphere in the country, the atmosphere of liberated creativity, which has come into being in the three years of *perestroika*.

The words from the rostrum were received by various delegates differently: there was none of the past proverbial unanimity. This different reception reflected the system under which the delegates were elected. The Party had not seen such elections for more than half a century. In many cases Communists really had elected those they deemed worthy, and not by injunction. Consequently those who were taking part in such forums previously saw many new faces. There were far fewer 'wedding generals' who had appeared in the Kremlin only to ensure that the report of the credentials commission should have the right percentage of workers, collective farmers, women and young people...

The existence at the elections of a so-called central list, under which senior officials from Moscow were elected as delegates by Party organisations in other republics and regions, sharply increased the representation at the conference of the Party and, to some extent, the state apparatus. Some of this group of delegates had obtained their credentials not for their merits in advancing *perestroika*, but as if they were owed there by virtue of the posts they held.

So it was only natural that apparatus officials reacted very coolly to such statements from speakers as the following:

'Such a system (centralised distribution of funds amongst the local Soviets) produces the illusion that a central apparatus is both necessary and important, and that one must go begging to it for every rouble' (Vadim Bakatin, First Secretary of the Kemerovo regional Party committee).

'It will be possible to take away from the apparatus the right to command they have usurped, and I am firmly convinced that this will only be possible if the economy is democratised. It must be made a law that only he who earns the money has the right to dispose of it'(Dmitry Motorny, Chairman of the Kirov collective farm, Kherson Region).

'In general we are used to believing in the power of decrees and the possibility of changing things by new decisions. But experience does not confirm this' (Leonid Abalkin, Director of the Institute of Economics of the USSR Academy of Sciences).

The few mistakes made in the elections did not affect the principal outcome of the conference: it approved the programme for the further development of *perestroika* and for democratisation. It happened just as Svyatoslav Fyodorov, the famous eye surgeon and delegate to the conference, had predicted. On the eve of the forum I asked him for his reaction to press reports of certain violations of democracy in the election of delegates. 'These reports,' he said, 'should be thoroughly checked. But in principle such cases change nothing. The conference will still come out in favour of *perestroika*. That is what the overwhelming majority of the people want. And I doubt if anyone will come out against.'

In the past it happened that delegates wrote their speeches well in advance and read them out, no matter what had been said by others. That was the general rule, and most people had more or less become used to it. This time the rule was entirely different. Most speakers obviously changed their texts so as not to repeat points that had already been made and to reply to questions that had come up in the debate. But not all. Y. Surkov, a worker from the Moscow factory for processing special alloys, remarked in this connection: 'The conference has very little time left. And I can't sit back and watch this time being wasted by some speakers. In this connection, I should like to draw attention to the fact that, strange as it may seem, in the speeches of the first secretaries one can sense the old stereotype.'

Having pronounced these words — absolutely unimaginable in the Palace of Congresses before, he continued:

'The Party is working badly at bringing up leaders... I believe that attention should be focussed on leaders, on training them and removing all the barriers in their way. If we had everywhere a leader who could find his bearings and get the masses to follow him, there would have been no such appeals as we heard here when some delegates appealed to Comrade Gorbachev to come personally to their place and see what's happening and resolve the problem.'

You don't know whether to be glad that such words should have come from the rostrum or to be sad that they reflect the realities.

The subject of leaders was also touched on by other delegates. The Director-General of the Microsurgery of the Eye scientific and technical complex, Svyatoslav Fyodorov, for instance, said that when the Public Health Ministers of the Union republics visited him they looked around, full of admiration, but said — we'd never be able to do such a thing. Why? 'We don't have the leaders', they explained. How can one believe that a great nation cannot produce leaders? What's the matter? Can't the Party train leaders? That is exactly what it ought to be doing! The conference did not specifically consider the problem of leaders, but it arose from the more general problem of the Party as the political vanguard. Under the command-administrative system, for instance, the secretary of the district committee was considered the leader, because he could command everything and everyone. And it was hard to draw a line between his personal authority and respect for his office. Now the Party is consciously renouncing the authority of the office a person holds. Party functionaries will have to prove their right to leadership each time by concrete actions.

I'm afraid that not all the Party secretaries who spoke in the Kremlin will be able to cope with such a task. And the more clearly they understand that, the harder they will find it to abandon the system that produced and maintained them.

'People say bluntly: if you find it impossible to control the departments, we shall find the means to bring you to heel,' said the First Secretary of the CC of the Latvian Communist Party Boris Pugo. Did you notice the new way the problem was put? The departments in question were the central ones, which republican Party bodies could do nothing about, while from their fellow citizens they were protected by the 'authority of their office' and could shrug their shoulders and reply, 'it doesn't depend on us'. A leader cannot take such a convenient stand. The people will no longer allow it. At no level.

'Incidentally, when we meet with the people they say bluntly: "We have no idea for what concrete issues each member of the Politbureau is personally responsible". The people should know such things so that they can see and judge how they cope. Whom to thank for successes or whom to blame for failures' (Veniamin Yarin, rolling mill operator at the Tagil Metallurgical Plant).

An interesting exchange took place during the speech of the General Director of the Broiler Producing Association Stavropolskoye Victor Postnikov. Turning to Mikhail Gorbachev, he said: 'Mikhail Sergeyevich, *perestroika* is a revolution. You said that we shall seek to carry it through calmly, using humane methods. But if it's a revolution then it can't be implemented by such methods. It's useless to keep trying to persuade people, to teach, for example, bureaucrats. We know that in this hall too there are opponents of *perestroika* and you can't do anything with them — they have to be kicked out and expelled from the Party.'

From Mikhail Gorbachev's reply: 'I think that if the CC again begins removing the bureaucrats sitting next to you in the Stavropol Area or even in your Association, or perhaps higher up, in the Russian Federation, or somewhere else, we won't get anywhere. That has already been tried. We have tried to do a great deal from the top. Nothing has come of it. Today we are trying to get all of society moving by means of an economic reform, a reform of the political system, an improvement in the general climate, through the mass media. Then the bureaucrat will have nowhere to turn to — the ground will sink from under his feet. That is what he is afraid of.'

That is the essence of the matter: to create a public mechanism through which the people themselves will be involved in deciding all issues, and no matter can be decided over their heads.

This mechanism presupposes the active daily participation of the mass media in the life of society. And although everybody seems to understand the role of the press in *perestroika*, the conference revealed that there were differences of opinion as to how it should play its role.

Grigory Baklanov, editor-in-chief of the magazine *Znamya*, said: 'Throughout history people have fought for their own enslavement with an energy and passion that is permissible only in fighting for their freedom. When the 1937 trials were taking place in the Hall of Columns and people came out with posters demanding the death sentence, they didn't suspect that soon they would be treated in the same way. He who today fights *glasnost* is fighting for his own enslavement. When he wants to speak out, he will not be allowed to. And what kind of socialism is it without *glasnost*? And, comrades, have we only just had a sip of freedom and everybody has choked on it? Have they started coughing?'

Some of those present did not like Baklanov's words. Perhaps he was saying something that everybody already knew? It would be fine if that were the case. But what makes one wary is the clearly approving reaction of delegates to any criticism of the press. One can only wonder if Party functionaries prefer an obedient press they can keep in their pockets.

The conference discussed changes not only in the style of work of Party bodies, but also in their structure. 'The truth today is also that many Party cadres, who for years have been orientated to technocratic methods, are not ready to work differently. We select for the Party apparatus, as has already been underlined here, not political commissars, but people working in industry, construction, trade, etc. Take a look at the structure of the apparatus of the CC CPSU: it is not only the Ministries and Departments, but also their sub-branches that are represented in the sections of the CC apparatus. That largely predetermines the structure and style of work of area, regional and district Party committees. We fully support the proposal to abandon the branch principle of the structure of the Party apparatus' (Ivan Polozkov, First Secretary of the Krasnodar Area Party committee).

Delegates were worried about the fact that the bureaucratic system still lives on, having remained virtually unscathed, and is prepared to defend itself.

In my opinion this well-founded alarm was expressed most vividly by the General Director of the Ivanovo machine tool production association Vladimir Kabaidze: 'Those damn papers are growing. I have realized one thing: it is hopeless to fight papers — one has to fight their authors.'

So it was only natural that the conference should have adopted a special resolution 'On combating bureaucracy.'

That resolution and all the others adopted by the conference are called upon to ensure the all-round democratisation of society.

Seventy years of the **Revolution**

What has changed

In his speech, 'October and *Perestroika*: the Revolution Continues', *Mikhail Gorbachev places the October Revolution in the context of the changing international situation and reaffirms his commitment to work for a world made safer by measures of nuclear disarmament and agreement amongst the great powers.*

The extract from the speech we include in Soviet Scene *is devoted mainly to the process of* perestroika. *In these passages Gorbachev is clearly at pains to emphasise that the break with old methods of work, bureaucracy and incompetence, the extension of* glasnost *and democratisation, does not imply in any way a dilution of the socialist basis of Soviet society, but rather a determined move towards the fulfilment of the socialist aims of Lenin.*

The celebrations of the 70th anniversary, for which this was the keynote speech, were conducted in a very different way this year. They were made the occasion for a businesslike review, focusing on outstanding problems. There was an absence of pomposity and rhetoric. The change in concept was evident from the visual aspect too: there were fewer banners, fewer posters with slogans. The military element was also substantially curtailed.

Foreign guests were agreed that the character of the event this time reflected the changes taking place in the country and that it gave a new importance to values that have been understressed—or ignored—in the past. Glasnost, *too, was alive and kicking on this occasion, and there were masses of witnesses!*

Many round-table meetings were arranged with foreign visitors, at which Communists, Social Democrats, Socialists, Greens and others from the advanced countries and the newly developing states got together to discuss common problems. Not so long ago this kind of social, political and religious

interchange of views in Moscow would have been unthinkable.
It is a good sign for the future, surely...

MIKHAIL GORBACHEV: HUMANITY'S FINEST HOUR

The year 1917 showed that the choice between socialism and capitalism is the main social alternative of our time..., stressed Mikhail Gorbachev, General Secretary of the CPSU Central Committee, in his report 'October and *Perestroika*: the Revolution Continues'.

Marxism-Leninism is a creative theory, not a set of ready-made guidelines and doctrinaire prescriptions. Alien to all forms of dogma, a sound Marxist-Leninist approach ensures vigorous interaction between innovative thought and practice, with the very course of the revolutionary struggle...

About Historical Truth

It is essential to assess the past with a sense of historical responsibility and on the basis of historical truth... We need honest assessments ... especially now with restructuring in full swing. We need them not to settle political scores or, as they say, to let off steam, but to pay due homage to all the heroic deeds in the past, and to draw lessons from mistakes and miscalculations.

Trotsky and the Trotskyists denied the possibility of building socialism in conditions of capitalist encirclement. In foreign policy they put their stakes on the export of revolution, and in home policy on tightening the screws on the peasants; on the city exploiting the countryside, and on administrative and military methods to control society. Trotskyism was a political trend whose ideologists took cover behind leftist pseudo-revolutionary rhetoric, and who in effect assumed a defeatist posture. This was actually an attack on Leninism all along the line. The issue was central to the future of socialism in our country, the fate of the Revolution.

In these circumstances it was essential to disprove Trotskyism before the whole people, and expose its anti-socialist essence. The situation was complicated by the fact that the Trotskyists were acting in concert with the 'new opposition' headed by Grigori Zinoviev and Lev Kamenev. Aware that they constituted a minority, the opposition leaders had again and again saddled the Party with discussions, counting on a split in its ranks. But in the final analysis the Party spoke out for the line of the Central Committee and against the opposition, which was soon ideologically and organisationally demolished.

In short, the Party's leading nucleus headed by Joseph Stalin had safeguarded Leninism in an ideological struggle. It defined the strategy and tactics at the initial stage of socialist construction and its political course was approved by most members of the Party and most working people. An important part in defeating Trotskyism ideologically was played by Nikolai Bukharin, Felix Dzerzhinsky, Sergei Kirov, Grigori Ordjonikidze, Jan Rudzutak, and others.

The end of the 1920s saw a sharp controversy emerge as to how to bring the peasantry over to the socialist road. It revealed the different attitudes of the majority in the Political Bureau as against the Bukharin group on how to apply the principles of the new economic policy at the new stage in the development of Soviet society.

The concrete conditions of that time — both at home and internationally — necessitated a considerable increase in the pace of socialist construction. Bukharin and his followers had, in their calculations and theoretical propositions, underrated the practical significance of the time factor in building socialism in the 1930s. In many ways, their position was based on dogmatic thinking and a non-dialectical assessment of the circumstances. Bukharin himself and his followers soon admitted their mistakes...

...The political discussions of that time reflected a complex process in the Party's development, and were marked by a sharp difference of views on crucial problems of socialist construction. In that unavoidable controversy the concept of industrialisation and collectivisation took shape.

The Party mapped out an entirely new approach to industrialisation: to begin building a heavy industry at once, without reliance on external sources of finance, and without waiting years for capital to accumulate through the expansion of light industry. This was the only possible way in those conditions, though it was incredibly difficult for the country and the people. It was an innovative step in which the revolutionary enthusiasm of the masses was taken into account as a vital component for economic growth. Industrialisation raised the country to a fundamentally new level in one jump.

...The period under review also saw some losses. They were in a sense connected with the successes to which I have just referred. Some had begun to believe in the universal effectiveness of rigid centralisation, and that methods of command were the shortest and best way of resolving all problems. This had an effect on the attitude towards people, towards their conditions of life.

A system of administrative command in Party and government leadership emerged in the country, and bureaucracy gained strength, even though Lenin had warned against the danger. And a corresponding structure of administration and planning methods began to take shape. In industry — given its scale at the time, when literally all the main components of the industrial scene were all in view, such methods, such a system of administration generally produced results. However, an equally rigid centralisation-and-command system was impermissible in tackling the problems of refashioning rural life.

Today it is clear: in a tremendous undertaking, which affected the fate of the majority of the country's population, there was a departure from Lenin's policy towards the peasantry... Flagrant violations of the principles of collectivisation occurred everywhere. Nor were excesses avoided in the struggle against the kulaks. The basically correct policy of fighting the kulaks was often interpreted so broadly that it took in a considerable part of the middle peasantry too. Such is the reality of history.

But, comrades, if we assess the significance of collectivisation as a whole in consolidating socialism in the countryside, in the final analysis it was a transformation of fundamental importance. Collectivisation implied changing the entire mode of life of the preponderant part of the country's population to a socialist footing. It created the social base for modernising the agrarian sector, and gearing it to accept advanced farming techniques; it made possible a considerable rise in the productivity of labour, and it released substantial manpower needed for other spheres of socialist construction. All this had historic effects.

To understand the situation of those years it must be borne in mind that the administrative-command system, which had begun to take shape in the process of industrialisation and which had received fresh impetus during collectivisation, had affected the whole socio-political life of the country. Once established in the economy it spread to its superstructure, restricting the development of the democratic potential of socialism and holding back the progress of socialist democracy...

Quite obviously, it was the absence of a proper level of democratisation in Soviet society that made possible the personality cult, the violations of legality, and the wanton repressive measures of the thirties. Putting things bluntly — they were real crimes stemming from an abuse of power. Many thousands of people inside and outside the Party were subjected to wholesale reprisals. Such, comrades, is the bitter truth. Serious damage was done to the cause of socialism and to the authority of the Party. And we must state this bluntly. This is necessary to reassert Lenin's ideal of socialism.

There is now much discussion about the role of Stalin in our history. His was an extremely contradictory personality. To be faithful to historical truth we must see both Stalin's incontestable contribution to the struggle for socialism, to the defence of its gains, and the gross political errors, and also the abuses committed by him and by those around him, for which our people paid a heavy price and which had grave consequences for life in our society. It is sometimes said that Stalin did not know about instances of lawlessness. Documents at our disposal show that this is not so. The guilt of Stalin and his immediate entourage before the Party and the people for the wholesale repressive measures and acts of lawlessness is enormous and unforgivable. This is a lesson for all generations.

Contrary to the assertions of our ideological opponents, the personality cult was certainly not inevitable. It was alien to the nature of socialism, represented a departure from its fundamental principles, and, therefore, has no justification. At its 20th and 22nd Congresses the Party severely condemned the Stalin cult itself and its consequences. We now know that the political accusations and repressive measures against a number of Party leaders and statesmen, against many Communists and non-Party people, against economic executives and military men, against scientists and cultural personalities were a result of deliberate falsification.

...The Political Bureau of the Central Committee has set up a commission to examine comprehensively new and known facts and documents pertaining to these matters. Appropriate decisions will be taken on the basis of the commission's findings.

In drawing up a balance-sheet of the period of the twenties and thirties after Lenin, we can say that we have covered a difficult road, replete with contradictions and complexities, but a truly heroic one. Neither gross errors, nor departures from the principles of socialism could divert our people, our country from the road it embarked upon by the choice it made in 1917. The momentum of the October Revolution was too great! The ideas of socialism that had gripped the masses were too strong! The people felt themselves involved in a great effort and began enjoying the fruits of their work. Their patriotism acquired a new, socialist meaning.

It may be said with confidence: the years of the Great Patriotic War are one of the most glorious and heroic periods in the history of the Party, marked by courage and valour, by the supreme dedication and self-sacrifice of millions of Communists. The war showed that the Soviet people, the Party, socialism, and the October Revolution are inseparable and that nothing on earth can shatter this unity.

Socialism did not just stand fast and did not simply achieve victory. It emerged from this most terrible and destructive of wars stronger morally and politically, having enhanced its authority and influence throughout the world.

It was the heroism inherent in the day-to-day work in those difficult postwar years that was the source of our economic, scientific and technical achievements, the harnessing of atomic energy, our first space flights, improved living standards and a higher level of education and culture.

But at the very same time a contradiction between the advanced society we had become and the old methods of leadership was making itself felt ever more. Abuses of power and violations of socialist legality continued. The 'Leningrad case' and the 'doctors' case' were fabricated. In effect there was a lack of genuine respect for the people. People were devotedly working, studying, seeking new knowledge, accepting difficulties and shortages, but experiencing a pent-up sense of alarm welling up in society. This gripped public consciousness soon after Stalin's death.

In the mid-fifties, especially after the 20th Congress of the Communist Party, a wind of change swept the country, the people's spirits rose, they took heart, became bolder and more confident. It required no small courage of the Party and its leadership headed by Nikita Khrushchev to criticise the personality cult and its consequences, and to re-establish socialist legality. The old stereotypes in domestic and foreign policy began to crumble. Attempts were made to break down the command-bureaucratic methods of administration established in the thirties and the forties, to make socialism more dynamic, to emphasise humanitarian ideals and values, and to revive the creative spirit of Leninism in theory and practice.

The desire to change the priorities of economic development, to bring into play incentives to stimulate a personal interest in work results was the keynote of the decisions of the September 1953 and July 1955 Plenary Meetings of the Party Central Committee. More attention was devoted to the development of agriculture, housing, light industry, the sphere of consumption, and to everything related to satisfying human needs.

In short, there were changes for the better — in Soviet society and in international relations. However, no small number of subjectivist errors were committed, restricting the advance of socialism to a new stage, moreover doing much to discredit progressive initiatives. The fact is that fundamentally new problems of domestic and foreign policy and of Party development were often being tackled by voluntaristic methods, by invoking the old political and economic mechanism. But the failures of the reforms undertaken in that period were mainly due to the fact that they were not backed up by a broad development of democratisation.

At the October 1964 Plenary Meeting of the Party Central Committee there was a change of leadership of the party and the country, and decisions were taken to overcome voluntaristic tendencies and distortions in domestic and foreign policy. The Party sought to achieve a certain stability in policy, and to ensure it was realistic and consistent.

The March and September 1965 Plenary Meetings of the Party Central Committee formulated new approaches to economic management. Economic reform and big programmes for the development of new areas and the promotion of the productive forces were worked out and put into effect. In the first few years this changed the situation in the country for the better. The economic and scientific potential was increasing, defence capacity was being strengthened, and the standard of living was rising. Many foreign policy moves enhanced the international prestige of our state. Military strategic parity with the USA was achieved.

The country was rich in resources for accelerating development. But to utilise these resources effectively, cardinal changes were essential in society and, of course, the corresponding political will. There was a shortage of both. And even much of what had been decided remained on paper, was left suspended in midair. The pace of development was substantially retarded.

At the April 1985 Plenary Meeting of its Central Committee and at its 27th Congress the party identified frankly the causes of the situation that had arisen and laid bare the bad practices retarding our development.

It was stated that in the latter years of the life and activities of Leonid Brezhnev the search for methods of advance had been hampered by an addiction to habitual formulas and schemes which had no connection with the new reality. The gap between word and deed had widened. Negative processes in the economy were gathering weight and had, in effect, created a pre-crisis situation. Many aberrations had arisen in the social, spiritual and moral spheres, which were distorting and deforming the principles of socialist justice, undermining people's faith in it, and generating social alienation and immorality in various forms. The growing discrepancy between the lofty principles of socialism and the everyday realities of life was becoming intolerable.

About *Perestroika*

Perestroika implies not only eliminating the stagnation and conservatism of the preceding period and correcting the mistakes committed, but also overcoming historically limited, outdated features of social organisation and work methods. It implies imparting to socialism the most contemporary forms, corresponding to the conditions and needs of the scientific and technological revolution, and to the intellectual progress of Soviet society. This is a relatively lengthy process of the revolutionary renewal of society, a process that has its own logic and stages.

The purpose of *perestroika* is the full theoretical and practical re-establishment of Lenin's concept of socialism, in which indisputable priority belongs to the working man and woman and their ideals and interests, to humanitarian values in the economy, social and political relations, and in culture.

Our aim of achieving revolutionary purification and renewal requires tapping the enormous social potentialities of socialism by invigorating the individual, the human factor. As an outcome of *perestroika* socialism can and must make full use of its potentialities as a truly humanitarian system serving and elevating mankind. This is a society for people, for the flourishing of their creative work, wellbeing, health, physical and spiritual development, a society where men and women *feel* they are in charge.

Two key problems of the development of society determine the fate of *perestroika*. These are the democratisation of all social life and radical economic reform.

Today we can say that we are entering a new stage of *perestroika*...

The difficulty of the forthcoming period also lies in the

fact that the transformations will come to affect the interests of ever greater masses of people, social groups and strata, and of all cadres. We are confident that widespread support for *perestroika* by the people and a profound understanding of the need for the changes, for the vigorous and unflagging pursuit of *perestroika*, despite the difficulties arising, will continue to shape the situation in our country.

But it would be a mistake to ignore a certain increase in the resistance of the conservative forces that see *perestroika* simply as a threat to their selfish interests and objectives. This resistance can be felt at management level and also in work collectives...

We should learn to spot, expose and neutralise the manoeuvres of the opponents of *perestroika* — those who act to impede our advance and trip us up, who gloat over our difficulties and setbacks, who try to drag us back into the past. Nor should we succumb to the pressure of the overly zealous and impatient — those who refuse to accept the objective logic of *perestroika*, who voice their disappointment with what they regard as a slow rate of change, who claim that this or that change does not yield the necessary results fast enough. It should be clear that one cannot leap over essential stages and attempt to accomplish everything at one go.

About the Philosophy of Peace

Comrades, without the Great Revolution in Russia, the world would not be what it is today. Before that turning point in world history, the 'right' of the strong and the rich, as well as annexationist wars, were a standard feature of international relations. The Soviet government, which promulgated the famous Decree on Peace as its first legal act, rose against this state of affairs and introduced into international practice something that had hitherto been excluded from 'big politics' — the people's common sense and the interests of the working masses.

It was a major achievement of the founder of the Soviet state that he discerned in good time the actual prospects the victory in the Civil War opened before the new Russia. He realised that the country had secured not merely a 'breath-ing-space' but something much more important — 'a new period, in which we have won the right to our fundamental international existence in the network of capitalist states'. In a resolute step, Lenin suggested a policy of learning and mastering the art of long-term 'existence side by side' with them. Countering leftist extremism, he argued that it was possible for countries with different social systems to co-exist peacefully.

Naturally, not all our subsequent foreign policy efforts were successful. We have had our share of setbacks. We did not make full use of all the opportunities that opened be-fore us both before and after World War II. We failed to translate the enormous moral prestige with which the So-viet Union emerged from the war into effective efforts to consolidate the peaceloving, democratic forces and to stop those who orchestrated the Cold War. We did not always respond wisely to imperialist provocations.

It is true that some things could have been tackled better and that we could have been more efficient. Nevertheless, we can say on this memorable occasion that the fundamen-tal line of our policy has remained in concert with the basic course worked out and charted by Lenin — consistent with the very nature of socialism, with its principled commit-ment to peace.

This was without doubt instrumental in averting the out-break of a nuclear war and in preventing imperialism from winning the Cold War. Together with our allies, we de-feated the imperialist strategy of 'rolling back socialism'. Imperialism had to curb its claims to world domination. The results of our peace-loving policy were what we could draw on at this new stage to devise fresh approaches in the spirit of the new thinking.

Naturally, there have been changes in the Lenin concept of peaceful coexistence. At first it was needed above all to create the minimum external conditions for the construc-tion of a new society in our country. Continuing the class-based policy of the victorious proletariat, peaceful coexist-ence subsequently became a condition for the survival of the entire human race, especially in the nuclear age.

The April 1985 Plenary Meeting of the CPSU Central Committee was a landmark in the development of Leninist thought along this line. The new concept of foreign policy was presented in detail at the 27th Congress. As you know, this concept proceeds from the idea that in spite of all the profound contradictions of the contemporary world, all the radical differences among the countries that comprise it, the world is interrelated, interdependent and integral.

The reasons for this include the internationalisation of the world's economic links, the comprehensive scope of the scientific and technological revolution, the essentially novel role played by the mass media, the state of the Earth's resources, the common environmental danger, and the crying social problems of the developing world which affect us all. The main reason, however, is the question of human survival. This problem is now with us because the development of nuclear weapons and the threatening prospect of their use have called into question the very existence of the human race.

This is how Lenin's ideas on the priority of the interests of social development acquired a new meaning and a new importance.

Acting jointly with the other countries of the socialist community, we have submitted several important initiatives to the United Nations, including a project for devising a comprehensive system of international peace and security. The Warsaw Treaty states have addressed NATO and all European countries with a proposal on reducing armed forces and armaments to a level of reasonable sufficiency. We have suggested comparing the two alliances' military doctrines in order to make them exclusively defensive. We have put forward a concrete plan for the prohibition and elimination of chemical weapons and are working vigorously in this direction. We have advanced proposals on devising effective methods for the verification of arms reductions, including on-site inspection.

It is true that, gauged against the scope of the tasks mankind will have to tackle to ensure its survival, very little has so far been accomplished. But a beginning has been made, and the first signs of change are in evidence. This is borne out, among other things, by the understanding we have reached with the United States on concluding in the near future an agreement on medium- and shorter-range missiles.

The conclusion of this agreement is very important in itself: it will, for the first time, eliminate a whole class of nuclear weapons, and will be the first tangible step along the path of scrapping nuclear arsenals, and show that it is in fact possible to advance in this direction without prejudice to anyone's interests.

The question is whether capitalism can adapt itself to the conditions of a nuclear- and weapon-free world, to the conditions of a new and equitable economic order, to the conditions in which the intellectual and moral values of the two world systems will be compared honestly. These are far from idle questions. The course history will take in the next decades will depend on the way they are answered...

Since an alliance between a socialist country and capitalist states proved possible in the past, when the threat of fascism arose, does this not suggest a lesson for the present, for today's world which faces the threat of nuclear catastrophe and the need to ensure safe nuclear power production and the elimination of environmental hazards?...

Indeed, the novelty of the international economic and political processes of our time has not yet been fully grasped and assimilated. Yet, this must happen because the ongoing processes have the force of an objective law: there will either be a disaster or a joint quest for a new economic order which takes into account the interests of all on an equal basis. We see the way to establishing such an order in the implementation of the 'disarmament-for-development' concept...

...Think, for instance, of the vast potential for peaceful coexistence inherent in the Soviet Union's *perestroika*. By making it possible for us to attain world level in major economic indices, *perestroika* will enable our vast and wealthy country to become involved in the world division of labour and resources in an unprecedented way. Its great scientific, technological and production potential will become a far more substantial component of world economic relations. This will decisively broaden and strengthen the material base of this comprehensive system of peace and international security. And that, by the way, is another highly important aspect of *perestroika*, the place it is assigned in contemporary civilisation.

Indeed, the grandeur and novelty of our time is determined by the peoples' increasingly obvious and open presence in the foreground of history. Their present positions are such that they must be heeded immediately rather than in the long run. The new truth thereby brought into sharp focus is that the constant need to make a choice is becoming increasingly characteristic of historical advancement on the threshold of the 21st century. And the right choice depends on the extent to which the interests and aspirations of millions, of hundreds of millions of people are heeded.

Hence the politicians' responsibility. For policy can only be effective if the novelty of the time is taken into account— today the human factor figures on the political plane not as a remote and more or less spontaneous side effect of the life, activity and intentions of the masses. It directly invades world affairs. Unless this is realised, in other words, unless a new thinking, one based on current realities and the peoples' will, is adopted, politics turn into an unpredictable improvisation posing a risk both to one's own country and to other nations. Such politics have no lasting support...

...The socialist system, the quests and experience it has tested in practice are of importance to all mankind. It has offered to the world its answers to the main questions of human existence, and its humanitarian and collectivist values centred on the working people...

Today the socialist world appears before us in all its national and social variation. This is good and useful. We have become convinced that unity does not mean identity and uniformity. We have also become convinced that there is no 'model' of socialism to be emulated by everyone, nor can there be any such...

...We can see today that humanity is not necessarily doomed always to live in the manner it did before October 1917. Socialism has evolved into a powerful, growing and developing reality. It is the October Revolution and socialism that show humankind the road to the future and identify the new values of truly human relations:

— collectivism instead of egoism;

— freedom and equality instead of exploitation and oppression.

The **Economy**

The big shake-up:
results are coming

Far reaching changes in the economy were mapped out by the Plenary Meeting of the CPSU Central Committee, held in Moscow in 25-26 June 1987.

Changes in management are central to all success; major experiments are encouraged. However, it is admitted that so far no dramatic results can be reported. Some resistance is more deep-rooted than expected, changes are being introduced far too slowly. Scientific and technological progress is also lagging behind.

The basic unit of the national economy — the enterprise (or production association) — does not as yet see itself fully responsible for satisfying society's needs and does not as yet make efficient use of the resources which are at its disposal. There has been very little change within individual industry ministries which persist in operating armchair administrative methods of management. The functions of the central economic authorities remain unchanged; the unresolved problems in planning, price setting, material and machinery supplies, finance and credit, the organisation of labour and pay structure are having a detrimental effect.

The Central Committee of the CPSU makes the solution of these problems its primary task. There has to be a radical reform which would provide efficient and flexible management, using to the full all the advantages of socialism.

Such a radical reform will:

— gear economic growth to satisfy all social requirements;

— ensure a fusion of interests of society and the individual worker;

— transform scientific and technological innovation into a moving force behind economic growth;

— ensure balance in the economy, eliminate deficits of ma-

terial resources and consumer goods which hamper efficiency and slow down production;

— provide the consumer with a choice worthy of developed society;

— create a reliable and efficient anti-waste mechanism for the basic unit (enterprise) and the economy as a whole.

Each enterprise must compile independently its own annual and five-year plans based on customer demand. The customer may be the state or an enterprise, or consumer demand. The enterprise bears full responsibility for the financial results of its operations, pay and rewards will be directly dependent on the success of each enterprise or unit.

During the transition period to full profit-and-loss accounting, the collectives of enterprises, depending on the specifics of their production, will be able to choose one of two models of full profit-and-loss accounting and self-financing.

The first model is based on a predetermined distribution of profit. The wage fund can be formed as a specific ratio to cash net output, while in the extraction industries — it can be to the sales of raw material quantity. Profit is used to settle accounts with the local and state budget and a superior body and to pay interest on credit. The net profit after these accounts have been settled is at the disposal of the work collective. It can be used to form an investment fund for further production, for the introduction of new technology, for the development of social amenities, or for material incentives. This model of accounting centres on the wages fund and residual profit.

The second model (the model of a collective contract) is based on a normative distribution of income allocated after all material overhead and development outlays have been covered out of the revenue. Profit is what remains after deductions are remitted to the local or state budget and a superior body, and interest on credit is paid out. Thus the wages fund is the residual fund after all expenses have been paid.

Such is the general outline of the June 1987 Plenary Meeting of the CPSU Central Committee. It would be a simplification to assume that changes can be made overnight even in relatively successful enterprises. Let us listen to VLADIMIR PAVLOVICH KABAIDZE, *General Director of the Ivanovo Engineering Production Association, who spoke to a correspondent from* OGONYOK *in late December 1987.*

Self-financing and profit-and-loss accounting is not a pana-cea or a magic wand. It is something new, so it must be tested thoroughly and adjusted, before it is to take the brunt of everything we could not do well in the past. We have the op-portunity to reorganise with speed. This is very important, for we must be aware at least of two factors which are inherent in any production: how to enter the market and how to quit it. The first one is given due consideration. But I have heard nothing sensible about the second one. Yet the second prob-lem is perhaps the one to be encountered most frequently. Who can admit to producing rubbish and not being able to stop? For instance, the Yenisei combine-harvester recently came in for criticism. No one needs it, yet it is still being pro-duced. The reason is that the machinery cannot be adapted to produce something else. For any Western firm, the inability to cease production when there is no demand is fatal. But here society has to pay for goods no one has a need for. I could find many other examples. Unfortunately, we have been driven to increase production and raise labour productivity for so long that we have forgotten to see what happens to it at the other end. I am afraid that profit-and-loss accounting and self-financing cannot guarantee us success.

What made you come to this conclusion?

First, self-financing does not yield returns immediately. We have the habit of unleashing a noisy campaign about any 'novelty', but when it does not yield the expected results im-mediately, we either forget about it or run it down. Second, it seems to me that many plants showing good profits at present might collapse without even understanding why.

How come?

They are loath to take risks. Risk-taking is not particularly encouraged. If you take a risk and it works — you may be praised. But if your risky experiment ends in failure or pro-duces no improvements, you will probably be punished, or even dismissed, in spite of the saying you can't make an omel-ette without breaking eggs. So someone 'encouraged' by being punished is hardly likely to risk anything again. Other people see this happen and are loath to take any risks also. So we lose an awful lot from the fact that many people have lost the risk genes.

What about you? Have you lost them too?

Fortunately, no. Although it might seem immodest to say

so. We have been operating for many years at our own risk. We are used to it. Our engineering staff, especially designers, have long understood that they don't need anyone else's consent. The Director General is where the buck stops!

Yet someone must have given you permission?

No one. At first we did come up against some resistance, of course, but later they just gave us up as a bad job, as some kind of desperadoes. After all, those at the 'top' also understand and can see our results: success follows success, and we have satisfied customers (the main clients of the Ivanovo Works are Western firms — Ed.), so they left us alone.

So you are now harvesting the fruits, as it were, of your 'genetic' inclination towards risk. But others might also develop a taste for working this way...

If only they would! I certainly did not mean that our collective has a monopoly on risk- taking. There are others like us. But I would like to stress that success in operating under the new conditions will be largely determined by a willingness to take risk. It must not be squashed, but encouraged.

The conditions of profit-and-loss accounting and self-financing will evidently help?

I'm not so sure. So far, at least, the opposite seems to be the case. As you no doubt know, all losses made by the enterprise in the form of various economic penalties are reflected in the part of profit left at its disposal. It is these funds we use to pay for short supplies under contracts, for dropping below the required standards, for excessive stocks, for delays in the commissioning of fixed assets and much more. It is obvious that any search for something new leads to certain interruptions in production. So it turns out that risk is punished materially. And when our room for manoeuvre is restricted to only 31.5 per cent of profits, it is understandable that it is much easier and more profitable not to take any risks.

Tell me, Vladimir Pavlovich, in January 1987 did you, in fact, count on more than you actually got from the experiment?

A year ago we thought we would be able to 'play the game' as they did in Sumy. But everything turned out to be both worse and more complicated. I think the Sumy experiment was a success because it was the first, so, as always, the conditions were particularly favourable: they were left 71 per cent of their profits, while we, as I have already mentioned, only

31.5. That is less than a half of the Sumy plant, and—a third less than we had before going over to the new operating conditions. The old story repeated itself: once an experiment is over and put into general use, the conditions are tightened... But I don't think this is the main question now. Events are now gaining pace; directors of enterprises are appearing on radio and TV, offering all sorts of advice based on their personal experience. For a time I was delighted by all this. But then I thought: who is going to judge? Who can judge local conditions? I know factories that haven't fulfilled their targets for years. What do the local authorities do? Complain to Moscow; ask for help. And what sort of help do they have in mind? A cut in the plan, additional resources. This means putting up someone else's plan and taking resources from elsewhere. We're too good to the 'lame and poor'. And if we put ourselves in their shoes again, once more those who are at the forefront will find themselves in an unfavourable situation. The aid will come out of their funds.

But, apart from profit-and-loss accounting, there is also the new Law on the State Enterprise (Association). It guarantees you considerable rights. Now you can hand the bill into your own ministry, if they took a wrong decision and caused losses for your enterprise...

Bill whom? Our own ministry? The law has been passed, but it has not put an end to administrative zeal. Even if something unlawful is done to us, I still won't be able to prove anything. An example? Willingly. Another new idea has now been adopted—the state order. A good idea. It should be welcomed, but we are battling against it, writing to all offices.

Why are you against it?

The idea is that the state order is, for any enterprise, a priority. Let the director general and his staff die in the process, but it must be fulfilled. In the GDR, this form has already existed for a long time. I went there to see how it works. Rudi Winter, an old friend and colleague of mine, and director general of a machine-tool factory, explained to me: 'Our state order is for only 15-20 per cent of the total volume of production. But it must be fulfilled. For the rest, the plant seeks its own customers, concludes agreements with them and, accordingly, determines the remaining range of production.' As we can see, they are granted quite considerable freedom and they operate on a long leash. I studied the German experience and decided that it is not realistic for us to expect a state order for only 15-20 per cent of output; about 50 per cent would suit everybody. I made my suggestion to the ministry and then went even higher. There the idea was chewed over and it was decided that 50 per cent freedom was too much for us — it was cut to 15 per cent. Only this part of our output can we dispose of at will; the remaining 85 per cent is the state order. A pity, I thought, that we've been curtailed so much, but it's still good: at least there's a precedent. On the basis of 15 per cent we can gradually gain new territory. Yet even this variant, cut to a minimum, was abolished without warning.

Why?

Wouldn't I like to know?! About three months ago we were sent additional state order data for 1988. Not only did they exceed the target figures for the production output by nearly seven million roubles: in addition they also contained 35 different items, of which 21 were not included in the previous plan at all.

Sorry, but I don't quite understand. The target figures are the enterprise plan for 1988. Corresponding assets have been allocated for it ages ago. It is a component part of the plan for the whole national economy. How could they hang another seven million roubles worth on you, without any back-up?

Ask me another, will you? But that's not all. Our business is to produce machine-tools. That seems clear enough. But they'd stuffed the new state order with anything they fancied. The collection of ferrous and non-ferrous metal scrap and waste, the production of consumer goods, as well as special technical equipment for ourselves and for the whole industry, saw timber, you name it...

What is that for?

You see, we despatch our machine-tools packed in wooden cases. We make the boards ourselves by sawing up whole trunks. We need this timber only for our internal use and for the number of machine-tools we produce: no more, no less. So we know, without Moscow's help, how much and what sort of timber we need to saw. But no, the capital sets this figure for us too, and even includes it in the state order...

It seems hard to imagine anything more stupid...

Hard, but not impossible. Tell me, why do they dictate to

us the amount of technical equipment required for our own needs? We will make only as much as necessary. We won't make too much — it's not profitable. Or too little — the main production would be slowed down. We can decide better for ourselves than anyone else. Yet some zealous official at his desk bothered to write it in. I naturally asked the Minister: 'What are you doing? Why are you undermining the authority of the state order?' The answer? 'That's what Gosplan (the State Planning Committee — Tr.) told us to do.' So I wrote to Gosplan, to the first Vice-Chairman. So far — no answer.

Sorry, Vladimir Pavlovich, but there's one thing I still don't quite understand. All the time you say: we will fight. But under self-financing, the main 'fighter' for justice should be the rouble and economic levers that would determine the logic of the enterprise's economic activities...

If only that were all true! You see, though I complain about us being left too little profit for social, cultural, domestic purposes and housing construction, do you think it would be any easier if we were left any more? At the moment, for instance, we have about 1,300,000 roubles for these purposes. I don't like money lying around idle, so I say to the builders: 'Take a million and build me this and that.' They reply by tel ling me where to go. They don't want our roubles. Part of the money we can find a use for, of course: the young pioneer camp, tourist trips, etc., but there's an awful lot left. If we had five or ten million do you really think we would live any better?

I suppose not.

And I agree with you. Following on from the problem of self-financing and the problem of how to earn money, is another equally difficult one — that of how to spend it and turn it into things. Personally I have to cope with this problem every month at home. I can't complain; I earn a good salary. I bring home a wage packet packed tight like a saddlebag, but my wife says: 'What do I want your money for? It'd be better if you brought home some sausage or some caviar.' Enterprises face the same problem. Many similar seditious questions arise.

Yet others manage somehow...

I've often had it suggested that we do the same. Build a cultural centre with your own resources, they say. I'm categorically against this. There are no bricks, no roofing, no panels.

Everything has to be obtained 'on the side', by getting in-volved in some sort of fiddling. There aren't any builders ei-ther. So we'd have to 'come to an agreement' with them, too; give them some semi-legal incentive... For me personally there is only one acceptable way: we make machinery and receive money for it, and everything we need must be done for us for payment. Any other way is against my principles. Policies cannot be based on such methods. To be 'naughty' once or twice and build something unlawfully (every director is guilty of this) is one thing; but to turn semi-legal methods into a constant activity — I'm sorry, but nothing good can come of it...

Such is the situation that has taken shape at one of the So-viet Union's best plants. Things cannot all run smoothly in an economy that was in a pre-crisis situation during the years of stagnation. This is demonstrated by the ideas expressed by Academician ABEL AGANBEGYAN, *the man at the hub of the new thinking on economy.*

NO RETREAT

We are all asking the same questions: how can the braking mechanism be eliminated? How can real acceleration be at-tained? Many people, remembering previous unsuccessful at-tempts at reform, believe we are now underestimating obsta-cles. Is this the case?

Yes, it is...

During the 1960s, attempts at reorganisation were made only in industry and agriculture. They did not affect fi-nance, trade, construction, supplies, branch ministries or regional bodies. In other words, the reform was narrow and superficial and did not embrace the whole economy. More-over, this restructuring was not accompanied by restructur-ing in other spheres of life.

The reform was the concern of an inter-departmental commission of the State Planning Committee (Gosplan), headed by someone who was not given the necessary powers. Any ministry or department could torpedo or der-ail the commission's measures. Decisions were taken behind closed doors and no one counted on democratisation.

Yet even under such limiting conditions this reform provided us with very valuable experience. Some important results were obtained.

What were they?

The chief one was increased rates of growth. The eighth five-year plan period (1966-1970) was better in all its indices than the previous one. The national income put to use increased from 32 per cent to 41 per cent. Labour productivity in industry — from 25 per cent to 32 per cent. Real per capita income — from 19 per cent to 33 per cent.

Did that reform help get rid of supply shortages? At least partially? Did it show up the reasons?

Indeed it did. Let me give a specific example. At that time there was a great shortage of petrol. We had to find out whether it was real or artificially created, whether rationing, especially with unrealistic quotas, was the reason for it. In five districts rationing was lifted: no limits were imposed, and one could buy as much as one wanted.

And what was the result? At first people were really greedy and started building up stocks... But the right to purchase unlimited quantities of petrol remained in force. And it then turned out that considerably less petrol was really required.

The case for setting quotas is clear. And there is obviously no point in reforming separate parts of the economy — restructuring must embrace the whole system. But, most important, we must understand perestroika's *real objective.*

The goal would seem to be clear: satisfaction of the requirements of people and society. All spheres of life, above all production, must be subordinated to this.

By people's requirements we mean, of course, not just material ones (food, clothing, medicines etc.), but also social ones. Requirements in the broadest possible sense.

Can we claim that human requirements are satisfied? Of course not. And not by anyone's evil design, but because economic development pursues unclear and often even false aims. In other words, production is divorced from the consumer requirements; it proceeds on its own, as it were, apart from people's needs.

Yet the way to achieve these aims is surely to do this gradually. For example, without acceleration of technological progress no restructuring is possible. What successes can be quoted?

Unfortunately, successes still number far fewer than failures. One success I can quote concerns the introduction of rotor and rotor-conveyor production lines; they are proving very successful.

The reasons for setbacks are mostly due to the conservatism of management. The majority of ministries are not going over to new methods, do not create incentives and do not encourage cross-industry cooperation. To find finances for such cooperation is very difficult. There is no encouragement for technological innovation. There is no clear appreciation of the line of development that would provide the highest potential for success.

We all know that the decisive factor in technological progress is information technology. In 1986 a major event occurred in the world economy: computerisation overtook electrification. That is, outlay on computers in the capitalist countries overtook expenditure on fuel and energy. Computer production is 10 per cent of total output in the capitalist world. It is considerably lower in the Soviet Union. It is deplorable that we are behind not only in total volume and net increase but also in the rate of development.

Nor can we see light at the end of the tunnel. Gosplan has four separate departments for fuel and energy supply, while there is no special department responsible for computers. Yet computerisation is key to future technological development.

How do things stand in traditional industries? Where are we diverging from the main objective?

There is one very characteristic example. We produce four and a half times as many tractors as the USA. What for? Our agricultural yield is a third less than the United States'. In addition, we produce only half of tractor driven equipment compared with other countries — in fact less than is required for normal functioning. The implication is that we do not intend to use the machines we produce. After all, tractors are supposed to drive other machinery and not become, as it were, an end in themselves.

Moreover, every tractor factory tries to increase the capacity of tractors, but the users need a variety: small ones (for lawns and gardens) as well as big ones (for logging).

Yet we produce only 60 h. p. tractors, and a 100 h. p. vehicle is in the pipeline. What for? After all, each new, more powerful model is less profitable as it requires an increase in the metal and fuel consumption. Yet here lies a typical paradox of our economy: this sort of over-expenditure makes the model 'profitable' for the manufacturer and the ministry running it.

Convenient models are taken out of production and the user is forced to accept an expensive one, one he doesn't need. He accepts, and not simply because there is no choice, but because this waste of money in no way affects his own welfare — he doesn't pay for it out of his own pocket. State and collective farms used to buy their equipment on credit from the state. They are now in dept to the tune of 100 billion roubles. The credit has never been paid off. It is easy, of course, to spend other people's money on a useless item...

So one of the reasons behind the shortages is the overproduction of unnecessary things, which are profitable only for the producers who fulfil their plans.

Yes. In many industries, in my opinion, almost a quarter of the output is unnecessary. The situation with lorries is similar. Eighty per cent of the lorries produced have a weight-carrying capacity of four or five tonnes. These are needed by the ZIL and GAZ motor works, not by the national economy! On a world scale, vehicles with this capacity constitute only three per cent. It is not surprising that the ZIL lorries run half loaded and for only one shift, or stand in the garages. About 40 per cent of them are not used at all!

If production investigated real demand before a new vehicle went into production, the manufacturer would have found out what sort of loads were to be transported.

That is, we need to determine the criteria first. What, in your opinion, should be regarded as an objective criterion of the efficiency of the national economy?

The extent to which requirements are satisfied. Only that which best satisfies real demand is efficient. That which diverges from this goal is inefficient. Demand and requirements are the key to everything.

The transition to self-financing surely calls for new managerial decisions. Here is an example. Collective and state farms have handed in orders for the next year for fewer lorries, tractors and combine harvesters than previously. As for combine harvesters, moreover, it turned out that only seventy per cent of the planned output was really needed.

Under the conditions of full profit-and-loss accounting and self-financing, the farms would have been satisfied even by fifty per cent less. I believe this because those farms which have adopted the new system pay out of their own funds, and therefore have cut their purchases of agricultural machinery exactly by half. When contract teams have to pay rent for equipment, they avoid taking on too much and take good care of what they have.

There are collective farms where contract units have hired only the exact number of machines needed even if more were available. It turned out to be half. The other half was purchased previously either without thinking or as a reserve 'for a rainy day'.

Given such surpluses, shortages are inevitable. Here is another paradox. In 1986 the USA produced 75 million tonnes of steel, while our output was 161 million. Yet the USA produced fifty per cent more products (machinery and machine-tools).

Virtually all our products are heavier and use more material. Thus metals, coke and iron ore are in short supply. Of course, we are short of capital investment in production. Capital is spent on coke, ore, sinter, steel, and, of course, on grain, too.

All this expenditure is inefficient precisely because our production is not geared to real demand. We use grain to feed cattle, of which we have 50 per cent more heads than the USA. Yet the yield is lower. It must be said, there is only enough fodder to keep the livestock just alive, not for the cows to produce high yields of good milk.

Enough examples, I think! So, our economic mechanism did not link needs to production.

What must we avoid when creating the new mechanism?

Producers' diktat. The imprimatur to produce, unhindered, product which nobody needs, such as the tractors, of which there are four and a half times more than required. The mechanism must be such that no-one will buy anything which is not required, either for cash or on credit.

With the tractors everything is clear. But what about con-

sumer goods? You yourself have written that the shelves are groaning. So what about 1988?

No better. In 1986 801 million pairs of footwear were made; in 1987 even more. In no country have families such stocks of shoes as here. Czechoslovakia (a well-known 'footwear' country) produces 1.7 pairs of shoes per person per year: we produce over three. The USA manufactures only 290 million pairs — yet no one complains about shortages. Of course, they import footwear from other countries, but we import shoes, too.

This isolation from real needs permeates all sectors. I say this to underline once more that the main task is the assessment of demand.

Is there any order of priority in the introduction of the new mechanism?

Yes. A specific timetable has been adopted and personnel has been appointed. But everything must be done as fast as possible. Over three years from 1987 to 1990 there will be a reform of finance, prices, banking and material supply. The changes are fundamental. For example, wholesale trade will now include capital goods (60 per cent from 1990, and 80-90 per cent two years later). But while we fulfil these provisions, we must go on fighting for *perestroika* and make sure the changes introduced are of practical importance.

What then is the most acute and pressing problem? After all, this might become the 'basis of growth' if everything works out well?

One burning question is that of quotas, especially the quotas of profits enterprises may have at their disposal. Ministries have theirs set by Gosplan. Individual enterprises receive instructions from the ministries. It is in their power to make the profitable unprofitable; anybody can be incapacitated by quotas.

In other countries there is a different procedure. A quota is an average norm for each and every enterprise. They must all pay the state the same percentage. In Italy, for instance, by giving the state half its profits, a firm may go bankrupt or it may become richer, but irrespective, the law remains the same: the quota is not changed. Rather like our taxes: no one cares about a person's starting abilities. He still has to hand over the set percentage of his wage packet.

Profit deductions vary widely. On average, light industry pays over 63 per cent. There are enterprises that pay 90 per cent. But ZIL pays only a few per cent. This is how much quotas fluctuate when they are individualised. Every production unit hands over a predetermined amount.

But if everything is regulated, where is the economic autonomy and self-financing? What is this regulation based on?

The same as usual — separation from the consumer. Producers' diktat. A five-year plan is determined for every enterprise — set out in great detail in advance. The work collective knows how big the incentive fund is and how much annual profit it should make.

We are now switching to a system of quotas but in conditions of the existing plans. The next plan will be drawn up in a different way. Unfortunately, we will have to live in the Procrustean bed of the old plan for another two and a half years — no room to stretch or grow.

But can things be run any other way during the current transition period from old to new forms? Do you think it is realistic to introduce new sets of quotas during the present five-year plan period?

Yes, I do. In industries it is quite feasible. True, this would demand a change in the interrelations between Gosplan and industrial enterprises. But the nation would benefit enormously. By delaying matters we are losing too much. We cannot let things go on as they are, with people working badly better off and those who work well worse off. If we continue to proceed from the 'level already achieved', even in respect of quotas, the form will be new but the outcome will remain unchanged.

Let me explain this in more detail. If an enterprise operates successfully, strict conditions are set for it (that is, less favourable ones), i. e. it should pay more to the state. But one that makes less profit pays less. This means that the funds that really belong to the better enterprises are simply handed over to the worse ones.

A whole series of exceptions are made for poorly performing enterprises; payment for assets is not deducted, and only a small percentage of profit is taken off them.

This inevitably holds back progress: today's quotas act as

a brake on development — it is not worthwhile for good enterprises to forge ahead.

Lenin's words come to mind here: correct in form but in essence a mockery!

The *acceleration* mechanism can be based only on one principle: encouragement of those who work well. And this means: an equal social demand on all enterprises. When demands are equal the ones that work well will earn more. Besides, when enterprises are transferred to profit-and-loss accounting and self-financing, the wage rates remain virtually the same. They are still calculated on the basis of the prescribed net output rather than the real commercial income.

And what about the directors of enterprises? Can they not try to defend their interests in ministries and Gosplan?

They cannot observe the situation in the country as a whole. They do their utmost to get quotas that suit them best. And each of them fights like a lion for this, that is (I want to stress it) for the quotas that are convenient precisely for their particular enterprises only.

And for some of them stabilisation of the old situation is convenient? There are no doubt some, too, that fear they might be closed down under the new Law on the State Enterprise?

Possibly. Yet, in spite of the supposition that such closures cause hardship to people, I believe this process will be carried out in a humane way in our socialist society. However, there can be procrastination. The following pattern is possible. First the enterprise gets into debt, asks for credit and is then refused; then it goes for help to the ministry, but eventually it, too, loses patience. During this time people working at the enterprise will earn less and less. Bonuses will no longer be paid; the staff will be cut. The unprofitability of the enterprise is felt keenly by the workforce. And by the management too — it is replaced. Only if measures to save the enterprise fail will it finally be closed down.

Excellent, if it is bought by some strong organisation. The Academy of Sciences, for instance, will evidently have an interest in buying up small factories, modernising them to its own requirements, turning them into specialised pilot plants.

Sometimes an enterprise is so run down, however, that nothing can be done to reinstate it. It is more economic to build a new one. Then it must be closed down, for which purpose a special commission is set up. The plant's workers receive three months' wages and go to jobs where they will be of more use. The property of the enterprise is sold off and the money goes to pay off its debts.

This is what happens in Poland, Hungary and China. The same is envisaged by the Law on the State Enterprise here, too, but closures are unlikely to be commonplace. At first they will more likely be single instances. But time will show. In the USSR, there are several thousands of obviously loss-making enterprises. Nothing can save them. In the interests of society they must be closed down. I don't suggest we copy the West, where tens of thousands of firms go bankrupt and disappear every year. But a few hundred enterprises would, in my opinion, be better closed down in the near future.

Is this also in the interests of the people? What of those who lose their jobs?

You're worried about jobs? You must understand clearly what it means for an enterprise to be loss-making. Let us assume that it shows a 5 million roubles loss. So it is stealing precisely this sum from all of us — from the nation. Everyone could have a higher wage than at present, but it is lower because such enterprises exist. They exist on the backs of those who really work.

In the Donbass Region there are about thirty mines that use up an enormous quantity of resources but produce a negligible amount of coal. The prime cost of their output is very high and their productivity very low. If these thirty mines were closed down resources would be released that would make it possible to mine three times as much coal.

But we are not used to it, and the mines continue to depend on the state subsidy. Now the ministry (under the new Law) must support them if it does not decide to close them. Such a burden would mean that the ministry could not develop other enterprises, and could not modernise deserving ones.

In my point of view closures should not be emergency measures resorted to only exceptionally. Of our 46 thousand existing enterprises only those capable of developing under their own steam should remain.

You mean self-development?

Precisely! Powerful incentives must be created to encourage self-development. Enterprises must develop on the basis of their own funds. The state should not pay for the engine of the new *Moskvitch* car. This is wrong. The motor works' design office should have built the heart of the car. The builders of the *Moskvitch* should set up their own plant out of their own funds. With its 'gifts', the state initiated a very harmful trend — the domination of monopoly enterprises. Lenin warned that any monopoly (any, you understand, not just capitalist) leads to decay.

Could you give an example of self-development apart from the Paton Inter-industry Scientific and Industrial Complex, which is well known?

With pleasure. *Cryogenmash...* But we'll never achieve self-development without properly substantiated rates and quotas, without profit-and-loss accounting, without self-financing and self-management. For self-development people must have means at their own disposal. And that is what will happen!

When circumstances demand change, sooner or later it takes place, irrespective of whether it is to everyone's liking or not. Those against them will leave, to be replaced by others who can cope with the new conditions.

There are objective laws of development. This is why a deficit economy by a producers' *diktat* will die a natural death.

Interview by E. MANUCHAROVA
Izvestia, 26 August 1987

What is the role and place of the central planning bodies in the current restructuring? The June 1987 Plenary Meeting of the CPSU Central Committee decided that enterprises (associations) will henceforth be responsible for drawing up their own five-year and annual plans.

PERESTROIKA AND PLANNING
ANATOLY REUT,

By USSR Gosplan First Deputy Chairman

USSR Gosplan has often been criticised for planning errors, disproportions and imbalance, for being carried away by its controlling functions. Its functions are now changing most decidedly. How do you envisage the new Gosplan? What, under the new conditions, will be the 'philosophy' behind the national plan?

For many years USSR Gosplan did, indeed, concentrate mainly on drawing up annual plans, while the five-year period became vague, especially with regard to the development of inter-sectoral links, to major structural shifts in the economy and to the distribution of the productive forces. The excessively planned annual regulation of economic operations of enterprises became ineffective. After all, the range of industrial and agricultural products now exceeds 24 million different items. Is it really possible to determine what to produce, for whom, in what quantities, with what outlays by means of directive to individual production units? An impossible task which inevitably bred a multitude of errors. What did happen was that enterprises which managed to fulfil the plan set for them carried on producing items for which there was no real consumer demand. By using their resources wastefully, enterprises covered themselves by inflating the wholesale price of their output.

The plan should be an instrument for the harmonious development of the national economy, a stimulus to the self-development of enterprises. Planning must acquire a fundamentally new role. It is required to determine the long-term strategy, the chief priorities and goals of the country's socio-economic development. It must also ensure the optimal combination of centralised regulation with individual enterprise independence. In my view, this must be the new philosophy of national planning.

But how can such a philosophy be implemented in practice?

The basis will be established by long-term scientific and technological programmes and concepts, mapping out the economic and social development of the country for the coming fifteen years. It must pinpoint priorities, determine the direction of investment policies, scientific and technical innovation, and the improvements in standard of living. It will also include directives for developing the educational and cultural sphere as well as the country's defence. For these objectives, Gosplan will issue guidelines.

From above, the enterprises will receive only four indicators which should be used in governing their own production programme: control figures, long-term stable economic indicators, state orders and quotas. These figures will ensure a balance in the national plan on the basis of sectoral contributions. In accordance with the initial data, as well as direct orders from customers, individual and corporate, enterprises will offer contracts and form their own plans. Henceforth they will have to tackle the market on their own, otherwise they will not earn enough even to pay the wages of their staff.

So there is really to be a democratisation of planning?

Absolutely. There will be direct links between manufacturers and consumers, there will be a wholesaling network providing machinery and materials (60-70 per cent of the total production will be transferred to this network). The wholesale trade will encourage competition among the producers of machinery. Previously, for example, the Ministry of Agricultural Machinery distributed machinery and equipment among farms, which willingly accepted any machine they were offered. After all, you don't look a gift-horse in the mouth.

Now with profit-and-loss accounting under way, people have started counting the outlay. Many harvesters and tractors have actually been refused. Industrial enterprises are refusing machine-tools they do not need. And as soon as there is a surplus of equipment, manufacturers begin to gear their production to real demand.

The Law on State Enterprise clearly says that quotas are set for state centralised capital investment, construction and installation work, materials and other technical resources. What can enterprises which have started earning considerable funds do to develop their production? Where will they get the cement, rolled metal, facing blocks and so on?

Perestroika, as we know, is being implemented in the course of this five-year plan period. The majority of materials have been allocated within the targets of this plan. We can only find new resources out of the output produced as an overfulfilment of the plan. Thus, for example, the motor industry received 300 million roubles increase in the quotas for equipment, transport and construction. This is because this industry is already fully operating profit-and-loss accounting and self-financing and has already increased productivity.

Enterprises have the right to design and work out estimates for technical retooling and modernisation, as well as for the construction of housing and other social facilities. There is priority for receiving material resources for these purposes. I believe that already in the 13th five-year plan — with setting up the wholesale trade in machinery and materials — we shall be able to provide enterprises with everything they need for retooling and for improving the living standards of their workers.

When I was the director of the Ordjonikidze Computer Technology Plant in Minsk, I was so bold as to build a preventive medicine clinic out of the social development fund. For two years the bank refused to recognise this expenditure as 'legal'. We had the means, but not the right to use it for this purpose. Now the rights of enterprises are being expanded, and we are striving to support their initiative in housing construction, especially those built with local building materials.

We are accustomed to Gosplan giving directives, including a multitude of indicators. What kind of directives can we now expect from Gosplan?

Gosplan — less than anyone — is interested in retaining its old directive role. Our directive is to ensure the fulfilment of the state order and the maintenance of sectoral proportions. It is backed up by economic incentives, including guaranteed sales and resource provision.

Specific work is now under way in USSR Gosplan to review and reduce substantially the various existing norms which in the past played a restrictive role. Out of the old 680 normative regulations, 432 have been abolished and 36 re-specified. In other words, 70 per cent of the total number are scrapped. Instead of this, USSR Gosplan, together with other central economic bodies, worked out 50 normative regulations concerning finance, credit and other aspects of economic management.

Formerly, the plan's directives were detailed down to every individual machine-tool. Now Gosplan has retained only one and a half thousand indices, and this number will fall every year. These are used for quantifying the state order and the state order itself will become the chief controlling instrument for the maintenance of balance.

But won't state order turn into a new version of the same old directives? It is not by chance that managers are proposing a limit for the state order to be from one half to two-thirds of the volume of production. What is Gosplan's attitude to this?

Our attitude is quite unambiguous: the state order must correspond fully to the purpose assigned to it by the Law on the State Enterprise and to the Guidelines for the Fundamental Restructuring of the Economy. This approach has already made it possible to reduce the number of indicators to less than a third for 1988. This applies only to centrally confirmed state orders. There will also be state orders from ministries and the Councils of Ministers of the union republics, but they will also be limited in range and be coordinated with Gosplan. One very important factor is that the ministries can place state orders on a competitive basis.

The draft plan for 1988 has shown that in the manufacturing industries, the state order will, indeed, embrace one half to two-thirds of total production. In the area of raw materials, fuel and energy, the proportion is somewhat higher. However, it is good that enterprises are given the percentage they have asked for.

Even so, the inclination of planning bodies to dictate a multitude of directives, including gross output, and to exert pressure is well known. Do you believe USSR Gosplan has changed already?

In recent years we have been concentrating on overcoming the gross output syndrome. Let us look at the figures. In the 1986 plan about 43 thousand targets were centrally confirmed, whereas in 1987 the figure was about 22 thousand. For 1988 it will be no more than eight thousand.

That's still rather a lot.

Yes, it is, but do not forget that we are talking about the whole economy. The number of target figures will continue to be reduced. There's another side to it however. I do not believe the consumers are quite ready for this. Most of them are used to receiving directives from above, so that they can pass the buck back if necessary. Nevertheless, we have persisted in the reducing the number of targets and this should give us credibility.

And, finally, from now on, we shall be looking at the previous year's growth rates when setting current targets. This will eliminate cases when this figure is used as a base minimum/maximum and foster initiative and utilisation of reserves. It is interesting that many enterprises have achieved in 1987 what would have been a target for 1988 using the old methods.

The June 1987 Plenary Meeting raised anew the question of control figures. They must no longer be directive in character.

Control figures are a starting point from which an enterprise works out its plan. They enable the management to plan for stability and for the creation of incentives. Of course, enterprises can depart widely from the control figures. They have the right to do so. But they will have to bear the responsibility.

Self-financing and full profit-and-loss accounting are already being implemented. Why does the attempt to set long-term indices arouse so much discussion? Or are we going the wrong way about it? We speak of the need for a scientific approach, but we continue to calculate standards on the basis of the targets set out for the five-year plan period. As a result, the wastage goes on.

The problem is that profit-and-loss accounting and self-financing is being introduced only *after* the plan for the five-year period has been adopted. The main task of the standards under these conditions is to ensure that the economy can function at least at the current levels. Where possible, we are untying the hands of work collectives and guaranteeing them that they receive additional rewards for the more efficient conduct of their enterprises.

So I disagree with you that today the wastage goes on. Even now, the standards set out for the current five-year plan period guarantee to each enterprise that a definite part of any improved operation will be at the disposal of the collective.

For many years unsuccessful attempts have been made to combine sectoral and territorial interests. How is perestroika going to go about this?

A great deal has already been done. Enterprises irrespective of their sectoral subordination must coordinate with local Soviets parts of their production which affect social services, the use of labour resources, the production of consumer goods, the development of service industries and the environment. These local aspects must be coordinated at union republic level. It is intended to set up district and area management boards the broad tasks of which would be to coordinate the activities of enterprises and organisations on their territories. Moreover, the system of deductions from profit into the local fund will encourage local government to help their enterprises to operate more efficiently.

In addition, one of the main directives remaining within the authority of Gosplan will be the long-term development of the key industrial regions. That for the Far Eastern Economic Region and the area beyond Lake Baikal was recently approved by the Political Bureau of the CPSU Central Committee. The development of the industries of Central Asia and Kazakhstan is being considered at present by the government. The long-term aims will be integrated into the succession of five-year plans.

With these new tasks for Gosplan, is the internal structure going to change as well?

Yes, inevitably. The structure of Gosplan is currently under review. There will be more weight given to combined departments — for the economy and social matters, for science and technology, for individual territories. We must get away from the very narrow sectoral division of our organisation. The sectoral departments were fully aware of the situation at local level but could do very little about it.

And what now? Will they be abolished?

To a considerable extent, yes. Take the engineering industry. Instead of sectoral departments there will be a department for economic strategy, for technological innovation and development. This applies to other industries. We intend to cut our staff considerably. To tell the truth, restructuring is no easy matter for us. We have these immediate problems, yet we must turn our attention to the global

plan of preparing our national economy to switch fully to
profit-and-loss accounting by the year 2005.

Interview by V. ROMANYUK and Yu. RYTOV

Izvestia, 17 August 1987

Those who read Soviet Scene 1987 *no doubt remember Nikolai Travkin — the model 'disturber of the peace' in the construction industry. In only four years a team leader from
Moscow Region has become an important industrial business
manager, renowned throughout the country. Something in
this rapid rise to fame is reminiscent of the turbulent twenties
in the Soviet Union's history. Yet is there anything to be surprised about in this:* perestroika *is a revolutionary process,
and consequently engenders its own revolutionaries. Men and
women who speak bluntly; with views that some consider extreme — but this is now increasingly a feature of today. These
are the qualities needed to sweep away the bureaucratic and
ideological obstacles to the progress of* perestroika.

*One interesting detail: N. Travkin was not trained as
a builder. He was a maths schoolteacher. He graduated from
a pedagogical institute, worked in a school before doing his
national service, and only later became attracted to construction work. In 1981 he graduated from a building technical college, but to this day he admits to feeling unsure of himself on
many technical matters. But he sees nothing wrong in this,
since he believes the most important thing for a manager is
the ability to deal with people without taking decisions for
them, to encourage or correct without interfering. Everyone
must master his or her job and feel a full sense of responsibility for the work undertaken.*

Let us now hear from NIKOLAI TRAVKIN, *head of
a mobile construction unit, manager of the Moscow District
Agricultural Construction Trust No. 18.*

A 'BOMB' FOR THE BUREAUCRAT

At one time I sharply criticised the organisation I am
now working with. Why? Because it failed to come up to expectations, even though the intentions when it was set up

were most progressive. It was presumed that the TCAs would separate from Glavk (Chief Department), assume current-production functions, as well as the technical, social and personnel policy responsibilities in their regions. In other words, they would acquire the status of design and construction firms, while Glavk, which, in our case, enjoys ministerial status, would become the strategic 'brain centre' with a limited staff.

But things turned out differently. Glavk, once it had set up the territorial construction associations (TCAs), did not relinquish day-to-day management or directing power. It still holds weekly intercom conferences and controls the incomes of each trust. The TCAs, moreover, became in a way additional levers in its hands, and certainly not independent units. The whole idea degenerated into a sort of 'curatorship', covering the trusts, while the management sat at the top. And, instead of being reduced, managerial staff actually grew.

Where exactly?

In the very same TCAs! Each of them has a staff of at least 80. Formally they are not supposed to belong to Glavk, so they claim to have reduced their numbers! In fact, however... It's simple arithmetic: Trust No. 18, from which I came, previously spent about 40,000 roubles on maintaining its supervisory body. The figure today exceeds 80,000.

I came out against this system when I was manager of the trust. But it's easy to criticise. I was offered the chance to go and put things right myself. That's how I became the head of the No. 2 TCA, covering fifteen regions to the south-west of the Moscow Region and nine trusts. What's more, the whole set-up was very run down. Seven of the trusts would automatically have gone bankrupt if transferred to self-financing.

And you want to transform this run-down organisation into a profitable construction firm?

There's no way back. Moreover, the task is quite realistic. Analysis has shown that not one of the loss-making trusts should be so. Say expenditure per rouble of construction and installation work was, for each of them, at least a little below the planned level. Where do the losses come from? From bad management. From enormous unproductive outlays. We have forgotten how to count money, or rather, we've never been taught to do so. We were taught to fulfil the plan at any cost, but only now have we started to think in terms of cost-effectiveness.

In other words, you want to apply the principles that at one time helped you create a strong contractual work team to make this trust a model for the whole country, yet it had been on the verge of collapse?

There's no other way; nothing will come of it until we close the circuit of the collective contract structure at the top. And if we do get a giant such as a TCA with an annual income of around 200 million roubles moving, then anyone can boldly apply our experience anywhere in construction! We are creating for the whole sector a model of profit-and-loss accounting from top to bottom and a model of the collective contract. This is why the Central Committee of the CPSU is supporting us.

I began with something basic: I wanted to unite the trusts with the mechanisation units which operated separately. On this basis I wanted to set up, within each trust, an engineering work directorate.

The EWD would lay down communications and organise amenities — in fact would do everything to enable the trust to operate as an independent economic unit.

The logic here is clear: to eliminate unnecessary organisational links. After all, while the mechanisation offices were separate from the trusts, the simplest question had to be decided via Moscow. To move a crane from one building site to another — permission from Moscow! In 'my' former Trust No. 18, we managed to get an EWD set up and the results were amazing!

In a word, an obvious decision. Moreover, back in December 1986 the Head Office of Glavk instructed that an EWD be set up in each trust — what could get in the way, one might think? Yet suddenly — stubborn resistance.

From whom?

First, from the Head Office itself. When, at the next session, I raised the issue of transferring the mechanisation offices to six of our trusts (in three of them, including No. 18, this had already been done), a heated debate broke out. It almost degenerated to the level of personal insults — how, they said, could someone who yesterday was a mere team leader, dictate policy to us? Of course, not all of them were in opposition, otherwise nothing would have come of it. We came to a compromise: I was allowed to 'reform' three of the six trusts. But this was not the end of the battle.

What do you think: will an order have any effect if the people to whom it applies are opposed to it? No! It's a hopeless task to reorganise a collective which is against any such reorganisation.

So, after the battle in Glavk I found out that the Naro-Fominsk mechanisation office had rebelled against merging with the trust. 'Work' had already been carried out there — you see democracy, not only we make use of it! So another general meeting of the whole work collective is convened, which will give a unanimous 'No!'. I rush off to the meeting understanding that this is the decisive moment, even though I have the order signed by the Glavk in my pocket. No order will help unless I can now manage to convince the people involved.

Did you?

I did...

Yet I still don't understand. Why, for what reasons, were they opposing you? In Glavk, yes, maybe someone thinks of you as an upstart, but at the mechanisation unit? The workers should have been attracted by the idea that Travkin was, until recently a team leader, one of their mates...

There are many nuances here. First: the structure had already taken shape and change in itself is a departure from a state of peace. Psychological inertia... But that wasn't the main thing. Everyone knows that mechanisation units are the most profitable elements in the construction industry. And everyone is quite aware that they get their profits at the expense of the prime contractor. He is unable to organise the work of subcontractors, of the very machine operators. They may work one shift, but get paid for two: it is cheaper for the trust not to argue.

For example, in Naro-Fominsk the trust is literally poverty stricken — almost two million losses in a year, and a total debt of 12 million. Next door — the mechanisation unit is just rolling in profits. So the workers and management got together but no one wanted to join hands with the poor relations.

How did you manage to change their minds? Did you play on their consciences?

Not only that. Though this, too, is important. Our people are clever; they understand everything if they have it explained to them properly. After all, we have been cultivating a feeling of Soviet patriotism for seventy years. So I said to them (about a hundred people had gathered): but it's your own state you are feeding on! Your profits are what you have grabbed off the impoverished trust: you look on while it collapses, and even warm your hands at the bonfire. Come on then, break it up completely! But then, what shall we need *you* for?

But you said it wasn't just a matter of conscience.

Any measure will be successful if the common interests coincide with personal ones. So I explained to them they would benefit from merging with the trust. Yes, I said, you will have to work harder, no one will write down two shifts for you instead of one, but if you really have worked two shifts, you'll earn more than if it had just been a 'paper' claim.

I went there together with the head of the EWD of the No. 18 Trust, Kharlamov, who also spoke to them. He told them straight: if anyone wants to earn as much as 700 roubles — then he can. But he'll have to work really hard, forgetting about weekends. From the audience came the retort: 'Perhaps we should work round the clock?' He answered that he wasn't forcing anyone, and added for some reason, no one complains about spending their spare time moonlighting. 'We provide your holiday pay, sick pay and housing', he said, 'but some of you go off to work for someone else. Is this the best use of labour power? And I, he went on, 'as the head have the obligation to provide everyone with an opportunity to earn well. Go on then! But here, for me, not for some other organisation.'

Well, there were some sarcastic outbursts, and at first they wouldn't agree, but eventually we brought them round. All of them, let me stress, all of them agreed. The next day at Glavk they asked how things were going. The work collective is for it, I said. They wouldn't believe me...

Who in Glavk will lose out from the introduction of profit-and-loss accounting and the contract system?

That's obvious: the apparatus that has become inflated beyond all measure. The collective contract system clearly demonstrates that this apparatus is redundant. Let's take as an example our TCA. Apart from the trusts, we shall also take under our wing the housing construction enterprises currently subordinate to the Large-Panel Housing Construction Office (LPHCO). There they have their own management apparatus, which will automatically contract by at least a hundred people. By a hundred respectable officials who do nothing but hand out directives and gather accounts!

The same thing will happen with the transformation of the design services. When the designers join our profit-and-loss system, a mountain of paper will be eliminated. Dozens of people in every trust, engaged in checking the design plans and specifications that come in from outside, will be without jobs. Or more accurately, they will have to become real workers, rather than just pretenders.

Now look: if we really carry out what we envisage in one of the three territorial associations of Glavk, do you think things will stop there? Of course, not! If the contract system proves its effectiveness and strength, many people will have to say goodbye to the quiet life, high salaries out of the state budget and privileges! 'You've come to destroy Glavk, to blow it up from the inside!' was what I had to listen to from some people. It's not a matter of my personality, but perhaps they are somewhere near the mark: for the bureaucracy, the collective contract is like a 'bomb'...

Over the last two years or so, we have seen the 'triumphal advance' of the collective contract through construction trusts. It's almost one hundred per cent. Does this mean that the problem is about to go away, and all that remains to do is to close the circuit in the upper link, as you are now doing?

This figure can be misleading. It is no longer possible to forbid or 'abolish' the collective contract, but emasculate it ... that's another matter. Sometimes, at a glance everything seems in order: there's an economic council in the trust and wages are paid according to the work input. But if you look closer, the very essence, managerial democracy has been reduced to nothing.

But in 1988 the new Law on the State Enterprise came into force: the financial welfare of each trust became directly dependent on the results of its operations. So, the distortions you mention will evidently disappear. To distort the contract will be to cut off your nose to spite your face?

But the 1988 plan was handed down from above. Each ministry and department is trying to pack it with more and more control figures, and if they succeed, everything will remain a fiction: full profit-and-loss accounting, and the collective contract, and the new law.

But the plan now is based on contracts that trusts conclude with the customers. The trust has reserved the right to sign or not sign the contract. And I made the managers understand publicly that this is precisely where the 'front line' runs today! To sign a contract which would bring an enterprise to bankruptcy is a crime against *perestroika*.

What do you think: will it take long to establish the new economic mechanism?

Perestroika is irreversible. But it could be faster. All the time we keep looking over our shoulder, fearing to overdo things. We introduce profit-and-loss accounting in an enterprise, then study the results of the 'experiment', then we expand it, and then expand it more... But profit-and-loss accounting makes harsher demands on the worker: if we bring too much pressure to bear, he's off to another job, and then another... So let's put each enterprise on full profit-and-loss accounting straight away! We'll get through the first year somehow, and after that we'll really get back on our feet.

Just like that, by direct order?

Why not? We assist a weak enterprise out of the budget, enabling it to keep its head above water, right? It doesn't want to learn to swim but we keep holding it up all the same! So let's cut off this lifeline; let it swallow some water and then start pulling with its hands! And if we see that an effort is being made, trying hard but still sinking — then we'll throw in a lifebelt...

Interview by M. KRUSHINSKI

Izvestia, 14 November 1987

Agriculture

The people, the weather and PERESTROIKA

In 1986-87, the first two years of the twelfth five-year plan, the gross grain yield in the USSR rose by 17 per cent. Over the same period, in comparison with the average annual output during the 11th five-year plan, meat production increased by 2.1 mln tons, or 13 per cent; milk by 8.2 mln tons, or 9 per cent; and eggs by 7 billion pieces, or 9.4 per cent. And, although during the 12th five-year plan the import of these foodstuffs was cut due to a decrease in foreign currency revenue, food supply in general was somewhat improved. The USSR Statistical Committee's data on per capita consumption of these basic foodstuffs (as of late 1987) are: meat and meat products including lard and offal in kind in meat equivalent 63 kg; milk and dairy products in milk equivalent 343 kg; eggs 270 pieces; fish and fish products 18 kg; sugar 46 kg; vegetable oil 10 kg; potatoes 105 kg; vegetables and melon crops 100 kg; fruit and berries (not including those used for wine production) 52 kg, and flour products (bread and paste in flour equivalent, as well as flour, cereals and legumes) 131 kg.

Unfortunately, we are still losing large amounts of potatoes, fruit and vegetables during transit, storage and sale, and in produce which is unfit for human consumption and used as cattle fodder. In 1985 we lost 1,115,000 tons of potatoes, or 10.8 per cent of the total amount produced, in 1987 this figure was 1,384,000 tons, or 12.5 per cent. The picture is similar with other foodstuffs. In 1985 1,385,000 tons of vegetables were lost, or 9 per cent, while in 1987 it was 1,195,000 tons, or 7.9 per cent. In 1985 130,000 tons of fruit (including citrus) were lost or 3.4 per cent, while in 1987 it was 179,000 tons, or 4.8 per cent. In 1985 99,000 tons of melons and gourds were lost, or 4.7 per cent, while in 1987 this was 129,000 tons, or 5.1 per cent.

The losses of potatoes, fruit and vegetables (including that used as cattle fodder) annually amount to 790-800 mln roubles in retail prices. This means that the losses of potatoes and vegetables in 1987 alone exceeded the joint annual consumption of these foodstuffs in Moscow and Leningrad.

On 23 November 1987 the front page of Pravda *carried an angry letter from one of its readers, Dudareva, entitled 'Everything in Short Supply'.*

'We live in a small town called Shahan, in Karaganda Region. We have three children, the youngest is just a year old. My husband works at the Shakhtinskaya Mine, I work at one too, but somewhere else. At the moment I'm on maternity leave. Do you know what made me write to you? I like reading Pravda's *section called "Letters about What Matters Most" because they are about real life. Well, I thought, I've never written to a newspaper before but I will now.*

'It was Sunday yesterday, and I went shopping. The elder children stayed at home, and I took the youngest one with me. I had to buy some butter. You should have seen the crowd in the shop. It was like queueing for bread during the war. How was I to get anything with a small child with me? I just turned round and went home.

'There's a well-known chocolate factory in the region but our children never see any nice sweets. There's only ever toffee or sometimes caramel. Life is supposed to be getting better, but we're always short of something in our town. Waffles are in short supply, and biscuits too, as well as sausages, cheese, halva, margarine, and a lot more. Yet judging by the papers, food production at agro-industrial associations is increasing every year. So where is this food then if the shops are empty? True, we've got canned fish, for which we thank the fishing industry. Meat is also sometimes available, but only in cooperative shops, where it is very expensive.

'Think about the problem of feeding a family in such conditions. The children are growing. And my husband works down a mine, not in an office job.'

Why is it so difficult to supply the population adequately with foodstuffs even now, when perestroika *is in full swing? What is hindering this? What can be done to end the difficulties which make agricultural production the acute problem it is?*

At the Party Central Committee Plenary Meeting in Feb-

ruary 1988 Mikhail Gorbachev said: 'If we are to change the situation, it is imperative to overcome dependence, the attempt of many local administrative bodies to solve the problem of food supplies by constant appeals to the centre. The most important thing here is to stop trying to run state and collective farms along administrative lines. It is important to open up possibilities for initiative and enterprise in the agrarian sector, to use all effective forms of organisation and labour remuneration: collective, tenant and family contracts within collective and state farms, as well as new approaches within the framework of the district agro-industrial associations.'

Mikhail Gorbachev, who spoke at the Fourth National Congress of Collective Farmers, said: 'We need to re-read Lenin in a way that will enable us to grasp fully what he has to say about creating a new society. His writings on the socialist cooperative movement provide us with a brilliant starting point for this.'

The growth of the cooperative movement is synonymous with the growth of socialism. The fewer cooperatives there are, the less there is of socialism. Or, to put it another way, the less there is in society of liberated labour, real democracy and genuine social transformation.

The issues of independence, autonomy and economic accountability were prominent on the congress agenda. The congress came to the conclusion that cooperatives have remained for too long the junior partners of the state sector.

THE REAL WORTH
OF A COLLECTIVE FARM

By ALEXANDER GUBER

How can collective farms be restored to their real worth? How can they once again become what they were originally intended to be — voluntary associations of farmers with total economic and organisational independence to satisfy public demand not by external directive but from the identity of their own interest with that of the public. It was the central issue discussed by some four thousand delegates to the Fourth National Congress of Collective Farmers.

When speaking to the delegates who represent collective farms with production levels on a par with the highest European and American farm performance, you get a strong feeling that these impressive results were attained in spite of the system of central command and bureaucratic management that prevailed over the years. The farms were most prosperous where the management was able to stand up to the bureaucracy and protect their independence.

But in former times such farms were the exception rather than the rule. The farm managers had to be daring, stubborn and have a keen business sense, and know how to deal with their superiors — abilities that were far from common. They also had to be wily as well as knowledgeable about the local situation, otherwise they would have no room to manoeuvre.

In short, in the past the poorer farms determined the overall situation in the countryside, and continue to do so today. Otherwise there would have been no need for the adoption of food programs, there would have been no shortages of meat and dairy products, and the government would not need to spend billions of roubles on food imports.

Here are some figures to illustrate the economic situation of the collective farms. In 1970 total collective farm basic assets (buildings, equipment, vehicles, livestock, etc.) were valued at 50.3 billion roubles. In 1987 they had grown by more than three and a half times to reach 180.8 billion roubles. But over these years farm output grew much more slowly, from 67.1 billion roubles in 1970 to 79.3 billion roubles in 1987.

The following facts were cited at the congress: one in ten collective farms have a profit rate of more than forty per cent, another ten per cent have a profit rate of five per cent or less, and nearly as many are completely unprofitable.

These last two groups of farms are largely responsible for the fact that, on the whole, Soviet collective farms remain a swamp into which are sunk billions of roubles of state investment with practically no result.

Despite this fact the state budget allocations for collective farm production is in need of certain adjustment, according to the congress delegates. They assert that the quality of new farm technology has not improved at the same rate as its rising costs. Putting it bluntly, a collective farm now pays twice what it did a few years ago for the same equipment.

Added to this, up to now collective farms were not consulted on, for example, what kind of tractor they needed and at what price. Tractors were simply delivered to the farms and payment for them was deducted from the farms' accounts. The farms were left without a choice: take what is delivered or go without.

This practice is now coming to an end. Collective farms now have the right to refuse delivery of equipment that is either unfitting or superfluous to needs. They invoke this right as often as they can. Yet, as before, they are left with little to choose from, thus the producer's grip on the consumer is perpetuated.

But, for instance, in Hungary, where the farm machinery industry is not as developed as in the Soviet Union, farms do have a choice. Farm machinery is not distributed, but sold. The collective farm decides on the kind of tractor or combine it needs, selects a manufacturer and determines how it is to be purchased, either on credit or by cash. Factories experiencing financial difficulties have been known to give considerable discounts to cash customers.

It is an open question as to whether such practices are applicable to Soviet conditions, but there may be no other way to break the grip of the producer.

At the congress it was repeatedly declared that collective farms which year after year constantly make a loss and factories that produce goods which consumers turn their backs on — are nothing but ballast that drags the economy down.

Another message signalled by the congress is that the economic bail-out of these enterprises at the expense of healthy ones is inappropriate and, basically, immoral. Collective farms that systematically operate in the red should lose their rights to the use of state land, that is, they should be abolished.

It is also time to sort out what kind of services are on offer to the collective farms, who offers them, and on what terms. In lining up suppliers of such things as mineral fertilisers, pesticides or building materials, or hiring contractors to do irrigation work, repair equipment and so forth, the collective farm is supposed to be treated as a paying customer. But can it choose a supplier or contractor and demand something from them? Only in rare instances.

A new draft of the collective farm charter discussed at the congress provides it with this right. But, as the delegates pointed out, the charter is binding only on the farms, and not on their suppliers. Only when the charter is backed by a law regulating cooperatives, mandatory for all parties, can the grip of the producer be broken.

New Times, 1 April 1988

Alongside organisational measures, the intensification of agricultural production presupposes significant advances in science.

The country's leading scientific centre in the field is the Lenin National Academy of Agriculture.

Founded in 1929, the Academy has nurtured some of the country's most outstanding scientists, among them a number of brilliant scientists known throughout the world. Some suffered tragic fates during the Stalin years. These losses could not but affect the performance of the Academy as a whole.

What changes are under way in the Academy now? What needs to be done to transform the food situation? These and other issues are discussed by ALEXANDER NIKONOV, *President of the Academy of Agriculture, and* VALERIA SHUBINA, *writer.*

MAN AND LAND

At the Academy of Agriculture

V. Sh. Once, at a conference devoted to nature conservation the work of the agricultural experts was dubbed 'intensification' in an altogether pejorative sense. The speakers attacked 'experts' in the field, made uncomplimentary remarks about the notorious 'black' session of the Academy of Agriculture in 1948, talked about its numerous blunders, and insisted it was going to kill us all off with its latest drive for intensification, reliance on pesticides and other chemicals. To a certain extent, I shared the assembly's indignation but could not help wondering if the Academy, which was doing its best to develop our agriculture, really deserved to be judged so harshly.

A. N. There is no other body of professionals that has been criticised so systematically as agricultural researchers, and it has not always been justified. Often the Academy has been made the scapegoat and found guilty of all innumerable crimes.

We should not forget one universally acknowledged fact, that the whip of the administrative management methods was felt the keenest in agrarian science. That was true of the 30s, and of the 40s and 50s too. Take Nikolai Vavilov, for example, whose strictly scientific approach did not fit into the accepted framework of the time. Lysenko and the like suited very well though. Science, production and the country as a whole have had to pay a costly price for all this. And we're talking of decades, not just two or three years.

V. Sh. But now the Academy has something to celebrate! I've heard that on 16 July 1987 a group of agrarian economists including Chayanov, Kondratiev, Chelintsev, Makarov and Yurovsky were rehabilitated. Fifteen people in all who were arrested and died during the Stalin period.

A. N. Yes, the USSR Supreme Court has found them not guilty. The majority of them belonged to school which was in the forefront of the world's agrarian science. They were actively involved in drawing up norms during the transition from farm produce requisitioning to tax in kind, and up to the 1930s were frequently called on by state bodies as consultants on agrarian policy.

A. V. Chayanov conducted major theoretical research in the field of cooperation and helped organise the cooperative movement in this country; N. D. Kondratiev invented the theory of 'cycles' in economic development which was later named after him, and was founder and head of the Institute of Topical Studies; A. N. Chelintsev researched into optimal location of agricultural production; N. P. Makarov was engaged in theoretical research on peasant farming, and later the organisation of socialist enterprises; L. N. Yurovsky was a specialist on money circulation.

Over the last 70 years Soviet agrarian science has traversed a difficult and controversial road, but its best representatives have never betrayed the truth. No one is going to absolve agrarian science from its share of responsibility for the current state of agriculture, but it is unreasonable to put all the blame on that quarter for social, moral, economic and other blunders. One more important point. Belief in the omnipotence of science is still universal, which is, of course, very flattering, but can it compensate for incompetent management?

V. Sh. Even today some agrarian specialists tend to be dogmatic. Their individual recommendations can take on an almost pathological form. A higher yield per unit of space is the key problem, especially now when all we ever seem to hear is, 'We're falling behind!' But do we want intensification at any price? That's what's worrying people. Indeed, who can guarantee the harmlessness of current chemical levels? It is true that we are losing a lot of produce due to pests, weeds and disease, but why the sole emphasis on chemicals? All these herbicides, fungicides, nematocides, acaricides and retardants make one's hair stand on end.

A. N. Unfortunately, many people believe it's a question of chemicals or nothing. Chemicals are a powerful means of raising agricultural efficiency, but there are others. Forests, uncultivated land, fertilizers and water all contribute in varying degrees. What we need is a rational approach, not blind worship of one idol after another. We are always calling for a comprehensive and systematic approach but rarely do we practise what we preach. So we continue importing grain. At the moment it's unrealistic to talk about abandoning the use of chemicals. What we must do is use them carefully. They should be applied at the right time and only to a certain depth, and not left lying around, or dumped along river banks and fields.

V. Sh. All the same, I think the present critical situation has arisen because plant protection has proved to be the weakest link in the chain of intensive technologies. In the whole vast region from the Urals to the Pacific there isn't a single Institute of Plant Protection, only an Institute of Agriculture and Chemicalisation. And we're talking about Siberia with its vulnerable ecological systems and extreme conditions, where even the remains of pesticides break down at a much slower rate than in Europe.

A. N. Beyond the Urals the level and scope of scientific research is far behind the country's European region. Giving it more impetus in Siberia would promote other industries as well. This is not only a practical but a social problem. Production of biological fertilizers and pesticides is a fairly new but very promising branch of science. In Siberia, it will be developed alongside the production of chemicals. We have an Institute of Biological Methods of Plant Protection in Kishinev. Useful work in this field is being done in Tashkent. For the moment we cannot give up pesticides, and I would be lying if I said anything else. What's important is to make sure that safety levels are not breached.

V. Sh. However, as far as I know we have not yet developed accurate methods of measuring the residual traces of pesticides in vegetables and fodder crops. Laboratories have been set up, but they are not fulfilling their function. On the one hand there are good harvests, on the other toxic substances are accumulating in the soil and in plants. Each plant has its own concentration level, with cabbage, cucumbers and melons at the top of the list.

A. N. I believe the medical science should carry out toxicological examinations. Just as the state control and test service are independent of the enterprises, so medical centres should be independent of the state agro-industrial complex (Gosagroprom).

V. Sh. In preparation for this interview I met V. Kiryushin, head of the Siberian Institute of Agriculture and Chemicalisation and a Corresponding Member of the Academy of Agriculture, and some of the staff of the plant protection department. Someone mentioned Academician Gilyarov, who popularised integrated or combined chemical and biological methods of combating pests and weeds. These are rarely used today. Why is this so?

A. N. That's not quite true. We are promoting integrated methods that combine biological, mechanical, chemical and other elements. However, whether chemical, biological or integrated, these are methods of suppresion, while the most sensible one is selection. We should concentrate on creating resistant varieties even though this is extremely difficult. There are still no absolutely resistant plants.

V. Sh. Is there any point in repeating for the hundredth

time that wherever land is concerned, the whole range of agricultural problems should be based on a moral and humanitarian understanding? It has to be admitted that in abandoning this principle we have lost a great deal. We did not even bother to leave some areas intact as nature reserves when exploiting the European part of the country. Today, before our very eyes, the last of the feather- grass steppe in the Ukraine is being trampled and eaten by the sheep of the Animal Husbandry Institute!

A. N. I suppose you are referring to Askania-Nova, about which so many people have expressed concern? At the moment the Askania-Nova reserve is accountable to the Ukrainian Scientific Research Institute of Steppe Animal Husbandry, but we are trying to bring it under the jurisdiction of the Academy of Agriculture's Presidium, which will monitor the native environment jointly with the State Committee for Hydrometeorology.

We have an agricultural institute in Voronezh Region where a hundred years ago Vassily Dokuchayev created a model of stable farming in the Kamennaya Steppe that still functions.

Our oldest agricultural scientific centre, the Nikitsky Botanical Gardens, is also of considerable interest. It is engaged in subtropical plant growing and nature monitoring.

V. Sh. If you remember, my article in *Literaturnaya Gazeta* was the reason for our first meeting. You invited me to a session of the Academy's Presidium, where my piece called 'Botanical Gardens' was being discussed. Listening to what was being said, I realised that the problem of old centres like the Nikitsky Gardens will never be solved unless we give priority to the question of protected territories, limits on land use, and possibly, keeping some areas intact as memorials. All kind of departments, some powerful, some not so powerful, are trying to get their hands on land to which they have no right whatsoever. In the past they used to build private dachas, now it's health and holiday homes for the *élite*. We're constantly fighting to get this land back. The threat of extinction is hanging over the Issyk Kul Preserve for useful insects, the first of its kind in the country and which has been in existence for 16 years. The section of feather-grass steppe near Tselinograd, enclosed thanks to

the efforts of Academician Barayev, has still not been granted any legal status. Meanwhile, the ploughing up of lands
in the Asian regions of the country is having fatal consequences.

A. N. Yes, in many parts of the country the ecological
balance and the sensible correlation between cultivated and
uncultivated land has been upset. The introduction of intensive technologies everywhere will make the expansion of
cultivated territories unnecessary. The ploughing up of
whole areas causes surface water drainage to carry away
particles of soil which dry up, and its fertile layer is blown
away by dust storms. As one scientist put it, the fields have
become a sieve letting through water and nutrients. Lakes
and smaller rivers are drying up and the microclimate
changing. The problem of land use would also solve many
questions of nature conservation. In relation to the Nikitsky Botanical Gardens, the Presidium of the Academy of
Agriculture has passed a resolution and its implementation
will be under our control.

The past few years produced a great number of time-
servers who couldn't care less about the future. Something
that Dmitry Mendeleyev termed 'depersonalisation in land
cultivation' took place. Now we are paying for this.
Frankly speaking, those working the land or using it —
builders, road-builders, electrification, communication and
irrigation workers — have for far too long been absolved
from material, administrative and legal responsibility. They
had no personal concern for its proper use. Up till now all
we've attempted to do is to scare people with fines that are
not in any way proportional to the damage. The culprits
were required to pay insignificant sums of money, and out
of state funds at that, while the losses sustained by society
were incalculable.

V. Sh. Suffice it to say that industrial and city dumps
alone occupy up to two million hectares; over the past
twenty years millions of hectares have been taken over for
non-agricultural use. We are not as rich in land as it would
seem, it's shrinking like shagreen leather.

A. N. Whereas 25 years ago there was over a hectare of
cultivated land per person, the figure is now only 0.82 hectares. The law obliges organisations and departments that
have had temporary use of land to restore it to its original

state, but this obligation usually falls to agriculture. Land, like water, has a price. For decades no one recognised this. And since there was no price on the land there was a correspondingly negligent attitude to it. But this will end soon.

V. Sh. Scientists predict that the amount of cultivated land per person will fall as a result of urbanisation, population increases and degradation of the soil. New territories, therefore, will have to be opened up, and, as a rule, these are located in either very dry or very damp zones. What do you think about melioration? Can we do without it, as some people believe.

A. N. Incompetent performance paves the way for extreme opinions. In places the soil is excessively damp; on large territories it is too dry; it can be acid, heavy or saline, stony or prone to alkalization. To ignore melioration, or land improvement, in such conditions means to impede the growth of agricultural production and progress in land cultivation. It is important that this work should be of an agroecological nature and not simply engineering as it has been up to now. Melioration should be comprehensive and cautious; water melioration (irrigation and drainage) should go hand in hand with other measures. We must stop thinking solely in terms of large-scale projects and combine them with smaller-scale ones, building new ponds and reservoirs, and so on.

V. Sh. I've got nothing against melioration. I am only indignant at people who carry it out in ways that damage nature, like thoughtlessly draining marshes which are the natural habitat of some rare birds.

A. N. What we need is ecological awareness. A man with a scythe could spare a nest, but a man in a combine harvester will not even notice what's below. Unfortunately we have never used a comprehensive approach when it came to the ecological problems.

V. Sh. This country, which under Peter the Great was the first to begin planting forests, and which has unique experience in creating oases in the desert (take, for example, Dokuchayev's famous Kamennaya Steppe, which you have already mentioned, Veliky Anadol not far from Mariupol, and the Starobelsky land) has recently slackened its efforts in shelter-belt planting. Many countries have far outpaced us in this respect. Over the past five years China has planted as many shelter-belts as our country has in seven decades. A 6,000-km long green shelter-belt stretches along the edge of the desert, and in the south of China a similar belt serves as protection from the monsoons. In England they plant belts to avoid using chemical pesticides. Arable land, eroded soils, pastures and sands (whose extent still exceeds that of arable land), all need forest shelter. State ecological strategy is unthinkable without forest planting.

A. N. You mentioned the reign of Peter the Great. At that time timber was mostly used to build ships and houses. However, it has gradually become clear that wind breaking plantation can help us to achieve better harvests, increase the humidity of soil and air, alter temperature and protect the soil from weathering and erosion. Unfortunately, we haven't got an agro-forestry-melioration service to speak of as yet. What used to be a large department has been reduced to two people, part of the agro-industrial centre. In its present form it can do nothing to alleviate the problem. The Academy has produced a programme for wind-break planting, and the Presidium has recently been considering it.

Last May at a session of the Academy held in Volgograd we discussed the problem of the stability of agriculture and ways of combating droughts. The global climate is getting warmer and this is liable to increase the likelihood of droughts in our latitudes and especially in the south. It's better to be prepared for the worst. We have drawn up a programme of measures aimed at improving the stability of agriculture, which should help us to withstand droughts and other unfavourable natural factors.

V. Sh. To sum up our talk, we could say that the relationship between man and land, and nature in general, has become extremely complicated over the past few decades. A host of problems has arisen which will have to be dealt with as a whole. Otherwise, a high yield, be it milk or meat, could spell disaster for the land. We must not miscalculate.

A. N. You're quite right. Competent use of intensive technologies requires a high standard of education, morality and conscience on the part of both farmer and scientist. Our land has suffered far too long from stereotyped approaches and indifference. It cannot take anymore.

I'd like to point out that we have only considered the ecological aspect of the problem. But there are also social and economic aspects, which are just as important. New methods are beginning to be introduced, particularly that of transferring land on a long-term basis to basic producer groups (contract teams, small groups and families). These first steps are encouraging. The land is finally getting a responsible and interested master. This is the right approach.

Literaturnaya Gazeta, 5 August 1987

In the summer of 1985 Izvestia *carried a story about* NIKOLAI SIVKOV, *from the Krasnaya Gorka farm hidden in the depths of the Archangel Region. He had signed a contract with the local state farm to fatten first five, then eight and finally 12 calves on his own farm. The project promised to be profitable both to Sivkov and the farm. No one denies this. But paradoxically, every new story about the man carried by the press, every television programme about him (the Moscow Documentary Film Studio made a film about him called 'An Archangel Farm Worker' which provoked lively interest throughout the country and equally lively irritation on the part of the local authorities) has compounded the difficulties of Sivkov's existence. Why is his initiative constantly coming up against a lack of understanding, unpleasantness and even hostility?*

The film incidentally put Sivkov under particular suspicion: attempts were made to cast aspersions on his past. Sivkov, described by everyone who knows him as a difficult and a rough man, immediately retaliated by writing to the Regional Party Committee and was eventually received by P. Telepnyov, the First Secretary. The interview proved to be fruitless and to this day passions continue to rage around 'the Archangel farm worker'. Sivkov has undertaken in the not too distant future to reduce the prime cost of beef to 75 kopecks per kg, while the average figure throughout the country is 3 roubles 68 kopecks. Yet the most common reaction to this is to call him a kulak and a money-grubber.

The relations between Sivkov and the state farm's director, Solovyov, are openly hostile. After the film about Sivkov was shown on central television, he received a visit from a couple from the Kuban area who wanted to join his project. Solovyov refused to grant permission and would not permit them

*to live in the all deserted village of Sluda. The same happened
to two young men from Moldavia, and two from Kiev. All of
them left. Only Vitaly Ivanov, an engineer from Obninsk in
Kaluga Region, found a job as a cowherd not far from Sivkov's farm, and is still hoping that permission to set up a cooperative will finally be granted.*

As Izvestia *reported on 21 August 1987, a dossier has been
opened on Sivkov. It consists of two folders, one containing
newspaper clippings, and the other, references, certificates,
money orders, Sivkov's complaints and the regional authorities' replies, together with a photograph of the calf-house with
a crow-bar in lieu of a lock on the doors.*

*'We're going to break off all business with Sivkov,' de-
clares Yu. Seliverstov, Chairman of the Vinogradov district
agro-industrial association. 'We've had it up to here with
him.'*

*'All we ever hear is Sivkov, Sivkov... I wouldn't have taken
him on at my farm, he'd eat up all my profits with his wages',
says the director of one of the district's state farms. 'What if
others follow suit? There'd be no one left on the farms.'*

*It gets curious more and more. It is no secret that the So-
viet press and TV enjoy such tremendous authority in the
country that virtually every critical report prompts Party or
state bodies to do something immediately to set matters right
and punish the culprits. Here it is quite the opposite: the more
the national press writes about Sivkov the more vigorously he
is attacked by those in power in the Archangel Region.*

*What is so special about Sivkov? Why is he still causing so
much fuss?*

PERESTROIKA AS SEEN
FROM KRASNAYA GORKA HOMESTEAD

Nikolai SIVKOV (farmer) and Lev VOSKRESENSKY
(journalist) on family contract farming

It is worth considering why Lenin's words still ring true
today after so many years: 'We look down disparagingly
upon cooperative societies, failing to appreciate their exceptional importance, first of all, in terms of principle (the

means of production being owned by the state) and secondly, in terms of their being the *most straightforward, simple and accessible form of transition for the peasant* to a new economic system.' Also: 'We should avoid philosophising and contortions as far as possible. In this respect NEP is a step forward because it can be adapted to suit even the most ordinary peasant.'

These words might have been spoken today. Does this mean that after seventy years of searching, of discoveries, failures and successes, we are finally moving towards that crossroads of ideas and historical experience that Lenin saw?

I did not ask Nikolai Sivkov whether he had read 'On Cooperation'. More important is the fact that this farmer from Krasnaya Gorka in the depths of the far north is discovering cooperative management for himself as a natural process, without philosophising.

A lot has been written about the documentary film 'An Archangel Farm Worker', which looked at the Sivkov family's farming team. A whole case study could be compiled from all the articles, letters and official papers, but only on paper — in reality the team no longer exists and the people concerned have left the state farm.

What happened? Is everything over?

No. We may have taken a step backwards, but that doesn't mean to say we've given up our ideas. We need to sit down now and think everything through calmly and thoroughly and then start from the beginning again.

The situation today is as follows: the 60 state-farm calves and heifers which the team got on contract have been fattened and sent to slaughter; the team has declined to sign a new contract with the state farm and Nikolai Sivkov's two team-mates, his son Sergei and Victor Yedemsky, have returned to their former jobs, while the team leader himself is leaving the state farm for good in early November.

If it was a purely personal quarrel between the administration and the team there would be little point in writing about it, but this is something far more serious. Two different approaches to the solution of the food problem (one of the most topical socio-economic problems today) have clashed, they possibly represent two different attitudes to *perestroika*. In theory everyone would appear to be for it. In practice, as far as the land round Ust-Vayenga village and Krasnaya Gorka farm are concerned — an infertile, boggy land, overgrown with forests and partially abandoned by agriculturists, but still capable of feeding a good herd of cattle and producing cheap meat — there appears to be nothing in common between this 'Archangel Farm Worker' and his opponents from the state farm office right the way up to district and regional level.

This dispute needs to be settled promptly. Sooner or later the system of state subsidies which keeps the retail price of meat artificially low in comparison to actual costs, will have to be abolished. When this happens the only way to prevent the consequent price increases would be to lower production costs. It is necessary, therefore, to ascertain the reasons for the increase in losses and overheads which raise production costs, and to find ways to make meat production cheaper. Nikolai Sivkov believes he has found the way. Not in theory, but in practice, not for general use, but for use on the land on which he lives. He is prepared to prove it by his own labour, without subsidy or exploitation, if only he is given the opportunity.

The state farm administration claims that the team violated the fattening process and failed to achieve the 500 grammes weight increase per head, per day, stipulated in the contract, thus not fulfilling the meat production plan.

This is true, but then the state farm itself failed to achieve its target under prevailing conditions in 1987. Its weight increases were even lower than Sivkov's team achieved. More importantly, the team itself laid in about two-thirds of all the fodder required to feed the cattle during the winter. It laid in 100 tons of hay for the winter, but this proved inadequate and the team was obliged to take an extra 20 tons from the state farm, for which it paid, of course. It took half the mixed feed which was due to it, and would have preferred to take none at all, making do with hay and potatoes.

In passing, let us note that this is a truly conscientious *strategically correct* approach to the job. One of the main problems in the field of agriculture is that we have started feeding cattle on grain, and in such a wasteful and reckless fashion that we end up having to buy fodder for hard currency. Sivkov, as a farmer, has understood the essence of the problem, without recourse to the State Planning Committee or the Lenin All-Union Academy of Agriculture calculations. He knows that it is unprofitable to overdo mixed feeds and that grain should not be wasted.

Sivkov may have failed to produce the amount of meat stipulated in the contract, but his meat was cheap. Preliminary estimates show a figure of 150 roubles per 100 kg increase in weight (1 rouble 50 kopecks per kilogram), which represents half the average price in the district.

This, apparently, worried the state farm administration and it quickly changed the system of calculating production costs as follows.

The team had planted, harvested and fed its cattle 11 tons of potatoes. They had planted their own seeds, fertilized the land themselves, and used their own horse to plough the land and dig the potatoes. They had paid for the loan of a tractor and potato digger from the state farm. According to Sivkov's estimates, the cost of producing a kilogram of potatoes was 2-3 kopecks or at the most 5. When the state farm received these potatoes, however, it entered the cost of production as 13.5 kopecks — the amount it spent itself on producing a kilogram of potatoes on its own fields. As the cost of fodder increased so, naturally, did the cost of the meat produced by the team. The same stratagem was used when estimating the cost of the 100 tons of hay laid up by the team.

Yet no matter how hard the administration tried to 'raise' production costs, Sivkov's meat proved to be cheaper!

So, your team's a bit of a sore thumb to the state farm as far as production costs are concerned?

More or less, says Sivkov. The administration is simply not interested in comparing production costs. But what's going to happen when they're forced to go over to self-recoupment and self-financing?

The whole point is that some farm leaders (and not only them) fear nothing more than real cost-accounting, self-recoupment and self-financing. They have got used to 'following the plan' at any cost, without regard to what, whom and how much it costs. They are used to being in debt to the bank — if the state doesn't actually cancel the debts, it'll prolong them. They are used to land improvement, centralised mixed feeds and credit coming like manna from heaven at the state's expense. When everything is like that there's no need to change, take risks, or reorganise one's way of working. Cost-accounting is the mortal enemy of such an approach to the economy.

Sivkov is in his element with self-financing. For him it is the only chance of surviving and getting established. That is why he always carries a newspaper clipping of the Political Report of the CPSU Central Committee to the 27th Congress in his wallet ('Like a prayer-book, always at hand,' he says). I can assure you that few propagandists preparing for a lecture or a seminar have studied the Report as scrupulously and painstakingly as this farmworker.

All he asks for is a clear picture of how self-financing works.

What's needed is an independent, self-financing unit — the cooperative, says Sivkov. First and foremost this cooperative needs land. And when we hire the land, of course, we need to know what we are paying for — what the soil and the terrain are like. Black earth is one thing, but what about sand, gullies and swamp? We need to be able to hire the land for not less than 10 years, otherwise there's no point in the farmer taking care of it.

What about hiring machinery?

Absolutely not! We'd go bankrupt. I've worked out it's more profitable to actually buy the machines.

Even at current prices and quality?

What's wrong with the prices? They suit us fine, provided we're given decent credit terms. The tractors are good, and we can fit the parts ourselves — we know how to.

Do you need much land?

In this district there are 22 head of cattle (35 including the calves) per 100 hectares of arable land — no more. A cooperative could fatten 60 head per 100 hectares, provided a third of the land could be ploughed.

What about people? You haven't got a team anymore.

As soon as the cooperative's been set up and the contract signed people will come back to work on the farm. Our indivisible fund at Krasnaya Gorka comprises a cattleshed for 40 head, a hayloft and a well. We've built it all ourselves, at our own expense. At the end of the year I'll expand the cattleshed to hold 60 head. Once you have that kind of solid base, there's no problem finding people.

How many people do you need in the cooperative?

We could take on any number, but you need to start from a nucleus of two or three families to build up trust and compatibility. After that people join this nucleus. We would like to mend the road so that people wouldn't get so worried that the school, hospital, post office and club are so far away. They keep trying to scare us with these distances, but what's the problem? My Dad wasn't afraid of going 11 km away from the village to Krasnaya Gorka in 1925, when there wasn't any electricity or telephone, and he had no car (all of which I've got now). People need space, so we'll find people who aren't afraid of living far away from everyone else. There are plenty of hard workers around. People are always nattering on about how farmworkers have got lazy, how they drink too much, and such like. It's a lie! Make them free men, untie their hands, let them get on with things without interfering all the time. Give them some real work to get on with so they feel they're in charge — and people will work willingly and put their back into it. The state'll get cheaper meat and the farmworkers — better wages.

I'm 56, I've got another three and a half years to go before I get my pension, but I'll work another 10-15 years. After that I'll be too old. I hope by that time the farm'll have 3 or 4 houses at least, not just one, like now. However northern it is with its cold and marshland and so on, it's still very dear to me: it's my home. I don't want it to fall into neglect or decay — that's why I'm all for the cooperative. We won't give in.

There is a clear decision of the Executive Committee of the District Soviet: 'To allow, as an exception, citizen Nikolai Sivkov ... to set up a cattle-fattening cooperative... The State Bank office to decide the question of opening an account for the production activities of the cooperative and to grant, if need be, short-term loans... The district financial department is authorised to draft a model charter ... with subsequent registration at the Executive Committee of the District Soviet.'

A sound decision. As far as is known this is only the second case of its kind in the USSR (the first being the Snyatinka cooperative in the Zagorsk District, Moscow Region).

But this was only the beginning of an uphill task.

Six weeks after the resolution was adopted Sivkov received a copy of the Contract Agreement with the Administration of the State Farm for the Fattening of Cattle. No mention of the cooperative. True, the team received 79 hectares of pasture and an island of 92 hectares on the River Dvina. (The island is not under cultivation, there being only 1.5 hectares of arable land on it, already cleared some time earlier by the team, the rest is sand and bush). But the team was bound hand and foot by restrictions and regulations. 'The administration undertakes to write out a receipt for the fodder produced by the team and to pass it on to the team head.' A taxing commitment indeed! The team produced the fodder, the state farm, as it were, acquired it, worked out the amount, adjusted the figure to fit its own average prime costs and then, as it were, returned the fodder to the team with an injunction to make thrifty and responsible use of it. So much talk about how to use the fodder and pastures — coming from people who knew a great deal less than Sivkov about how to do so. Matters standing as they did, the cooperative was not its own master but a mere cog in a far from perfect machine.

Would it be any use if the cooperative become a branch of the state farm?

'None at all,' insists Sivkov, 'what I'm suggesting is that they allow us to decide for ourselves what is best. We want a clear agreement on plan targets for meat and the terms for selling what is produced over and above these. Who will the agreement be with? I've no idea. With the state farm, the district agro-industrial association, or the consumers' cooperatives? What's important is that there be an arbiter, or a second, to look after the interests of the state (and **not** some department or another), someone with a knowledge of economics, who could sort things out. But if the arbiter's functions are usurped by one of the signatories to the agreement (the state farm administration) we shall only be independent on paper.'

Surely the role of arbiter should be taken on by state and Party bodies? Who if not they should rise above parochial interests and 'look after the interests of the state'?

Let us, however, see what P. Telepnyov, First Secretary of the Archangel Regional Party Committee had to say in his open letter in reply to Professor Stanislav Fyodorov, who had publicly asked the following straightforward and natural question: 'Why can't you allow the hard-working Sivkovs to act freely? Why are you afraid of them?' Referring to the District Soviet's resolution quoted above, P. Telepnyov asked in turn: 'Are we afraid? What more freedom are you asking for? Everything has been done properly. It is quite another matter that, after the District Executive Committee's resolution (or so we have been informed), the "team leader" has to date shown no initiative in setting up the cooperative, although considerable time has passed. There's been so much hullabaloo about it all that it looks as if the baby's been thrown out along with the bath water. We believe it's time to stop.'

Is the team leader guilty? Has he really shown no initiative, this very same Archangel farmworker who forced the authorities into giving him a family contract on his farm, who forced them to agree to the idea of a cooperative, and who is now fighting for a legally valid agreement, having shouldered all the hard work involved in its economic, organisational, financial and juridical substantiation, and toiling away to finish building the cattle yard, which is the cooperative's material base?

Oh no, there is still a lot that has not been *done properly*. In fact, Sivkov is only now about to get the chance to *start work*. Once his cooperative, or 'mini-farm', 'cooperative farm', or 'cooperative business'—the name is unimportant—is set up. Then prime costs will be reduced, meat will be cheaper, and the paper work can stop. But only then. Not a day earlier.

Moscow News, 8 November 1987

WHAT IS 'FAKT'?

By G. PALAMARCHUK

Not long ago the appearance of each new cooperative in Moscow was a memorable event. At present there are more than 1500 of them in the capital and it can be assumed that this number will continue to increase. We cannot be but happy that these cooperatives have taken it upon themselves to unburden us of many of our everyday problems, helping us to save time and avoid frayed nerves. If you need to change flats, have repairs done quickly or build a dacha, if you urgently require someone to look after a child or invalid, there is now a number of cooperatives to which you can turn to find qualified people. This new system of cooperative ventures is also attractive to many people in that it gives them opportunity to use their skills and talents in their spare time and put into practice whatever original ideas may have been buzzing in their heads during their leisure time.

Of course, there are still many difficulties in this new line of business and another cooperative, 'Fakt', a paying information service, has set about helping to smooth these out. As an efficient intermediary, it puts cooperatives in touch with each other, provides them with the necessary documentation and information on business propositions from state organisations, on available raw materials and equipment of all kinds, helps in the selection of specialist personnel, and passes on innovatory commercial ideas.

'Dial 299-00-04', explains Mr. V. Yakovlev, head of the information service, 'and one of the 12 telephonists working in our bureau will answer your queries for a set fee. You can get more detailed information by calling into 'Fakt' for a consultation. We send out regular information packs to our subscribers.'

'Fakt' employees —lawyers, economists, journalists and sociologists— help organising bodies wishing to set up a cooperative to draw up draft rules, prepare technical and economic groundwork, and necessary documents. 'Fakt' also warns against pitfalls and unexpected misjudgements, not least the unpropitious choice of name for a new cooperative. According to 'Fakt' statistics, in the course of a month more than 100-150 cooperatives change the nature of the service they offer and operate new forms of business. Commercial success, therefore, depends on a thorough study of consumer demand.

'We believe that ample and timely information will strengthen confidence and trust in cooperatives,' says S. Aleksandrovich, one of the members of the management board of 'Fakt'. 'The suspiciousness we're still encountering will disappear and we believe the cost of the services provided by cooperatives will be stabilised. Already many cooperative workshops are claiming their prices are only a little higher than state prices.

Curious — and heartening — news items can be picked up from the 'Fakt' bulletins. To mention but a few, miners in Vorkuta have started growing button mushrooms in exhausted underground pits along cooperative lines, while a cooperative in Kishinev by agreement with a carpet factory there, is restoring old furnishings to their former colours... State enterprises are now looking with a more commercial eye at their waste and outdated equipment, offering cooperatives apparently valueless oddments of tinplate, paper dust, plastic shavings and so on. With initiative and ingenuity, the coops can turn these into useful goods for the public to buy.

Pravda, 8 April 1988

The process of renewal is continuing in Soviet society. Renewal, as the word suggests, must bring forth novel forms, methods and attitudes, abandon hackneyed, worn out practices and, on the contrary, actively seek new ones. Recently, there have been quite a few interesting discoveries. Doubtlessly, not all of them will be approved of unanimously by society, but that must not become a pretext for discarding new ideas before they are examined. This applies particularly to the Provesin agricultural firm's initiative in Lvov.

BUY SHARES IN THE PROVESIN AGRICULTURAL FIRM!

By ALEXANDER GUREVICH

By customary standards the above invitation may be unusual but nevertheless it is soon to be published by an agricultural firm in Lvov. The Ukrainian word *provesin* means 'the coming of spring'. The firm has been set up on the basis of a state farm supplying the city of Lvov and neighbouring towns with fresh vegetables, flowers and mushrooms.

The population of Lvov—some 800,000—has constantly suffered from chronic shortages of early vegetables, which the firm has been unable to alleviate with the 16 hectares of greenhouse space at its disposal. The Lvov Region Party Committee has, therefore, decided to build a further 40 hectares of greenhouse facilities by the end of the current five-year plan to improve the situation, using money provided by the city's industrial enterprises and other organisations.

'But what have shares to do with this?' I asked the firm's General Director, Ivan Piven.

'The firm's staff have decided that they have had enough of complaining about the lack of organisation, enough of lamenting and looking for a scapegoat. We must stop wasting time and get down to business, acting on the decisions of the Party and government and proceeding from the principle that "everything is legitimate which is not illegal".

'From 1988 onwards, the firm will become a society of individual and collective shareholders. All organisations and enterprises, irrespective of the ministries or departments they belong to, are welcome to invest money in it. Genuine economic initiative can make no concessions to parochial, bureaucratic limitations.'

According to Ivan Piven the shareholders' society will operate on the following basis. The agricultural firm itself will be the major shareholder. It will likewise retain a 60 per cent vote on the society's managing committee, which will also include representatives of the various shareholding enterprises. As many as 22 industrial enterprises in Lvov have already expressed interest in becoming shareholders. They include the Lvov railway company and industrial enterprises such as Lvovkhimselmash, Avtopogruzchik and others. Enterprises with disposable funds will make money payments that will be put towards financing the firm's construction projects. Enterprises without such disposable funds may help on a practical basis with the construction work. Individual groups will work as cooperatives within the overall framework of the society. For example, the firm will supply seeds and fertilizers for growing onions or celery and teach them how to cultivate them. The entire crop will be bought by the firm.

'Everyone stands to gain: the people themselves, the firm, which gets extra money and labour, and society as a whole,' Ivan Piven is positive. 'State help is important, but it has its limits. Why not use various enterprises' and the population's uninvested money for developing our firm? The Law on State Enterprise allows us to use our capital freely to the best advantage of the work collective and production. Any shareholder may leave the society and take his or her invested money, as well as a share of any profits that have been made. Our society will guarantee its shareholders interest at twice the 2 or 3 per cent rate of an ordinary bank or savings bank.'

I asked the General Director whether he was afraid of going bankrupt.

'No,' he replied. 'I share Mikhail Gorbachev's opinion that the biggest mistake lies in being afraid of making mistakes. Our produce will always find a ready market. Moreover, we are determined to expand the firm's activity within the framework of CMEA. We have good ties with an agricultural enterprise in Rzeszow, Poland. They gave us the idea of growing mushrooms and cauliflowers, and now that it's worked out well we're sharing our know-how with them.

'Our direct contacts with two Hungarian agricultural enterprises — the Pecsi state farm and the Novotrade shareholders' society — promise profitability for both sides. With their help we plan to modernise production and step up output, maintaining a quality as good as anything on world market. Novotrade, for example, has offered to set up a joint enterprise with us for growing seed potatoes and other vegetables. We have accepted their offer.

'Perestroika is slowly but surely removing the barriers that hinder initiative and creativity. Work itself has become much more interesting, inspiring and productive. Take my advice: join our Provesin society without delay. Our bank account number is 40615 at the Chervonoarmeisk Branch of the USSR State Bank, Lvov. We pay interest either in money or fresh vegetable, if you wish — quite an advantage in wintertime.'

Moscow News, 20 December 1987

Science and Technology

New worlds to win

When President of the USSR Academy of Sciences GURIY MARCHUK *was asked what he thought was the goal of Soviet science in the restructuring drive, he replied:*

'The aim of science in perestroika is to attain pre-eminence — or at least world level — in many branches of scientific research. A second objective is to bring into existence the conditions that will link science and industry more closely, especially at enterprise level.

'Of course, it would be naive to assume that in Soviet science — or for that matter, in world science — major discoveries are made every month of the year. Yet, reflecting on the most impressive accomplishments of Soviet science in 1987, several breakthroughs merit attention.

'Firstly, there is the work of a team of researchers headed by Academician R. Petrov of an AIDS diagnostic test employing artificial antigens. The AIDS virus has many forms. The method devised by Petrov's team makes it possible to detect the different modifications of the AIDS virus. This method has brought us one step closer to creating a vaccine against the virus.

'Another valuable development is the achievement of unique results in the field of high-temperature superconductivity independently in the Soviet Union, the United States and Japan. It is impossible to overestimate the significance of these results for fundamental science and the practical application of superconductivity.

'A third breakthrough worth mentioning is the successful application of hard-body lasers, which holds out vast technological prospects and new industrial concepts.

'Fourthly, substantial progress has been made in thermonuclear synthesis. In August 1987, at the Joint Institute of Nuclear Research in Dubna, outside Moscow, an international team of scientists headed by Academician GEORGI

FLEROV, *director of the laboratory of nuclear reactions, synthesised the 110th element of the Table of Elements and set out to synthesise the 111th element.*

Of course, Soviet scientists are conducting successful research in various other fields, of which more later.'

Those who read Soviet Scene 1987 *may recall that Academician Valery Legasov was one of the ten most famous people in the world for 1986. A holder of a USSR State Prize he has done distinguished work in the chemistry of rare gases and the chemistry of plasma. Legasov came to the attention of the world through his heroic efforts to tame the damaged Chernobyl reactor. In the Soviet Union Legasov is also known for his work on a project to devise a model of modern industry that would best protect man and his environment from unpredictable emergency situations.*

In fact, alarming reports from all corners of the earth give grounds for both specialists and the general public to be seriously concerned. Among such problems are acid rain, the consequences of pesticides, pollution of the oceans and waterways and accidents causing human suffering and great property losses.

Experts in various fields work constantly to increase the reliability of every operational device and devise new technical and organisational means for protecting mankind and the environment from harm.

Yet, despite an overall improvement in statistics (such as accidents per thousand operational devices), the cost of a single flaw or technological mistake has increased manifold. There is an irony in this! While the probability of a single negative event occurring has fallen, such as an air, rail or ship accident, the destruction of a dam or a chemical enterprise, or even a nuclear accident — the scale of the consequences from that accident, should it occur, has risen manifold and at times assumes catastrophic dimensions. Here is just one example: whereas in the 1940s, in dozens of air disasters the death toll amounted to dozens of people, today the more rare, single air crash costs hundreds of lives.

Thus, while the need to protect people and the environment has provided a powerful impetus for the development of reliable technology to preclude negative consequences, the development of technology has also drastically increased the extent of human risks.

How can these apparently contradictory tendencies be reconciled? Valery Legasov, reflecting on this subject, wrote recently in Kommunist: *'For scientific and technical progress, which has already demonstrated its vast possibilities, to continue to serve people, it is necessary for experts in all fields of knowledge to work together to see that their achievements are used with greater circumspection and safety. These efforts must be made both in the institutions that are responsible for the development of technology and in specially created centres for industrial safety.'*

FROM THE PRESENT INTO THE FUTURE

By Academician VALERY LEGASOV, Deputy Director, Kurchatov Atomic Energy Institute

(Note: as the book was being prepared it was learned that Valery Legasov had taken his own life at the age of 51, on 27 April 1988.)

Today people have mixed feelings as to the usefulness and finality of changes taking place everywhere, and sense the existence of a large abyss between their hopes of world we live in and what actually happens. We now possess an abundance of contrasting images of amazing technological and organisational achievements as well as economic and organisational acts that are totally unacceptable and devoid of any common sense.

In this context, in the totality of separate facts, it is not always easy to grasp the whole picture of the colossal scale and importance of the scientific and technological revolution taking place in the world, in which the socialist community, having gotten off to a late start, is obliged to partake and obtain the best results by virtue of being adequately prepared socially for all the implications of the current stage in human development.

We are experiencing the culmination of the industrial revolution that has been proceeding for several centuries. The historic mission of this stage, which began with the invention of the steam engine, was to develop magnificent examples of engineering everywhere. At the turn of the 20th century there was an inordinate preoccupation with records: farther, higher, faster, stronger. People became good at setting records.

In one way or another the industrial revolution has given humanity astonishing advances, fueling a natural desire to possess all that the human mind has fashioned.

Yet the attempt to satisfy this desire, to saturate the market with mass produced goods by standard technological methods, has spawned a series of crises that has afflicted our community.

Initially these crises were of different types and causes: a food crisis, brought about by a shortage of proteins for an expanding population; an energy crisis, rooted in dwindling supplies of easily extracted fuels; and an ecological crisis, stemming from the paucity of resources allocated to setting up purification facilities.

But, as the years passed — years of intense labour by the scientific community — it became increasingly clear that the earth was capable of sustaining the lives of ten to twelve billion people, and that energy sources were abundant. It also became obvious that even an all-embracing network of purification facilities would not be able to save the earth from ecological upheavals caused by accidents, the threat of which hangs like the sword of Damocles over the industrial landscape.

Conventional wisdom dictated that industries be arranged into high capacity enterprises specialising in a single product, such as mining, iron and steel production or chemicals. This allowed engineers and scientists to focus all their energies in a single area, on the creation of mechanisms for extracting the requisite element; and all the rest was considered to be waste materials.

The point I would like to make is that the main problems causing universal alarm today are rooted in traditional approaches to production. This danger threatens the onset of a technological crisis, and what is going on today in the world's laboratories, in the halls and forums and political centres must lead to a new stage of the scientific and technological revolution.

The task of this new stage, increasingly known as the technological stage, is not just the development of new equipment, or continuing present production. But to begin asking what should be produced and how much, why, and at what cost materially and socially.

The Communist Party of the Soviet Union has made such notions as *'perestroika'*, *'glasnost'* and 'new thinking' by-words, not only and solely because of the existence of specific negative phenomena over the last several decades of the country's economic development, but because the communist world view and the dialectical materialist outlook underlying this approach have enabled the CPSU to realise earlier and more keenly than anyone else how critical the inertia of the human community really is.

The preceding rapid economic development, which brought into existence a highly developed social and political infrastructure, has exhausted itself, bringing about the danger of formidable crisis phenomena. Today the contours of this multifaceted danger stand out in bold relief. I have in mind the threat of a global military catastrophe. But also the threat of the destructive power of major industrial accidents which are comparable to the effects of war. For in the energy sector alone some 10 billion tons of conventional fuel, capable of burning and exploding with a force comparable to the arsenal of nuclear weapons amassed in the world over the entire history of its existence, is produced, transported, stored and used worldwide. Such chemical components as arsenic, barium, phosgene, ammonia and prussic acid are processed, stored and transported in quantities ranging from hundreds of billions to trillions of lethal doses, which is ten to a hundred times greater than the accumulated radioactive substances as measured in the same units.

I also have in mind the growing influence of modern industrial processes on the environment and human health. Another area of concern is the breakdown of the social, economic and resource balance on the regional as well as interstate level. And there is the draining of surplus brainpower away from the humanities into technical fields and the increasing alienation of people from modern production processes and the management of these processes.

The new leadership of the CPSU and the government have proclaimed with a great sense of responsibility the need to develop new thinking and carry out a restructuring drive in today's conditions. They have also reliably formulated the country's goals, which can be summed up by the term 'security'.

Security is first defined literally as ability to survive, the prevention of military confrontation at all costs.

Security also means safety from the influence of the high-capacity industrial infrastructure. Over the last two years, the leadership has taken a number of decisions to protect human life and limb and the environment. But, the decision-making process still needs to turn all attention to industrial projects, both those already started and those still on the drawing board.

The *third* meaning of *security* (particularly for our country) — safeguard against any further economic inefficiency. This represents the most complex part of the programme.

Fourth, it concerns measures to prevent a possible departure from the agreed course and any attempted restriction of the ongoing processes which are beginning to involve the whole of society. This meaning of security, which has yet to be defined in legal terms, has to do with greater public openness (*glasnost*), public control over the conduct of officials and organisations, and the promotion of a broad democracy combined with compliance with the principle of individual responsibility.

Fifth meaning concerns the preservation of the cultural and historical heritage of each of the Soviet Union's ethnic communities and the prohibition of incitement to ethnic or religious strife in any shape or form.

Sixth involves *security* against the conformism of orthodoxy and lack of principles, against a disregard of the finest human traditions, human values and achievements, and against the excessive influence of technocratic trends.

Finally, it means *security* against the loss of the great social gains of 70 years of the country's socialist experience.

The sweeping scope of restructuring launched on the initiative and leadership of the CPSU is a matter of universal importance, having objective implications and specific features for each country.

Several industrialised countries have already moved towards the new technological age by having created a series of production units based on new principles. Such innovations as miniaturised factories, mass computerisation, robotics and complex communications systems have allowed managers to cut energy requirements by 25-30 per cent, while expanding output and creating new types of materials based on ceramics, polymers and composites.

In a number of instances technological innovations have already had far-ranging social implications. At the same time, many of these countries have to deal with a host of serious social and racial problems and also confront the risk of ecological or psychological imbalances.

Our problems are more related to a delay in technological advances and the failure to act in time to solve a number of social and cultural problems.

All of these, to be sure, are cumbersome problems. But in broad concept the outline of this technological society is fairly clear to us today. First of all, we must use substantially less energy and resources. The opportunities here are immense. Normally we compare the economic performance of the USSR with that of other countries and draw attention to the fact that, on average, we are falling behind the West technologically. Our industries consume some 20-50 per cent more energy than in the West to produce such things as steel, aluminium, cement or paper. But if you sit down and calculate how much energy is theoretically required to produce a unit of a given material, you find that even the best Western technologies exceed estimated energy consumption rates by four times for steel, six times for aluminium, five times for cement, nine times for oil refining, and 125 times for paper.

Obviously, none of the world's scientists today can give any advice as to how to produce paper at one-hundredth of the current cost, or cut the amount of electricity used in steel production by one-fourth. In fact, no one expects any industrial process to cost what it is calculated to cost theoretically. But the examples cited above show how far away modern technology is from the ideal and how big are the still untapped reserves. These figures indicate the road researchers have yet to traverse.

But is it reasonable to put the matter this way at all? Even now it is clear that improvements in existing technology will have relatively minor consequences. The next stage of the scientific and technological revolution will have to be centred on new processes based on different principles.

To create something that has never existed before requires that science take precedence over industry. Only then can the normal flow of scientific and technical progress be ensured.

Let us now look back to the time over forty years ago when the USSR tackled the nuclear issue. The first nuclear reactor required uranium to fuel it and graphite to act as a neutron moderator, with a minimum amount of admixtures. We then lacked both the materials and the technology to produce them. We would not have been able to cope with this challenge if at the outset we thought only in terms of existing industrial capabilities.

Kurchatov, Khariton, Aleksandrov and other leading scientists were put in charge of the project. They were given the final say on the establishment of new plants and institutes, laboratory programmes and industrial research. In other words, all decisions were handed over to science.

Chernobyl is a tragic illustration of an opposite approach. Science was in this case subordinated to production, and this had an immediate effect on quality and paved the way for decisions that were certainly not optimal. This is why we now stress basic research.

It is a strong indicator of the times that new chemical, electronics, nuclear and space technologies increasingly emerge from universities or private companies whose leading researchers are university graduates. A university education is understood to be indispensable for basic research.

When new technology demands are seen in this new relationship to basic research, the next major step will be to replace the diversified structures of raw materials and power generation with integrated schemes based on synergetic effects which are safer and more efficient.

The living world around us testifies that the most compact and flexible systems consist of multipurpose components. In contrast, the industrial structures developed by man employ a principle opposite to this, one of single-functional components. The macrostructure of modern industry illustrates this point, particularly that of the power industry, where energy is separated in space and time from its transportation and use. All this makes the system cumbersome and dangerous and necessitates excessive flows of raw materials and energy.

The combining of different technological processes is

a field with great prospects. For instance, a nuclear reactor can simultaneously produce heat and electricity as well as useful nuclides and radiations for medical and other purposes.

Combined systems easily synchronise processes and even out workloads. Another aspect of an advanced technological society would be its preference for chemical processes over mechanical procedures.

In a display of deep understanding of this issue, the Politburo of the CPSU Central Committee has decided to prioritise the growth of the key sectors of chemistry and technology. This is heartening news.

All of us know the present well enough — with all its pros and cons — and have a more or less clear opinion of what our future should be like. The key question on the agenda is how to prepare for a rational transition from the unsafe and critical state of the present to a safer future.

A strategy has already been formulated and proposals have been advanced concerning disarmament. What remains is a tactical battle for the assertion of reason.

Take technology. While the country is restructuring, some enterprises may embark on their own form of 're-structuring' which may waste resources on the production of goods and services that no one needs.

Efforts have been stepped up everywhere. However, we often embark on practices which may not be decisive for the future development of technology.

Our colleges train specialists in such fields as timber chemistry, tunnelling machinery or the study of rare elements. We need people who will eventually become good professionals. Yet we forget to train people in broader fields such as safety, transitional processes or deployment. Such people are indispensable to the current transitional period.

The production targets of new and existing industrial sectors and enterprises have been fixed, quantified. This system of targets will not provide us with technologists and managers who will be able to display initiative and think creatively in the technological society of the future.

The failure to co-ordinate the restructuring processes is a major defect. Not infrequently, the success of a producer does not mean success overall as both his supplier and clients may not be as successful.

Most executives look with hope upon the planned reforms. However, a warning must be sounded that performance-related leverage is no cure-all.

We must set up a brains trust which would direct technological innovation to bring society from the industrial age to the technological age. I for one believe that only a combination of technology and correct utilisation of manpower resources can catapult us into the 21st century.

Pravda, 5 October 1987

There is hardly any need to introduce NIKITA MOISEEV, *the world-famous scientist whose brilliant mathematical models revealed the catastrophic consequences a 'nuclear winter' would pose after a third world war. The extraordinarily erudite and hardworking scientist unexpectedly announced his retirement in 1987. The academician explained he was leaving in order to make room for younger scientists.*

Nikita Moiseev did not, however, stop his work after vacating his position. He has been using his spare time to write more articles for Soviet newspapers and magazines (in addition to his scientific abilities, he is a gifted writer).

We would like to introduce the reader to a new work by Nikita Moiseev in which the scientist attempts to draw a general picture of the development of science from its origins up to the present, and discusses the role of the scientist in the world today.

SCIENCE AND ETHICS

Sometimes I envy the ancient Greeks who believed that they lived in an integral world, and did not seek to control it. Their world was ruled by beautiful gods who were well-disposed to men and often mixed with them on equal terms. For centuries well-balanced ancient Greek culture stimulated the progress of civilization and no other mythology meant more to Christianity than that of ancient Greece, which pictured the earth, cosmos and man as an integral whole.

**From the apple of discord to the
law of gravity**

In the Middle Ages the rigid formulation of ideas into an established canon of beliefs impeded the development of European culture, which all but fossilized. The Renaissance, the revival of the ideals of antiquity, which seemed to have had sunk into oblivion never to return, proved that the links had never really been broken. The new philosophy brought with it a breakthrough in science in the age of Newton, Copernicus and Galileo.

After Copernicus had worked out his heliocentric system in which the planets revolved round the sun, the Ptolemaic tables (which even today can be used to determine the exact positions of planets and luminaries at any moment past or future) fell out of use. Only a century later did Kepler discover new laws of celestial mechanics.

However, the rationalistic approach to deciphering the mysteries of nature had, as a concomitant, the paradoxical vision of the world formulated by Laplace, which goes approximately as follows: 'An empty Universe, with heavenly bodies in motion and man existing in accordance with his own laws.' Asked by Napoleon, who thought highly of his work, had he reserved a place for God in his system, Laplace replied: 'Sire, I have no use for this hypothesis.' The entire subsequent record of scientific progress has corroborated his approach: if a hypothesis can be dispensed with, it must be abandoned.

Vernadsky's cosmism

At the end of the last century there emerged a trend in science known as 'Russian cosmism,' which had a formative influence on many future outstanding Russian scientists, Vernadsky and Tsiolkovsky in particular. Cosmism is a school of thought according to which man and nature are one, and thought is a phenomenon as material as planets, outer space and life on earth. Vernadsky's teaching on the noosphere marked a new step in the development of the scientific vision of the world. By the noosphere he meant a qualitatively new state of the biosphere, with mankind, equipped with the knowledge of the principles that underlie universal development, creating a new organisational social structure scientifically correlated with the laws of evolution and social progress. Vernadsky started to build a bridge from the age of spontaneous development to the age of development controlled by reason. Science resumed its concept of the fundamental integrity of the earth, man and the cosmos.

According to Vernadsky, any theory in the field of natural science had to be founded on a specific empirical generalisation. For Vernadsky himself, this was the emergence of life on earth, which he regarded as an occurrence which required no explanation. Today astrophysics and physics have accumulated a sufficient body of knowledge about the development of the Universe for us to be able to conclude that we inhabit a colossal system which is never in equilibrium but is continuously evolving by virtue of a constant exchange of energy and matter between its constituents. Far from all the processes described have so far been understood; nevertheless we know that matter always tends towards greater complexity. This is an empirical fact. If we work on the assumption that life is a cosmic phase in the development of nature, then life on earth emerged as a result of the increasing complexity of molecular structure. The phenomenon of living matter's optical activity, discovered simultaneously by Louis Pasteur and Pierre Curie, consists in living matter polarizing light. Analyses of cosmic matter have revealed that in outer space there is no optically active matter—i. e., no living matter or matter born thereof. To me, this is the most convincing argument in favour of the terrestrial origin of life on earth.

Our planet is slightly over four billion years old, and life emerged on it some 3.8-3.9 million years ago. The fact that the earth and life on it developed almost simultaneously gives us grounds for speaking of a qualitatively new organisation of matter. Vernadsky's hypothesis comes down to the assumption that the transition to the age of the noosphere will be a switch to an entirely new terrestrial state with the earth's further development determined by collective reason and joint efforts by society. Unless this happens, mankind will degenerate. We must make such a leap, otherwise human society will cease to develop.

Scientists will be in doubt for too long

By now science has come to realise how extremely precarious the world we live in. It has already been established
what level of discharge of soot into the atmosphere is lethal
to mankind. The loss of genetic diversity of living things is
now a danger as real as that of the irreversible pollution of
the ocean. People are already capable of destroying civilization even without going to the lengths of armed conflict.
That science has come to realize this is a signal achievement. But all of us must be aware of it. The chief purpose of
science, as I see it, is to draw a hypothetical picture of the
development of matter (i. e. of the material world), and develop the theory of integrity. Mankind, regarded in antiquity as a mere constituent element of nature, has become
the determining factor in its existence. While in the New-
tonian scheme of things man was a mere onlooker, today he
is an active participant in progress and, as such, must find
a way of looking at himself from the outside, evaluating his
actions, and predicting his future.

In its modern form, the notion of man as an integral
component of nature presupposes our common responsibility to ourselves, the earth, and the Universe. Therefore, human responsibility is now an issue every bit as important as
human rights — something our foreign colleagues are, unfortunately, not always aware of.

I have just returned from an international conference on
human rights and European security, where I spoke on the
concept of ecological imperatives. At our present technological level just one careless step could prove fatal to civilization and all life on earth; hence the need for political and
moral imperatives. Disputable international issues can now
be resolved solely on the basis of the new morality which
has taken shape in the new ecological situation. Therefore,
I consider the following to be the three most important missions of science.

First. Science must explain, in lucid terms, mankind's responsibility today. It is no longer enough to bring people to
the door of the truth — this door must be kept ajar or, better still, flung wide open. Creating new means towards this
end is the job of the natural and social sciences alike.

Second. Scientific knowledge must be brought within

everyone's reach. Ecological, moral and political imperatives must become common knowledge.

The third mission is linked with the political responsibility of science. Science must provide the criteria for the per-
missibility of concrete political actions.

In general, science, like a solicitous nurse, must keep
mankind from wrong-doing. This brings us to the question
of scientific ethics. As a member of the International Life
Institute I share the organisation's view that bans ought to
be imposed not on specific research trends, but on the publication and use of dangerous technologies. This should be
done for ethical reasons rather than for fear of legal punishment.

Can scientists replace politicians? I do not think scientists
should be entrusted with the reins of government, if only
for the reason that their doubts would prevent them taking
prompt and decisive action. This is all the more so now that
the time for resolution has come. The late Academician
Mikhail Lavrentiev's suggestion that a special committee of
scientists commanding absolute trust and independent of
state and scientific organisations be set up under government auspices seems the most acceptable to me. Decision-
making should remain the prerogative of politicians who
ought, however, to be fully aware of the consequences their
decisions could entail. I believe this would play a positive
role in international affairs.

Neanderthal man at Oxford?

At one time I was busy, along with other experts, constructing a model of the nuclear winter. Besides the consequences of nuclear war, I was interested in the possibility of
a compromise. It stands to reason that a mutually acceptable decision can be arrived at, given even the least ambitious aspiration in common, which, as I saw it, was to mini-
mize the danger of nuclear war. I came to the conclusion
that although the two nuclear powers were effectively poles
apart on the issues of war and peace, they could nonetheless
effect a compromise. In other words, a mutually beneficial
compromise making further social progress possible remained a realistic proposition. This is the cornerstone of the

new thinking, a prerequisite for the radical restructuring of relations, which calls for the replacement of antagonism and rivalry with compromise and cooperation. The results will be a new way of life, a new morality and a new scale of values.

Has human history ever witnessed situations calling for a similar restructuring before? Yes, it has. Archeologists tell us of the 'hunter's crisis' — the extinction of mammoths and large hoofed animals, when pre-historic men had to take joint action, to change over to crop farming and cattle breeding in order to survive. It cost mankind nine tenths of its population to emerge from the crisis. Only those who had joined hands in the face of adversity managed to survive.

Another such episode was the transition from the herd to the community. Anthropologists can trace today the incredibly rapid development of man, and the striking evolution of his brain structure. It took the Australopithecus about two and a half million years to become Neanderthal man, whereupon evolution came to a standstill. Modern man does not differ much from the last Neanderthal men or the first Cromagnons. A British professor once said at a lecture that a Neanderthal man would be perfectly capable of completing a course at Oxford. Whether it was a compliment to primitive man's mental faculties or a dig at the University is anybody's guess, it doesn't much matter. What matters is that human history has already known radical changes in ways of life, for which people paid a heavy price. Today we build space bridges and solve complex technical problems, but must effect a compromise again, as our remote ancestors did, because historical progress presupposes not only the struggle of opposites, but also compromise between opposites. Realizing this will help us survive without forfeiting nine tenths of our kind.

New Times, 12 February 1988

The ecology and environmental protection are global problems today. Australian scientists conducted an experiment whereby they released the largest weather balloon in history. Even at a height of eleven kilometres, the instruments showed that the Earth's atmosphere was polluted with industrial wastes.

What is being done in the Soviet Union to improve the situation?

It should be noted that perestroika *and* glasnost *have entered this vital area as well. Thanks to the energetic efforts of the Soviet public and the support showed by the Soviet press, plans to divert the flow of some of the northern rivers to the south have been halted; a government resolution has been adopted to preserve the unique body of water, Lake Baikal; voices are being raised to save the Aral Sea and Lake Ladoga. The first positive results are now evident: an interesting experiment showed that sterlet hatchlings, which live in crystal clear water and have become a rarity in their natural environs of the Volga, could survive in the Moscow River; city air has become cleaner and the forests are more healthy. Answering the questions of a* Pravda *correspondent in September 1987,* YURI IZRAEL, *Chairman of the USSR State Committee for Hydrometeorology and Environmental Control said: 'Environmental control is organised and is functioning in all the major cities in the country (450 cities), at water reservoirs and rivers. Emission norms for the major enterprises have been set (for 15,000 enterprises) and the observance of these norms is monitored. Violators receive warnings, and those found guilty are denied bonuses and fined. More serious and effective measures are also being taken: some facilities, workshops and enterprises are being shut down... Everyone remembers the closing of the Priozersk cellulose plant, as well as a number of enterprises in the vicinity of Yasnaya Polyana, and the biochemical plant in the city of Kiroshi. In 1986 this Committee issued 1,559 orders to halt different production facilities, and more than 300 cases were turned over to Procurator's Office.'*

Does this mean that the ecological situation in the country has radically improved? No. The Soviet public today is most alarmed by the widespread chemicalisation of the national economy. Academician NIKOLAI ENIKOLOPOV, *a leading Soviet chemist and Lenin Prize winner, comments on this problem.*

ECOLOGY FIRST

You have devoted your entire life to chemistry. Now it is becoming more and more evident that chemistry can not only be useful but also harmful. Perhaps, as some people suggest, chemical production should be curtailed and no new plants constructed?

I am convinced that it is impossible to stop the development of civilisation. The good old days, so to speak, will never be back. The population of our planet is continuing to grow; and the people must be fed, provided with water, clothing, and decent living conditions, and their spiritual needs must be satisfied. Of course chemistry has a role to play in this. Computers, television, radio, movies, tape recorders, and photography would be unthinkable without chemistry.

Today our country must switch from an extensive to an intensive mode of development. In many cases this means the utilisation of the latest achievements in chemistry. Without them, it would be impossible to meet the tasks of the Food Programme, for example.

In many cases chemistry has led to a saving of human labour resources, and because of that it successfully competes with many traditional industries. Unfortunately, we lag behind world trends in this area. There has been a thoughtless increase in metal production in our country, while all the industrial countries have realised that it is more feasible to develop plastics. This requires less energy, and plastics are less susceptible to corrosion, manufacturing goods from plastics is less labour-intensive than with metal; and means of transportation, made completely or partially from plastics, consume less fuel. The benefits are evident, and we should restructure.

Let's not argue about the undeniable usefulness of chemistry. But on the other side of the balance we have the ill-fated insecticide DDT, streptocide rubrum, 'phosphorescent' clocks and ornaments, saccharin, tetraethyl lead, which is everywhere added to fuel to increase its efficiency, pesticides and other 'achievements' that have caused harm. The rapid development of chemistry and miscalculations associated with it have led to the pollution of water reservoirs, acid rains, the destruction of plants and animals, and a threat to the pe-

*ople's health. And these unfortunate results of chemical deve-
lopment are being felt around the world. For example, many
scientists have linked the threat to the ozone layer, which protects all living creatures on Earth from the destructive influence of ultraviolet radiation, with the wide use of refrigerator
coolants and aerosol containers. The volatile combination
of fluorine and chlorine found in these products spread to
the upper layers of the atmosphere and begin to react
with ozone. Do people need 'boons' like this from chemistry?*

Yes. The chemists are to blame. The long-term consequences of the use of different chemical products have been
insufficiently studied. There is no government procedure to
certify the harmlessness of chemical products, but they
should not leave laboratories without such a certification.
As a chemist I know that if one thinks enough and the appropriate research is carried through, harmless products
can be created. This is within the competence of modern science. Harmful and hazardous products simply should not
be put to use. There should be some kind of state inspection
agency responsible for predicting the far-ranging effects of
utilising a particular chemical substance.

*You are talking about a final product, but it is production
itself and its technological wastes which are often more dangerous. In large-scale production the amount of wastes is
enormous, and the natural environment can no longer cope
with them.*

It is not the development of chemistry alone that is to
blame, but general processes of industrialisation. And the
scale of the danger obliges us to take measures. But I would
like everyone to understand that from the point of view of
the majority of scientists the problem of eliminating
hazardous wastes and by-products in effect does not exist.
A harmless way of obtaining needed chemical substances
can always be found. This is not a scientific or engineering
problem, it is an economic one. Unfortunately, the additional costs of utilising harmless technology can become
comparable with the costs of main production and even
surpass them.

*Why are chemists not searching for ways to utilise harmful
wastes effectively and economically at the stage of development of new technology or new materials?*

The existing system of priorities and the economic levers works against it. The first priority has always been the main process, the new product or material. In academic research the problem of wastes and by-products is considered to be a trifle and is completely ignored. In industrial research institutes these questions are usually postponed until the very end, and then the excuse is that there is no more money. On all the directive levels a common stereotype exists: 'we' (the industry, state) need this product and we know how to make it. So, it has to be made, and the wastes are of minor importance.

For those who design, finance and locate chemical production, the problem is even more difficult. Economic feasibility demands lower capital and operational expenditures for the organisation of any production. Everything 'superfluous' must be sacrificed. It goes without saying that waste treatment systems that 'burden' the project are subject to almost automatic cuts, and that they are the last to be constructed or simply remain on paper.

And the situation will not change if a narrow institutional approach continues to dominate. A state or public approach is needed. The USSR Council of Ministers and the USSR State Planning Committee (Gosplan) must issue state contracts for developing clean production. And the recently established USSR State Committee for Nature Protection must defend the people's interests. The potential risk of chemistry should be taken into consideration, and no new enterprise should be put into operation without ensuring its safety and without permission from the State Committee for Nature Protection. It is very difficult to bring existing production to a halt, for this could have serious consequences for the national economy. It is easier not to 'let it go' to the design stage or the final stage of construction. And waste-processing installations should, in my opinion, be constructed first of all, so that there will be no way back and no room for compromise.

A Comprehensive Programme for the Chemicalisation of the USSR National Economy for the Period up to the Year of 2000 has been adopted. It states that the implementation of the programme will save more than 450 billion roubles. The share of chemistry in total industrial production is projected to reach 8 per cent. But the Programme does not specify how

*and in what way obsolete plants hazardous for the population
will be shut down.*

I don't think this is right. The Programme has been
drawn up in the old manner: to increase production of such
and such a product by so many tonnes or by so many times.
I think another task, which is of no less importance, should
be formulated simultaneously: to decrease at the same time
harmful emissions by, let's say, 50 per cent.

If some minister tells you we can't do this, that we just
have to accept the costs of scientific and technological progress like the rest of the world, don't believe him. In a three-
year period, from 1983 to 1985, for example, the US reduced the emission of harmful chemical substances by 27.8 per
cent while the volume of chemical output increased by 10
per cent. This is the result of goal-oriented measures.

Can we do the same? Of course. It is precisely these measures that should be envisioned in the chemicalisation programme. I have not heard about even one competition held
in our country to create harmless chemical production.
Why not? Why do we try to follow the same path when
many processes could be made less dangerous? For example, most of our chemical processes are carried out in water
solutions which then flow into sewage. Now the chemistry
of solids is successfully developing, which makes it possible
to do without water and solvents entirely. It has already
been found that many classical processes, from producing
soap to processing cellulose and wood, can now be conducted in the solid phase rather than in solution, suspension
or the gas phase. Yet these solid phase processes are being
implemented very slowly.

Why are we spending billions to renovate old plants,
some even built before World War II? On the average,
technology is now being replaced every 7-10 years with
more effective and less dangerous processes. But we spend
decades trying to patch up old factories. It is time we stop
this erroneous practices once and for all.

*We now have a contradiction between the traditional paro-
chial approach to the development of the chemical industry
and the processes of democratisation. Working with chemical
substances has been considered dangerous for centuries. The
greater the development of the chemical industry, the greater
the incidence of work-related diseases. This is why chemists*

*have more vacation time, a shorter working day and retire at
an earlier age. But the work-related diseases of chemists are
now becoming territorial illnesses affecting people living in
the environs of chemical plants. Of course the public does not
like this. Spontaneous protest meetings have been held, and
grass-roots 'survival groups' have been formed. People have
become more particular about their life conditions.*

I agree. Chemical production definitely must be viewed as
a social factor. This should be the concern not only of
chemical agencies but also of the Bureau of the USSR
Council of Ministers for Social Development, of the scientific community and of all the people.

The role of the public is great, but it must be channelled
correctly. When a grass-roots organisation is formed it
usually includes both competent and responsible people as
well as blatherers and demagogues. Responsibility is what
must win out. It is right that such organisations should
work in close contact with the USSR State Committee for
Nature Protection, local branches of the USSR Union of
Scientific and Engineering Societies, and the USSR
Academy of Sciences.

Until recently three agencies controlled a plant's dangerous emissions — the USSR Ministry of Health's Sanitation and Epidemiology Services, offices of the USSR State
Committee for Hydrometeorology and Environmental
Control, and the plant's own department. Nonetheless, it
frequently happened that emissions contained a concentration of harmful substances 200-300 times more than the acceptable level. The light fines imposed on a plant were paid
out of the state's pocket and essentially had no effect.

The transfer of chemical plants to self-financing may exacerbate the situation. It will be beneficial to turn off the fil-
ters, save electricity, make a profit and not give a hang
about anything else. This predatory thinking must be
fought without compromise.

In my opinion, all chemical plants operating today must
be studied to determine whether they fit the modern demands of world technology in both efficiency and safety.
We must draw up an ecological passport for each plant.

*What about the groups and local agencies that are demand-
ing the shut-down of chemical plants and their relocation?*

Don't Soviet people live there too? Egotism is not a solution. What we have to do is join efforts to organise harmless production. In some instances it might be necessary to close down old plants where emissions are a part of the technological process. This was what was done in Yerevan, for example. The production of petrol-resistant rubber was shut down even though the product was much needed by the country.

I think we must gradually remove all chemical plants from city centres. They were originally built on the outskirts and now they are surrounded by housing. This is unacceptable. And plans to construct new chemical plants in city centres, as was the case in Ufa, for example, represent the epitome of voluntarism.

We must also guard against grandiose projects. Even in purely economic terms, it is feasible to increase the power of chemical reactors only to a certain degree. We often exceed that optimum today by building both economically unfeasible and potentially dangerous facilities.

It is important to stress that we must control the situation, and not let it develop to the point when the public is faced with emergencies. A special supervisory committee for safety has been created for the atomic and power production industries, but it is not realistic to create such bodies for the chemical, petro-chemical, cellulose-paper industries, metallurgy and other branches where chemical reactions play a significant role. In my opinion, we should rely on existing control organisations and the more widespread involvement of the public.

The symbol of medicine is a bowl and a snake. The snake can, of course, either bite or give a healing substance. Chemistry also has a dual role. To ensure that it will not be a 'biting snake' traditional approaches must be changed, an entire range of measures implemented, and efforts to provide for safe and useful chemistry conducted along the entire chain—from the stage of research and development to the control over production. There is no alternative.

Interview by B. KONOVALOV

Izvestia, 13 March 1988

*Theoretically a satellite could have been launched even in
the days of Newton. However, it took centuries before it actually happened. But the time between the theoretical idea of
semiconductors and its realisation was a matter of a few
years. It is self-evident that basic research is affecting the
economy, and every aspect of man's life ever more rapidly.*

*It would seem we are approaching the time when it will take
just a few months, a year at most, between the development of
a theory and its practical application.*

*If only this were the case. In science, as in other fields in the
Soviet Union today, inertia is still a problem. Academician*
JORES ALFEROV, *Director of the A.I. Ioffe Physics-
Engineering Institute in the USSR Academy of Sciences, has
described this situation.*

WHAT HAD TO BE PROVED

Basic Research and Perestroika

*The acceleration of basic research is viewed today as an im-
portant principle of* perestroika *in science. But what is new
about that? After all, basic research has always entailed profound and far reaching changes.*

Much of what was accepted blindly yesterday is being
tested in practice today. Academician Lev Artsimovich
long ago appealed to scientists not to deify basic research,
not to regard it as a truth that does not have to be proved.
Presenting his thought as a paradox, he said that the difference between applied and basic research was quite simple to
define, since the former would find application and the latter not. Well, it might not, unless people and organisations
grasped not only the theoretical significance of fundamental knowledge, but also how this knowledge can be put to
practice.

The targets set by the 27th Party Congress cannot be reached without science, but not without science 'in general',
but without an assessment of which aspect or which application would promote a revolutionary leap in society's development. That is only possible if new discoveries are closely integrated in a revised mechanism of economic mana-

gement. After all, scientific and technological progress in the USSR has slowed down because it was not an organic part of the economic processes.

What do you mean specifically by a different attitude to basic research?

Firstly, it is necessary to increase social consciousness, (primarily the consciousness of managers of the economy and science) and promote correct understanding of the powerful and far reaching role of science.

Secondly, it is necessary to create favourable conditions for unhampered search. The first of these conditions is the encouragement of a strong base for experimentation. Genuine science cannot exist without such a base.

Thirdly, in fundamental research, it is necessary to establish continuity between generations of researchers and, building on the best traditions of Soviet science, to develop excellence among scientists, ranging with the world's best.

A correct understanding of the role of basic research... Would you say it is not understood correctly in the Soviet Union today?

Yes, this is true to a large extent. To this day officials come to our institute checking up on our work, asking such questions as: 'What is the economic implication of your work? How many roubles in profit are made by each rouble you spend?' How can I explain to them, for instance, that the first semiconductor laser operating continuously in room temperature led to the application of fiber optics communication lines? That this meant the creation of a completely new branch of industry? That we are coming up with completely new communication lines and information systems?

The economic result of basic research is measured by the rate at which it gives birth to new areas in science, and these areas, in turn, by the rate they give rise to the most advanced methods of engineering.

This is the way this question was adopted recently by the Central Committee of the Communist Party and the USSR Council of Ministers. Research organisations were transferred to complete profit-and-loss accounting and self-financing: 'Research organisations under the Academy of Sciences and institutions of higher education must develop basic research in the natural sciences, in engineering and in social sciences.'

What kind of criteria can be used in evaluating basic research in the new conditions of profit-and-loss mechanism?

The only correct criterion is whether the research meets world standards or better still, overtakes them. If you use such a strict criterion you will find that many academic institutes which appear to be doing serious work are actually standing still. Just close down those 'areas' of work, laboratories and institutes, and you will achieve economy.

Every five to ten years we should compare our work with research under way abroad. This could be accomplished by qualified commissions of specialists who would identify and evaluate key areas and growth centres. Long ago we learned to reach world standards, or surpass them in certain small areas, yet in terms of science in general, they were insignificant.

What's important are not these small successes, but a quick identification of the 'growth centres'.

A good example is today's boom in physics around superconductivity which arises at a temperature liquid nitrogen. You do not have to be a specialist to understand what practical applications can result from this new discovery. Does that mean we must rush ahead with this? The answer is no. Once the feeling of sensational success subsided, lots of 'whys' began to be asked. The problem today is not which laboratory will be working on this, but who will be the first to provide a complete answer to all the 'whys', who will come up with a scientific concept with which all experimental data would agree, and which would pave the way to practical application — to the creation of hitherto unparalleled superconductive materials for industrial uses.

Technology which revolutionises production is always the result of concepts which revolutionised science itself. They can be developed only by major research collectives reaching world standards. The very existence of academic centres, such as the Institute of Chemical Physics, the Institute of General Physics under the USSR Academy of Sciences, our Physics-Engineering Institute, and a number of other organisations, would not make any sense if they lagged behind modern science.

It is a rather widespread opinion that we are lagging behind other countries in technology, but that we are either equals or ahead of them in basic research. How does that correspond to your claim that genuine science cannot exist without a powerful experimental base?

This is an example of the sort of thinking that persists, although it has not been true for a long time. I have contested this point of view many times, including at general meetings of our section of the USSR Academy of Sciences.

I will cite an example from my own field, for which I am responsible to a certain extent. The idea of semiconductor lasers was first raised by Soviet scientists, but put to practice abroad. The idea gained its second wind in lasers on the basis of heterojunctions. The idea and the experimental confirmation were ours. We were the first to understand the importance of heterostructures in semiconductor electronics. However, its subsequent elaboration was slow in our country, whilst in the West many laboratories engaged in research and development.

Today semiconductor lasers are used in video and audio recorders, in computer memories, in laser printers, etc., all produced by foreign companies. We are behind; now we have to catch up.

Why am I saying this? In modern science it is important not only to pronounce 'A'. The first 'why' is followed by numerous others. The answer to these questions signifies that a real development is taking place. Without a serious experimental base it is sometimes impossible to get the answer. In other words, the truth is that whoever lags behind in technology does not jump ahead in science. This is because science itself today is Technology.

Is this technological panache always useful? The acute problem of applying scientific ideas has led to a situation in which major academic centres strive to create their own 'small industry', while the most progressive branches try to gain essentially their own 'academies'. Is this trend justified?

If what is meant by 'small industry' is attempts by academic research centres to turn experiments into industrial series, I do not see anything good in this. It inevitably lowers the level of research. The industries do not need their own academic research centres either.

The technological aspect of science is directly linked with the state of its experimental base. In order to conduct some modern experiments new equipment and buildings are needed.

Today serious measures are being taken in our country to develop the production of scientific instruments. Here I must admit, we are quite a bit behind. For many years we were encouraged to import equipment, we did not develop our own industry. Now we have to pay for it by lagging behind the West.

Do you think that the development of an experimental base was also slowed down for reasons of economising? It was, perhaps, considered a luxury to have alternative projects, to have competition between different possible solutions. Was it not that one scientific school, one institute, or even a whole project had a kind of monopoly of the truth?

Yes, there were such cases. Actually that kind of mistake has cost us dearly. Not twice, but thousands of times!

A sign of the times is that we finally understand that spending is inevitable if we do not always want to be in a position of having to catch up. The common belief is that two teams working on the same problem, but in different ways, are more expensive than one. In fact, the more far-sighted organisers of research projects always did it that way. The monopoly status of research teams has always been more costly for society.

We should remember one other thing: the results of basic research cannot be measured in new equipment (even if it is created), but in the introduction of new thinking. Yes, the laboratories of Basov and Prokhorov were the first in the world to come up with masers, and the first Soviet lasers. But they began to play an even greater role when they became centres where the new scientific concept was introduced to scientists and engineers.

It is extremely important that research centres become generators of ideas, and attract increasingly more advocates of these ideas. What do we see happening in practice? Major academic collectives produce very few specialists for industrial application. Meanwhile, in American universities which are equivalent to our leading academic research centres, specialists for industry are being educated on a large scale. This is more important than the simple introduction of the latest technology.

The Presidium of the USSR Academy of Sciences should

work together with ministries so that in their institutes and laboratories they educate scientists in the most promising areas, and on a nationwide scale. This would be a genuine introduction of new thinking and of new scientific ideology, because researchers trained in advanced scientific schools will become the best protagonists of their innovative ideas.

Science needs a more democratic mechanism for discussing and supporting new ideas. Therefore the overwhelming majority of research should be open. I do not mean special defence research or technological secrets which exist in every country. I am against bureaucratic secrecy.

Scientific ideas should be published, discussed and should produce a chain reaction of new ideas.

Today we must speak primarily of the responsibility of scientists themselves. They are the first to notice what no one else has yet seen. It is unfortunate when their social vision blurs, when they do not want to take responsibility, do not want to take risks. Risks are noble acts, truly noble acts. They are related to honour. Much about science is unexpected. Without taking risks based on inspiration and foresight, nothing serious in science can be accomplished.

Interview by V. NEVELSKY and K. SMIRNOV

Leningrad

Izvestia, 16 November 1987

The Church

Christianity a thousand years old in Russia

One thousand years ago, in 988, Kievan Rus joined the union of European Christian states. The interest now being shown in this event, both in the Soviet Union and far beyond its borders, is perfectly understandable.

Viewing historical monuments in the Soviet Union one often happens to overhear the explanations which the guides are giving to groups of tourists. Describing the events connected with the adoption of Christianity in Rus, the guides carefully stress the religious aspect and only mention in passing the socio-economic and political aspect of this process. First and foremost Rus gained access to European culture. They invariably emphasise, for example, the forcible nature of the baptism. The history of the spread of Christianity does indeed give certain grounds for this. Take for example the so-called baptising of pagan tribes in the Baltic region by the crusaders. The latter acted with ruthless simplicity: a host of knights would crush the opposing forces, seize the land, build their castles on it, turn the free population into serfs and give this brigandage an air of 'respectability' by baptising those who remained alive. It is obvious, however, that the main objective was not baptism, but seizing of the land. The aboriginal tribes in America were also baptised by Spaniards in the same way. Nothing of the sort took place in Rus, however, where events took a different course.

What happened at the end of the tenth century in Old Rus was outstanding in our country's history. Grand Prince Vladimir carried out a bold state reform, which had far-reaching consequences, comparable perhaps only with the reforms of Peter the Great. As in Peter's day, great advances were needed in the country's development in order to get anywhere near the highest achievements of the leading countries of that period. Vladimir sought to put Kievan Rus on a level with the developed feudal monarchies. This required an energetic feudal reform and all the profound changes associated with it.

In order to understand better the processes which determined the life of our ancestors in those remote times, we must make brief reference to the events of the preceding century. The originally separate Slav tribes united from time to time to fight against their neighbours, sometimes even making inroads on the outskirts of the Byzantine Empire. In the middle of the ninth century the first big campaign against Byzantium took place, linked in the chronicles with the name of Prince Askold of Kiev. This was a period when the patriarchal communal system was breaking up and feudal relations were forming. These were still in a primitive form; in autumn and winter the prince and his armed men would travel round his territory collecting tribute; feudal land-holding did not yet exist. In spring the surplus tribute (furs, wax, etc.) was shipped down the Dnieper to Byzantium and even farther afield. It was exchanged for articles which were not produced in Rus. Askold laid siege to Constantinople, lifting it in return for a large ransom, and concluded a treaty with Byzantium which probably contained some benefits or privileges for the Russian nobility. This was Byzantium's first clash with the emerging state — Old Rus. It was no longer a question of 'barbarians' looting border provinces, but something more serious.

At the end of the ninth century Prince Oleg of Novgorod captured Kiev and united northern and southern Rus (Novgorod and Kiev). The contours of the future Old Russian state emerged. The as yet precarious unification of Rus into a single state was sustained by constant fighting against recalcitrant tribes. Another successful campaign against Byzantium ended in a treaty favourable to the Russians and an undertaking to pay annual tribute to them (payment for non-aggression).

With Oleg's death (in the early tenth century) the fragility of the union of Slav tribes was exposed immediately and their alliance fell apart. Prince Igor was compelled to restore it by force. He was killed in a campaign against the Drevlyane tribe for fresh tribute. His wife Olga, who ruled until her son Svyatoslav came of age, took cruel vengeance on the Drevlyane for Igor's death. Bitter experience forced Olga to regulate the tribute and dues from allied tribes. This was a step to-

wards a feudal state regulated by laws.

On his accession to the throne, Svyatoslav directed all his energies against the external enemies of the emerging state. After conquering the Khazar Kaganate (Khanate.— Ed.), his troops reached the Northern Caucasus. His campaign against Byzantium was also marked by victories (although not always). On his return Svyatoslav was killed in a battle with the Pechenegs, whom the Byzantines had told in advance the route his troops would take. But Rus' potential enemies in the east and west had been neutralised.

The internecine strife between the brothers after Svyatoslav's death brought his son Vladimir to the throne in 980. What was the legacy inherited by Vladimir from his forebears? To put it briefly, he became the head of a somewhat precarious union of Slav tribes, the stability of which required constant recourse (or at least constant threat of recourse) to armed force. In order to strengthen this union, the young prince took two important decisions. First, he settled in Kiev so as not to leave the government of his principality for periods of several months or even years (such was the length of his predecessors' military campaigns). Second, he tried and united ideologically, to use a modern expression, the allied Slav tribes with the assistance of a common religion.

The transition to a settled life in the capital was a major step towards the feudalisation of the state: in the kingdoms of Vladimir's day the monarchs usually governed their countries from capitals. Having settled in Kiev, Vladimir set about constructing defences in the east, thereby confirming that he intended to reside permanently in the capital and defend it against the nomads. A calm and secure life in the town was also an important basis for the success of his far-reaching state reforms.

The second problem, that of uniting the allied tribes, he at first tried to solve by putting all the main tribal gods 'on an equal footing'. Any traveller from afar could see that in the capital they worshipped not only their own gods, but also the god of his particular tribe. Thus there arose in Kiev a pantheon of six pagan gods, remains of which have been discovered in modern times by archaeologists. According to a different point of view, the gods in the pantheon symbolised the main elements of the ancient Slavs' picture of the world— the sky, the earth, the Sun, etc. The main deity in this group was

*the Grand Prince's god Perun. But in this case the pantheon
also had a pan-Slavic, unifying character.*

*It soon became clear, however, that the path on which Vla-
dimir had embarked so successfully in fact led to an impasse.
There were two main reasons for this. First, even after Vladimir's innovations pagan religion presupposed the old way of
life. It was suited to the patriarchal system, but seriously impeded the formation of the new production relations of nascent feudalism. There was a need for new laws, new customs,
a new social consciousness, and new approaches to events.
The old paganism could not provide this. The second reason
was that Kievan Rus could not achieve an equal footing with
the advanced countries of Europe and the East, could not
reach the 'world standard', to use a modern term again, without
mastering their trades, building techniques, learning, culture
and a great deal more. Meanwhile both the former (religion)
and the latter (trades, building techniques, learning, culture,
etc.) were readily available in Byzantium.*

*Why Byzantium? In deciding which one (or ones) of the
existing countries to take as a model, Vladimir could have
turned to the Moslem East or the Catholic West. Yet his
choice came to rest on Orthodox Byzantium (the formal division of the originally united church into Orthodox and Catholic did not take place until 1054, but in fact they became independent much earlier). To a large extent Vladimir's choice
was determined historically, but to an equal extent by his wisdom as a statesman. Kievan Rus already had fairly extensive
economic relations with Byzantium; it was geographically
close; Bulgaria, another Slav country, had embraced Christianity about a century before Kievan Rus, largely thanks to
the activity of Cyril and Methodius, who created a Slav al-
phabet and preached Christianity in the Slavonic language.
Thus, Vladimir's decision may also have been influenced by
the fact that in the Orthodox Church, unlike the Catholic, the
services could be held in a language understandable for the
congregation. It should also be noted that at that time Byzantium was still flourishing; the traditions of Ancient Greece
had not yet died out — Homer and other ancient classics were
studied in Byzantine schools, while Plato and Aristotle continued to live on in philosophical disputes. The Byzantine version of Christianity met the needs of feudal society and was
therefore consistent with Vladimir's intentions. At the same*

time all the tribes of Old Rus were embraced in a single religion.

Neither Rus nor Byzantium saw the forthcoming baptism as a purely religious act. To put the matter in a somewhat simplistic and extremely brief form, Byzantine's point of view was as follows: since Rus was to embrace the Orthodox faith, and the Orthodox Church was headed by the Byzantine Patriarch and Emperor, Rus was to automatically become a vassal of Byzantium. However, the growing and already fairly powerful old Russian state, which had campaigned successfully against Byzantium on several occasions, did not have the slightest intention to play such a role. Vladimir and those around him took a very different view of the matter. The baptism and the consequent borrowing of Byzantine culture and technology should by no means deprive Rus of her independence. As the Grand Prince saw it, Rus would turn into a state friendly to Byzantium but entirely sovereign. This essential difference of views on the consequences of the baptism greatly complicated the event itself.

But fate proved to be on Vladimir's side. In 986 Emperor Basil II of Byzantium suffered a crushing military defeat, barely managing to survive, and in 987 the mutinous Byzantine general Bardas Phocas approached Constantinople with his troops and proclaimed himself Emperor. In this desperate position Basil II appealed for help to Grand Prince Vladimir of Kiev. Vladimir agreed to provide military aid, but on the following terms:

— the baptism of Rus should take place 'Kievan style';

— Vladimir should marry the emperor's sister and thereby take his place among the leading rulers of Europe.

The emperor had to agree. This was a great diplomatic victory for Vladimir. The prince's army helped to defeat Phocas, and Basil II remained on the throne.

The year 988 arrived, and with it the baptism of Rus began. Basil II did not keep his word, however. His sister Anna's departure for Kiev was continually delayed. Vladimir took resolute action: he laid siege to Korsun (present-day Khersones in the Crimea), one of Byzantium's most important strongholds on the Black Sea. Korsun fell, and Vladimir threatened to extend military operations to Byzantine territory. Basil II was compelled to give way. Anna's fate was mourned for a whole week in Constantinople, and it is not difficult to imag-

ine what her thoughts were as she set off to marry Vladimir.
Those who like to talk about the 'enforced baptism' can see
from this example that recourse was in fact made to 'force'. It
can be said ironically that having defeated the Byzantines the
troops of Old Rus forced the latter to baptise them.

We bring the reader's attention to the following article by
Academician BORIS RAUSHENBAKH, *Lenin Prize win-*
ner and a member of the International Academy of Astro-
nautics, a specialist in the field of mechanics, combustion
theory and space vehicle orientation control. He worked to-
gether with Sergei Korolyov in preparing the first space
flights. He is also highly productive in the humanities and is
the author of the monograph Spatial Constructions in Old
Russian Painting *(1975), and 'Iconography as a Means of*
Conveying Philosophical Concepts' in the collection Problems of Studying the Cultural Heritage *(1985).*

DOWN THE CENTURIES

At first glance it may appear that the social role of any religion is always the same, since they all recognise the existence of a mystical force which influences what takes place in
the world. In fact, however, the matter is more complex.
Religions have their own complicated history and, in particular, Kievan Rus' transition from paganism to Christianity should be evaluated positively, as a progressive process, as a transition to a 'civilised' religion. For example, an
element essential to the pagan cult of many of the tribes po-
pulating Europe was human sacrifice. It was performed on
various occasions, including certain annual feasts. At the
funeral of a rich man one of his female slaves was killed,
sometimes even several male and female slaves. There was
the custom of sacrificing a warrior before battle. Human
sacrifice as a form of expressing gratitude to the gods was
also practised.

The question naturally arises as to how the spreading of
Christianity took place. Did this process meet with resistance? It must be stressed that this process was a domestic
matter of Kievan Rus. The transformations took place on
the orders of the Grand Prince and those close to him, the

'government', so to speak. The country did not experience any external, coercive pressure. Moreover the population was already familiar with Christianity: for many years in the towns of Old Rus there had been small Christian communities which appeared during the reign of Olga, Vladimir's grandmother, who was the first of the rulers of Kievan Rus to embrace Christianity (if we discount the tales about the baptism of Askold). This also promoted the establishment of the new religion.

As with any cardinal transformation, the new and progressive met with resistance from the old and obsolete. It is therefore worth discussing who benefited from the new changes and who did not.

The prince stood only to gain. Whereas before he was simply the head of a tribal union, now his power was consecrated, 'God-given'. Vladimir's closest associates did not suffer any loss of property or anything else. The same can be said of his armed force. For those engaged in trade with Byzantium the reform opened up new opportunities. Whereas before they had been 'savages' and 'Scythians' in the market places of foreign lands, they now became respected 'fellow Christians' in Byzantium and Europe, and representatives of a world-wide religion in the Moslem Orient. As long as the process of feudalisation had not yet gained momentum, ordinary commoners did not suffer particularly either. Christianity promised freedom to slaves. As we know, there were only household slaves in Old Rus. Slaves were not used in production, but they constituted a considerable stratum of society. Slave-trading was widespread, however. Even today in English, German and French the word for a slave is derived from 'Slav', because Slav slaves were greatly valued at slave markets. Slavery is not characteristic of feudalism, and the Church was strongly opposed to it, particularly slave-trading, when fellow-tribesmen were sold 'to heathens'.

The people who lost everything were the pagan priests. This influential caste suddenly became completely superfluous. In this new situation the pagan priests had recourse to two fundamentally different tactical devices; the first was to 'go underground', as a result of which the worship of idols and the performance of magic rites continued in border areas and other places where it was possible; and the second was open (even armed) resistance to the whole system of Vladimir's reforms.

Vladimir's reaction to these two tactics was different. He paid scant attention to the 'underground' priests and chose to leave them alone because they did not present a threat to his main intention, feudal reform. Here is the source of the so-called double faith. Vladimir believed that as a result of the activity of the Christian clergy these pagan elements would gradually die out. In such sweeping reforms it would have been unreasonable to expect everything to change at once.

His reaction to the resistance to his system of feudal reforms was different. Here Vladimir showed firmness and ruthlessness, making recourse to armed force when necessary. What is important for us to understand, however, is that 'fire and sword' were used not simply to introduce the new religion, but to create a centralised feudal state.

The process of Christianisation took place gradually and, according to present assessments, took about a hundred years. This is a very short time if one bears in mind the size of the country: in the case of Sweden and Norway, which adopted Christianity at about the same time as Russia, it took 250 and 150 years respectively.

Vladimir's state reform released, as it were, the potential which had been gradually building up in Old Rus. A period of intensive, rapid development began, showing how timely the reform was.

Craftsmen invited from Byzantium erected stone buildings and churches and adorned them with frescoes, mosaics and icons. Alongside them worked Russians learning hitherto unknown arts and crafts. The next generation was to build complex edifices and other structures in Russian towns without recourse to foreign help. Agriculture changed too, with the availability of traction, instruments, and so on.

The clergy newly arrived from Byzantium not only officiated in the new churches, but also trained 'national personnel' for the Church and, as a result, literacy and learning began to spread. Schools were organised, to which Vladimir sent the children of the nobility, in spite of their mothers' tears. Young people were sent to study abroad. Chronicle-writing began. Like any developed state, Kievan Rus began to mint gold coins.

Old Rus was gradually becoming a state with a new, highly developed culture. It should not be thought, however, that in pagan times it did not possess a culture which was perfect in its own way. This popular pagan culture was to survive for a long time to come and give old Russian art distinctive and entirely original features. In speaking of the new, I have in mind mainly that sum total of knowledge (from the writings of Aristotle to ways of building a stone arch) which already formed part of world culture.

Strangely, the chronicles of Vladimir's day tell us very little about him. Perhaps this is due to the fact that they were written by Byzantines who undoubtedly wanted the adoption of Christianity by Rus to yield different results. Vladimir did not heed his spiritual fathers when their advice was of use only to Constantinople and contrary to the needs of Kiev. It was not these foreign churchmen who 'laid down the law' to Vladimir, but vice versa.

But whereas the chronicles are silent about Vladimir, he is extolled in folklore, and this was the highest praise that a political leader could receive in those days. Vladimir the Red Sun remains forever in the popular memory. And this is no accident. Throughout the ages people have always wanted the present to be better than the past, and the future to be better than the present. The faster the rate of improving life, the happier people are. In Vladimir's day the rate at which all aspects of the life of society were renovated was quite staggering. Only a short while before the Kievans had gazed in amazement at the wonders of Constantinople, yet now they saw something similar arising in Kiev. This filled them with great pride in their native country and confidence in its great future.

During this period everything was surrounded by an aura of optimism, the optimism which was inherent in the early Christianity of Kievan Rus. This early Christianity in Rus was joyous. It did not renounce earthly passions and was alien to monastic asceticism. In Vladimir's day there were no Russian monks or monasteries in Rus. All this is quite natural. For anyone to feel the need to go into a monastery, he would have to have grown up, preferably from childhood, with Christian notions and ideals. And that took time. Moreover, the first generation of Russian Christians regarded the very fact of Christian baptism as such a great

feat of personal piety that it did not need to be supplement-
ed by enduring the rigours of monastic life. Of all the vir-
tues preached by Christianity the most prized was love of
one's neighbour, which can be seen, *inter alia*, from the
practice of arranging feasts and giving alms to the poor.

There had been princely feasts in pagan times also. Vladimir retained this custom and gave it new content. Here,
among the representatives of the prince's armed force and
the tribal aristocracy there was free discussion of 'current
politics' and this served to strengthen the class of feudal
lords. As for alms to the poor, the Kievans could eat freely
at the royal court. Vladimir gave orders that food should be
taken to the houses of the very old and sick. One form of
charity was to buy a captive (slave) in order to give him his
freedom.

When feudalism became sufficiently fully developed, the
Church helped the ruling class hold the oppressed peasantry in submission. What is more, it became a most powerful
feudal lord itself. But all this was still in the future. For the
time being Kievan Rus was ruled by that 'gentle prince',
Vladimir the Red Sun.

Vladimir's well-considered energetic policy brought Rus
into the system of European Christian states. Her international status grew ever stronger. Rus was becoming 'known
and heard ... in all corners of the earth.'

The rapid rate of change in Vladimir's day was nevertheless unable to ensure the completion of the feudal reform
during his lifetime. This required more time and was accomplished by his son, Yaroslav the Wise. As the chronicles
say, Vladimir ploughed, Yaroslav sowed, and we (that is,
the next generation) reaped the harvest. What precisely did
Yaroslav 'sow'?

Having ascended the throne after a bitter internecine
struggle, Yaroslav began just as energetically as his father
to continue the reform. Like his father, he built fortifica-
tions to protect his lands, now, it is true, mainly in the west.
Also like his father he made sure that nothing obstructed
the feudal transformations. In this connection a word must
be said about the 'sorcerers' revolt'.

In the hungry year of 1024 in Suzdal, then a remote
border area of Kievan Rus, a revolt flared up. It looked like
the pagans fighting against the Christians, but in fact it was

more complicated. As the chronicler tells us, the rebels were fighting against the 'old *chad* (tribal chiefs)'. This reveals exactly what was taking place. The time in question was witnessing the gradual stratification of what had been the free tribal commune. The tribal chiefs, or 'old *chad*', were expropriating the common lands and gradually turning into feudal lords. They collected tribute for the prince and, of course, did not forget about themselves in the process. In years when food was short these nascent feudal lords stored up supplies, growing rich and enslaving their fellow tribes-men. Thus, the revolt of 1024 was a typical uprising of the enslaved against their oppressors. It was the prototype of the peasant uprisings which came later in Russian history.

At this moment the sorcerers emerged from the 'under-ground' and tried to use the revolt for their own ends, namely, to re-establish paganism. The revolt was put down by Yaroslav. It is noteworthy that as long as the Suzdal sorce-rers simply performed their pagan rites, Yaroslav left them alone. He intervened when an anti-prince (only outwardly anti-Christian) revolt broke out. For him, as for Vladimir, it was important to consolidate the feudal reforms.

Yaroslav continued his father's intensive building activ-ity, seeking to make Kiev rank with Constantinople. Con-stantinople was famous for its Cathedral of St. Sophia, so a magnificent Cathedral of St. Sophia was erected in Kiev too; and in Kiev the city walls were crowned with a Golden Gate just as in Constantinople, and so on. Yaroslav also de-voted much energy to the development of trade: during his reign Kiev began to mint silver, as well as gold coins.

Yaroslav's main concern, however, was the creation of a Russian intelligentsia (for all the conventionality of the application of the term to that age). Vladimir did not have the time to accomplish this task. It required more than just literacy. It was also essential that Kievan Rus should not need to 'import' the Greek clergy, that it should have its own scholars, writers and philosophers, so that it could wage an ideological struggle, if necessary, against the im-perial ideology of Byzantium.

In the Middle Ages the only places where a person was provided with all the essentials and opportunities to study were the monasteries. They performed the function not only of religious centres, but also of academies of sciences and universities, one might say. Here treatises were written on a wide range of subjects and a new generation of educated people emerged. Princes and tsars visited monasteries not only to pray but also to obtain counsel, for often their most learned fellow-countrymen were to be found there. It is not surprising that Russian monasticism and cloisters appeared during the reign of Yaroslav.

Inventories of the 15th to 17th centuries (no earlier ones have survived) show that most of the books in monastery libraries were of a secular, not a liturgical nature. They contained chronicles, chronographies, various geographical writings, philosophical and military treatises and such classical works as Flavius Josephus' *History of the Jewish War*. A learned monk had to be widely educated. This can be seen, for example, from the beginning of the *Tale of St. Stephan of Perm* in which the fifteenth-century author, Epiphanius the Wise, a monk in the Trinity-St. Sergius Monastery, belittles his own talent, as was the custom in those days: 'I was not in Athens in my youth, nor learned I from philosophers their cunning word braiding, or wise words, nor did I master Plato's or Aristotle's discourses...' From this passage we can form an idea of the ideal monk-scholar.

In the monasteries chronicle-writing continued (Nestor), works of a polemical nature were written (often with an easily understood, although deliberately concealed, political message), manuscripts were copied (it is thanks to these monastery scripts that we can read ancient annals and that such works as *The Lay of Igor's Host* have survived), and icons were painted (Alipius). Monastery physicians gave free medical aid to common folk. Another important point is that the monasteries produced Russian priests and hierarchs who replaced the ones from Byzantium.

Relations with Byzantium varied, sometimes improving, sometimes deteriorating. In 1037, taking advantage of Yaroslav's difficult position in his struggle against the Pechenegs, Byzantium forced him to organise the Russian Church as a metropolitan seat of the Patriarchate of Constantinople, with the metropolitan of Kiev (a Greek appointed by Constantinople) at its head. Thus the Russian Church became formally subject to Constantinople. Byzantium was still hoping to make Kievan Rus its vassal. When a military conflict arose between Kiev and Constantinople a little later, the Byzantine historian Psellus called it 'Russians' uprising'. Not an attack, but an uprising! He clearly would not accept the idea of Kievan Rus' independence.

In 1051, after the death of the Greek metropolitan something quite unprecedented happened. Yaroslav himself (without the Emperor and Patriarch of Constantinople), 'did gather together the bishops' and appointed Ilarion, a Russian presbyter from the prince's village of Berestovo, metropolitan. The Russian Church again asserted its independence.

Metropolitan Ilarion was undoubtedly a most talented person. He is the author of that fine specimen of ancient Russian literature, the *Treatise on the Law and Grace*. Judging from the title one might think it was a classical theological treatise. For it was the Apostle Paul in his *Epistle to the Hebrews* who raised the question of the relationship of the Old Testament (the law given by Moses) to the New Testament (the grace bestowed on mankind by Christ). Naturally this problem was solved in favour of grace. In his work, however, Ilarion gave a new, politically topical twist to the classical theme.

Insofar as grace is above the law, it follows that the new is often above the old. Hence, peoples who embraced Christianity later were not inferior to those who had been baptised long before them, and consequently, Byzantium's claims to seniority in relation to Rus were unfounded. In narrowing down the subject and speaking of the baptism of Rus Ilarion particularly stressed that this was not thanks to Byzantium. The baptism had taken place in accordance with the wishes of the Russians. It was only a first step, and the Russian people had a great future ahead of them, he said. Narrowing down the subject even more, Ilarion praised Prince Vladimir, the baptizer of Rus, and his policies. In so doing he raised the question of canonising Vladimir, as a 'new Constantine'. Emperor Constantine, who many centuries before had made Christianity the state religion of the Roman Empire, introduced it into a country where it was in fact already widespread. Vladimir, however, introduced it into a pagan country, which was far more difficult. Therefore Vladimir's services were greater than Constantine's, Ilarion went on to describe and praise not only

Vladimir's 'charity', but also his activity as a statesman and to pay tribute to his ancestors, Svyatoslav and Igor, in other words, to praise pagans!

In fact this work of Ilarion's was a trenchant ideological weapon in the struggle for the independence of Kievan Rus. This did not go unnoticed by Byzantium, and the suggestion that Vladimir should be canonised was rejected at that time.

Under Yaroslav the spread of literacy and the building of schools (not only in Kiev) continued. Evidence has survived of the opening in 1030 of a school for 300 children in Novgorod, where they 'did study books'. There were also schools for girls, as well as boys. Gradually literacy spread among all the estates. This can be seen from ancient birch-bark documents. The population of ancient Rus enjoyed a rapid cultural growth.

Civilised states cannot exist without written laws, and Yaroslav compiled the *Russian Law*, and also a series of other written laws. In short, Yaroslav, who completed Vladimir's reform, made Kievan Rus a freely developing feudal state on a level with all the others. Not only the prince and his entourage, but the whole people were proud of their country and felt the desire to be independent of Byzantium, to be its equal. A few decades after Yaroslav's death this was shown by the higumen Daniil who went on a journey to Palestine and described it in his *Pilgrimage*. Seeing that in the Church of the Holy Sepulchre there were many lampions from different countries, including Byzantium but not Rus, he requested King Baldwin (Palestine was at that time in the hands of the crusaders) to let him hang up a lampion 'from the whole Russian Land'. Rus should never lag behind Byzantium.

What then were the main results of the reigns of Vladimir and Yaroslav? First, Rus became united into one feudal state. It was united by what was then a progressive culture, by written laws and by religion. The old tribal divisions disappeared. The united ancient Russian people, from which the Russians, Ukrainians and Byelorussians later developed, was finally moulded into a state.

Second, as a result of these reforms Rus finally occupied a place on a level with the whole civilised world. It was not inferior to the other countries either in its socio-economic formation (i. e., feudalism, which continued to develop) or in respect to its culture, crafts as well as militarily. The adoption of Christianity, which became the ideological foundation of the united feudal state of ancient Rus, played a progressive role in the early Middle Ages.

The rapid flowering of the ancient Russian state made a great impression on the rest of the world. The Western chronicler Adam of Bremen called Kiev 'the flower of the East' and 'the rival of Constantinople'. But perhaps the most eloquent testimony to the international authority of Kievan Rus is to be found in dynastic marriages. Whereas Vladimir won a 'worthy wife' for himself by force of arms, we find a quite different picture in Yaroslav's reign. He himself was married to the daughter of the king of Sweden, his sister to the king of Poland, three of his daughters were the wives of the kings of Hungary, Norway and France respectively, his son was married to the king of Poland's sister, and his grandson to the king of England's daughter, while his granddaughter was the wife of the German king and Holy Roman Emperor Henry IV. This is a clear indication of the ancient Russian state's international authority as a major power. It has emerged from a conglomeration of 'barbarian' tribes before the eyes of an astounded Europe in the short space of two generations. Thus had Vladimir 'ploughed' and Yaroslav 'sowed'!

Today we have every reason to be proud of what our great forebears did and to remember their noble labours with gratitude. What happened a thousand years ago was a great step forward on the long path of history.

Kommunist, No. 12, August 1987

Not long after this, on May 31, 1223, on the River Kalka (now Kalchik in Donetsk Region, Ukraine) the first major battle was fought by the united Russian and Polovtsian forces against forward detachments of Mongolo-Tartar cavalry which invaded the country. This battle, which ended in the defeat of the Russian and Polovtsian forces, was the prelude to the long and bitter period of the Mongolo-Tartar yoke which lasted right up to the end of the 15th century. Rus, which had attained the same level as the most advanced countries of

Western Europe by the end of the first millennium, was now set back a whole epoch in its economic, political and cultural development.

The interesting thing is, however, that after the adoption of Christianity, the Russian Orthodox Church continued to strive hard for independence during the period of the Mongolo-Tartar yoke, with the result that in 1448, i.e., almost fifty years before the end of the Mongolo-Tartar overlordship, it succeeded in breaking away from the Patriarchate of Constantinople and becoming autocephalous.

How can we explain this determined striving of the Russian Orthodox Church for independence even at a time when, one might think, the Church should have concentrated above all on seeking economic, military and political support from the Christian West? There are many reasons, and one of them was touched upon in passing by Academician Raushenbakh, when he noted that neither Prince Vladimir nor his retinue paid any attention to the 'underground' pagan priests and did not prevent them from performing pagan rites. 'Herein,' he remarked, 'lies one of the roots of the so-called double faith.'

This double faith, or to be more precise, the pagan elements in the religious consciousness of Russian people, retained its power for a very long time, right up to the 20th century. It included belief in mermaids, house-spirits and wood goblins, various rites which had nothing in common with Christian rites, belief in good and evil spirits and so on. Traces of paganism have survived to this day in Russian national costume, in rural architecture and in certain festivals (such as Pancake Week, the festival of bidding farewell to winter), even in our language, although we Russians usually say these words or expressions without being aware of their pagan origin. That eminent specialist on the history of paganism in ancient Rus, Academician BORIS RYBAKOV, persuades us to take a new look at much of what has survived in the Russian language and acquired considerable artistic and aesthetic force today. Thus, for a long time after the adoption of Christianity the people of Kievan Rus denied the Church's monopoly on cult activity, believing that one could pray to God at home and not only at church. For a long time the home remained the place where each pagan rite began and finished; it is not surprising that the expression 'home hearth' acquired a definite social meaning in the Russian language. The mediaeval

*sect of Strigolniks also based themselves on the firm an-
cient Slav tradition, maintaining that 'my home is my temple'.*

*Speaking of homes, many foreigners who visit our country
are struck by the rich carving on Russian peasant houses: the
carved barge-boards and window surrounds and the protrud-
ing end of the roof beam (finial), which is often in the shape
of a horse (sometimes other animals or birds). The word for
a roof beam (*konyok*) does not come from horse (*kon'*), but
from Old Russian* kon*, which meant a limit, border, and
sometimes a beginning and an end. These things which today
arouse our admiration with the richness of their patterns that
mean nothing to the uninformed eye, had a much more significant function in the old days. They were intended to protect the
house from evil spirits. The places through which the dwelling
was most likely to be invaded by evil spirits, in which the paganism of the ancient Slavs abounded, were, of course, the windows
and doors. This is why windows and doors in particular had
surrounds adorned with intricate symbolical carving,
in which the evil spirits would get 'entangled' or from which
they would run away. These evil spirits were, above all,
the spirits of the dead of other tribes (the Russians respected
their dead and believed that they protected them from trouble), the spirits of enemies and ill-wishers and the spirits of
those who had been punished by the forces of nature for wrong-
doing (drowned, eaten by wolves, struck by lightning.)*

*The beautifully finished, brightly painted and ornamented do-
mestic utensils and the rich embroidery on the national costume
of the Slavs were intended to serve the same purpose. People believed that cloth would not let in evil spirits. But the open places:
the neck, the arms and the legs, were vulnerable to the influence
of evil spirits, and that is why the neck, the cuffs and the hem
were decorated most lavishly with symbolical embroidery. The
ornamentation and embroidery on dresses varied considerably
depending on whether the dress was to be worn at home or outside. At home a person was protected from evil spirits in any
case, so the ornament on domestic clothing was simpler and less
lavish. It was quite a different matter when a person went outside
and thus became unprotected from evil spirits. This is why such
clothing was intricately adorned with richly ornamented embroidery. Both men and women wore high boots, also decorated
with patterns, as well as embroidered mittens, etc. So it is not*

*surprising that to this day clothes worn outside still differ consi-
derably from those worn at home.*

*In referring to these enduring pagan elements in the Russians'
consciousness we do not wish to suggest that the Russian Orthodox Church, which is today the largest of the world's fifteen autocephalous Orthodox Churches (suffice it to say that the Russian Orthodox Church consists of four exarchates, 76 dioceses,
11 vicariates, including some foreign ones; it has two theological
academies, three seminaries and sixteen monasteries and con-
vents, publishes the* Journal of the Moscow Patriarchate *and
has been a member of the World Council of Churches since
1961), bears the imprint of a primitive animist world outlook.
This is not the case, of course. But those who would like during
the celebrations of the millennium of Christianity in Russia to
acquire a deeper knowledge of the history of the Russian Orthodox Church, would be well advised to begin by taking a look at
paganism in ancient Rus. They will then be able to understand
the reasons for Patriarch Nikon's reforms in the middle of the
17th century and the schism in the Russian Orthodox Church
which followed immediately after these reforms, the emergence
of sects, including that of Old Believers.*

*The following article, about Old Believers in Moscow, was
written by* Alexander Nezhny, *a specialist on the history of
Orthodoxy in Russia. He describes his article as 'modest remarks on Old Believers, on the trials which have been their
lot, on the priceless treasures of Russian culture which they have preserved, and finally, on how they live today in Moscow,
at the Rogozhsky settlement, not far from their old cemetery'.*

IN ROGOZHSKAYA ZASTAVA.
VISITING OLD BELIEVERS

By ALEXANDER NEZHNY

Inheritors of a Priceless Legacy

The faith of the Old Believers is an amazing phenomenon
of Russian life, beyond compare with anything else. It has
made a permanent impression on our lives — in literature it

was expressed by the gigantic figure, Archpriest Avvakum, a writer of stunning strength and ferocity; for our culture it has preserved the tradition of Old Russian icon painting, handwritten and printed books; and also the old church music. Without attempting to explain the different trends in old believers' faith, I would simply say that today its main centre is in Moscow, in the Rogozhsky settlement. Some 200-odd years ago at the time of the plague in Moscow, a cemetery was started here and a chapel built. Soon afterwards the Cathedral of the Intercession was built by Matvei Kazakov, the outstanding Russian architect, and after it the Cathedral of the Nativity: both were painted by Palekh masters. The majestic belfry church which soared to a height of 70 metres was built early this century. It seemed to gather round itself all the other buildings — the almshouses, monasteries, the theological institute, the choir house, the house of the clergy, the archpriest's chamber — all of them, big and small.

These were built exclusively at the expense of Old Believers, without help from the state, even though the Old Believers helped society a great deal, and did so eagerly. I mentioned the almshouses — they gave shelter and food to hundreds of poor and sick people. There is also the Botkin Hospital, known all over our country. It was built and equipped by Kozma Soldatenkov, a notable figure in the Rogozhskaya community, a merchant and book publisher. He laid down that treatment at the hospital would be free. The Moscow city No. 1 children's clinic is still called 'Morozovskaya' in the vernacular, after the name of its founder Morozov, a merchant and industrialist, and a representative of the famous family of merchants, industrialists and generous providers of charity. Savva Morozov built the Moscow Art Theatre in the Kamergersky Lane and financed the publication of Lenin's newspaper *Iskra*. It is to our shame that some five years ago the Morozov family tomb in the Rogozhskoye cemetery was put in order not by the Moscow Art Theatre and not by the Ministry of Culture, but by relatives from France.

Happily, and thanks to the Old Believers' infinite patience, we've inherited a truly priceless treasure. The Old Believers from Rogozhskaya Zastava have saved over 2,000 icons — and what icons! Works from the school of Andrei

Rublev, Dionysius, icons from Novgorod, Pskov and Tver dating back to the 14th-16th centuries. My heart fluttered when I saw all that. What a pity it is that so few people get the opportunity to see the stunning St. Nicholas (15th century), with its sincere, penetrating look, or the very noble 14th-century Nativity, or the wonderful Saviour (also 14th century). But this is not due to reluctance on the part of the Old Believers. They are prepared to show people the icons. I was told this by Archbishop of Moscow and of All Russia, Olimpi (Gusev), and by R. Khrustalyov, chairman of the community. But there is nowhere to display the icons today. And the books—handwritten and in old print (including some made by Ivan Fyodorov), in ancient leather bindings, with wonderful multicoloured headbands and capital letters—all of them still have to wait their time to be put on display.

Academician Dmitry Likhachev said: 'This is a living example of ancient Russian culture, which has retained all its wonderful qualities. The collection of icons is a great treasure of worldwide importance. The Old Believers loved and prized books. They were all literate people, though they registered as illiterate... And the old church music—thanks to the Old Believers we can still hear them live and not from a tin can. Their aesthetic, historic traditions enable us to glimpse the manifold art of Ancient Rus—in the combination of singing, painting, architecture and literature.'

Reservation Zone Needed

The Rogozhskoye cemetery—a centre of culture of the Old Believers—has lost much in the last decades. The Cathedral of the Nativity was closed down a long, long time ago; first it housed some sort of small factory, then—a canteen, and now it is a depot for the museums of the Moscow Kremlin. When I went to see what the Kremlin museums keep in storage, I saw old office desks, chairs and empty crates. I thought—can it be that in all our fatherland there is no one sufficiently interested to find a more fitting use for the Cathedral and give it back its original dignity and beauty? Because if we are fortunate enough to see a reservation area set up in Rogozhskaya Zastava, then why shouldn't the Cathedral be used, for example, as a museum of culture of the Old Believers? Realizing very well the irreversible nature of many of the changes that have taken place here, we should be as careful as possible with what remains. Yes, in its time, attempts were made to close down the Cathedral of the Intercession, too; the 1,000 *poods* bell was thrown off the belfry, and after that it was decided to blast away the entire majestic building but either the charge was too small or the building happened to be extremely resilient. We, however, accept the guilt of our fathers, and realize — at least! — that you can't achieve anything through destruction, and that without our past we are utter nobodies.

The former house of the clergy, a two-storied building of graceful proportions, was used as a hostel for people working at a vegetable depot and has been left vacant for two years. It has burned many times, has no windows and practically no roof; one other small, two-storied building, which in its time served as a shelter for monks and afterwards housed various sorts of offices has been abandoned and now only the walls are left standing. Would it not be reasonable, would it not be fair, to give back to the Old Believers these almost dead buildings, taking into account both their needs and the present-day, somewhat cramped circumstances of their activities? Shouldn't we meet them halfway by setting up a historical-architectural reserve here?

These quite proper proposals made Alexander Udaltsov, Chairman of the Executive Committee of the Zhdanovsky District Soviet of Moscow, feel somewhat uneasy. However, today, it is not so good even for a Chairman of the Executive Committee to be looking at ruined architectural relics, which the buildings are. Udaltsov said: 'All right, we'll return the house of the clergy to them. But they must set up a picture gallery in it and let people see the exhibits.' And then it got round to the idea that a museum of icon art should also function here, on somewhat different lines (like, for example, the historical-architectural room of the theological academy in the Holy Trinity-St. Sergiy Monastery), and that the second house, or rather, the remaining walls, should be returned to Old Believers; this re-raised the question of a reservation area — and one could see in the Chairman's eyes a cautious, obstinate expression of opposition. Opposed to what? I thought bitterly that the irony of fate can be really merciless. The Old Believers had to live through the most terrible suffering and persecution for three centuries; Avvakum was burned on the tsar's fire and tens of thousands of Old Believers burned themselves alive for their faith; the Old Believers had to suffer their altars being sealed at their Rogozhsky sacred places; they had to save during all the sufferings of these times the immortal creations of the people's spirit for our common glory—they went through all this, just to be confronted, finally, with an obstacle at the District office.

Confrontation

Tolerance of dissidence is certainly not the first virtue of our Fatherland. The moral vulnerability of the dominating idea did not lead to self-examination, but rather to violence, to the desire to quash any other opinion; the ensuing silence, full of hate and terror, was read as a sure sign of universal accord. The Old Believers were well-nigh the first ones in Russia to be persecuted for their faith. Their distressing sufferings started immediately after the reforms introduced with such cruel zeal by Patriarch Nikon in the second half of the 17th century, leading the Russian Orthodox Church and Russian society to the tragic split which was to have such serious spiritual and social consequences. And this cannot be reduced to adherence to procedures—for example, crossing oneself with two fingers, which Nikon replaced with crossing with three fingers. It was the Old Believers' understanding of the church and also of social life, their world outlook, if you like, that was of greater importance in their unshakeable confrontation.

The state joined the official Church in the persecution of the old faith. That is why the Old Believers' protest went beyond religious limits, and had a social dimension too from the very beginning. Archpriest Avvakum deemed it necessary to pose the question of the limits of the tsar's power, and when he was already a stone's throw from the fire to which he had also been sentenced 'for great aspersion of the Tsar's House', he wrote with amazing lack of fear about Tsar Alexei Mikhailovich: 'Oh, ye poor, poor and mad little tsar! What have you done to yourself? Well perish though to hell, ye whore's son!' After suffering the violence of Peter I's years, getting a breather under Catherine II and then coming under the merciless hand of Nikolai I, the followers of Avvakum displayed amazing political sobriety when appraising the April 1905 decree on freedom of conscience. 'No, the Russian people, including us Old Believers, will not be lured now by this bait any more; everyone can see that this is merely lip service, in order to win time while giving nothing to anyone, or, having given a little, to take away even more,' we read in the protocols of the representative meeting of Old Believers, held in Nizhny Novgorod in August 1905. 'It is high time ... to demand that the war be ended and the Constituent Assembly be convened immediately on the basis of universal, equal, direct and secret ballot, that guarantees are given of unconditional freedom of conscience and faith, freedom of speech and the press, of movement, assembly, unions and strikes, personal immunity, sanctity of the home, and amnesty in all political and religious cases.'

So that the thread is not severed

'I think a course for singing should also be established,' I told Udaltsov. 'It is an ancient art — it should be taught! No matter what happens we must not allow it to disappear. We must not sever the thread, Alexander Nikolayevich!'

But he shook his head — no teaching of singing.

However, I returned to the subject of the reservation area over and over again. I tried to prove that any civilized society would go out of its way to set up a cultural centre here with various exhibitions, a history museum, restoration and other workshops, a publishing department and a research service. Everything that shames us here is exclusively our fault — garages, a former pub, litter of all sorts, and houses that are falling apart. Why not give these houses to the Old Believers? Why not give them the opportunity to work here now — both for themselves and for us? The more so that they are ready to cooperate with the state, with the Soviet Culture Foundation! I repeat that only a step in the right direction to meet them is needed. And once again I pointed to the house of which only the walls are left. 'Impossible,' Udaltsov said.

'There are blocks of flats nearby and a school. The teachers will be against it. You know — bad influence on Young Pioneers.'

Believe me, please, I'm not trying to make Udaltsov look bad. He is, I'm sure, a good worker, who performs well his far from simple duties. But he should not be entrusted to deal with questions whose importance he does not understand. And that's that — he doesn't understand.

But I do fervently hope that we'll not miss the opportunity of setting up in Rogozhskaya Zastava a reservation area — to preserve the culture of Russian Old Believers.

The **Human Factor**

At the nub of it all

Soviet society has embarked on a thoroughgoing renewal, and it is not just empty words when the USSR describes perestroika *as a continuation of the social revolution. But if people from all walks of life are to be actively involved in this revolution, it calls for a number of democratic reforms. Uppermost among these is a reform of the judicial system so as to guarantee any individual or group of individuals the right to go about the activity of their choice so long as it does not conflict with the Soviet Constitution. It must likewise ensure that any person or organisation without distinction engaging in unconstitutional acts is made to answer for them before the court.*

Then if we understand perestroika *as a continuation of the social revolution it raises yet another demand. This revolution has been initiated by the Communist Party, which is not only the party in power in the Soviet Union, but the only one. Just like any other party it has its progressive elements which endorse and actively support the new political line adopted by the leadership. But there are also elements which find* perestroika *not to their liking and are seeking to sabotage it behind the scenes. The Soviet press regularly carries reports of dismissals from Party organisations of people opposing* perestroika, *or slowing it down. It goes without saying that the democratisation of Party life and methods of running society needs to be carried out in the open and publicised to the full, since only openness and the clear subordination of the Party to the norms of Soviet legality can guarantee public confidence in the new political line and ensure a growth in grassroots activity. People set great store by the resolutions adopted at the 19th All-Union Party Conference in summer 1988.*

The ideas behind perestroika *enjoy the support of people from all walks of life, and evidence of this is not hard to find. Society's healthy forces are ready and willing to press on with the matter in hand. But it would be a mistake to idealise this readiness. It mainly rests on hopes, but it needs to be based on interests and clear organisation at all levels of society. The tactical objectives, methods and procedures involved in* perestroika *are being refined and amended and will be refined and amended many a time yet. What matters most of all is that the initiative behind the renewal should not be lost as it finds its way all the way down from the highest levels of social management to the very lowest levels; it must become the concern of millions of individual people.*

Conservative forces are certainly to be found in our society, and it would be a mistake to underestimate their retarding effect. The magazine ECO, *published by the Siberian Department of the USSR Academy of Sciences, set out to model a number of scenarios for the behaviour of various social groups depending on the course of events. It based its work on a host of forecasts devised by economists from both the theoretical and practical fields, works managers and sociologists.*

Below we present several models for the behaviour of certain social groups during perestroika.

1. 'OSTRICH' SCENARIO: burying one's head in the sand. This is based on a blind refusal to accept changes and the considerable inertia inherited from the period of stagnation. It finds its supporters among the most conservative and inactive forces in society, people who have become accustomed to receiving payment by virtue of their position rather than for their work, who enjoy privileges through their involvement in the distribution process against a background of shortages. 'They'll kick up a fuss, criticize each other and sack a few,' is what they think. 'Of course, we're not perfect, but who is? After all, things were comfortable enough and we didn't wash our dirty linen in public.' And to protect their cushy existence, this type of person will try to block any major change. In their efforts to do so, they are not be found lacking for a justification: the slogans calling for thoroughgoing revolutionary reform represent a leftist deviation, they say, and are a departure from socialist principles. Their entire repertoire consists of a handful of impressive-sounding quotes and facts unrelated to our history. Their objective is to return to that serene self-satisfaction that leads nowhere, to ideological dogma and to brushing problems under the carpet. On this scenario, the present deformities of socialism would even-

tually become worse and would slowly but surely lead to its degeneration. It would be a mistake to think this course of events is totally out of the question. It has no lack of advocates, particularly among those employed in that oversized sphere of highly paid professions which makes little demand on personal skills.

2. 'FOX' SCENARIO: evading actual problems. This rests on an understanding that something has to be changed coupled with primitive fear of renewal. The irresistible conclusion is to play at reforms. How might this approach look in practice? It could manifest itself in countless cosmetic reforms. Minor changes might be made at the focal points of everyday life to demonstrate a concern for, and appreciation of, 'ordinary people's needs'. Part of the population will be only too ready to respond to this subtly disguised 'demagoguery', to lend it support and denounce the troublemakers and extremists who call for profound, revolutionary changes. The sum total of numerous minor improvements will be presented as the revolutionary renewal of society.

This policy also has its advocates, not among the most hardened elements of the bureaucracy, as is the case with the 'ostrich' factor, but among the middle level of officials employed in the omnipresent management apparatus, the most cynical of all. Though they realise the need for change, they are confident that 'large sections' of the population will be quite satisfied with the semblance of reform present in the most minor improvements. A policy of evading the cardinal problems involved in renewal will exacerbate the tendency to stagnation. Both these strategies testify to political blindness and cowardice, a pretence that things will turn out better without rocking the boat.

The following two options are based on a readiness to make many fundamental changes. But how?

3. 'BEAR' SCENARIO: putting things in order with an iron fist. Growing openness has revealed long-existent but carefully concealed instances of the most blatant wastefulness, moral decay, abuse of power and other unlawful acts. Being quite unprepared for such frankness and self-criticism, public opinion (this is particularly true of the older age groups, who have given considerable service to society) took this torrent of negative reports as an indication of the disorders peculiar to the last few years. To compound this general state of shock, we have a widespread fear among officials that they will lose their social status, a dread of shouldering responsibility and a complete inability to put their house in order using the methods laid down by economic practice and the law. There remains but one salvation: a return to draconian methods, 'tightening the screws'. And to support this claim they have a historical precedent ready and waiting. 'Remember,' the 'bears' say, 'what things were like in Stalin's day. Everyone knew their place, did a decent day's work: there was no mischief and the prices came down — in a word, general enthusiasm and one success after another.' The saddest thing about it is that even today there remain a sizeable number of people who prefer to ignore the truth about our past. They see 'tightening the screws' as a method which will settle all conflicts, and are prepared to restore Stalinism and condemn only its greatest excesses: the camps and mass reprisals. Everything else will suit them fine. Sure, the 'bears' are prepared for certain reforms so long as calm is maintained and no conflicts arise. Certainly, they say, who could object to the use of economic methods of management, a democratisation of the management apparatus, the election of all those carrying responsibility and so forth? But when there are severe political tensions internationally and economic difficulties domestically this is no time to 'cultivate' democracy. Only an iron fist can shake people up and channel their endeavours into tackling the urgent matters in hand. Such is the ideological foundation of this approach. Its political and social foundation may be seen in innumerable threads leading to the past: insufficient legal safeguards, the ever-present responsibility of the grassroots to the top, decision-making from the top to the bottom, blinkered perceptions, the habit of blind obedience. What such a scenario ultimately leads to is quite clear: the definitive loss of socialist achievements and the 'barrack-room socialism' of which Marx warned as far back as the 19th century.

4. 'GO-IT-ALONE INDUSTRIALIST' SCENARIO: give me full freedom of action, the right to buy and sell, the right to dispose of money, housing and other assets, and all your problems will be solved. This approach is based on the illusion that purely economic methods are sufficient to solve the problems facing society. This scenario is the brain-child of a certain section of economic managers and their ideological backers in the academic world. The advocates of this approach are convinced (and numerous negative examples from the recent past have strengthened them in this conviction) that the entire management pyramid and the entire nonproductive sector are nothing but 'loudmouths and hangers-on'. The only real force is represented by themselves, their teams, their production capacity, their resourcefulness, cunning, intuition, their ability to take risks and come out on top and their contacts with those of the same ilk, fellow businessmen. Everything else for them is just empty words. So the country needs an efficient economy? You can have it tomorrow: just give us complete independence and real power!

Who would deny that independence is one of the conditions of success? At the same time, it is quite clear that it would be a dangerous course indeed to divorce economic freedoms from political and moral freedoms. Little by little, we are witnessing the emergence of 'go-it-alone' attitudes, covert efforts to 'divorce' the individual team from the countless concerns of the broader community, of the country as a whole to make it like the crew of a ship steering its own course on the high seas, taking its own risks and reaping its own rewards. However, the 'freedom of action' demanded from society, no matter how innocuous it may appear, and the concentration of all power in the hands of one person, could quite easily make the individual worker defenceless against the 'ship's captain', the government department, the local authority, the tyranny of the collective or the despotism of the family unit.

A dangerous variation on the 'go-it-alone' industrialist is the 'go-it-alone' manager on the level of a region or a republic. He views perestroika *as an opportunity to make the most of his position — be it by virtue of natural, national or historical reasons — and to use this as a way of favouring his 'own' people to the detriment of others.*

It should be noted that all four of the scenarios examined constitute an indirect disregard for working people as individuals for the sake of goals inimical to their interests: the retention of privileges, the attainment of power, the settlement of purely technical matters, the satisfaction of nationalist ambitions. Humanitarianism, ethical considerations are incompatible with such approaches.

We are left with but one choice: perestroika viewed as a continuation of the social revolution — *precisely what we*

10–867

*started out with. Our friends abroad who take a genuine inter-
est in the processes taking place in the Soviet Union today
often ask: 'What do you expect to build with your* perestroika? *Communism?' What can we say?*

*There's a long, long way to go before there can be any
thought of communism. So what were our objectives in em-
barking on* perestroika? *The main objective should be clear
enough: we are out to revive and advance the most appealing
features of socialism: its humanitarianism, democracy, its vitality and commitment to the cause of peace. We want to advance our society to a position from which it will be able to
embark on the most arduous and noblest of all tasks, implementing that ideal of the future which has been the dream of
humanity's most outstanding thinkers from time immemorial,
the Great Ideal which guarantees the Happiness of All.*

*What we understand by the 'human factor' should not be re-
garded as some kind of 'mechanical adjunct' to* perestroika,
*as an 'adjustible screw' designed to ensure the reliable and
smooth functioning of all branches of the economy. The human factor is first and foremost concerned with individuals
and their personal ties, their ideas, the sincerity of their actions and the genuineness of their feelings.* Perestroika, *let us
remind ourselves, begins with human beings. The goal of* perestroika *is the creation of a harmoniously developed human
being. It is enlightening to recall the words of* Goethe: *'Before a great mind I bend my head, before a great heart my
knees.'*

Lev Tolstoy *could also get to the heart of the matter. He
said that the best kind of people were those who lived mainly
by their own thoughts and the feelings of others, and the worst
those who lived by others' thoughts and their own feelings.
For Soviet people,* glasnost *encourages the need to live by
their own thoughts, to ask themselves questions, like what is
peace, what is truth, what is kindness, what am I, what is the
meaning of my individuality? The first advances in reforming
the economy will inevitably arouse (or should arouse, otherwise the moral foundations of* perestroika *will be seriously
lacking in meaning) in people a desire to be sensitive to the
feelings of others, to perform acts of kindness for others, notably in the sphere of social needs.*

Here, and particularly at the initial stages of perestroika, *a great deal depends on the moral climate generated in collectives, whether at school, college, places of work or elsewhere. This moral climate is engendered by those who lead the collective. Their role is, by far, the most important one.*

Let us give an example. The Elektronmash works in Leningrad were heading for bankruptcy. The factory failed to meet its targets and cut back on social amenities. There was pressure for a change. And then PAVEL RADCHENKO, *a new general manager, was appointed, a leader full of vitality and with organisational capability.**

The new general manager Radchenko set about organising the factory in a way which, he considered, had brought results elsewhere. But success was not apparent. Surprise ... surprise. Perhaps the people were at fault? But it turned out it was the leader. Instead of working together with the staff on the shop floor, Radchenko immersed himself in paperwork. He introduced 6,000 norms for measuring the performance of workshops and individuals. At a time when team work was showing results in many places elsewhere, it was undermined at Elektronmash. People were not concerned so much with how to help each other, but how to shift the blame for deficiencies onto others. For all his shortcomings, Radchenko was not given to modesty either. 'I believe in proper organisation,' he would proclaim, 'and I see to it that proper organisation is observed.' Things became so bad that the work force demanded a general meeting at which they expressed lack of confidence in their general manager. Radchenko was forced to resign, and the ministry lost no time in accepting his resignation.

We chose to relate what happened at Elektronmash for this reason: two or three years ago there could have been no question of subordinates expressing a lack of confidence in their managers: they were compelled to obey managers who were imposed on them from above.

Today, things have changed beyond recognition. Nowadays it is not ministries and government departments which appoint heads of enterprises, but collectives themselves elect their leaders at all levels, from the lowest (team leader) to the highest (department manager, general manager, rector of

---

*   He is the author of a book entitled *Iskusstvo rukovodit* (The Art of Management).

a college, etc.). The first example of high level post election occurred in January 1987 at the minibus factory (RAF) in Yelgava (Latvian SSR). Before that date, the factory was in a sorry state. It failed to meet the plan and the minibus it produced was downgraded by the quality control, which further worsened the factory's finances. In this way it was deprived of funds urgently needed for the construction of housing and communal facilities.

We have reported in Soviet Scene 1987 *how* Komsomolskaya Pravda *carried an advertisement, inviting applications for the post of factory manager. The response was overwhelming — about 4,000 applicants. The top twenty of these were invited to take part in the final election procedure. This was followed by a national contest lasting no less than ten days in Yelgava, at the end of which democratic elections were held for the post of the factory manager. On 2 February 1987* VICTOR BOSSERT'*s post was confirmed by the Automobile Industry Ministry and he took up his duties.*

He kept a diary, excerpts from which we publish below.

'I BELIEVE IN MY FACTORY...'

By VICTOR BOSSERT

10 February. Morning. First day at work.

An elderly woman at the gate jumps to it, nods her head as if she's known me for years. Chilly and misty is the office outside. Quiet and deserted. Take a look at the office. Uh, no direct link with department heads.

The conveyer belt, I hear, has stopped. There are no spare parts, and the deputy manager responsible for supplies and three dozen workers of the supplies department sit in their offices keeping warm by the radiators. (For some reason or other almost all of them are women.)

It's crazy — alone in an empty office. It is my first day after all, and a few kind words might be called for, but all I can think of are instructions and orders.

11 February. Evening.

Attended the factory meeting. Too much talking.

A strange conversation materialises. They'll do it by the end of the week, they tell me. I ask exactly when: on Thursday or Friday, at what time? They look at me quite dumb-struck. But finally we agree: Friday 3.00 p. m. on the dot, they must report back on what they've done.

Forgot to have lunch. Together with the Party and the trade union committees I give first written guarantees to improve housing conditions for young families. Now it's time to get down to business.

12. February. Evening.

Did a round of the workshops. People willing to talk. Concerned about their work, give advice, suggestions, wish me success, invite me to meetings. It's good to see. But that's not all. All at once four announced they were leaving for 'objective' reasons.

Heads of department came to the Party committee. Worried, don't know how to cope with a situation like this. The Party committee secretary apparently calmed them down. They're all working. Had a look at the flat where I will be living with the family until it's our turn for a flat in the factory block. Rang Ella. She's coming on 26 February with the children. I'd better get things ready. But when? In the middle of the night? Mother will remain in Omsk with her sister. I'm worried about her, we ought to live together.

13 February. Morning.

Woke up at 5.00 a. m. Damn it: I keep working and giving instructions in my sleep.

Things are pressing at the works. A lot of parts are missing. And what about the conveyer belt? The mechanical shops are not getting all the metal they need. Sheet steel is in short supply. Whose fault is it? To a large extent our own, the fault of those responsible for supplies. They are in no rush themselves to get involved where the heat is on and prefer to send others. Incidentally, today is Friday, so what about the work? Forget it, not finished at 3.00 p. m. or 8.00 p. m. either.

14 February. Evening.

From 4.00 to 7.00 p. m. attended a gathering of Pushkin enthusiasts. A lot of talented people. It's raw outside, and you can feel the moisture in the air. Wife rang from Omsk. It's minus 30 there.

15 February. Sunday.

Got away from the factory for the first time in the last month. Took a walk around the old town of Riga. Looked around, but didn't notice anything, can't stop thinking of the factory.

16 February. Late evening in the office.

A hectic schedule today. Began at 6.00 a. m. Examining the first week's results.

Meetings with Komsomol activists went well. Seeing workers to discuss personal problems. I should be more friendly and welcoming towards them. But they're guarded and inhibited. Distrust has set in. They're not used to the idea of a free-and-easy talk with the boss. Out of 14, ten wanted the same.

17 February. A hard day.

They decided not to let anyone leave, from the cleaners to the deputy manager, without first seeing the works manager. The benefits? Of the five people I spoke to, two agreed to stay.

Complete panic due to the lack of parts. Met drivers: they had come from far away, from all corners of the country, for our minibusses. But there are none. They're not ready. Masses of complaints.

Here and there it's our fault, as well. I keep thinking we need to start from scratch again, to improve the factory management structure. Agreed to an increase in the number of lawyers today. That will pay for itself.

18 February. Evening.

We discussed cooperation with the head of the Latvian student builders. The factory still needs workers. And all this because of the lack of technology. Manual labour wherever you look.

19 February. A memorable day.

Met a delegation of experts from socialist countries (Yugoslavia, Poland, Czechoslovakia, Romania, Hungary). Talked about joint ventures.

In his speech to senior Latvian figures from the Party and economy, General Secretary Mikhail Gorbachev referred to my election at our factory. But he also mentioned that the workers had not kept their promise to modernise the minibus.

22 February.

Woke up on my own. It's 6.24 a. m. The alarm will go off in a minute. But why create a din. Switched it off and, would you believe it, overslept. Awoken by a knock at the door. The driver was worried. It's Sunday today, but the shops that were standing still are working.

23 February.

The morning began with sorting out an argument between a worker and a foreman. The workers invited me to attend a shop floor meeting. Will make sure I'm there.

Must help the lads from the factory band, provide them with better costumes. Appointments with workers to discuss their personal problems began at 5.00 p. m. Of 20 people, 17 had complaints about accommodation. This was the first series of meetings in the presence of the trade union committee chairman, the Party committee secretary and the welfare representative.

24 February.

Today gave a whole group of managers a good ticking off for the first time. It's time they matched words with deeds and showed some commitment. Yesterday, the lack of personal discipline of a number of managers was the sole reason for our failure to meet the day's plan.

Had a fruitful meeting with the three different teams responsible for various supplies and cooperation with other enterprises. For many years these teams made claims on each other, but you can't carry on like that within the con fines of the same factory. They became bureaucratised beyond all measure. There was a very interesting joint meeting of the Party branches of the pressing, repair and tool shops. A majority were in favour of reorganising the management structure, of decentralising certain services so that they are provided by the shops. We jointly came to the conclusion that we all need to learn economics and how to make the operation pay its way. Maria Kozima, head of the labour and wages department and an opponent of decentralisation, sat with a dejected look on her face. The meeting demonstrated that the workers are more in touch with the situation than she is.

25 February. Evening.

An analysis of the last few days shows that the quality control department is not doing its main job. There is no procedure to sort out rejects at every stage of production, and this goes in particular for the stores and the pressing machines shop. The head of quality control adopted a wait-and-see attitude, sitting back and watching the battle between two giants, the production control and the state quality control.

This morning I was forced to dismiss the head of the quality control department and temporarily transfer these responsibilities to his assistant, with whom it was agreed that nothing must escape the attention of quality control.

26 February. A very important day.

Following 'tough' measures, I think the departmental heads have understood they will not be allowed to get away with neglecting their jobs. Nobody is irreplaceable. Elections were held for the post of deputy chief engineer in one of the workshops. There were five candidates. Ivashin was elected by secret ballot.

By 3.35 p. m. I have arrived at Riga Airport to meet the family at last. I have bought carnations for the occasion. So now the family is at full strength again, the rear is secure, and things at the factory will be better.

But we've still got some catching up to do. Tomorrow is the penultimate day of the month. Will we make it, will we meet the plan target?

27 February. Penultimate day of the month.

The day begins with a call from the Ministry. They want to know how pressed we are to fulfil the month's plan. It was not until after 22 February that things were more or less clarified with the main supplies. Engines are still a problem... So what will it be like when we have to pay our way, with self-financing and self-recoupment to boot?

28 February. Last day of the month.

The whole work force turned up for today's *subbotnik*.* They knew the figures and the plan for February, and so they really got down to work. A man needs some reward — satisfaction with the result, with the open discussion of the result, with his competitive performance. And the plan for February was fulfilled.

1 March. Late in the evening we welcomed the spring. It had crept up on me entirely without my noticing.

2 March. In the office. Late evening.

I really feel like shouting at someone. What on earth is happening to the workers? They seem to find it quite normal to sit back for the first couple of days. But then comes

---

*   *Subbotnik* — voluntary free work on a day-off.— *Ed.*

the rush to catch up. At 12.00 noon I gathered together all those who are supposed to ensure normal working, living and free time conditions. They have been telling those in the hostel to buy their own taps, lamps, paint, etc. Incredible!

We reviewed the results of competition between the shops and handed out certificates — to the great pleasure of those receiving them. But didn't they do this before? In the auxiliary shops (repair, tool, transport, etc.) apparently not. There was a total lack of discipline and there was drunkenness in these shops.

3 March. Evening.

All day at the Ministry in Moscow. Began with the central board. I was spoken to for two hours by the Number Two and taught how to live. We have different approaches and will never agree. The talk with the head of the central board lasted for three hours... Moscow supports the factory's strategy. We should be aiming for a new model and use it as a basis for the manufacture of a series or a range of vehicles for different purposes.

4 March.

Received by the Minister today. I was a bit worried, particularly about the short term plan (up to 1992). We did, after all, devise it in just two weeks. How will Nikolai Pugin respond to our proposals? My fears were groundless. I read out the draft order, and the Minister listened. Then he re-read it carefully, took a fountain pen and crossed out the word 'draft'. At the end he wrote, 'Fulfilment of order to be monitored by deputy minister.' Everyone in the office at that moment looked in disbelief at what had happened. After all, that's not the way things are done here. The accepted way is for a draft to make a tour of the various offices and to become an order in a curtailed form.

5 March. In Moscow.

Meeting with management of the central board in charge of bus and coach manufacture. Decisions contradict each other here. You get the feeling that *perestroika* has still to make its impact felt on quite a few individuals. Someone back at the works had had their 'encounters' with these people and had warned me not to 'offend' them without approval 'from above'. What should I do? After all, among our 'trustees' here are those responsible for the loss of the works' good name.

6 March. In Moscow.

Noon. Meeting with the management of Avtoexport. I must quickly find out: if we produce 1,000 extra of the RAF-2203 minibusses, will we be able to sell them abroad?

7 March. Saturday.

Straight from the train to the factory. What is going on? The first week's schedule has only been fulfilled to the tune of 60 per cent. What on earth have you been doing, assistant production manager?

8 March. At home. International Women's Day.

Gave the women in our house my best regards together with a large bouquet of tulips. This is the first time the whole family has been able to spend a full day together. The children are joyful.

9 March. Morning.

7.20 a. m. Suggested to assistant production manager that he make way for someone else. The reason? Inability to manage. His expression betrays disbelief; he considers my objections unjustified.

12 March.

Today we have a general meeting with a secret ballot.

The choice is between two alternatives: either we continue working at the same pace or adopt a counterplan. I spoke in passionate terms, but I don't think eloquence won the day (since I'm no expert at it anyway). The clarity of the plan was the decisive factor. If we work properly profits will grow and everyone will enjoy the benefits themselves. Around six per cent were against, but the majority voted in favour. This means that in 1987 1,000 minibusses will leave the works in addition to those originally planned. Now things will be easier.

1 April. Morning.

Pranks apart, we've fulfilled the plan for the first quarter. Marvellous!

8 April. Sverdlovsk.

Andreika was born today, a son! But again I am thousands of miles from home. The comrades from the Sverdlovsk Regional Party Committee found me at the Uralmash works. This is the venue for the regular meetings of the All-Union Managers' Club. They passed on the news and the chairman of the meeting offered me his compliments. Then I got up to speak — about the contest and elections back at the RAF factory. It's a pity that most of my fellow managers were against such contests and the idea of elections in general. They think that team leaders and departmental heads can be elected. But top-flight managers? That won't lead to anything.

15 April. Evening.

This afternoon I was called on by Belozub, the head of the body shop and a one-time candidate in the competition for general manager. Looking dejected and tired, he said:

'I can't go on. I see no way of fulfilling the plan.'

What was I to say? We sat in silence, without looking each other in the face. I told him that I would think about it.

And I thought of an unexpected twist. Let us see which of us turns out to be right: him or me.

30 April. 11.00 p.m.

Last day of the month and last day of my management ... of the body shop. After talking to Belozub, I had firmly decided to do the job of factory manager in addition to my job for a week. And the shop fulfilled the plan. But for me personally this was not the most important thing. I had given some thought to the following question. Why do so many managers collapse under the pressure of unforeseen crises? Because they can only manage in overall terms, but they often cannot imagine what is involved in the job of a foreman, a team leader, a head of shop.

1 May. International Workers' Day.

Our contingent was the largest at the May Day parade. The first time for many years, so they say. And their mood didn't seem bad either.

2 May. Evening.

Today I spent the whole day with the family in Jūrmala, at the seaside.

4 May. Morning.

We have a new assistant production manager. Alexander Panov, a native of Minsk. One of the candidates in the contest for the post of general manager. How will he fit in?

11 May. Evening.

Problems with the body shop. Vassily Belozub is on holiday. He has been temporarily replaced by Igor Ignatushkin, a chap of about thirty with secondary technical education and a flair for organisation. I have high hopes for him. Up to now, around twenty of the former heads have been re-lieved of their posts, some of them at their own request, others because they couldn't cope with the job. It's unbearably difficult working with the head of the labour and wages department. She knows everything — all the instructions, directives, prohibitions, clauses, paragraphs. But she can't manage the simple task of paying someone for their hard work. People want to earn, but with our Maria Kozima it's impossible. But the man has doubled his productivity. How do you explain this to someone with a degree in economics?

Dogmatism on financial matters on the part of the administration and economic departments is tantamount to crime. They have made an incredible mess, in effect destroying the entire system of material incentives at the works.

8 June. Morning.

Not the best of moods. Make a fuss, do what you want, but today the twin penalty comes into operation for the downgrading of our products which took place last year. Deductions from profits to the state budget have been doubled, which will mean about two million roubles less this year alone. Why? That's enough to build three nine-storey blocks with one hundred flats each. And where are we going to make the cuts? These penalties seem something of a paradox to me. It was thought that they would be an incentive to the administration, make them get down to some proper work. But those who ruined the factory are no longer at the helm. They have all been found cosy jobs elsewhere — as deputy general managers. Now they are laughing. Let Bossert do the work. But it's not up to me. A work force trying to get out of a mess is made like a horse with a rope around its neck with these penalties. It can be tugged along in whatever direction outside forces see fit. Common sense is called for here.

It seems to me that those who are actually guilty should be the ones to be punished, and severely at that. They should be made to feel it in their pockets.

17 June. Wednesday. Evening.

Today I signed the resignation of Maria Kozima, head of the labour and wages department. At her own request; it appears she's not pleased with me. It's a great pity that she didn't understand what *perestroika* involves economically. She believed that work is just an object of standardisation and not a form of creativity, the manifestation of talent and initiative. If you reduce everyone to the same level you cannot expect any success, and if successes do occur for all that, they will only be coincidental and short-lived. Success, stability and plentitude are brought about ultimately not by statistically average individuals, not by nuts and bolts in a system, but by human beings.

18 June. Afternoon.

Democracy is striking deep roots at the factory. In April the young specialists' council was re-elected at a lively meeting. In May a foremen's council was elected, and now it is the turn of team leaders. The initial meetings of the councils already show that people are straightening themselves out.

This is becoming a habit: in the last week of June I am to deputise for the head of the pressing shop. This is the greatest challenge yet. The system of pay had been changed there. Taking into account the quality of their work, they are now the best paid of all.

30 June. Evening.

The second section of the shopping centre has been completed. A few months ago nobody would have believed it. At a general meeting workers told me: 'We have great doubts, and if it comes off, we'll erect a monument to you.' A monument I don't need, but there's no getting away from the truth: the building workers have earned themselves great credit.

3 July. Evening.

I'm off on holiday, as is everyone else. You have to take it easy sometimes. We've completed work on the intermediate model of the new minibus and in January 1988 another will follow. From the second half of the year we'll be starting bit by bit to produce minibusses with a new type of suspension. We've launched a competition in Latvia to design an entirely new car. The first batch is planned to leave the factory in 1993. Orders are already arriving from all parts of the country.

The first 100 children have gone to a Pioneer camp near Sevastopol. For the first time ever we've managed to provide all applicants with a spell of spa treatment and stays at holiday homes. The factory's medical preventive care centre opened work in Jūrmala, although it's not very big as yet. We have agreed that in the first year it will be open only to workers and will make sure this is strictly adhered to. Oh, I almost forgot. We've fulfilled the plan for the first half-year. We're now producing half as many consumer goods as in 1986 and to date have turned out 211 minibusses in excess of the plan.

3 August. Morning.

I never wrote a word throughout the holidays. Which must be a good sign — at least I managed to switch off for a while.

The first news I hear on returning from holiday is that the chief engineer has been sacked. He failed to fulfil the recommendations of the industrial safety commission on time. An accident did happen, as a result of which one worker was seriously injured, and the industrial trade union committee decided he had to go. Another piece of news is that Panov is leaving. He doesn't feel at home in the factory, didn't manage to get along with his colleagues. Well, that's life. It just didn't work out this time. It was too hard a nut for him to crack, so now we're left without an assistant production manager yet again.

4 August. 11.00 a.m.

Strange things are happening at the factory. The conveyer belt has been stopped for a full day. The state quality control authorities are making checks on the output of all the workshops. In July when I went on holiday they were using 2.5 mm alloyed steel. This is the raw material for almost 100 different parts. The factory has fulfilled the plan for the month. The state quality control people had no objections to this steel. And suddenly such a fuss — the head of state quality control notices that the technical documentation calls for ... 3 mm steel. Should we argue? There's no point. Two research institutes tested 2.5 mm steel and came to the conclusion that it serves the purpose quite adequately.

23 August. Midnight.

That's it. The 'battle' ended with us on top. The workers have achieved the impossible. In the space of twenty days, or rather days and nights, they have remade thousands of parts. No less than 130 of them were transferred to the pressing shop to make up for lost time, keeping the presses going around the clock. The people from state quality control have changed their tune and are looking rather despondent. Do they really mean to say they didn't want us to save the situation?

25 August. Tuesday. Noon.

The motor has burned out on one of the automatic presses for producing seat supporters. The atmosphere in the assembly shop suggests impending disaster.

26 August. Wednesday. 7.00 p.m.

The new motor has been tested and is ready to start work. What a relief!

26 August. 9.00 p.m.

The drive belt pulley has disappeared from the motor. They've searched the entire factory, but it's nowhere to be found. They spent all night turning the pulley in the workshop, and minibusses left the conveyer incomplete.

27 August. Thursday. 7.00 p.m.

We must have been cursed. The die for casting a part in short supply has disappeared. Minibusses are still leaving the conveyer incomplete. Try to make a die. This is a bit too much.

28 August. Friday. 7.00 p.m.

The die still isn't ready. Damn it, is somebody playing games?

29 August. Saturday. Evening.

Incredible! Found the die at the bottom of a waste bin!

30 August.

No engines left. Again the engine factory on the Volga is failing to deliver the goods...

1 September. Late at night. At home.

This is my second night without sleep. I just haven't got time for anything. The children went to school on their own, and now they're fast asleep. They shared their impressions of the first day with their mother; father, as usual, is not at home. But otherwise things are OK. We met the plan for August after all. These past few days have been a nightmare.

4 September. Evening.

Met a representative of Avtoexport. Discuss our potential for competing with Western firms. Incidentally, on 1 September the factory fulfilled the year's plan for the production of export models. Present at the discussion, though in body only, was our chief designer. But I felt ashamed. The man from Avtoexport listed regions and whole countries where we couldn't sell our minibusses. Why, I wondered? The trouble is that we don't produce any with right-hand drive. I look at the chief designer to see what excuses he had. He says that it's nothing out of the ordinary and we have no reason to blame ourselves. And anyway, the Soviet vehicles industry is not capable of producing anything with right-hand drive. Not a single factory does so, he says, sounding convincing enough. But what technological shortcomings, provincialism and simple laziness is costing our country doesn't bear thinking about. With a chief designer like that, we haven't a hope in hell of competing with the rest of the world.

5 September. Saturday. Working day.

Received an invitation to take part in the *Komsomolskaya Pravda* festival in Czechoslovakia. Journalists from *Rudé Právo* asked me to provide answers to readers' questions. They want to know how things are progressing at the factory. On the whole, in just little over six months we have managed quite a lot. Maybe it has taken an enormous effort up to now, but we do fulfil the plan every month. Work has started on retooling the works. And then there are plans to produce intensive care ambulances as a joint venture with foreign firms. There's a suggestion about producing a minibus for large families. We have started work on a project to turn out series of vehicles, and to set up a large technological centre, which would fit with our factory into one enterprise. In August, the number of workers began to increase for the first time in many years. About forty top managers have been replaced. We now have a new chief engineer. Things will be easier from now on: the present management is about fifteen years younger than previously. At the end of September, we will have completed a block of 52 flats. The foundations have been laid for another with 76 flats.

Yet for all this, for all this I can not say that the entire work force has an unshakable commitment to *perestroika*.

There was a call from Omsk. Things are fine in Siberia at the moment. The air is wonderful, and mushrooms are growing everywhere. And then there's the hunting. But what is hunting when you have the sea just down the road? I look out of the window and see nothing but autumnal mist. And it crossed my mind that I managed to swim in the sea only a few times...

Komsomolskaya Pravda, 9, 10, 11, 13 October , 1987

Readers may well ask whether the democratic elections of managers at Soviet factories really has solved all the problems. Are we actually saying that all Soviet workers, as soon as they have the concern of their managers behind them, are able to achieve miracles?

Not at all. Unfortunately, we still have a long way to go. The account below of a three-day strike at the Likino bus plant near Moscow shows what an uncaring attitude towards people and production can lead to. This strike again underlines the importance of the human factor in the process of perestroika.

AN EMERGENCY

By YURI TEPLYAKOV

How Things Used to Be

Alexei NEGAZOV, assembler-fitter:
Our standards of work have been simply unacceptable for the last few years. Our main aim was to push the bus out of the gates; what happened to it after that — we didn't care! We fulfilled the plan no matter what happened and at any price. At a certain period they even paid us two salaries. People were brought from other sectors to work on the line, and they got paid both for this and their former job.

There was always a feverish atmosphere at the plant. What can you expect when there was practically always a shortage of something or other? A bus comes on the production line with a part missing. It wouldn't be a bad idea to stop it, but instead it is pushed forward. What, no doors? Never mind. Continue, it has to go forward to the finish line. And the bus would arrive at the finish more or less half-assembled.

Sometimes the conveyor would stop for 2-3 hours, or for a whole day, even though the parts needed were not from suppliers outside our plant, but parts which should have been made here in the shop next door.

Early in the year we began to lag behind the plan quite drastically. The workers had to work two hours more per shift for two months and every week-end, too, in order to fulfil the quarter plan.

But from April we were in a slide-down. Instead of 33-34 buses every day, only 20-25 rolled off the line. We were not paid any bonus. And we are talking about quite a lot of money: I, for example, would have got 100 roubles bonus. Each worker had lost 60-70 roubles.

Many people think that we have been hamstrung by the state quality control, and that we are, therefore, to blame ourselves for neglecting the quality of output. But I think that the SQC only clarified the situation. The standard of work did not become worse, the workers simply got fed up with covering the sins and inactivity of others. How long can anyone work, fulfilling and 'storming' the plan by enthusiasm alone?

Everybody needs money. But the conflict flared up not because of the bonus money. Three-quarters of the collective took action with the sole purpose of letting everyone concerned know what the situation at the plant was like so that something might be done about it at long last.

Yevgeny CHEPURIN, member of the SQC team at the assembly shop:

I've worked at the plant for over 30 years. The conflict matured under my very eyes. In the past the plan was fulfilled through the money incentive. Whether you earned the money or not, you were paid anyway. The main thing was to clock in at work. Now the money must be earned. And how can you earn it if the equipment is obsolete? The bus made at Likino first went on the line in June 1970. Since then little has changed, and even then the jigs were of an old-fashioned design. Some of the presses are more than 40 years old. So, how can you talk about quality? The technical control department accepted the bus so long as it could last out the drive to the depot. Now SQC reveals even the slightest error.

But are the workers to blame for making such a machine? I don't think so. You can't make a watch with an axe.

The pressing shop is the plant's most critical and outmoded sector. Practically everything in it needs to be changed. But when? No time is given. No physical or technical changes could be achieved in the period between October 1986 when SQC started to operate experimentally, and January 1987 when we were functioning already officially. But no one expected that the inevitable fiasco would end in such a scandal.

I think the assembly shop stopped work out of desperation. In the past, of course, they wouldn't have risked it, but times are different now.

Gennady TARULENKOV, General Director of the Likino bus plant (a newcomer, the former director — Litvinenko — was dismissed from his post by order of the minister immediately after the conflict, for failing in the administration of the plant):

There was a time when the plant was famous all over the country. The collective was even awarded an order. Now it has become notorious. However, it is amoral to blame the workers, though there were those who did just that. The people are working normally. The bus does not meet the present-day state standards which SQC operates.

The bus is obsolete. As a result the plant is already paid 5 per cent less, and yet SQC was introduced.

A radical reconstruction of the plant was needed two five-year-plan periods ago. In 1978 it was decided to erect a new production building — 30,000 square metres in size. But later on, in 1981, the minister for the automobile industry decided that the Likino plant could be transformed without new and costly construction, without extending its size and area.

'The economy must be economic' was the fashionable slogan. Superficially it seemed fine. The weakness was that it was applied to everything without account being taken of the specific problems. Someone at the top approved the 'calculations' of the ministry and the interests of the moment took the upper hand. This proved to be damaging for the Likino plant. Two sheds were built and reconstruction stopped.

Boris KAMINSKY, head of the central board which supervises the country's bus plants:

When I came to Likino the shop wasn't working, but the public prosecutor had already left. Generally speaking, calling in the public prosecutor was an unwise thing to do: somebody wants to scare people. How can this be described as a crime — it is a production conflict, the reason for which is blatantly clear. Production organisation is archaic in the extreme. Innovations are only for reports. For example, start-to-finish teams have been set up. But the team leader hasn't the least idea what his worker is doing on another shift. This leads to misunderstandings in paying people when the common bonus fund is being shared out. Moreover, the directors were constantly being changed. Plus the obsolete model of the bus. Plus the bad supplies — you would be glad to make something but lack the materials.

The plant operated for a long time on enthusiasm, on deception and on groundless promises. I wouldn't blame the workers. At the shop, in a heart-to-heart talk, it was revealed that they regretted not so much the loss of money as the time lost through bad administration.

How Things Are Now

Alexei NEGAZOV:
Our plant should be stopped for about three months. We should re-adjust everything and start anew. There's no point in trying to patch things up continuously, nothing will come of it. I don't think the new director will manage to achieve anything, though he is bold and full of energy. He has introduced a third shift so as to fulfil the annual plan. I'll go on working and stay at the plant, though others are thinking of leaving.

Gennady TARULENKOV:
Yes, we're introducing a third shift so as to make up for the losses. To catch up on the plan we must produce 45 buses per day. Two shifts would not be enough for this. When we fulfil the plan bonuses and all the other social benefits will be restored. There is no other way out.

The collective voted for the third shift. Out of the 700 workers only one was against, and 15 abstained. This support is the main thing for me. Now we must adjust the work, set a certain pace and everything will be all right.

It is different with the administrators. We'll have to part with some of them. Here on my desk is the draft order — to dismiss Chistov, the head of the production-controller's office from the plant. This office has effectively disorganised the work of the shops. I only have to sign it. But phone calls started to come from the city Party committee: 'Couldn't you do it in a different way?'

This is a renewal of the 'telephone law'. I'll not retreat. Let the minister sack me. But if he does it will not be for inactivity on my part!

Boris KAMINSKY:

I know who phoned the new director. Farafonov, the second secretary of the city party committee, is concerned with the old methods most of all. Apparently he failed to learn the lesson. You see, the regional Party committee issued a reprimand to him after the conflict. It is correct that the director first of all sought advice among the collective. When the people know the truth then both the administration and the workers will be at one and will not be pulling in different directions.

How Things Will Be in the Future

Gennady TARULENKOV:

We'll get out of this fiasco in 3-4 months. Then we'll start work on the long-term projects at once. A research-technical centre of our own will be set up at the plant to design new models of buses. In the past the institutes of our ministry were doing this. We'll also set up a construction trust of our own. We'll start real reconstruction. It is high time we got rid of everything old — and not just the habits.

Boris KAMINSKY:

The ministry has given, as urgent aid, 800,000 roubles to the plant's wages fund. However, that's really chicken-feed compared with what the Likino giant needs.

There is no sense in refurbishing the old. The main assembly shop will get a new production line. Tens of millions of roubles' worth of purchases have been made (including abroad). 25 million roubles' worth of equipment is to arrive this year. And as much again a bit later. The main thing now is to make space for the new production lines and machine tools.

We adopted the decision to begin the production of a new bus in January 1988. Cautious people tell us — you're in too big a hurry, mind you don't break your necks.

We don't want to break our necks, but it is worthwhile and necessary to take the risk. The needs of the moment and the people demand this.

The times are really different. Risks, of course, must be taken. But, first of all, people should think. And learn the lessons from what has happened. And better do it without thunder. And what's more, in order to go forward we must remember that the success we wish ourselves is now in our own hands.

Moscow News, 18 October 1987

The subject of the next piece is known throughout the country. Frequently on television, she is holder of several government awards. On public holidays she dons her Order of the Red Banner of Labour and medals. In December 1987 she became Hero of Socialist Labour. What else can be said about her? For some reason, every encounter with ANTONINA KHLEBUSHKINA, *Honoured Teacher of the Uzbek SSR, First Deputy Chairperson of the Soviet Children's Fund, is an intensely moving experience which never fails to reveal new qualities in a woman who is widely know as 'Mother'.*

KHLEBUSHKINA'S SCHOOL

By Mirzaahmed Alimov

'Why did they choose me of all people?' she asked in distress. 'I haven't even been to university. How many deserving people do we have up and down the country, and who am I? The head of a children's home like any other...'

There is no doubt, a person's character is shaped right from childhood. And Antonina Khlebushkina's childhood was far from easy. When she was just a year old her father left home to fight in the First World War, and never returned. Together with her mother, she went to live with relatives in the village of Novo-Klyuchi, Samara Province. She went to school in Samara and joined the Komsomol. In the early thirties she went to work in Central Asia on the recommendation of the Komsomol Central Committee. She worked as an instructor for a local Komsomol city committee and as head of a tourist centre.

At the beginning of the war the Komsomol Central Committee of Uzbekistan opened up a centre to help accommodate children who had been evacuated. Antonina Khlebushkina was among those who spent long anxious nights waiting at Tashkent railway station for groups of evacuated children. And her heart missed a beat each time a train arrived with the children, many of them full of tears.

'Builders from the Central Board of War Industry Engineering were working and fighting at the Stalingrad defensive positions,' Antonina Khlebushkina recalls, and in 1942, Komsomol members in Stalingrad asked the Komsomol Central Committee to establish in the rear a home for the children of the military construction workers with the money raised by the youth organisation. This home was located in Tashkent (Uzbekistan). Antonina Khlebushkina recalls that she was told to take things in hand and receive the children from Stalingrad. So she picked up her two-year-old son and set to work.

They lived in mud huts without food or clothing. The stoves were kept going with anything burnable. Electricity was totally absent. At night light was provided by a primitive lamp with a wick made of old rope.

Five hundred children separated from their families by the war — Antonina Khlebushkina gave love and kindness to them all.

'To begin with, I felt uneasy about the children calling me mother. But then I got used to it, I began to feel I had earned their respect and trust. But it was a real battle.'

Several of the children, though still of tender years, had stared death in the face. Misha Mikhailov, Igor Matveyev and Vanya Tertichny were all sons of senior officers. Quite often at night when the snow was falling outside, little Vitya Glebsky, whose father had been hung by the Nazis in his presence, would need comforting.

She told the children fairy stories. And the snow continued to fall outside. Crammed two or three in a bed, the children did not sleep very soundly. But Antonina Khlebushkina's sleep was even more troubled: 'Poor things, what am I going to feed you on tomorrow,' she would be thinking.

When the war ended, those who had been fighting at the front returned and came to collect their children from the children's home. But Antonina Khlebushkina was left with a hundred orphans who had lost both parents. And they couldn't continue living in such miserable conditions. So she called the staff together with the children's council and they decided that she should go to Moscow. Having arrived in Moscow, she went to see someone she knew from Tashkent, a certain Vassily Kopeiko, head of the Central Board of War Industry Engineering for Central Asia. He expressed sympathy with her problems, left the room for a moment and warned her not to touch the phone, saying it was a direct line to the minister. But as soon as he was out of sight, that is exactly what she did.

'So you're that head of the children's home in Tashkent,' Minister Nikolai Dygai said in amazement. 'And how are you getting along with them?'

She told him everything: how she had saved the children from hunger and the cold, how they were crammed together in little rooms, about the shortage of beds and desks. The minister asked her to repeat all this at a meeting of the senior staff of the ministry.

The decision was to build a new children's home in Tashkent. And Antonina Khlebushkina left Moscow with a waggon full of furniture, clothes, textbooks and toys...

The entire children's council was at the station to meet her. How pleased they were when they heard that they would be getting a new home. But they nearly didn't. In 1950 a large number of repatriates returned to Tashkent and the town fathers decided out of the blue to give them the building. But Khlebushkina refused to give way. She moved with her children into the new building where the plasterers were still at work. They even threatened to throw her out of the Party for that, but Minister Dygai stood up for her.

But what trouble Antonina Khlebushkina had with Anatoly Uss. He even set the home's bus alight and burgled a haberdashery kiosk. She was summoned to appear before the court. And as his legal guardian she had to answer for him. She vouched for him. Many years later she was to receive a letter from distinguished machine operator Anatoly

Uss of Tselinograd Region: 'Dear Mother, I and my entire family bow down before you.'

And then there was another episode. A dishevelled, slovenly dressed woman smelling strongly of alcohol, shouted at Khlebushkina: 'Give me the kid back! Give me him or otherwise...'

For several years, this 'mother' had forgotten all about her son. And suddenly she turned up and demanded him back. Khlebushkina didn't argue, but simply said: 'Let him decide for himself.'

As fate would have it, his natural mother had the same name as Khlebushkina. And there they stood before the confused little boy: the one who had given birth to him and abandoned him, and the one who taken tender care of him — two women of the same age.

The little boy made his choice, and now he's called Khlebushkin.

On the subject of surnames — her very first charge, Volodya Ananiev, took hers for himself and his children without even asking. He entered her office with his new identity card and his children's birth certificates and said: 'Look, mother, we're all Khlebushkins now.'

Before the war there were only two people called Khlebushkin in Tashkent, but now there are more than forty. And they are all her children. There are now Khlebushkins to be found living in Russia, the Caucasus, the Ukraine, Kazakhstan... And all of them, be they Russians, Uzbeks, Koreans, Tartars, Latvians, Jews, Kazakhs, Byelorussians, Greeks or Bulgarians, are proud to have this surname. Can there be any other such family in the country? Khlebushkina's story would not be complete without a word about weddings. There have been 65 of them to date, all celebrated in the children's home.

Unfortunately I didn't manage to attend the sixty-fifth. Antonina Khlebushkina was giving away Natasha Tkacheva. But they tell me it was just like all the others. In one room, the bride put on her white wedding dress, the well-laid tables were surrounded by older children, and waiting at the gates was the mother of them all. A minister, an artist, an engineer, a worker, a machine operator, a builder, an officer ... all of them brought up by Khlebushkina, and now they number more than 3,500. There are hundreds of teachers among them. There is even team of builders — and they are always to be found among the best! They are known as *Khlebushkina's school.*

So what is so peculiar about this school? Right from the outset, all matters have been decided by the children's council, the council of pupils (as it is called nowadays), a body for children's self-government. There are no maintenance workers at all in the children's home; they attend to everything themselves. They also nominate a 'grocery team', which is responsible for taking delivery of food supplies. The pupils' council is responsible for organising work at the summer house, which has a large orchard, a kitchen garden and even produces melons.

The former chairman of the council, Bulat Nugmanov, is now the Uzbek Minister of Construction. He has this to say:

'Mother took all of us, six brothers. We're a lot older now and finished our higher education long ago. And now my daughters Malika and Nargiza and son Nadyr keep asking to see their "granny". We all owe an unrepayable debt to her.'

There were never any locked doors in the home. Trust was encouraged here. The secret is very simple.

And what does Khlebushkina say about this?

'I have no special secrets. You just have to act like a mother.'

She makes it look so easy.

Sobesednik, No. 40, September 1987

In August 1987, a plenary meeting of the Moscow City Committee of the CPSU took place. The meeting listened to the sharp, vigorous criticizm of shortcomings in the capital from BORIS YELTSIN, *First Secretary of the Moscow City Party Committee. 'There are many sore points in the city,' he noted, abcesses must be opened so that they can heal more easily. The sooner we perceive deficiencies, the quicker we can act. All this requires maintaining a strict tone. And if anyone gets offended it is a clear sign that they personally are a long way removed from* perestroika...'

The next plenary meeting of the Moscow City Party Com-

mittee held on 11 November 1987, 'dismissed Comrade Yelt-
sin from his functions as First Secretary and bureau member
of Moscow City Committee of the CPSU for serious shortco-
mings in leading the Moscow City Party organisation'.

So what had happened? Why had Boris Yeltsin, who en-
joyed undoubted popularity among the people of Moscow, al-
lowed such 'serious shortcomings' to vitiate his work and what
exactly were they?

On 22 November Moscow News carried a short item from
Moscow University Professor GAVRIIL POPOV, which
read in part: 'Perestroika is a revolution, a revolution now
two and a half years old, a revolution which has entered its
second, perhaps most difficult, stage. The difficulties are sur-
mountable, but there is no doubt that they will be, and already
are, used by the conservative opponents of change.'

Was Boris Yeltsin a representative of the conservative op-
position to change? Popov's article gave rise to more ques-
tions than it answered. And then the professor made a further
statement.

THE KIND OF *PERESTROIKA* WE WANT

Some ideas about political avant-gardism

By GAVRIIL POPOV

My notes published by *MN* a month ago giving my first
impressions of Boris Yeltsin's dismissal from the post of the
Moscow Party organisation leader, evoked numerous telephone calls and letters c/o *Moscow News*, to say nothing of
dozens of questions. I think all of these entitle me to
another attempt at singling out the 'rational kernel' from
among the event's numerous repercussions.

Without naming the authors of particular letters or questions, I would like to note that many of them believe the
former First Secretary of the Moscow Party Committee had
no special concept of *perestroika* to speak of. I believe that
he had one, and presented it in his address to the 27th
CPSU Congress and in other public statements. He put that
special concept to work in his practical activities, too.
I would define his position as 'authoritarian conservative

avant-gardism'. It is authoritarian because it is the leaders rather than the masses who are proclaimed the main motive force of *perestroika*. It is avant-gardism because, as an enthusiastic supporter of *perestroika*, Boris Yeltsin tried to achieve its goals in one or two leaps, while ignoring the unavoidable fact that numerous problems could only be solved step by step through sustained and strenuous daily effort. His avant-gardism is conservative because its methods are doomed to failure and will do nothing but discredit *perestroika* and play into the hands of our conservatives, regardless of the avant-gardists' declared intentions. To substantiate this, it is enough to recall that some of the speakers at the Plenary Meeting of the Moscow Party Committee condemned Yeltsin for preferring spontaneous meetings with Muscovites in the streets and visits to factories and institutes to participating in plenary meetings of district Party committees. This in fact constitutes a criticism also of the entire new-style leadership approved by the people and the Party.

To my mind, the truth of the matter lies in the fact that certain sections of society, avant-gardists included, do not see the solution to *perestroika* problems as requiring the restructuring of the Party apparatus, state and public life, do not see the need to bring urgency to the concept of radical economic reform, along with the organically related democratization of society. They see the solution to *perestroika* problems in terms of changing personnel.

Such an attitude reflects the views of a certain group of state apparatus personnel who implicitly believe in the omnipotence of the state machinery, the leaders' ability to resolve any problem without stirring from the office or stepping down from the rostrum. This group of functionaries see the absence of appropriate leaders within the framework of the state apparatus as the only reason for slow progress.

Furthermore, this attitude sums up the views of the biggest part of our apparatus personnel whose duty it is to serve the people. However, they have been disposing of the valuables created by the working people for so long that their concern for the interests of the people is conceivable in just one form — that of paternal tutelage over them, of guardianship and high-handed benefaction from above, whether in terms of material conditions or democratic involvement.

Lastly, the attitude is rooted in those conservative strata of the population who fear the prospect of a transition to economic methods of management. Wage levelling has divorced them from the habit of hard work. They have been corrupted by the unearned, even if low, wages and bonuses they have received for decades. They have lost the habit of independent thinking and became accustomed to the role of executives. They fear the prospect of having to *earn* their wages and face up to responsibility. The view prevailing in these quarters puts the blame on bad leadership. One can almost hear the echo of the Russian peasants' age-long yearning for a good tsar: replace the bad tsar with a good one, and life would be better.

In the final analysis, this is just another attempt to find a quick and easy way to catch fish without getting wet. No country or people in history has managed to resolve cardinal problems this way.

Moscow's experience was that this approach brought a second wave of personnel reshuffle, giving no guarantee against a third or a fourth one. The unity of words and deeds, the only reliable criterion for a serious evaluation of personnel suitability for carrying forward *perestroika* was not considered, so all one could hope for was that the First Secretary could discover the knack of finding the right people to superintend *perestroika*.

Over the years of stagnation numerous 'black holes' accumulated in Moscow's municipal economy. A record of sorts was set even by public toilets, numbering one per 20,000 residents (not including visitors). No apparatus can possibly darn these holes unassisted. What we need is an organised movement of masses of people, the conversion of disinterested bystanders or sympathizers into becoming the real motive force of *perestroika*. But the avant-gardists' concept does not provide for this.

But wasn't Boris Yeltsin one of the leading lights in the struggle against the braking mechanism? Yes, he was. I am perfectly aware that he had to engage in combatting the most powerful taskforce of this retarding mechanism, its Moscow division, where people like Tregubov, Churbanov, Shchelokov and Sushkov thrived. It must be acknowledged, too, that Yeltsin not only overcame their resistance, but also dealt them crushing blows, for which he was greatly admired by all honest Muscovites. The one important thing that escaped their notice was the fact that success on that front was safeguarded not simply by the First Secretary's personal courage, but by the vigorous effort of the Party's best forces and the support of its leadership.

I am deeply convinced that *perestroika* can be accomplished only if it succeeds in involving the entire people, if it becomes the vital interest of every one of us.

The support and efforts of the masses should have been mobilized to realize the constructive programme of *perestroika*. To achieve this changes were needed in the Party's role as the political vanguard of society (and the role of the Moscow Party organisation as the front battalion of the vanguard) to bring the Party's methods into conformity with the requirements of the new stage in the development of socialism. That was not done. Hence the stubborn adherence to the 'forceful' personality policy, which cannot resolve the problems of today under today's circumstances.

The situation in Moscow presupposed only one hero of *perestroika*. The rest of us were to admire and applaud the solo performance in this one-man theatre. As is well known from Marx' and Engels' works, benefactors from on high invariably degenerate into one or another variety of 'barrack-room communism'. In our national history, calls for 'imposing the revolution', 'forcing' it and 'reshuffling personnel' were widely promoted by Trotsky, and consistently used in practice by Stalin.

Such are the roots of present-day avant-gardism, the haven for the Devils of *perestroika*. One can predict the consequences should avant-gardist methods prevail.

Presumably, having spread the 'forceful' personnel policy to all levels of state control throughout the country, its advocates would then discover, sooner or later, that they were hopelessly lost in the labyrinth they had promised to find a way out from. At that point they would have to return to the concept of real *perestroika*, which presupposes the involvement of every citizen in the renovation of society through the processes of democratization — or else to continue 'exposing the enemies' preventing them from achieving the successes promised to the people. Should that hap-

pen the ruthless logic of high-handed management by decree would lead once again to the situation known to us in
the 1930s.

To my mind the situation is further aggravated by the
fact that there are quite a few undoubtedly honest, sincere,
courageous Communists and competent leaders among the
supporters of avant-gardism, generally prone to overuse
pseudo-revolutionary rhetoric. When people like that
(Boris Yeltsin is undoubtedly one) discover that the problem lies not so much in replacing the crew as in rebuilding
the ship, when they realize that the task might take years of
hard work without spectacular results, they tend to panic.
Then come the doubtful calls for an unprepared, untimely,
unsupported by the majority (and consequently doomed)
attack. When such calls evoke no response, are ignored or
rejected, the question of resignation arises. Thus, the avant-
gardism of *perestroika* turns into the avant-gardism of de-
featism.

Boris Yeltsin's resignation *per se* is an event normal in
any democratic society. I personally find the leader openly
admitting failure and requesting a more suitable job very
understandable. However, the public reaction to the resignation proved much stronger than the event justified. This
was not because people are not prepared for *glasnost*. The
matter is more serious than that.

The letters and notes I've received breathe passionate
support for *perestroika*, but I found certain conclusions
alarming. 'His resignation is a triumph for *perestroika* opponents', 'The departure of the First Secretary of the Moscow Party Committee is the end of *perestroika*', etc. Where
does this personification of *perestroika* come from? It
would seem to date back to the tradition of the personality
cult when the fate of the nation and the Party was considered the personal burden of one man, one leader. But my
letters are from people nurtured in different, more rational
times.

The more I think about it, the more clearly it seems to me
that in the case under discussion we encounter one of the
most unhealthy aspect of the *perestroika* process. Political
avant-gardism appears to be attractive to a sizable section
of the working people, who would like to have *perestroika*
accomplished by somebody else and presented to them as

a gift on a silver platter. For supporters like these, who see *perestroika* as the exploit of individual heroes, the resignation of their idol is tantamount to the end of the world, a tragedy. They would rather sit through the cold and stormy period in their warm flats waiting for 'someone from the outside' to change winter to spring.

Sentiments of this kind provide the culture medium for political avant-gardism. On the one hand they are impotent themselves to further the cause of *perestroika*, and harbour a craving for pseudo-revolutionary phraseology and ultra-*perestroika* slogans that disguise a lack of faith in the workers' active role in *perestroika*. On the other hand, it is in this 'waiting room' that the myth of individual heroes about to work wonders for all is created. Here another analogy from our history comes to mind, I refer to the theories of 'the hero' and 'the crowd'.

Thus, the political avant-gardism of some and the passivity of others walk hand in hand — backwards. But our marching orders are different. We can't *wait* for *perestroika* to be accomplished by somebody else. We must *act, each and every one of us.* There are ample opportunities for urgent action today. Since resistance to *perestroika* is not subsiding, urgency is added to the need for concerted effort by the healthy elements in our society to overcome the resistance — even if we see people among the resisters whom we used to admire and respect.

Soviet Youth

A turbulent factor

Komsomolskaya Pravda *printed a letter from O. Sklyrenko, a Moscow State University student. It deserves to be quoted in full:*

'At nineteen I'm one of those young people who are the subject of so much talk, one of those young people "opportunities" are being "opened up" to. But I envy those younger than myself.

'Our misfortune is that we knew everything at sixteen. We didn't necessarily understand but we were certain what we knew and thought was the real thing. It is sad to reflect that in that brief span of awareness we concluded from what we read, heard and saw what was permissible and what wasn't. I remember my country when it was "immune" from catastrophies and natural disasters. I remember the infamous lists of rock groups whose music was "banned in public places".

'We, too, had our shock, our mourning ceremony at school. I remember the feeling of confusion and uneasiness... Later we learned to take nothing seriously. But that was the first time — and the mournful faces of the adults, and the unspoken question: "What'll happen now?" And the long, agonizing wait. Later we acquired a phlegmatic attitude to everything. It was later that we discovered that awful variety of atheism — no faith in anything at all.

'We subdued ourselves without ever having had the desire to fight. Fight for what, if everything is okay the way it is? We had the example of our parents. Their generation may be able to rise from the ashes — they suffered more when they were young. We grew up in relative comfort. It will be a thousand times harder for us to rise to our full height, because we didn't manage to gain faith, let alone lose it.

'If a generation that comes of age in adventurous, questful times encounters difficulties it will search high and low for *a way out of the situation. But we grew up in calm and quiet, when "no" was the watchword. If the biological makeup of an individual is conditioned by his genes, a generation's makeup is shaped by history.*

'We're often accused of being callous and cynical. Not so. Rather, my generation is just distrustful. We have developed a fool-proof mechanism. We are smarter than previous generations and, more importantly, we are more calculating. We will not put ourselves out for nothing. There are times when I think that generations like mine do not make history. History makes us and will move us, like chess pieces, one square at a time.

'We do not talk politics, for instance. I avoided those pointless discussions ever since I was in school. And now I feel out of place as society is moving forward.

'We knew what our future was to be—gray and immutable. We grew up in the seventies—that was all we knew. And everyone told us that it was the best, in fact the only possible way. We simply lived the life you laughed about once you had put us to bed and firmly shut the door. No wonder you have turned out to be better prepared for the gust of fresh air which has knocked us off our feet.'

The letter's honesty is startling. So are the bitter truths it tells. It gives us an insight into the minds of some sections of the young. Their mixture of skepticism, bravado and maximalism, their sense of frustration in spite of changes; their confusion resulting from unpreparedness. Let us not disclaim at least a share of the responsibility for some of the disagreeable responses that have been showing themselves.

NIGHT ESCORT

By ANDREI LAPIK

What Is Going On?

The image of the Rocker created by newspapers and television is so offensive that it stays in the mind. The 'night riders', undaunted by the militia, bound together in a romantic brotherhood, are natural heroes. Furious speeds and incredible stunts are their trade. And what if some people can't sleep because of them, or if they break a law or two? That's not so terrible. After all, enthusiasm and a desire to be noticed, to show off are all part of being young. They have a hard life. They are put upon. It should be our duty to help them ... every one of us should abandon his or her affairs to figure out how to come to the rescue.

Then it was discovered that Moscow wasn't the only place with motorcyclists who liked to drive around at night. Leningrad had them, Minsk, Riga... Even the most remote provincial towns began to turn out their own Rockers. Are they indigenous products or is it simply a case of copying Moscow? Or is this phenomenon greatly exaggerated by the town fathers who invent it simply to be able to say: 'We are dealing with this problem.' Of course, there follows the danger of suspecting all motorcyclists, even those who ride in the day.

In short, there has been much ado about this matter. The word 'Rocker' has become a Russian word.

What do we know about them? Apart from the usual stereotype image of the 'outsider' motorcyclists who are ignored by the Komsomol and every other organisation except the traffic militia, practically nothing.

A Special Score

The taxi rank at Domodedovo Airport on a foggy day. Cabdrivers stand huddled in groups, chatting as they wait for fares.

'What associations does the word "Rocker" have for you?' I ask, after explaining that I am writing an article for a newspaper.

'Oh, those...'

They agree to talk to us if we agree that no names will be given. Some vernacular language has been 'edited out'.

'I wouldn't put this in the paper, but we have brushes with them, serious ones sometimes,' Sergei says.

'Lately they've been scared to muck about with us, but they still do, sometimes,' adds Victor who is about forty.

'Why are they scared?'

'Because we've got a special score to settle with them. We don't like those punks... And when we've got something to tell them we make it short and sweet.'

'You mean you beat them?'

'Sometimes...'

'And what would you do?' Sergei asks, getting heated. 'Once I had this fare: they surrounded me and put their brakes on. You should have seen their ugly mugs... And I had a pregnant woman in the back seat. I told her, "Close your eyes." Then I stepped on the gas and went straight at them. They made way but then they went after me. Well, I forced the first one into the ditch. Over he went. It was all right, he survived, there was earth there. The others stopped and waved their fists at me... The first one, he was about to hit the windscreen with a chain. Maybe he wanted to frighten me, I don't know. I didn't wait around to see. I had a fare, you know...'

I heard a lot of stories that day. Frankly, they were pretty horrifying. It would seem that 'vigilantes' are in action. Go to any taxi garage and talk to the drivers. You will hear about clashes with Rockers. And they'll name names. Of course, if matters didn't go too far...

Why cabdrivers? Because they work at night.

'Look how much time the militia has spent on them. How many people they take away from their jobs — doctors, militiamen, mechanics...'

Cabdrivers and traffic militia have a special attitude towards the Rockers. And there's no doubt what it means: 'Things have come to a boil.'

What About the Rest of the Population?

'To the Chairman of the Moscow City Council Executive Committee:

'Dear Comrade Saikin:

'Haven't our Moscow law enforcement bodies fooled around long enough with those "Rockers"? They are really just nasty hoodlums rudely disturbing the citizens and should be dealt with.'

(From a letter)

'Dear Editor;

'What have things come to? Gangs of crazy youngsters carry on in the city and we just say, "Can you believe it!"

'...Some may think that I'm opposed to motorcycles. The fact is that I got my license in 1947 and became a Master of Motorcycling. True, at the time we didn't have such fine machines. And we didn't ride them at night ... we didn't take the silencer baffles out nor did we bother people, we didn't want to. Now they don't care.

'...I'm sure militia officers have means they can use to control this motorcycle mafia. There's the Moscow City Council's decree on disturbing peace after 11 p. m., the article on hooliganism...'

Yes. And there is also another regulation not everyone knows about: the Moscow City Council's ban on motorcyclists travelling in groups.

This is really what started it all.

The order was given, the militia said OK. But as it turned out, the job was far from simple. Who the Rockers were, how many they were, what could be expected of them — no one knew. Crucially, how were they to be stopped? As in the 'good old days', directives were issued:

'1. Prohibit until further notice the movement of groups of motorcyclists in city streets and arterial roads.

'2. Instruct the Internal Affairs Commissioner to ensure that this resolution is strictly enforced as of 28 February 1987.'

That was all!

The objective was set. But how to go about it? The first encounters with the Rockers revealed that they would not obey. They did not stop when flagged down. They openly ignored the police.

The militia were given no additional rights. What could they do?

Change their tactics, perhaps.

The militia decided to badger them into submission. They started checking every motorcyclist's papers. The training course in Luzhniki Park was a popular gathering place for dozens of Rockers. As long as they drove around it, showing each other what their Javas, Chezetas and Hondas could do, no one bothered them: training courses are intended to be used for driving. As soon as anyone left the course the militia asked to see the driver's license and vehicle registration. For some reason the Rockers did not want to comply and sped off. As a rule the fugitives weren't

caught. Militiamen in cars were no match for the motorcyclists!

'They're not criminals, either,' Lieutenant-Colonel
O. M. Butakhin says. 'I know a lot of them. I spent a whole
month at the course, talking to them, trying to understand...'

The Rockers were supposed to be organised into registered motorcycle clubs which would rule out nocturnal esca-
pades. However, they deliberately zoomed down the Arbat,
a pedestrian zone. Not long after that they rode around
Red Square.

In short, the attempt to talk things over and find agreement failed.

Then the militia motorcycle platoon appeared on the
Rockers' horizon.

When Captain Sergei Novikov turned up in Luzhniki for
the first time on his BMW the Rockers were thrown into
confusion. Very respectfully they examined this famous
make. Clearly it was 'one hell of a machine'.

'Even so you won't catch us,' a voice broke the silence.
The Rockers were worried.

'Okay,' Novikov said. 'Race you over there on one
wheel. If only one of you can keep up with me I won't come
back. A deal?'

There were a lot of takers. The race began. Novikov
came in well ahead, his 'rivals' far behind. Quite a few
couldn't keep on one wheel the whole way.

'We can do it on two,' Novikov said. But it was more
a gesture than a real wager. No one was interested.

'We won't be able to get away from those wheels,' the
Rockers thought and their belligerancy diminished noticeably.

'So don't try it on,' Novikov said. 'You won't get anywhere.'

It didn't stop them.

In one of the first encounters they ran over Lieutenant
Palchik. He was badly injured.

'We'll mow all you creeps down,' Misha Lo crowed.

But there was not much joy. With their Javas they didn't
have a chance of shaking off the BMWs. This was the beginning of the end.

What's at the bottom of this unwillingness, fear even, of having their papers checked? Most of the night bikers do not have licenses and many do not even have license plates. But why should they risk breaking their necks to get out of paying a ten rouble fine? Something is wrong here.

One keen motorcyclist, a Master of Sports, is up in arms. 'They show these Rockers on television. But no one is asking where do they get spare parts from. On the black market? Do you know what they cost? If you used your salary to buy them you'd die of starvation. I say they must be stealing. Maybe it's not them, who knows? Whoever steals is a thief — not a Rocker or heavy metal freak. And that's that.

'One thing bothers me. A lot of the motorcycles impounded by the militia are never claimed. When they are caught they give false names, pretend to go to get their paper and disappear, leaving their motorcycles behind...'

Now, when democratisation has allowed greater freedom, the situation has changed. More and more informal groups are emerging. We need to pay attention to them.

Many violate laws and are provocative. They are detained for identification. That is when the tricks begin. For example, a young man throws himself at the militia's car windscreen and is taken to hospital. He is seen to be the victim. Another kicks in the door of the militia car and breaks his leg. In the hospital he says that the militia broke it, and so on...

This gives rise to rumours of the militia's 'brutality': it is the 'poor' Rockers who are being harassed. The rumours spread like wildfire.

Democracy is great. But it has to be learned. Some people see democracy as anarchy, and cherish their rights while ignoring their duties.

The Rockers, who have contributed nothing to society, demand every advantage. And we adults are afraid to tell them to behave. After all, that wouldn't be kind or democratic...

I was interested in the Zakharenkov brothers, especially the eldest, Valery. I wanted to see him 'in action', surrounded by his pals.

The youngest, Albert, was there but he did not take the initiative in the conversation. The lads came in and took seats in the small room. What did they have in common? Valery will soon turn thirty. He has two convictions, the latest for gang rape. He has spent eight years in jail. What about the rest, how old are they? Seventeen, eighteen, twenty. In their eyes he's a hero, of course. Because he was probably innocent. Besides, 'Who said and where's it written that ex-cons are not people? They may even teach other folks to keep away from crime...'

'I teach them not to behave like hooligans, not to steal,' Valery says. 'There's nothing good about prison. No fun in that...'

But if he works so hard to keep them on the straight and narrow, why has his own brother done time, too?

I don't hear anything new and switch off. In any case, no one pays any attention to me. They are spoiled by the media. TV drools over them, film-makers come, hat in hand. They have given several interviews to foreign correspondents. They even thought of petitioning the United Nations Organisation.

My interest stirs as Valery becomes more impassioned. We, Rockers, are the greatest. We are fearless, we are noble. We could teach any driving instructor a thing or two. Leave us alone, give us our freedom, or else we'll take it ourselves. The others listen to him spellbound, ready to agree with anything he says, ready to go anywhere he tells them. They believe in him. The outcome?

'June 6th a group of motorcyclists, approximately 100-120 in number, drove into Luzhniki course. At 10:45 p.m., when people came out into the street after the film show and headed for the Luzhniki bridge, the motorcyclists started up their vehicles and, sounding their horns, drove full speed into the crowd.'

(From a traffic control report)

'...Yesterday I was sitting in the square outside the Brest Cinema. At first I was alone, then a young mother arrived, pushing a pram with a sleeping baby. Suddenly an engine roared and this punk swept down on us out of the blue on his motorcycle... He pulled up alongside the pram and revved his motor. The little boy woke up and began to cry. The woman leapt to her feet, she was in tears... I jumped up and he stepped on the accelerator, choking me with a cloud of gas and took off...'

(From a complaint lodged with the Moscow City Committee of the Communist Party)

What about their parents? Some shake their heads in defeat, others think that everything is all right — the kids never moped around the house. And then, Rockers are so varied. The bulk are young workers, technical school students, and idlers.

There are students, office workers and schoolkids among the Rockers. But in some way they are all very much alike. When I met their parents I suddenly realized what it was: all of them came from bad homes. I do not mean that they lack for anything materially, although I visited some squalid flats where the sheets hadn't been washed for months and where there were more bottles than books. I mean morally lacking. When the father isn't interested in knowing where his son got his new motorcycle, and when a mother doesn't care where her daughter spends the night, you cannot call that a good home — although it may not be short of creature comforts.

People aren't born bad in this society, nevertheless bad people appear. Because they weren't taught what's what at the start. Because they never learned the meaning of the word 'no'.

Yet it must be said they are not all criminals. It is what they could become. They are ready. It is not at all an innocuous phenomenon.

One out of every ten Rockers has already committed a crime. Without doubt many of the Rockers are good kids, not yet spoiled, who naively believe in the romanticism of the night riders and Rocker brotherhood. The gang idea is a deception.

Zakharenkov breaks the window of the militia car with his head.

So what? He did the right thing. He did it for his fellow Rockers.

They tell a militiaman, 'Be careful or we'll write a letter saying that you beat us and we'll all sign it.' And the militiaman leaves because neither he nor his partner are accepted as witnesses in the eye of the law.

Can they really be our children? Why did they come to be like that? We don't know how to win them. Apparently we don't even want to. It is so much easier to pay them off: give them what they want, let them do what they please, asking nothing in return just as long as they leave us alone...

Moskovsky Komsomolets, 15 November 1987

CLOISTER WALLS

Dialogues with Future Novices

By SERGEI FILIPPOV

I first saw them in the abandoned Intercession Cathedral outside Moscow. It was a cold, nasty day. The enormous cathedral, totally covered with scaffolding, seemed to swallow up the six female figures.

The young women piled the rubble onto wheel barrows, and chipped away at the loose plaster. Very little remained of the cathedral's old decor, just a few pieces of marble windowsills.

Their feet grew cold on the stone floor. Small hands reddened from the chill and from the weight of the barrows. At last it was time for a break. The young women formed a semi-circle and got ready to sing. A hymn rose to the vaulting of the empty cathedral...

That was my first acquaintance with the future nuns.

How often, wearied by the rat race, we say, 'I've had it! I'll join a monastery!' The expression is meant to be funny. For these women it was otherwise. They have decided to spend their lives in a monastery.

I talked to these young women for quite a long time. I argued what might seem so obvious — to become a nun is unnatural — until I realized: they had made their choice. Simply a different choice from ours.

It is easy to decide that we alone are right and those who don't agree with us are deluded. How often do we declare the right of every individual to his own opinion but become irritated by those who act contrary to our expectations. We try to explain it as a consequence of an unenlightened up-bringing or the effect of life's disappointments.

I think our attitude to democracy is formed to some extent by our attitude towards believers. Let's listen attentively to the other view and try to comprehend why these young women — who did their homework in subjects they liked and disliked just as we did, who besieged the theatres in the hope of a free ticket, and played the Beatles over and over again just like we did, who fell in and out of love like we did — suddenly decided to become nuns. Why?

Tatiana S. is planning to enter the convent with her mother and younger sister. She was baptised at 16, although her family has always been religious. Orthodox believers are people she feels very close to. She can share with them what she might not tell her family.

'They're always kind, always understanding... Not like those who have no knowledge of God and are bogged down by worldly cares.'

Tatiana works at a maternity hospital with other young women. How does she see them?

'You should hear what they talk about! It's all clothes and parties. How to find a way to save enough money to buy a 400 rouble hat. Utter spiritual poverty. They don't like work. They aren't really interested in women in child-birth. I don't know how they stuck the nursing school out.'

'Some of them are surprised that I haven't got married and started a family. What's there to be surprised about? Look around. The girls I went to school with have already managed to jump into marriage and out again. Some more than once. They're going around in circles, confused by themselves and by others. They can't tell good from bad. But it's all very simple: what's good is from God, what's bad is from Satan.'

There you are. It's sad, of course, that Tatiana will never experience the deep wells of human happiness and emotion, cannot see that there are many genuine individuals whose lives are a tireless search to discover right and wrong. She has chosen her path for all time...

Truth has been attained, doubts have no place. But what

is 'good'? What is 'bad'? And can those categories exist in their pure form?

Accustomed to regarding religious faith and atheism as opposing world views, we listen to what a believer says with hostility. When I heard Tatiana say that divorce and abortion are evil and the handiwork of the Devil I was ready with my side of the argument. But I stopped myself. She was right in a sense: the abortion and divorce rates are horrendous. And we talk a great deal now about the consequences of the mistakes in bringing up our children, and the fact that young people today are unprepared for marriage and parenthood.

Irina N. was baptised two and a half years ago, while attending the Moscow Institute of Architecture. Her parents are academics. She grew up surrounded by families like her own and from an early age heard that science was the ultimate and that man was omnipotent; scientific and material progress held the only key to eliminating society's ills.

At school she was one of the first to join the Komsomol. 'Active, always in the thick of things,' said her school and college reports. She was a Komsomol committee member, all her free time was devoted to the restoration of buildings. Then she met some believers and it changed her life completely.

'I chose to be baptised after careful consideration. Every church, every stone used to build them was sacred. And here was I trying to restore them. What right had I to do this work without sharing the spiritual faith our people were imbued with for centuries? The idea of serving God was essential to the building of our Orthodox churches, these ideas preserved our ancient culture. To continue the work I felt morally obliged to be baptised.

'The Russian Orthodox culture is disappearing day by day. Why is there so much dissipation, why have so many people rejected their history, their roots? Why have drug addiction and drunkenness become widespread? We have forsaken our past. Just try saying proudly that you are a Russian. You will be immediately accused of nationalism.

'Our architecture today, all our residential areas, lack human feeling. I am not talking about those ugly concrete boxes. Even our "greatest" achievements are nothing but cold handsome objects. They lack spirituality.' Irina spoke with the strong conviction of the newly converted, occasionally presenting her own thoughts as the teaching of the Church.

The accusation that our architecture lacks spirituality stung. I recalled heated discussions over models of tomorrow's streets at exhibitions of designs by young artists and architects. They showed real knowledge of our traditions and attempted to apply it to every house and every shop. They responded imaginatively to every bit of free space.

Irina contrasts modern art with medieval iconography. To me, it is like comparing a caterpillar with the butterfly it becomes, and asserting that the larva is 'more perfect'.

Irina says that she does not need the kind of life the people around her are living. To be a nun is a higher state of being.

It is her right to choose, but I was reminded of my son who grabs one toy in each hand and still reaches for a third. Human beings have a natural desire to learn. We reach for one thing, then another. We make mistakes but that does not stop us. That is part of life.

Irina Z. is quite different. I would say she has qualities of leadership. The story of her search is interesting. Many years she was actively interested in sports, in the sciences, in photography and painting. She went to a school for gifted children where physics and math were the main subjects. Flying captured her imagination: she entered the Moscow Institute of Aviation. She 'hung out' with hippies and wore patched and faded American jeans. A member of the institute's volleyball team, she was admired as a good athlete. Then she transferred to Moscow State University to study journalism. Developing a keen interest in avant-garde art, particularly cubism, she took up painting. The relationship between objects and space particularly fascinated her and she tried to apply Malevich's suprematist theories to her own work.

Then Russian philosophy inspired her. She defended a thesis on Dostoyevsky in the Department of Russian Literature and then — the convent. She went there not as a tourist, but to 'cleanse' her soul. Then she was baptised and began her pilgrimages to many monasteries.

'Deep down I was not satisfied. One day I decided to show an elderly monk my work *A Tree and the Cosmos*. It was painted as a flight of fancy. The old man turned it this way, that way and finally advised me to burn it. And all my other paintings, too.

'I set out for home and agonized over it — would I really have to throw them away? I'd put so much work into them. People had praised me. Besides, how could I get them back — I'd given a lot of them away to friends? But as soon as I got to Moscow I realized that I had to do it. I collected them all to the last one and carried them to the rubbish heap myself. And when I did it I experienced a tremendous sense of liberation. I felt I was freed from evil.

'Every object contains truth. When that truth is distorted the object loses its morality, its purity. Purity is an integral consciousness, encompassing truth, morality and beauty.

'For a long time I had a distorted view of the world. Once I was painting a column in a cloister and suddenly realized that it was straight! It stayed the same no matter how I looked at it and I could feel its smooth concrete surface with my paint brush. It's hard to express the realisation that you have been accustomed to visual lies and suddenly your eyes have been opened.

'A similar thing happened to me when I began to pray regularly. At some point I noticed that I could not concentrate and direct my thoughts to prayer. Snatches of worldly thoughts and images from television would flash through my mind. It was as though they had a will of their own. My brain was sapped. The word had lost its value from overuse. The word, which had meant everything in the beginning.

'Sometimes at home we don't turn off the television and radio. They babble on and on, warring with each other. There are times you think that you know everything but when it comes to the point it turns out that you don't know anything, all you've got are bits of other people's views and opinions. It turns out that man is not capable of historical knowledge, he is powerless to think independently. All thoughts are alien, they are foisted on us. Satanic forces are to blame.

'Unaided, man cannot find himself and keep his thoughts

and deeds clean. But if he turns his eyes to God he can conquer any evil.'

Irina is an unusual woman. She is consumed by a thirst for knowledge. Her only regret is that women are not allowed to study at the ecclesiastical academy. Nothing gives her greater pleasure than wrestling with the knotty questions of the church dogma. Irina is strong-willed. Yet others might say she is weak. Irina, her friends, are strong individuals who have either lost or never found ideals and values outside Christianity. Life in a convent is not the easiest course to take. Conquering temptation demands courage.

Tatiana Belyavtseva, an artist, writes:
'I have heard of people joining monasteries before, so these cases do not shock or surprise me. It is just that it makes me sad. The point is that I respect those people. It seems to me that they have a potential to do good. They are not interested in personal gain. In fact, they deny themselves normal pleasures and comforts. And then it strikes you that these are people with a great sense of self-denial who could do a lot of good for others in society. The reason for their withdrawal from the world is not solely of their making, it has to do with the world around them. One of the reasons, I think, may be that they never met the one person whom they could love.'

Alexei Nerlin, a serviceman:
'In the first place, it seems so unnatural. In the second place, they just want to run away to some quiet, swampy backwater so they won't have to help to tackle the difficulties we face today. They want to avoid responsibility for society around them and probably dream secretly of getting a free ride into the future.'

Valery Pustovoitov, a driver:
'Before we start denouncing them we must try to understand them. I think they have done what they've done because they grew up when honesty and fairness were in short supply, because they found that the words uttered from rostrums frequently did not match deeds. So in many ways it's their misfortune, not their fault. It's their misfortune because now, when our life is changing before our eyes, they

are looking for an answer in the past. And it is not there. I disapprove because I think they are wasting their minds and their hearts.'

Some people are simply horrified: 'A convent—in this day and age?'

Moskovsky Komsomolets, 23 October 1987

TO UNDERSTAND AND TO ACT

By I. KOROLKOV

The debate in Taganrog lasted for four days. They argued at lunch and on the way to their hotel, went to bed in the early hours of the morning, and at 9 a.m. made their way back to the park. They forgot all about the warm sea and the water-melons and grapes at the market place.

How different it all was from the innumerable meetings, seminars and conferences to which people were lured by boxes of chocolates, oranges and volumes of foreign mystery stories.

Here is the list of books they brought with them and studied at the meeting: Karl Marx and Frederick Engels, *Manifesto of the Communist Party, Karl Marx, Frederick Engels, and V. I. Lenin on Social Justice*, V. I. Lenin, *Materialism and Empirio-Criticism*, V. I. Lenin, *The State and Revolution*, and *Political Report of the CPSU Central Committee to the 27th Congress of the Communist Party of the Soviet Union*. The margins of the volumes were filled with notes.

Almost all young people are ready to join actively in *perestroika*. I have not said 'almost' by accident. At the Taganrog meeting, some people made one wonder at the way they argued, persisting as they did in the habit of phrase-mongering, exhibitionism and intolerance of other people's opinions. While talking about democracy they would try to force their views on others.

Some of this is particularly true of Yuri Shevtsov, a history teacher from Brest. I heard him speak at the Moscow conference. There was a lot of complacency, plenty of promises and wishful thinking. I had the impression that the painful processes under way in society do not really touch him personally. He was in the public eye and that is what mattered to him most. He seemed to be more than ready to set up a clamour if that would put him in the lime-light. His pushy egocentrism has a bad influence on every-one who comes under his sway.

However, to give credit where it is due, members of the SPCC quickly realised what they were dealing with. He was not elected to the Club Council, which was a severe blow to his aspirations.

The SPCC stresses the study of revolutionary theory. Knowledge is power. It helps a person straighten up, walk into his superior's office with confidence, and defend his opinion. This is all very well, but there is also the question of the practical application of knowledge, the revolutionary application of theory to the problems of today. One has to admit that young people do not always come up to scratch in this area.

The suggestions which Komsomol Committees used to produce often resembled a childish game that could not possibly be of any practical use to a factory, a farm, or the country at large. Young people are tired of playing games, of imitating public and political activity. They want to make a real impact on real life.

This peculiar unreality is potentially very dangerous. If young people do not get a chance to influence economic, political and cultural life, why should they believe the decla-rations being made, or why should they believe that the country really needs them? Current difficulties and the wish to help overcome them is at times tinged with scepticism, which can breed an unhealthy, unprincipled approach, ei-ther from the right or the left. Who can be certain that some young people will not eventually cross the bounds of lega-lity, especially since the democratisation of society stimula-tes not only healthy elements but also some adventurists.

Democratisation is impossible without a sustained strug-gle to win over people's minds. One thing in particular was demonstrated in Taganrog: it was that over the past de-cades we lost the skill to conduct effective political work based not on authoritarian principles but on knowledge, not on withholding information but on openness, not on bans but on the force of persuasion. From the window of the Taganrog City Komsomol Committee office there is a fine view of the park where the discussions were held, only a minute's walk away. But this distance has proved too much for Sergei Vasin, the Committee's First Secretary, and also for Vladimir Getmanov, head of the Rostov Regional Komsomol Committee propaganda department. Even my persistent invitations proved futile. I am firmly convinced that the club frightened them, as it did the First Secretary of the Rostov Regional Komsomol Committee, Valentina Petrenko. She told me quite frankly:

'Please don't think you are talking to a dyed-in-the-wool bureaucrat. I've had a lot to do with informal youth groups. I mix with hippies and with heavy metal fans. They visit me at home.'

But, Valentina, the hippies and the heavy metal fans will never ask you: 'If society has so far failed to carry through the basic principle, "From each according to his ability, to each according to his work," what kind of society is it?'

I think that there are two main reasons why Komsomol leaders are afraid of such clubs. The first is that they do not feel up to equal discussion, having no thoughtful, digested knowledge of either Marx, Engels or Lenin. I'm not exaggerating. This is our common misfortune. A knowledge of the classics of Marxism-Leninism was previously not obligatory. It was enough to take them on faith.

The second reason... At the Komsomol Central Committee I was told a revealing story. Leaving for a meeting of an informal group, a staff member said to his colleagues: 'Look here. If tomorrow The Voice of America says that a representative of the Komsomol Central Committee was present at the gathering, please confirm that it wasn't of my own free will that I went but because it's my job.'

It would have been funny were it not so sad, as they say.

Is it fear of a slap on the hand that paralyses political fighters? But where then can they learn to argue and debate, how can they know what people think and talk about?

Very well, so the first time the Komsomol leader will be the loser. That's certain. The second time may not be much better. Even the third. But after that he or she will be transformed. Then, with first-hand knowledge and experience, rather than hearsay, the Komsomol functionary can be counted upon to refrain from statements of this kind: 'Each member of the SPCC is working in the conditions prevailing in his district. These conditions have shaped his views. One district suffers from a shortage of sugar. Another district has plenty. All first secretaries should be convened to find out the concrete reasons why people are coming to the SPCCs. I am responsible for my region only. Let others, who are so authorised, accept responsibility for the country at large.'

I'd like to say that members of the club have a much broader range of interests than the absence or availability of sugar or the quality of the roads in the area where they happen to be living. They want to grasp the in-depth processes under way in society, discover the sources of stagnation and regression, find ways out of the situation that confronts us, and use whatever abilities they have to help. To accuse them of being shortsighted, lacking vision, as the Rostov Komsomol Regional Committee has tried to do, means to indulge in demagogy.

Young people's desire for frankness and truth, their attempts to be useful, their effort to change society for the better are bound to go hand in hand with illusions and errors. That is as much true of the SPCCs as of others. But does this mean they need help or that we should mount a crusade against them? Lenin wrote: 'Of course, the youth organ *still* lacks theoretical clarity and consistency. Perhaps it may never acquire them, precisely because it is the organ of seething, turbulent, inquiring youth. ...Such people must be given every assistance. We must be patient with their faults and strive to correct them gradually, mainly by *persuasion*, and not by fighting them.'

I'd like to emphasise: persuasion, not fighting.

The Komsomol Central Committee resolution on organising the political education of young people provides for establishing a large number of political debating clubs. The Komsomol committees should take an interest in the work of these informal associations. When this has been accomplished the young people may no longer be so keen on SPCCs and other similar associations.

The Komsomol congress has expressed its anxiety over the falling prestige of the organisation. But, no doubt, it will get a boost when the young people have reason to believe that the Komsomol is, above all, a body of daring people. It will improve when Komsomol members demonstrate courage and determination in their public efforts to defend principle in thought and action.

Socialism will not be won without a struggle. It is a hard path. But in order to appreciate the value of mankind's greatest achievement we must all assume some responsibility for its future.

This is each person's duty, and each person's right.

We have all grasped the fact that society has entered a new stage which requires a new outlook, a new mentality, and new youth leaders. They are sure to come. As soon as the work of a Komsomol leader becomes synonimous with studying, energy, principle and courage, time-servers and fellow-travellers will immediately look for cosy niches elsewhere. The role of leadership will be taken away by genuine leaders.

There is no reason to be afraid of vigorous diversity. What is far more dangerous is somnolent uniformity.

Komsomolskaya Pravda, 23 October 1987

The subject of the next article is a man of very modest means. In this summer, he can be seen with a broom in his hands sweeping the yard of a Moscow kindergarten; in the winter, he clears the snow with a large scraper, or breaks the ice on the paths. He is a caretaker and only a few people know his name. VICTOR KALMYKOV. *But there is another side to Victor Kalmykov.*

If you happen to be one of the lucky ones to get a ticket to the Taganka Theatre you will be able to see a portrait of the famous Soviet actor and singer — Vladimir Vysotsky. The portrait was painted by Victor Kalmykov. He is an amateur artist, with no academic training, and he is not a member of the Artists' Union. Vysotsky is Kalmykov's hero. Kalmykov saw Vysotsky as a kindred spirit, someone like himself whose achievements were won without professional training or institutional backing.

HIS CITY IS CLEAN AND BRIGHT

By VLADIMIR BARKOVSKY

To begin with, let us say something about the strange choice made by a young and talented (I do not hesitate to use this word) self-taught artist. Let us try to explain it and show that you reap what you sow.

Back in his schooldays Victor's art teacher used to call him 'another Levitan', being aware of his extraordinary talent. This prophesy was a veritable inspiration to Victor the pupil, who was certainly no genius and never got near the top of the class. Even a little praise is precious for such youngsters, and can actually determine their path in life.

Victor had plenty of choice. He attended a music school where he learned to play the piano, sang in the boy's choir which, together with the band, performed works by Georgi Sviridov that were even issued on record. He took part in the play *Pugachev* at one of Moscow's popular theatres. At the age of ten Victor Kalmykov was one of those few chosen to play alongside the famous Vladimir Vysotsky. He has never forgotten these encounters.

On leaving school Kalmykov began work, convinced that he had made the right choice ... in a laundry. He was subsequently employed to assemble *bayans*, a kind of Russian accordion and to hang paintings at Moscow's Tretyakov Gallery. Although this brought him closer to his final objective — art — it will nevertheless appear to be the wrong route to some. What he should have been doing was learning to paint, but there was no point in remonstrating with Kalmykov. He's not the sort that changes his mind easily, though this is probably a sign of considered conviction rather than stubbornness on his part. Ever since his national service in the army (Victor was a radio operator in the Air Force), his inclinations have been the same. He became a caretaker, his latest job being right next to where he lives. In a city the size of Moscow this is convenient. Kalmykov did this so that he would have the opportunity to devote more time to his passion for painting.

He displayed his paintings around the family home, and as their number began to increase, taking up space in the room where his daughter watched television and his son

played, their flat seemed smaller than ever. The difficulties
are obvious. Not even all members of the Artists' Union
have their own studios, let alone the self-taught. Kalmykov
knows this only too well and doesn't complain too much.
He feels he is the master of his own fate. The young artist is
in no hurry for fame and success. He is confident that if he
produces really outstanding work he will be acclaimed
sooner or later. But he has no confidence in officials from
the arts scene, and this is probably why he tries to avoid
everything that entails intrigue, administration, form-filling
and minutes. His desires are very simple — to paint without
copying from a famous teacher, without being constantly
prompted by members of some jury. He has something to
say and he has the ability to express it. He is a painter pure
and simple.

1980, the year the poet and actor Vladimir Vysotsky died,
marked a turning point in Kalmykov's life, and his portrait
of this famous bard was his first serious work. He painted it
in one session, relying simply on the image of Vysotsky he
recalled from childhood all those years ago. There are those
people whose courage and steadfastness are a source of inspiration. This is how Kalmykov always saw Vysotsky and
how he depicted him. Caretaker Victor Kalmykov wants to
become an artist who has made a name for himself. Without idealising his present situation, it is the life that suits his
independent manner. The most important thing for him is
that he is master of his own destiny.

His works inspire optimism. Anyone will appreciate this
if they take the time to peruse his *Woman in White* or
Koktebel. Incidentally, Victor has not yet given any names
to his pictures. We thought them up together when looking
around. You should have seen how Irina, the artist's wife,
was eager to help. She's also an artist in her own way, she's
a lighting engineer at the theatre, and did her best to show
the paintings to best advantage.

It was a long time before he showed the paintings to anyone at all. Frames were lacking and he had no money to
buy them. There are times when he spends a large part of
his wages on just one frame. Whenever Victor is to be seen
carrying his latest purchase across the yard, the old women
complain about him squandering money on such useless
items. But Kalmykov does not let them into his secret.

Everything in its own time, he feels. He's quite calm about it, but you still get the feeling that you'd like to help him reach a wider audience.

A caretaker... If I could, then I would certainly paint a friendly caricature of Victor: a caretaker sweeping the street not with a broom, but with an enormous paintbrush. I would add a caption: 'When Kalmykov is at work, our city looks brighter and cleaner.'

Sobesednik, No. 48, November 1987

Bitter Lessons

Readers of Soviet Scene 1987 *will recall our discussions about Chernobyl, about the wreck of the ship* Admiral Nakhimov *and about the dramatic events that took place in December 1986 in Alma Ata. Can we now say any more about these bitter lessons?*

In the summer of 1987, the Criminal Cases Division of the Supreme Court of the USSR, presided over by R. K. Brize, heard the criminal case against the former managers of the Chernobyl station. It was recognised that one of the principal guilty parties was the former Director of the station, V. Bryukhanov. Although he was in charge of a very complicated technological enterprise, he did not maintain the essential safety requirements, nor enforce strict labour discipline among the personnel. This lack of discipline and control had existed at the station long before the accident... Instances of breaches in technical procedures had been concealed with his knowledge, and the root cause of problems had not been eliminated. All of this had contributed to the catastrophic situation and had meant that wrong action was taken in the critical situation.

Bryukhanov lost his head and displayed cowardice during the catastrophe — he did not take measures to limit the scope of the accident, and did not carry out the emergency plan to protect the personnel and the population from radiation. He deliberately presented incorrect information about the actual level of radiation and thus hindered the timely evacuation of people from the dangerous area.

The court revealed the facts demonstrating the gross neglect of duties by the former chief engineer of APS, N. Fomin, and his deputy, A. Dyatlov. Bryukhanov, Fomin, Dyatlov and the former head of the reactor system, A. Kovalenko, decided to carry out an experiment in the fourth reactor before its plan-

ned repair. However, they were not in agreement on how it should be done; they did not thoroughly analyse the specifics of the experiment and did not introduce any additional safety measures.

The personnel on duty in the reactor block turned out to be completely unprepared to cope with an accident. The former head of the shift, B. Rogozhkin, declined to take charge of the experiment and to control the work of the reactor. When he learned about the accident, he did not inform the personnel according to the emergency rules.

Former inspector of the USSR State Agency for Atomic Energy Supervision, Yu. Laushkin, was criminally negligent in fulfilling his duty. He showed neither principledness, nor persistence in fulfilling the safety regulations.

The Supreme Court Division gave V. Bryukhanov, N. Fomin and A. Dyatlov the maximum sentence allowed by the law for these crimes — ten years of deprivation of liberty. B. Rogozhkin was sentenced for five years, A. Kovalenko for three and Yu. Laushkin for two. An additional investigation of the ill-timed measures intended to improve reactors of this type was announced by the Supreme Court Division, which also passed two special riders addressed to the USSR Ministry of Nuclear Power Industry and the USSR State Agency for Atomic Energy Supervision.

Until the Chernobyl disaster we could only imagine the scope of destruction that could be wrought on people and nature by radiation. Now we begin to know...

ON THE DEFENSIVE AND ON THE ATTACK

An exchange between YURI KANIN, science reviewer of Novosti Press Agency, and NIKOLAI LUKONIN, Soviet Minister of the Nuclear Power Industry

N. L. Let me first make a brief introduction. Since the accident at the US power station on Three Mile Island, and especially the Chernobyl disaster in this country on 26 April 1986, as well as a long list of minor accidents at nuclear plants in various countries, it has become unrewarding and even risky for nuclear experts to discuss their trade in the press. 'Here's another advocate of the indomitable atom out to prove the unprovable,' people jump in with. 'That's his job and he gets paid so long as nuclear power stations exist.'

Yu. K. *For this reason many in your line of work today prefer to keep silent.*

N. L. Right. Remember the biased coverage nuclear power engineering received in the world press following the Chernobyl accident. There were clear political allusions to Hiroshima and Nagasaki. Some reporters alleged that radioactive clouds were sweeping across the world, spreading panic. Western embargoes on imports of agricultural produce from socialist countries were an obvious attempt to harm socialist economies. Some farmers in the West suffered, too, even those who were paid compensation as part of the political speculation. The mythical numbers of projected deaths from cancer caused many people to picture themselves and their relatives as future patients in cancer wards.

Yu. K. *Too often in the past nuclear power engineering has been portrayed as almost completely safe. The illusion has now been replaced by a deep mistrust of this source of energy.*

N. L. I would say it is excessive mistrust, or perhaps a lack of faith in the ability of modern science and engineering to solve safety-related problems at nuclear power plants. I think that nuclear experts, researchers and practical scientists should use the press to inform the public about measures being taken, the real state of things in this area and also its importance for the further progress of civilisation.

We experts in the field are not turning a deaf ear on our opponents. We, too, have children and grandchildren. We are not their enemies, nor are we the enemies of humankind.

Yu. K. *Incidentally, what do your children do? What do they think of the nuclear power industry?*

N. L. I have two sons. Both have followed in my footsteps. The elder is a foreman at the Leningrad Atomic Power Station (APS). The younger is specialising in the operation of nuclear power plants at the Polytechnical Institute. They both believe, as I do, that there will never be another

Chernobyl, that nuclear power can and will be safe, that humankind currently has no other alternative. It is wrong to think that we defend nuclear power plants because we operate them. I've been in power engineering since 1952. I've worked my way up from being an engineer at nuclear reactors to being the director of the Leningrad, and then of the Ignalina APS. I've built up knowledge and experience. That's the position from which I approach this problem, which worries so many of us today — particularly experts like myself.

Yu. K. *The main problem with reactors of the Chernobyl type, experts believe, is what they call the steam ratio of reactivity.*

N. L. The ratio has now been sharply reduced because each RBMK-1000 reactor at present has 81 neutron absorbers; the RBMK-1500 reactor in operation at the Ignalina APS has 52 absorbers. The absorbers are rods of boron steel. Today, if there were for any reason a sharp drop in the level of water, there wouldn't be a power burst like there was at Chernobyl.

Besides, emergency protection has been improved: safety rods in all Soviet reactors in use can now reach their active zones one and a half times faster than before. The length of the absorption part of the rods has been increased and other structural improvements have been made.

Safety systems are being continuously improved. We now have the first prototypes of an even faster emergency protection system. Testing is under way at the Ignalina APS of systems whose rods can reach the active section in as little as 2.1 seconds. Under the programme for 1988-1989 this system will be installed in all reactors of the RBMK type. We are also working to equip all types of reactors with special systems to check their equipment. These systems are being installed first at the Chernobyl and Armenian nuclear power stations among others. The system can detect even incipient faults inside metals, say in the pipe of the primary loop, so that repairs can be done in time.

As a result of these additional safety measures, reactors of the RBMK type, i. e., the type installed at Chernobyl, are no worse than any others, including the water-cooled reactors widely used throughout the world. As for the stability of their operation, they were never worse than any other

and have even been improved in this respect. In 1986 each
RBMK generating unit was shut down 2.6 times on average. In 1987 the figure was 1.3. As far as I know, the USA
and France are aiming to reduce shutdowns to an average
1.5 per unit by 1990.

Yu. K. *What do you think about the present radiation safety around the station and inside its control rooms? What are
the working conditions like? In Britain, for example, they
hold the popular Monopoly championships inside the technical maintenance room at the Albury nuclear plant (built in
1967) as a way of winning back the public's trust in the safety
of the nuclear power industry. Last year the premises were
used by 200 doctors for a conference. Are you ready to stage
something of the kind at the Chernobyl APS?*

N. L. A nuclear plant is, of course, not meant for enter-
tainment or scientific symposia. Nevertheless, there was
a pop show broadcast on TV last year from Chernobyl. Various shift workers and other personnel from the Chernobyl
nuclear power station live in Pripyat, 3 kilometres away,
with the permission of the Ministry of Public Health of the
USSR. At the power station we've got no rooms large
enough to hold 200 people but at different times we have received many more from many countries: scientists, engineers, state, political and religious leaders, journalists, authors and medics. I remember Hans Blix, director-general
of the IAEA, standing right up against the wall of the crip-
pled reactor as he checked the radiation level. In 1987 the
level of radiation inside the Chernobyl power station control rooms was one-third of the norm.

Yu. K. *Some countries have renounced the nuclear power industry...*

N. L. They include those which have no nuclear power
stations or are just taking their first steps in this area.

Yu. K. *True. But others have stopped the construction of
nuclear plants, and Sweden is planning to close down the
plants it has by the year 2010.*

N. L. Provided there is an alternative. As a means of
calming public fears, we can understand such an assurance.
Incidentally, both Sweden and the USSR are vigorously
working to improve the safety of reactors in operation as
well as those still on the drawing board. At the same time
Japan, whose experts can hardly be mistaken in their pre-

dictions, has increased the share of electricity produced by nuclear plants to 31.7% (in the USSR nuclear plants produce 11.2% of all electricity). The *Japan Times* recently reported government plans to increase the share of nuclear energy in the country's overall energy balance to 40% by the year 2000.

Yu. K. *What are the main arguments for the continued use of nuclear power at this stage? Wouldn't it be better to invest more in alternative energy sources such as solar energy, the heat of the earth's interior, wind and tidal waves?*

N. L. No nuclear industry expert would say 'No' to those sources. But they simply cannot compete in terms of the amount of energy produced. They are a useful addition to the overall production of electricity and heat, but can only be used locally.

No one, I think, would contest that the world's living standards and economic development largely depend on the availability of energy. According to rough estimates, the demand for energy in the first quarter of the 21st century will double. If we exclude the nuclear power industry before we have found a viable alternative, how can we manage? Using organic fuels? These are already beginning to be exhausted. Besides, we need oil and gas badly for other purposes.

But let us imagine that we have closed down the nuclear power stations which currently generate 17% of all electricity in the world. We will be obliged to burn more coal, gas and oil. What does this mean for global ecology? Wouldn't it mean the final blow to an atmosphere already devastated by acid rain?

The second critical issue is the disruption of the established structure of generation and consumption of energy. France's nuclear power stations generate 70% of its electricity. What should it do? What about other countries, especially developing ones, which have no other energy resources? There would obviously be another and more intensive energy crisis followed by another peak in political tensions and instability.

I still vote for the nuclear power industry for the safety of which numerous teams of experts in the Soviet Union and many other countries are working in a dedicated way.

In an interview published on 21 March 1988 in the newspaper Izvestia *the historians* LEOKADIYA DROBIZHEVA *and* YURI POLYAKOV *had something interesting to say about the national question in the USSR.*

In the early years of Soviet power the creation of national republics was of enormous political and also economic importance. In just six or seven years — war-torn, hungry years! — the majority of the republics and regions which now make up the Soviet Union were established. Creating these republics was particularly difficult as there was no precedent or model to use as a guide. Most nations, when creating their republics (and the Soviet Union comprises more than one hundred different nationalities), had previously not existed as independent states.

The situation was further complicated by the fact that there was migration on an unprecedented scale. Hundreds of thousands of people from different ethnic groups were moving to new regions, taking with them their culture and traditions. Of the total number of Armenians living in the USSR, for example, 66 per cent (according to the census figures for 1979) live in Armenia, 11,5 per cent live in Azerbaijan, nearly 11 per cent in Georgia and about 9 per cent in the Russian Federation. Over 20 per cent of the Tajiks live outside the Tajik republic. Only 26 per cent of the Tatars live in Tataria. This mass migration raised the problem of adaptation. Estonia, for example, needed to intensify its development of natural resources and provide a workforce for several branches of its economy. What might the social consequences be? Some Estonian experts are of the opinion that the flow of specialists into the republic from outside should be halted, because this reduces the proportion of Estonians making up the population, particularly in sectors of material production. Other experts, however, believe that to halt this flow would damage the economic development of the republic. Clearly this problem cannot be resolved by arbitrarily adopting one or other of the proffered solutions; what is needed is a careful analysis of the demographic situation in the republic.

There are also two points of view as regards national schools. Why, for example, is Byelorussia reducing the number of schools where lessons are taught in Byelorussian? The usual answer is that the number of pupils whose parents wish them to be taught in Byelorussian is falling, and therefore few-

er such schools are needed. Others say that new schools are needed so that children can be taught in Byelorussian, and then the pupils will be there for them. What is the decisive factor here — pupils for the schools, or schools for the pupils?

This question can, of course, be resolved: in a number of republics there are schools with parallel classes in which lessons are taught in different languages. It is not a question of schools but rather of qualified teachers. If, for example, a Kirghiz family sees that education in Kirghiz is at a low level, then, without asking anyone's permission or agreement, they transfer their children to a class where the lessons are given in Russian. And vice versa.

Interaction among different nationalities has always led to mutual enrichment. This, however, does not exclude the preservation of the fundamental values of individual national groups, their culture and interests. On the other hand, certain nationalities within the Soviet Union have lived through dramatic events in their national history, events which until recently were not referred to. There was, for example, the mass deportation of entire ethnic groups living in the North Caucasus, and their subsequent return. The Chechen, the Ingush, the Balkars, the Karachais remember what happened to them between 1944 and 1956, even if nothing was said about it in the history books. The same can be said about the deportation of the Crimean Tatars to Central Asia...

The nationalities issue is far from being an easy one. As regards the Crimean Tatars, on 5 September 1967 the Supreme Soviet of the USSR repealed that part of a decree issued by the state authorities which contained accusations against the entire Tatar nation living in the Crimea, and fully restored their constitutional rights. Since then around 10,000 Crimean Tatars have returned to the Crimea, where there are now about 20,000 Tatars. This process of resettlement is continuing. However, it must be remembered that the demographic situation in the Crimea today is quite different from the one before the war. The population of the Crimea now comprises about 2.5 million people of various ethnic origins, that is, twice as many as before the war. These 2.5 million people enjoy exactly the same constitutional rights as the Crimean Tatars. The question, as we see, requires a calm, responsible and balanced approach.

All the republics of the Soviet Union are now multinational (in Georgia alone, a relatively small republic, the population of just over five million people includes over 80 different nationalities), and people of different ethnic origin work side by side in factories and institutions of various kinds. In such a multinational milieu, any discontent is easily given a national bias.

The events which took place in Nagorny Karabakh in February and March of 1988 shook the whole country. One could explain the excesses which occurred there and in Sumgait in Azerbaijan by arguing that anti-social, extremist elements exploited national tensions. This is quite true. However, it is apparently not the whole truth, since to suppose that large numbers of people are likely to be misled by a few irresponsible extremists is to bring into question the political credibility of a lot of people. The explosion of national sentiment in the Nagorno-Karabakh Autonomous Region had tragic consequences. Two people were killed and about fifty wounded. Even more tragic in their consequences were the disorders in Sumgait. Here 32 people of different nationalities were killed, 197 people were wounded, 12 women were raped, more than 100 flats were plundered, 26 consumer service facilities and more than 20 cars were damaged. Troops had to be sent in to the town to restore order and protect life...

NAGORNY KARABAKH:
A PROGRAMME OF DEVELOPMENT

Interview with VLADIMIR LAKHTIN,
First Vice-Chairman, Bureau for Social Development,
USSR Council of Ministers

Q. *Vladimir Petrovich, you went to Nagorny Karabakh only a few days after we, a group of correspondents for the national press, had been there. We have already shared some of our impressions with our readers. What was your impression of the situation in and around Nagorny Karabakh?*

A. In my opinion the situation remains tense, and this is the greatest single obstacle to any sober examination of the problem and its solution to the benefit of all concerned.

Q. *That is to say, it is also an obstacle to the very mission*

*which brought you to Nagorny Karabakh? And what was that
mission precisely?*

A. We went in order to study the situation with a view to
helping draw up a programme of economic and social development in the region, intended to raise the living standards
of the local population. In other words, a programme designed to satisfy the interests and demands of the working
people of the region as expressed in the course of the local
campaign to change the status of Nagorny Karabakh.

Q. *The question of whether a change in status would bring
about the desired changes in other areas of life is an issue requiring special discussion. I would like to ask you something
else. The newspaper* Bakinsky Rabochy *recently published
a long discussion entitled 'Round Table', based on material
provided by a number of experts. The aim of the discussion
was to show that the Nagorny Karabakh Autonomous Region
is one of the most prosperous regions in the republic. Do such
conclusions perhaps reveal only one side of the story?*

A. These conclusions are based on precise data. In terms
of the housing index, for example, Nagorny Karabakh has
a lead of 40 per cent over the rest of the republic. There are
other indices which show the region to be ahead of both the
Union republics of Azerbaijan and Armenia.

Q. *If that is so why the need for an additional programme
of socio-economic development, which was the reason for
your visit to the region? Simply to multiply its advantages?*

A. Two factors have to be taken into account. In the first
place, alongside these achievements in the social sphere
there have also been a number of failures. There are considerable problems with the water supply. The road network
lags behind the average for the republic, and there is
a shortage of cultural and leisure facilities. The sports centre in Stepanakert, for example, has been under construction for more than nine years, and there is still no Young
Pioneer centre. Let us take the largest enterprise in the region, the silk combine which I visited in Stepanakert. The
impression it created was one of a total lack of management. Local colleagues told me about the exceptional order
which reigned in the town during the round-the-clock dem-
onstrations. Even food for those taking part in them was
organised to perfection. Yet when it comes to the provision
of meals for those working at the silk combine, it is a very

different matter. That is just one example of the failure to cater for people's basic requirements.

Secondly, if previous negligence is to be corrected, previous achievements must also be further developed and not merely left at their present level. Therefore the development programme for the region provides for a 1.4 increase in new housing over the next five years. As a result, by the year 2000 each family in the area will have a separate flat or house. The average living space per person will be about 20 sq. m., which is higher than in the country as a whole, and considerably more than in Azerbaijan and Armenia.

Q. *Did you come across any difficulties while working on the programme?*

A. On the whole, no, as the requirements have, in my opinion, been correctly identified and adequate finance and resources allocated. However, there is one difficulty which I think ought to be mentioned. Surprisingly, this concerns the attitude of the local leadership, and above all the Party leadership headed by the new First Secretary of the regional committee of the Communist Party of Azerbaijan, G. Pogosyan, who do not see these problems as being the most important.

Why do I think this view is mistaken? Although the housing situation is, on average, fairly good, there are still quite a few people in the region who require better housing conditions.

Q. *What does the programme consist of? What can people hope to gain from it?*

A. The programme envisages a complex of measures to provide more material and technical resources for the social sphere, and to accelerate the development of the productive forces and the infrastructure of the region. I have already spoken about the housing situation. In addition there are plans to build a cultural centre in Stepanakert which will seat 850 people, a regional hospital with 400 beds, and a clinic able to handle 600 consultations per shift. There will also be a Young Pioneer centre, a town library, and a further 9-10 general schools so that the two-shifts-a-day system can be done away with in school education over the next few years.

One of the problems facing Nagorny Karabakh at present is a lack of local enterprises where the young school-leavers can find employment and settle in the region. As a result, large numbers of young people move away. The programme provides for existing enterprises to be expanded, reconstructed and re-equipped, and for the construction of more than ten new branch enterprises. There will also be 14 new enterprises producing cheeses, meat, sausages and canned food.

In order to improve the water supply in Stepanakert and the district towns of Nagorny Karabakh, two large new reservoirs are to be built and the water supply system expanded. Roadway construction will be almost doubled. Gas pipelines will connect local villages and towns to the gas supply. There is already a large increase in the volume of work being undertaken by the construction industry.

All these measures will require considerable financial outlay; up to 400 million roubles. Even this year expenditure will go beyond the planned amount.

Q. *We have been talking primarily about the material sphere. However, in their demands many of the residents of Nagorny Karabakh placed as much, if not more, emphasis on the cultural sphere, on more and freer contacts with Armenia.*

A. First, free contacts. There should be no restrictions. As regards the programme, it contains, on the basis of the expressed desire of the Armenian population, such points as the provision in Nagorny Karabakh and adjacent areas in Azerbaijan and Armenia of reliable and high-quality reception of three television channels, including the Armenian republican channel. Historical and cultural monuments in the region are to be renovated with the help of Armenian experts. Local publishing facilities are to be expanded in order to increase the output of literature and educational material in Armenian.

The programme also contains a special item on work in schools where lessons are given in Armenian. It is proposed that, beginning this year, places should be allocated in Armenian institutes of higher education for students from the Nagorny Karabakh Autonomous Region.

I have mentioned only a few of the points in the programme. If it should prove necessary this programme can be extended. In my opinion the planned measures constitute, taken overall, the care of *perestroika* in the main spheres of life in Nagorny Karabakh.

Q. *An important aspect of* perestroika *around the country is that local authorities should have greater freedom of initiative and independence. When we were in Nagorny Karabakh this subject was brought up more than once.*

A. It was mentioned during our visit as well. It had long been a sore point. However, this is a question which lies outside our competence and our programme.

To return once more to the programme itself, it is of considerable political as well as economic importance. People must see clearly for themselves the gulf separating the demagogy of particular individuals and the real, practical activity of the Party and the state and their concern for the vital interests of the people.

Izvestia, 25 March 1988

On 8 March 1988, an Aeroflot plane en route from Irkutsk to Leningrad, with a stopover in Kurgan, was hijacked by eleven people, all members of the Ovechkin family of Irkutsk. The family consisted of the mother, her seven sons and three daughters from the age of nine to twenty-six; the father had died in 1984.

The Ovechkins were known to many people in the Soviet Union. The brothers had a band called the Seven Simeons, a film had been made about them, and they had been written about in the Moscow News *in July 1985. In the autumn of 1987 the group had a successful tour of Japan. Thus it was shocking to hear about the hijacking which resulted in the death of nine people, including the four older Ovechkin brothers and their mother. A total of nineteen were wounded, including two members of the assault team. And the plane itself, a TU-154, as a result of the explosion of a homemade bomb on board and the subsequent fire, was totally destroyed.*

There was controversy in the Soviet press about whether the plane should have been landed on Soviet territory, or flown to Britain as the criminals demanded, where, under international laws against terrorism in the air, the hijackers would have faced life imprisonment. Some argued that the behaviour of the hijackers was unpredictable, so there was no guarantee that the airplane would have reached London.

However, no one can change what happened. What follows is an account of the tragedy given by crew members.

AN INTERRUPTED FLIGHT

Flight Captain Valentin Kupriyanov:

At 2:53 p.m. we were approaching the city of Belozersk when our chief stewardess Irina Vasilieva brought me a note. It was a piece of paper from a school notebook with a message written in blue ink: 'Head for England (London). Do not descend, or we will blow up the plane. You are under our control.'

We looked at each other. Irina said, 'I can't tell if this is a joke, or if they're serious.' Whatever the case, the situation was extraordinary and a decision had to be made. I immediately notified ground control. Someone had to negotiate with the bandits. Irina said there were eleven of them, and that they were armed. The flight engineer, Innokenty Stupakov, said he would go to them.

Flight Engineer Innokenty Stupakov:

I went to the second passenger compartment. The moment I entered I saw guns pointed at me and someone shouted: 'Don't move an inch!' I said, 'One of you come over here, and let's talk.' We agreed to meet in the middle of the compartment where there were not any passengers. We sat on opposite sides of the aisle. The hijacker, who was nervous, said, 'We demand you fly to London.' I explained, 'We don't have enough fuel. We barely have enough to get to Leningrad. We need to refuel'. He said, 'Okay, then land abroad.' I promised to report back to the captain.

Captain Kupriyanov:

For the sake of the passengers' safety we decided to agree to the bandits' demand, and fly abroad. Ground control approved. But the closer we got to Leningrad, the clearer it became that we would not make it even to the nearest Finnish or Swedish airport. When we left Kurgan we had just enough fuel to get to Leningrad or, in an emergency, to Tallinn. But if we had to fly, for instance, to Finland, we would have to do some manoeuvring over an unfamiliar airport, and perhaps the fuel would not last. The question was, what to do?

We could not land in Leningrad or Tallinn because the bandits, who had threatened to blow up the plane at the slightest suspicion, might have been in Leningrad or Tallinn before, and could have recognised them from the air.

Ground control advised us to land at an airport outside the city. We had to make a nearly 180 degree turn.

Stewardess Irina Vasilieva:

The bandits were nervous as it was. But at this point they became particularly excited. One of them was especially on edge — he shouted and darted around more than the others. I noticed that they had pasted some kind of cross on the wall. Then they demanded the crew tell them where we were flying.

Captain Kupriyanov:

We could not tell them we were landing in the USSR: there was no guarantee the bandits would not blow up the plane. The nearest airport was Kotka, so we told them that was where we were headed. They could not see anything from the air because the clouds were so thick. They realised we were on Soviet territory only when they saw the soldiers surround the airplane. It was the beginning of three and a half difficult hours.

It was at this time that our stewardesses were at their very best. I cannot find the words to express how wonderful they were! When the situation became extremely tense, Irina Vasilieva and Tamara Zharkaya tried to calm down the hijackers, saying the plane was just refuelling, that it would take off again. Suddenly two of the bandits grabbed Tamara, and sat her down between them as a hostage.

Stewardess Vasilieva:

One of the bandits demanded that I contact the captain over the intercom system and tell him that if the plane did not refuel in five minutes he would blow up the plane.

Captain Kupriyanov:

I replied that the engineer would have to leave, or the plane could not refuel.

Flight Engineer Stupakov:

I came out of the cockpit, opened up the entrance hatch, and lowered the folding ladder. It took me a long time, but finally we got more fuel, just enough to reach some foreign airport if need be. Upstairs I heard a lot of hysteria, demands to take off immediately. The captain said we could not fly without the engineer. I came up, pulled in the ladder, and told one of the bandits: 'Hold on to the ladder while I close the hatch.'

Captain Kupriyanov:

While he was putting the steps together, the flight engineer quickly ducked into the cockpit, not giving the hijacker a chance to get in too. Just then we were called over the intercom. The leader of the band — that is what I thought he was because he was the calmest one — took the intercom from the stewardess and said: 'Captain, why aren't you taking off?' I replied, 'We have to turn around; we're waiting to be pulled.' The response was, 'I'm giving you five minutes. If we don't take off, we're blowing up the plane.' They were already hitting the door of the cockpit with the ladder, and broke the peephole. By then there was no alternative. The assault team, which had already got into the cockpit, rushed out into the passenger compartments. Simultaneously, from the other side of the airplane, the second group attacked. I could hear shooting over the intercom. Two men from the assault team had been hit at close range, and were lying on the floor bleeding. Then the bandit shouted over the intercom: 'Captain, tell your men to stop shooting...'

Flight Engineer Stupakov:

Just then we heard what seemed like an explosion. We were informed from ground control: 'You have a fire on board, turn on your fire extinguishers.'

Captain Kupriyanov:

I looked out of the window and saw flames, there was already smoke filling the compartment; the passengers were being evacuated. All electric currents were immediately switched off and everything was subordinated to rescuing the passengers. Ground control gave us permission to leave the plane. When we got out we learned how well our stewardesses and steward had done their jobs. Alexei Dvornitsky had quickly put down the cushion ladder; he was helped by an unknown cadet who happened to be nearby, and an air controller from Kurgan. They had also opened up all the emergency exits.

Then we found out that three passengers had been killed by the bandits. Our friend and crew member, Tamara Zharkaya, had also been killed.

Sovetskaya Rossiya, 11 March 1988

'UP AGAINST THE MAFIA'

As Seen by the Hero of the Story

By VICTOR LOSHAK

The Uzbek case has been the biggest in Soviet postwar history in terms of the sums stolen and the political, economic and social damage caused by the crime. TELMAN GDLYAN, *senior investigator of major cases under the Procurator-General of the USSR, has been investigating this case for five years.*

Gdlyan always keeps at hand the 'List of Deputies to the 11th USSR Supreme Soviet'. He uses it to specify details in the biographies of those with whom he is now dealing. A couple of years ago, those in Gdlyan's care, if taken together, would probably have been deciding the major questions of Uzbekistan's life. Today the Chairman of the Republic's Council of Ministers, four Secretaries of the Central Committee, two Ministers, and six First Secretaries of the Regional Party Committees are only answering questions.

It is usually believed that a criminal always expects to be put behind bars at any moment. But the Uzbek case has, in many respects, refuted this notion: the very criteria of legality were somehow lost in the Republic. Keeping up only the appearance of order, the militia became simply a faction in the war between different groups. 'The first year we were lucky in that they weren't united against us and did not consider us a serious threat,' Gdlyan maintains.

Gdlyan was sent to Uzbekistan in the spring of 1983, a few months after Leonid Brezhnev's death. The republic was still under the command of Sharaf Rashidov. For five years 'Rashidovshchina' (loosely translated as the times of Rashidov's rule) was the term used to describe many things: corruption, bribery running into thousands of roubles, the oppression of millions of people to the accompaniment of noisy reports and loud speeches...

Investigators would inevitably have to reckon with the almighty Rashidov. On learning who had exposed the bribe-takers in Bukhara and caused the investigators to come from Moscow, the former First Secretary of the Central Committee of the Communist Party of Uzbekistan did all he could to remove the leaders of the republic's KGB (State Security Committee) from Uzbekistan, and succeeded.

Telman Gdlyan and his group found themselves to a great extent isolated.

This was, perhaps, the crucial moment. Many would have preferred the widely advertised case of bribe-taking in Bukhara, involving the regional militia and trade bosses to remain a local affair and be regarded as the result of 'isolated shortcomings'. It is hard to imagine how many millions the ringleaders of the Uzbek mafia would have paid this investigator, on a modest salary of 365 roubles, if only he would 'lash out at the leaves without touching the roots'.

Further investigations promised no joy — just a long search for the truth and five years of work without leave (in Moscow his wife, son and daughter were waiting for him). It should be said that during all the 47 years of his life Gdlyan had never been considered either submissive or compliant. Was it due to these qualities that he remained in the lowest procurator's rank — that of a junior jurist — three times the usual duration?

...The investigation continued. Abduvakhid Karimov, First Secretary of the Bukhara Regional Party Committee, whom Rashidov had once included amongst the 'gilded society of Uzbekistan', turned out to be 'gilded' in the literal sense of the word. There are three photo albums held at the Procurator's Office these days: the pictures show heaps of gold tsarist chervonetzes (ten-rouble coins), watches, jewellery and trunks filled with money from Karimov's 'personal collection'. One photograph, incidentally, makes it clear how Gdlyan feels about all this wealth: he stands beside a box of treasures, an expression of weariness and disgust on his face.

It seemed convenient to stop at Karimov, but not even half the truth had been revealed. Gold busts, gold-embroidered portraits, gowns decorated with astrakhan and embroidered in gold were made in Bukhara for Brezhnev and Rashidov... In the court, which sentenced Karimov to be shot by firing squad, it was stated that the First Secretary of the Uzbekistan CP Central Committee alone had received 300,000 roubles from Bukhara. Karimov had also managed to hand over dozens of thousands of roubles to Usmankhodzhayev, who replaced Rashidov.

Why? As hush-money. Some time after an earthquake in Gazli, Yu. Churbanov, First Deputy Minister of Internal Affairs of the USSR, came to check on how its aftermath was being dealt with. 'There aren't any cigarettes in the shops!' he scolded Karimov right in the street. The latter drew certain conclusions from this incident and that same evening, at someone's dacha, handed over 10,000 roubles to Churbanov in exchange for his gracious promise 'not to report his shortcomings at the top'.

Gdlyan understood that the interests of the investigation demanded maximum information. Hundreds of times before the publication in May 1986 of the Resolution of the CPSU Central Committee and the USSR Council of Ministers 'On the Repeal of the Resolution on Perpetuating the Memory of Sh. R. Rashidov', he drove across Tashkent past the Rashidov memorial, very much aware of the charade entailed in the visits of Young Pioneers and foreign tourists to this grave.

It was perhaps here that what was yet to be combatted became particularly obvious. At this grave Rashidov's successor Usmankhodzhayev pledged that the republic would fulfil the deceased's behest to produce six million tons of cotton! And it did... Usmankhodzhayev summoned the Chairman of the Council of Ministers and ordered him to 'add' to what had already been collected another 240,000 tons of raw cotton. All in all, that year, nearly a million tons were 'added', by distorting the results achieved. A quarter of a billion roubles received for this was embezzled.

After his five years in Uzbekistan, Gdlyan now and again uses Uzbek words in conversation: 'opa'—'wife', 'aka'—'esteemed', 'tukhmat'—'slander', and again 'Rashidovshchina', which for him means also an extreme degree of cynicism. For instance, pinning a Hero of Socialist Labour Gold Star on someone, while whispering in his ear: 'This isn't gratis ... it'll cost you money'.

Taking the offensive against an all-round defence is how one could, perhaps, best define the work of Gdlyan's investigating team during the first four years. They heard about 'fascism', about 'repressive measures', and about a secret assignment 'to discredit the republic' ... And they worked, living like monks, resorting to ruses, flying from region to region in a military helicopter, or buying tickets in someone else's name. They had to be ahead of the enemy by at least one day, one move, one step. The investigating team, which numbered by that time more than a hundred people from all over the country, counted the confiscated property. They were dealing with in sums of tens of millions, while borrowing roubles from each other: even investigators only get a 2.6 rouble travel allowance per day.

They worked hard. Evidence, photographs and voluntary acknowledgements of guilt built up to a picture, previously hidden from the public eye, showing the involvement of hundreds of people — in effect, the whole ruling stratum of Uzbekistan. The picture even shocked the investigators: these people held nothing sacred. They sold government awards, dachas, Party membership cards, seats on presidiums and places in cemeteries, official posts and deputy mandates. The most horrible implication of this was that people knew what was going on, but kept silent. In one of the *kishlaks* (Central Asian villages), to which they flew to confiscate what had been stolen from the people, Gdlyan was amazed: collective farm wages had not been paid for half a year, and there had not been a single complaint.

The work of Telman Gdlyan's investigation team may well be used eventually as a case study in the law faculties. It would be good if it also included a short story, as told by the investigator, about how they flew to a distant *kishlak* to the well-known potter Kulol-bobo who, as was known, became one of the obedient 'keepers' of a highly-placed official's treasures.

'No,' he said, 'I have nothing, don't even search.' Then I took his hand in mine. 'Look what kind of hands you have, *usto* (master). Such hands are priceless! As for me,' I said, 'if they sack me, it will be difficult to find a new job, but everyone needs you with your hands of gold. Why do you disgrace them? Why do you hide what has been stolen from the people?' He took me to an old mulberry tree out in the fields. What for, I thought? But Kulol-bobo, it turned out, had a box containing 3,000 gold coins hidden in the bottom of an irrigation ditch... 'Dig here!' he pointed.

Hidden meanings of long compliment-strewn conver

sations over cups of tea, exchanges of courtesies with people on whom you know you're going to put handcuffs in a week's time... This investigatory work seemed more akin to diplomacy. Even the smallest detail could not be neglected.

It was decided to bring a charge against Ruzmet Gaipov, First Secretary of the Khorezm Regional Party Committee, the biggest bribe-taker, at the Procurator's Office. His mansion was encircled. Gdlyan and his colleagues went in to ask Gaipov to come with them. They were asked to take seats and offered tea. 'At Ruzmet Gaipovich's former workplace he was called the "Lenin of Kashkadarya"...,' Gaipov's wife said, as the host brought in his jacket covered in government awards. Then he returned to the wardrobe, and suddenly there was a cry. By the time Telman Gdlyan got to the bedroom Gaipov had already managed to inflict 13 knife wounds on himself...

It is customary to judge the success of justice in terms of roubles, but, having returned only a fraction of what had been plundered by the *'bais'* (rich landowners in Central Asia), Gdlyan's team have been working all these five years as profitably as any well-organised business. However, there are bribes which no investigator can confiscate. Bribes of fame and spiritual values. Rashidov was made into a great writer, the Tashkent militia head Sattarov arrested for bribes — into a journalist... Portraits, busts, giant murals — the thirst for money paralleled by a craving for fame. After the court had witnessed this horrible picture of personal degradation, the former First Secretary of the Bukhara Regional Party Committee addressed the judges with these final words: 'I beg you to take account of my personal contribution to the development of agriculture.'

It took five years of investigation to shed light on these silent intrigues behind the heavy curtains of Republican power. Now the stage is becoming more brightly lit and the once heroic leaders diminish in statue as the floodlight of truth reaches them. It has already caught in its light the former Minister of Internal Affairs of the USSR N. Shchelokov, and his First Deputy, Yu. Churbanov, implicated in the Uzbek case.

This exposure is due to the efforts of Gdlyan and his aides, men with an independent outlook, not the usual justice department bureaucrats. As Nikolai Ivanov, Gdlyan's deputy in the investigating team, investigator of major cases under the Procurator-General of the USSR said: 'We are not the sort of people who enter the chief's room with our own opinion and leave it with the latter's. To defend the law honestly you have to have your own position.'

Moscow News, 3 April 1988

On 15 February 1988 a fire broke out at the Library of the Leningrad Academy of Sciences. Founded in 1714 at the height of Peter the Great's progressive reforms, the library is the pride of Russia. It held some 12 million items.

Academician **DMITRI LIKHACHEV** *gives some details of the consequences of this tragedy.*

THE 'FIRE' CONTINUES

The fire which raged for 19 hours in the priceless archives of the USSR Academy of Sciences Library in Leningrad, was a catastrophe for our culture equivalent to Chernobyl.

According to official figures published by the library's administration after many days of overt misinformation, the fire completely destroyed 400,000 books, including 188,000 foreign-language publications from the world-famous Baer Archive, which included books from the 18th, 19th and early 20th centuries. There are no longer any foreign books from the Aptekarsky Prikaz (Medical Department) library, a collection begun as early as the 17th century, no volumes from the library of the dukes of Courland, no personal libraries of the physician in ordinary Robert Areskin and the diplomat and translator Andrei Vinnius. Many books from the private library of the Radzwill family were destroyed, a collection amassed over two centuries and the biggest of its kind at the time.

But that is not all: the fire destroyed a quarter of the library's unique newspaper archive—many of these old newspapers are no longer to be found anywhere else.

But even that is not all: what wasn't destroyed by fire, was damaged by water and high humidity (the fire was extinguished by an antediluvian method: for 19 hours 25 fire engines pumped water into the building). The entire archive of reference publications was virtually destroyed by water; 150,000 storage units from the Baer Archive, the Slav Archive and the oriental languages archive of rare books were flooded — a total of 3,602,000 storage units were damaged by moisture and water. But even this does not complete the list. The 'fire' continues: now black mould and fungi are threatening to destroy whatever was saved from fire and water...

This appalling damage might well have been even worse but for the help of enthusiasts. Unfortunately, the library's administrative director Filov and his deputy Leonov were not revealed in their best light in that crisis situation: they deceived Party bodies, local authorities and the mass media by deliberately minimizing the real extent of the disaster and giving public promises that the library would be open for work in just a few days. It was probably the desire 'to keep their word' that explains the incredible fact that an order was given to clear the yard where books have been heaped during the fire with a bulldozer. Thanks to volunteers the vehicle was stopped and about 60 rare books about to be pulverized were thus saved. Is it any wonder that after the fire the most contradictory rumours circulated in Leningrad, including one (so convenient in that it excuses so much!) that the fire had been started by enemies whose aim was to destroy our national culture.

The disaster could have been prevented. The hazardous state of the USSR Academy of Sciences Library has been known for some time. As early as 1986 Academician I. V. Petryanov-Sokolov and I wrote an article in *Sovetskaya kultura* warning of the likelihood of a fire, but we were written off as scaremongers. The public also warned about other likely accidents. But... How long shall we continue to multiply our losses? The library of Leningrad University's History Faculty has burned down; the department of rare books at the Krupskaya Library of the Institute of Culture has been reduced to ashes in a fire lasting for more than 24 hours; the Plekhanov Archive has been flooded; hundreds of thousands of books have been irretrievably lost at the Rostov Regional Scientific Library; things have gone from bad to worse at the Lenin State Public Library; the library of the Gorky Institute of World Literature has been closed for 15 years. Meanwhile disaster hovers over the Institute of Russian Literature of the USSR Academy of Sciences — the famous Pushkin House — where all of Pushkin's manuscripts are kept, as well as most of the manuscripts of Lermontov, Dostoyevsky, Saltykov-Shchedrin and Blok — in short, 500,000 volumes are on the verge of destruction. Little wonder: the building has had no drastic repair work done since it was built in 1832. Experts have assessed the state of ceiling supports, external and internal engineering networks as hazardous; in 1986 and 1987 alone the hot water pipes burst more than 40 times — Pushkin's manuscripts survived by a miracle, but the unique archive of phonograms suffered. It has been estimated that in the event of a fire it would take a mere 19 minutes for Pushkin House to burn down. If this is the state of one of the centres of our literary culture, what can be said about the hundreds and thousands of libraries right across the country?

It grieves me to think that our country was once considered the European treasure-house of books — now specialists on Russian books go to Helsinki. It grieves me to say that Academician A. A. Shakhmatov, director of the USSR Academy of Sciences Library, died in 1920, while bringing by sleigh a private collection bequeathed to the library. It grieves me to recall how books were preserved during the Leningrad blockade. Now, in these peaceful and happy times, books are being destroyed... Incredible!

This incident, of course, hasn't been passed over in silence. In the past, too, articles were published, followed by official replies with promises to put things right, threats to punish the culprits and pledges to earmark finances. And in those same cities where libraries were destroyed and book depositories flooded, before those promises were honoured there grew up splendid district Party committee and regional Soviet's executive committee buildings in whose fine offices those who had signed these official replies discussed problems of leisure, deliberated on the declining interest in books and the crisis of moral integrity. This 'upside-down' *glasnost* is worse than silence because it creates the illusion that things are being done and makes people believe the train is picking up speed when in fact it is standing stockstill.

All this is not just a question of individual negligence: it is a consequence of underestimating the role of culture in our country's life and of literary and humanitarian tradition as part and parcel of that culture. Without such a culture society cannot develop, for the abscnse of humanitarian culture also influences adversely material culture and production — they begin to malfunction. Chernobyl is a case in point.

The situation demands serious measures. When Florence was flooded experts from the Hermitage helped Italian museum experts. Now we need UNESCO's aid — aid which would enable us to invite, for instance, Polish book restorers, the recognized masters in this field, and to receive special equipment indispensable for the restoration and normal functioning of libraries, including the USSR Academy of Sciences Library. There is nothing to be ashamed of in this aid — from time immemorial specialists of different countries have pooled resources — especially when it was a question of world cultural values. What is disgraceful and criminal is that books and manuscripts, which ought to survive for centuries, should be burnt and flooded.

Moscow News, 27 March 1988

In an interview with NBC Mikhail Gorbachev formulated the Soviet Union's position on the Afghanistan question as following: '...The situation requires a solution. We are looking for ways to bring about an honest and prompt one.' The outcome of our efforts depends on whether or not a will exists to resolve the issue by political means. Analysts estimate that the withdrawal of Soviet troops could be effected in a few months' time.

The inhumanity of war is obvious. We see the faces of young Soviet soldiers who, performing their internationalist duty, have fought in Afghanistan, and try to understand what marks them apart from other young men of their age. The newspaper Komsomolskaya Pravda *has written about their heightened sense of social justice.* Pravda *relates how torn they are at the sight of human callousness...*

What follows is a story about some of these former soldiers who deserve a little more care and attention from society.

WHAT SOCIETY OWES
THE AFGHANISTAN VETERANS

By VICTOR TURSHATOV

When they first arrive, they assemble in a big room to hear the following honest and straightforward address: 'You have fulfilled your duty and have sustained serious wounds. Many of you have lost arms or legs. Life is going to be very difficult, but you must summon up your courage, accept the terrible truth and remember that you are citizens of this country and makers of your own destiny.'

These are the words that young men aged 19 or 20 who have been through Afghanistan hear at the Saki military rehabilitation sanatorium in the Crimea.

They arrive here in Saki having already undergone several operations in military hospitals. They are sore from countless injections, and sick and tired of treatment. Doctors know the seriously wounded need to relax from time to time, and send them off for a month to breathe the salubrious steppe air and take the famous mud baths which have helped so many people before them. After the sanatorium, they usually return to the hospital for further treatment.

The rehabilitation centre in Saki opened in the early 1980s when few people thought our presence in Afghanistan would last. The sanatorium therefore was built on a small scale. But soldiers with back wounds, fractured bones, multiple operations and amputations continued to arrive, and another wing had to be added.

From a purely medical point of view the conditions here are ideal.

It has the latest in laser therapy equipment, muscle electrostimulators, and training apparatus the like of which can only be found at the Cosmonaut Training Centre. The rooms are clean and comfortable, complete with colour TV, video and game machines. But what about the young men themselves?

We have seen them many times on television, clad in khaki running into battle from the right, from the left, from the air. In the newspapers we have read about the wounded being decorated and returning to active service after hospital treatment. But those were stories about men 'fit for frontline service'. What about those who lost their good health in Afghanistan, received the appropriate medals but are now invalids? How much do we know about them?

In Saki people have long since got used to them. At the market a seller will sometimes give one a bunch of grapes or some apples, saying: 'Forget the money, lad, help yourself.' Shoppers standing tiredly in a queue, already fed up and ready to explode at the slightest pretext, will make way for them without a word.

Young radiant faces and ... a wheelchair or crutches. Any normal human being feels guilty at the sight of such a heart-rending, incongruous combination. It is hard to put my own feeling into words. I can only say that after an hour at the sanatorium the photographer put his camera back in his bag, sat down, covered his face with his hands and said: 'That's it. I can't take any more pictures.'

Their service cards show various military specialities: sappers, infantrymen and drivers. But the most popular item on sale at the local army supply shop is the commando vest. All of them want this 'symbol of valour and strength', as the papers call it. The war is over for them. Why do they need this 'symbol'? Perhaps it's a game only the veterans know how to play?

The most popular items at the nearby grocery shop are chocolates and condensed milk. Sweet-toothed like children, not quite the heroes one expects.

But not all are like that. My interview with Igor Ovsyannikov, commando platoon leader and bearer of the Order of the Red Star, began with small talk, then turned to the war. 'Igor, you closely follow all the latest reports from Afghanistan. How do you assess the latest events there, the policy of national reconciliation?'

'To be honest, I don't know. They show dushmans on TV laying down arms, but the number of seriously wounded isn't decreasing. I'm going to have to change profession. I want to become a historian. By studying this war, I hope to understand it better.'

Yes, he can think for himself and is confident about the future. I'm only sorry to have to write about this handsome big-hearted Russian in such a telegraphic style. The strongest impression of our first interview, however, was of the

bleeding stumps I saw as he removed his artificial legs after
a trial walk, and the artificial legs themselves which have
nothing in common with the words 'humanity' or 'high technology'.

'When I look at the sophisticated artificial limbs in foreign medical journals, I wonder why our boys have to put up
with worse? There's no comparing the present times to the
1940s. The number of invalids is far lower, and the country
is much richer now. But are we more merciful?' said Captain Mikhail Babich, acting chief of the rehabilitation centre.

In the second half of the 1940s a wave of war invalids
swept across the country, swearing in public places, begging
for alms at railway stations and fighting to death among
themselves, their war medals jingling. We were poorer then,
and could not help them much, so we simply removed them
and their home-made carts from sight. Have they forgiven
us for that? Will the new wave forgive our formal condolen-
ces and aid going hand in hand with antiquated crutches,
wheelchairs and artificial limbs?

It must be difficult to learn to ignore long and shamelessly curious glances, especially when you are 20, but they
are learning to do so. They go to dances at the neighbouring
sanatorium, standing in a circle, all by themselves, crutches
in one hand, and trying to dance to the loud, rhythmic music.

They crave a normal human life with all its temptations
and disappointments. The people of Saki still remember an
incident triggered off by a slightly drunk local lad calling
out 'Hey, cripple!' to an invalid. Not maliciously, but as
a statement of fact. The man he addressed, turned round,
hobbled over to the offender and dealt him a fatal blow
with his crutch. A casual word cost the lad his life.

'Many of our patients suffer from shattered nerves in addition to serious physical afflictions. They need more than
good medical treatment. They need extra attention, support
and love from the people around them. But unfortunately,
most of these are indifferent. What's worse, some encourage the lads to drink,' said Lieutenant-Colonel Gennady
Dorofeyev, Deputy Chief for Political Education.

What about letters? Tender letters from girl friends, caring letters from parents, and cheerful letters from friends

have always warmed soldiers' hearts. Alas, the sanatorium is a 'dead zone' in this respect. Former girl friends have long since married: life does not stand still while soldiers are fighting and recovering from wounds. Parents are often told not to write because the Crimean holiday is only a month long. Of course, there are more expedient forms of communication, so many of the young men get telegraphed money orders. As for friends... Mostly, it's only former patients who ever write to Saki.

Andrei Zaitsev served six months with the commandos, lost a leg, and spent 18 months in hospitals. He said: 'The other day I got a letter from a fellow patient who's disabled and confined to a wheelchair. He had to go from his village up to town to the commission which awards disability pensions. The first time he went the necessary doctors were absent. The second time the same thing again. He said there is no way he'd go again but how can he survive without a pension, and no legs?

'Only a short time ago the Minister of Defence issued an order prescribing all formalities to be completed at the hospital. I have seen the order, but have not had the time to collect all the necessary papers. Without a leg, I'm not very good at running bureaucratic races, but compared to that other fellow, I'm lucky!'

There are other disquieting reports from disabled veterans. Some write that local recruiting offices often offer them the inferior 30 hp model Zaporozhets (automobile) instead of the 40 hp. Artificial limbs, however imperfect, are hard to obtain. So are jobs. The most cautious estimates show that it is hard to subsist, even the first few months, on a disability pension.

On the way back from the sanatorium I popped into the local Komsomol committee. The secretary, a nice young man who didn't strike me as the type to mouth formalities, told me about a recent get-together of local ex-internationalists. That summer they had met for the first time to set up a council and a march. 'The council helps young veterans to get flats, buy cars, and basically settle down.'

'Do they visit the wounded?'

'They are planning to. So far they have organised fruit parcels to be sent to the sanatorium from nearby farms.'

Marches, flats, cars, fruit... What's the matter with us? Fellow soldiers seem to be paying their comrades off with melons and grapes...

November saw an all-Union meeting of young reservists in Ashkhabad. Most of the delegates had fought in Afghanistan. The programme included shooting practice, military vehicle-driving competitions, and discussions. One issue discussed was that of disabled veterans. Unfortunately, the final document did not contain a single clause about assistance to those who need our help most.

Moscow News, 13 December 1987

Social Conditions and Living Standards

The PACE of advance

We would like to open our discussion about social conditions and a rise in living standards with what would seem to be just an ordinary letter*:

'The "human factor" consists of such people as myself, those who have believed wholeheartedly in the inviolate principle "to each according to his work". I am 47 years old and my son is 18. I passed my high school exams and could have gone on to university, but at that time, there was a campaign for high school graduates to go to work in production. The district committee of the Komsomol was supporting the idea, so we went to the factories. I spent three years on the production line and my photograph was posted on the factory bulletin board as a front-rank worker. The district Komsomol Committee decided that I, one of the top workers, should work with young people. In short, a school in a remote village which has no Pioneer leader. Well, if they need me — I must go. And so I went. After a while, the teachers there were convinced that I was a "born educator". You must go to a teacher's training college and come back to teach at our school. So I entered a college to study for what was supposed to be a five-year course. But after only four years we were called to take our state exams earlier in order to be able to take up duties in Magadan region where there was a dire shortage of teachers. I taught the local children to the best of my abilities. Dogs, reindeer, helicopters, camps of nomads and temperatures of $-50°C$. But if they need me, I must stay.

'And so it has been all my life. Teachers were needed to work till midnight at the agricultural training school, a job

*   *Kommunist*, No. 3, 1987.

nobody wanted. I did it. Somebody was needed in a far away school where once every ten days or so a ship, or in good weather a plane, delivered supplies. I went there. I never looked for the "cushy" jobs, I always went wherever the Komsomol, and later the Party, sent me. Even my present job was suggested to me by the district Party committee. Throughout my life I have gone where I was needed and firmly believed I got my due reward. Now, at the age of almost fifty — a tragic revelation. My son gave me his opinion. He has always been a reserved person, but when he learned that it was still not clear how long we would have to continue tripping over each other in our 12-meter room, and that we would soon be taking in grandma as well (in the last distribution of better accommodation I was left out yet again) he could not restrain himself any longer: "Mum, you're gone about your life all the wrong way. People like you are active in community affairs and others get the apartments and other advantages. Not you, the 'principled' people. Your life has taught me a lesson. I'm not going to be like you..." And how will he live his life? By deceiving others, looking for the "cushy" jobs or washing his hands of any responsibility?'

One of the most negative features of the period of stagnation was the glaring gap between words and deeds, between the slogan 'everything for the sake of man, for the benefit of man' and true concern for each individual.

To change a person's consciousness, to create a new way of thinking, and a new attitude to work and society, to create conditions under which everyone's potential can be developed to the fullest, and to reward people according to their true contribution to society is today a very difficult task.

One cannot say that we have made impressive gains in this aspect of perestroika. *On the contrary, the Party and the state leaders, as well as the media, are reminding us constantly that the period between 1988 and 1990 will be the most crucial and the most difficult yet.*

It is sometimes said that there is no political opposition to perestroika, *yet we know that there are many factors which impede its implementation. What is worse is that we lack objective criteria by which to judge an individual persons' contribution. We cannot explain why a graduate engineer earns less than an ordinary worker, or why the head of a laboratory earns less than his subordinates.*

The causes behind such anomalies are varied and not easy to fathom. A lot is due to whole sectors getting priority whilst others, what involve equal effort, lag behind. Whether we intended it or not, earnings in our country have taken on a 'class' nature. Many departments that are in no way connected with material production provide their personnel with special benefits and privileges. At the same time, many other people believe that the labour of those engaged in material production must necessarily be better rewarded than the labour of those who work in other fields (health, education, etc.)

It is understandable that such a disparate system cannot be rectified overnight. The problem is complex, many-sided and requires thorough analysis. It calls for a reform which takes into consideration the entire system of pay and social benefits, it must also revise the system of wholesale and retail pricing of consumer goods and services.

The question of prices will be a topic for particular discussion. One comment made by an Izvestia *reader on Mikhail Corbachev's speech in Murmansk — 'with all due respect, we are being led to believe, of all things, that price increases will improve our standard of living' — is a good indication of how people feel. Below, we offer two more opinions on pricing.*

WHY IS A PRICE REFORM NECESSARY?

By VLADIMIR PAVLOV, Dr. Sc. (Econ.),
Chairman of the USSR State Committee for Prices

Each one of us is a consumer. Therefore, prices naturally concern everyone, including those of us who work for the USSR State Committee for Prices.

Why has the issue of price reform arisen? It must be remembered that the basis of our pricing policy was laid down in a period when there were large reserves of natural resources and a constant supply of labour. In the last thirty years major changes have taken place in our economy. The method of setting wholesale and retail prices created under those conditions and maintained for many years without any change has become totally unrealistic.

Let us turn back to an even earlier period. From 1928 to

1940 the level of retail prices of basic goods provided by the state and the cooperatives increased 6.2 times. This applied both to foodstuffs and to manufactured goods. For example, the price of meat products increased 5.7 times; butter, 6 times; fish, 3.8; shoes and clothes material, 2.2 times. Earnings were increased in order to keep to pace with the rising prices and a balance was maintained.

In December 1947 there was a reform of retail prices. In comparison with 1940 prices rose on average threefold (food products, 3.6 times, manufactured goods, 2.2 times).

What happened to earnings? Factory and office workers' wages increased by only 45 per cent over these years — from 33 roubles per month in 1940 to 48 roubles per month in 1946. Collective farmers' earnings were considerably less. In spite of this, the population provided 26 billion roubles of state loan for reconstruction. Young people today have probably never heard of this. Older people will remember that most of the population lived in very poor circumstances. I am bringing all this up in order to point out that the so-called 'golden age' to which letters in the newspapers often refer, pointing out annual reductions in prices during that period, was far from 'golden' It would be true to say that in the early 1950s many stores in Moscow, Leningrad and other cities had caviar and similar delicacies, but people could not afford to buy them. The apparent abundance on the shelves was due to the consumer's low purchasing power. Annual meat consumption per person stood at 26 kilograms in 1950 (today it is more than 62 kilograms). Consumption of milk and other dairy products was 172 kilograms per person (today it is 333 kilograms).

So what about price reductions? It must be remembered that this was only after a sharp, threefold, increase in prices, and that it occurred at the expense of a virtual wage freeze. Earnings did rise, of course, but much more slowly than labour productivity. In the period between 1950 and 1955 labour productivity increased by 48 per cent in industry, by 49 per cent in construction and by 39 per cent in transport. Earnings, however, increased by only 12 per cent. How did this come about? By the very simple fact that production quotas were being continually put up from above, while remuneration rates remained the same or even decreased.

Finally, there is yet another very important factor which

had a bearing on price reduction in those years: the standard of living in the rural areas dropped considerably. To be frank, collective farmers at that time earned very little. In the early 1950s 16.4 roubles per month compared with 64 for factory and office workers. Take into consideration that at least half of the population at that time lived in the countryside...

Wheat was purchased from collective farmers at one kopeck per kilogram, while the retail price of flour was 31 kopecks. Rye was bought for 0.6 kopecks per kilo, while rye flour sold for 25 kopecks. Beef was obtained at collective farms for 23 kopecks per kilo and sold at an average price of 1 rouble 50 kopecks; milk, respectively, for 2.8 kopecks a litre — with the retail price at 22 kopecks. Purchase prices brought a totally inadequate income to the farming population. So, first a vast increase of prices, then a freeze in wages, and the purchase of food products from the countryside for next to nothing made it possible to carry out a small annual reduction in consumer goods prices. But one could hardly call this system efficient or just. Can we possibly carry on in this way? I think the answer is obvious.

Such a system did not hold out for long even at that time. There was a veritable exodus from the countryside and labour productivity there was low. In 1956 the danger of a food crisis seemed imminent. The country's agriculture had to expand, leading to the conquest of the virgin lands. This became a dire necessity. Industry also expanded without regard to efficiency, involving an ever greater workforce made up mainly of those who had come from the countryside. When these possibilities were exhausted, what then? There was no 'second source' of virgin lands in the country. It became clear that the economic mechanism was not operating efficiently. Economic reforms were called for and as a first step purchase prices were raised.

We gradually 'ate away' the difference in prices (remember that wheat was bought at 1 kopeck per kilo and flour sold at 31 kopecks) that had been artificially created after the war.

Towards 1962, reserves were again used up and it was necessary to raise both the purchase price and the retail price of meat and milk by 30 per cent. It should be noted that the production of foodstuffs did run at a loss at that time.

A balance was being maintained but it was clear that this could not last for ever.

In 1965 state subsidies of food products were introduced for the first time. The balance was tipped the other way and purchase prices exceeded retail prices. With each year the value of subsidies continually rose.

In the early 1970s the Soviet Union became an oil exporter. The Samatlor deposit was tapped and with the current high prices of oil, further subsidies were an easy matter. But everything comes to an end.

Efforts to intensify farming — supplying machinery, fertilizers and improving the living conditions — provided for a certain growth in the food supply. Yet it had its paradox: higher yields meant more subsidies were required. Now it became inevitable to raise the prices of certain consumer goods, particularly non-essential items such as gold, crystal, carpets and cars. The difference between wholesale and retail prices (turnover taxes) went into the state coffers. In the late 70s and early 80s 30 per cent of all revenue was used for subsidies; 70 per cent was spent on pensions, public health, education, construction of state housing, child-care centres, etc.

Today as much as 50 per cent of the state revenue from turnover taxes is spent on subsidizing food. This amounts to 57 billion roubles, a very large sum indeed. Now state revenue is cut further by the reduction of the sale of alcoholic beverages. So where can additional revenue come from? From lowering pensions? From cutting down on housing construction? From retraining doctors and teachers to be workers or engineers? The situation requires drastic remedies.

It is true there is still one other possibility — the printing of money, that is, the issue of additional paper bills. However, this is no real solution. It would inevitably lead to the weakening of the economy. Issuing additional paper is the worst form of lending money to the state. It is a process that places the greatest strain on the shoulders of those who have the least. It is no secret that for a number of years there has been a discrepancy between the amount of money held by the population and the availability of goods and services. One of the reasons for this is that during the period of stagnation the growth of earnings was greater than the growth of labour productivity, and the production of consumer goods failed to meet demand.

Where do matters stand today? Every increase of one per cent in agricultural production demands additional subsidies of hundreds of millions of roubles. And there is nowhere to get them from. Therefore, 'to leave everything as it has been' is impossible. After all, we are all interested in an increase in the production of foodstuffs.

Agriculture can become more efficient. No one disputes this. But there would need to be a change in personnel, technology, fertilisation techniques, etc. And this takes time.

So we are still confronted with the problem of prices. If it is not resolved we cannot move forward. Today, almost all foodstuffs are produced at a loss — rye bread, potatoes, meat, milk, cheese, sour cream, sausage, carrots, beets, fish, buckwheat, millet. Current retail prices of food products are on average priced at half the production cost.

This causes enormous disproportions in the national economy. The need to procure more funds would cause further hardship to the population. Wholesale, purchase and retail prices are lumped together without any real relation to the production costs. Under these conditions prices have ceased to serve as a socially useful indicator of labour and productions costs. Undervaluation of goods and of labour hampers the introduction of new technology, automation and mechanisation.

Moreover, the system of profit-and-loss accounting cannot function properly because subsidies require the appropriation of funds from well-run enterprises. We would be forced to set high quotas to well-run enterprises. There is hardly any justice in that.

There are many discrepancies in prices, especially those of beef, poultry, whole milk, cheese, sour-milk products, rice and other types of grain, domestic and imported clothing, footwear, children's clothes, synthetic and natural material and knitted fabrics. The current system of retail prices is full of contradictions and often in breach of social justice. Such a system has no future.

A reform of retail prices and the development of a corresponding compensatory mechanism is an extremely complex task; it has economic and political significance. Certainly it is impossible to look at the reform of retail prices as a means of filling state coffers at the expense of working people's standard of living. We must create conditions and incentives to develop a new efficiency of production which would lead to an increase in real incomes. A wide-ranging discussion is being encouraged by the Party and the government. It must be ensured that the reforms accord with the idea of social justice.

Virtually all sectors of the price setting mechanism are in need of substantial restructuring. At the June 1987 Plenum of the CPSU Central Committee Mikhail Gorbachev noted that 'we need not to partially improve the system of pricing, but to radically reform pricing with an interconnected restructuring of our entire price system — wholesale, purchase and retail prices, and tariffs.'

In its scale, depth and economic importance, this task has no precedents. For the first time in the whole history of building our socialist economy it is necessary to create a virtually new system of pricing. This system must meet many, often opposing, demands.

The reform must be carried out in a short span of time. We need to enter the 13th five-year plan period with the new system of prices and tariffs in all sectors of our economy. Wholesale prices in industry and transport rates should be set in time to be able to take effect from 1 January 1990. New purchase prices and construction rates are planned to take effect from 1 January 1991. It would be expedient to carry out a reform of retail prices and their coordination with the incomes of the population by the beginning of the next five-year plan period.

Radical reform of pricing policy is the most important economic and political measure of the new economic mechanism. When and how it is carried out will determine the effectiveness of the new mechanism and the speed with which profit-and-loss accounting and self-financing can be introduced. We are aware that prices directly influence working people's standard of living, but they also influence the monetary incomes of enterprises operating on a cost accounting basis.

Trud, 22 November 1987

Izvestia *of October 10, 1987 published the statistical data of the average earnings and total incomes of Soviet people, based on a study of the income of 62,000 families.*

Average monthly earnings of a factory or office worker—200.5 roubles.

Average monthly income of a factory or office worker, including social benefits—279 roubles;

Average family monthly income, including social benefits—500 roubles.

Until recently this kind of statistic information would have been taken on trust, without any kind of discussion. Today, these figures raised an uproar of indignation. 'These figures are not statistics, they're fantasy! My relatives working in Moscow receive between 130 and 160 roubles (and they have good education!). Their situation is not how to buy a car but how to afford even the most modest daily items. The State Statistics Committee should give the press more truthful information about the material circumstances of the working people,' wrote Muscovite L. Korzenkov. 'As I read the article "Family Budget" I had to laugh,' writes E. Draga from Kishinev. 'But then it struck me it was laughter with tears. Why print such nonsense? In order to justify an impending price reform?' 'Once again—exaggerated reports and percentage nonsense,' writes V. Semyonov indignantly. 'What is this—have we gone back to former times? Or could it be that perestroika *has not reached* Izvestia?'

Yuri Rytov returned to these letters in Izvestia *of 18 December 1987. The objections fell into five categories:*

Objection No. 1. *In such a delicate matter as the calculation of family income, it is impossible to lump together the earnings of high- and low-income families, they are simply not comparable. Naturally, in the Soviet Union there are families whose earnings total 800 or more roubles a month; but we also have quite a few families whose monthly income does not top 200 roubles. The average figure—500 roubles—in this case can in no way reflect the real situation. A. Grigoriev, V. Shpeyer and I. Zargarian summed it up as follows: 'Averaging incomes and expenses of families tell us as much of their true standard of living as would an average body temperatures in a hospital about the condition of each patient.'*

Objection No. 2. *Family income should not include social benefits since the figures published lump together pensions, grants, benefits, education grants and medical care. Any one person receives only some of the whole list. Furthermore, payments of benefits are just as unevenly distributed as earnings. 'The very idea of including in the family income the means used for maintaining schools, child-care centres and hospitals,' angrily writes L. Polyakovskaya from Irkutsk. 'In my opinion, earnings mean what I have in my hand, my take-home pay, and the money I leave at the check-out counters in the stores. That, and only that, is what determines my budget.'*

Objection No. 3. *In estimating the income side of the family budget, the USSR State Committee for Statistics includes alimonies, contributions from relatives, and payments for work received from individual citizens. If contributions from relatives are included in the budget, E. Petrova from Kherson Region reasonably notes, then the same sum should be subtracted from the relatives' budget. And indeed, even among the relatively small circle of families studied — 62,000 — it is difficult to determine whether alimonies, contributions from relatives, etc. fall under the 'plus' side of their budget or whether, in the end, they balance each other out.*

Objection No. 4. *concerns mistakes made in determining the expenses side of the budget. According to the statistics, it appears that the share of the family budget spent on food constitutes 28,3 per cent. I. Petrakov from Moscow remarks: 'No doubt the cost of food was arrived at according to prices in state-run stores. But this is very far from the real situation. The population is compelled to shop at cooperative stores and at the markets. And there, prices are a completely different story!' Incidentally, even if this were so, pensioner G. Gorlova from Lutsk disagrees with the calculations. Having compared the 28.3 per cent with her pension, she reached the caustic conclusion that such an amount wouldn't be enough to feed anyone ... except perhaps a cat!*

Objection No. 5 *boils down to the fact that in averaging the figures people with extremely modest earnings are 'out in the cold'. I. Mamedov from Baku writes: 'You proudly announce that 65 per cent of the population have a monthly income of more than 100 roubles per family member. This also means that 35 per cent receive less than 100 roubles per family member! Why do you say nothing about how these people live?'*

It appears that the statistical data provided by the State Committee for Statistics did not find much support among the population. The question arises: does it mean that it is impossible to gain information on the actual standard of living of Soviet people without revising the whole system of what actually constitutes an income and what goes into the 'consumer's basket' as expenditure? Today, in spite of all the shortcomings of the current methods of collecting statistical data we are able to give our readers a sufficiently objective view of the Soviet people's standard of living.

WHO DICTATES PRICES?

By Prof. R. KHASBULATOV, Dr. Sc. (Econ.)

I would like to point out straightaway that I firmly oppose the view that people today 'have more money than they know what to do with'. I am absolutely convinced that the majority of people who have savings in the bank earned this money through hard work, by their talents offered in service to the state. After all, it is well known that less than one half of Soviet families have a savings account. Forty per cent of the families have an income of less than 100 roubles per family member. And in many cases savings accounts are small, holding a maximum of 100 roubles. It is also a known fact that thieves, embezzlers and bribe-takers are not overly fond of keeping their money in the bank.

However, more and more often, under the mistaken assumption that the entire population has a surplus of money, the tendency for price increases is stubbornly justified and foisted upon society as the 'law of rising prices', a 'law' which suddenly appeared in the 70s.

The economy suffers from disruption and society's standard of living stagnates. Psychologically, price increases produce insecurity in people.

People look at things simply. Why, they ask, should prices of our goods — both means of production and consumer goods — be higher than those on the world market? Our adversaries answer unanimously: your economic system is ineffective. We are entirely convinced that this is not so. We believe that the State Committee for Prices, together with the appropriate specialists, must ensure that our prices are no higher than those of the world market.

The main indicator for setting prices should be the socially necessary expenditure of labour. Conditions are being created in which enterprises can operate with high efficiency, without manipulation of prices, producing high quality product, matching world standards.

What is the situation today? Let's take an example of blue jeans. To buy them abroad for 20 dollars a pair and sell them to the population at 100 roubles can hardly be called normal. No matter how great the commercial profit of such operations, one cannot overlook the moral damage; after all, the main buyers here are young people. And that's not all. Why must Soviet-made jeans sell for 50-60 roubles when they justify a price of 15 to 20 roubles? Low-priced items are fewer and fewer and no ceiling has been placed on the prices of popular items, including those which are not in short supply.

Now let's look at cars. Maintaining a high price on cars is justified by the high demand. Is it acceptable that high prices are justified where there is greater demand than supply? We think not.

At worst it would have to be admitted that there are 'two economies' operating in our country: for the consumers — a market economy based on the principle of 'supply and demand'; for the producer — a planned economy.

Furthermore, basing prices on shortages is untenable. Karl Marx wrote: 'Whatever the manner in which the prices of various commodities are first mutually fixed or regulated, their movements are always governed by the law of value. If the labour-time required for their production happens to shrink, prices fall; if it increases, prices rise, provided other conditions remain the same' (Karl Marx, *Capital*, Vol. III, Progress Publishers, Moscow, 1986, p. 177). As we see, the major factor in price changes is labour productivity, the saving of time.

Now let's take a look at different groups of buyers. For example, car buyers. One group are those who deny themselves many other things like buying new furniture, stylish clothes or nutrient foods, economise on everything and start a savings account, into which each month for many years they deposit a portion of their modest earnings. Then there is a second group. Those who are not concerned with prices; they have the means to buy things if only the item can be found. Moreover, the higher the price, the more 'prestigious' the item. It would make sense, of course, to analyze which group is predominant among those buying cars and other expensive durables. However, that's another subject.

Let us return to the question of demand. Why is it that whenever talk turns to the incredibly high prices of certain goods, they are explained by high demand? Take, for example, refrigerators for which there is no demand. Where, in this case, is the connection between price and demand, why has this dependence suddenly disappeared? Every day we see hundreds of items which remain unsold for years. This is because people are responding to the disparity between their prices and their usefulness. There can be no talk of demand, it serves only as a convenient cover for continuing in the old way; it leads the economy into a dead end and prevents restructuring.

In my opinion these arguments are offered only as an excuse because it is impossible to explain the confusion over prices in terms of economic laws. Throughout the 60s and 70s there was no unified policy within the State Committee for Prices. By trying to uphold what is virtually a supply and demand mechanism, the Committee is at the same time demanding the continuation of dictating prices. Because it is unwilling to work out an economically sound method of pricing it is in no hurry to change. The economically sound basis includes high labour productivity.

Let us turn to the low price of food. Low in comparison with what country? The US? Great Britain? West Germany? Sweden? It is true that our prices are somewhat lower. But not by much, and certainly not by as much as the State Committee for Prices would have us believe.

In discussing the low price of food, those who like to make such comparisons seem to forget about the average pay in our country and in industrialized capitalist countries. Food expenses in the capitalist states family budget constitute 15-35 per cent. Now let's ask the readers of *Komsomolskaya Pravda* how much they spend on food. Much more, I think. The same could be said about books, children's clothing, toys, etc.

But if we continue on this subject we must bring in the low efficiency of agricultural production and the incredibly high purchase price of meat, the latter being the only way for farms to make a profit. Opinions supporting the view that prices of consumer goods are kept at a high level by a number of supposedly unprofitable sectors have also become outmoded. In an article in *Komsomolskaya Pravda* A. Komin of the State Committee for Prices, admitted that state subsidies for food are 50 billion roubles. It should be noted that ten years ago these subsidies amounted to 20 billion roubles.

What is going on? The efficiency of agricultural production is abysmal. If we follow the logic of Comrade Komin, the ever increasing size of state subsidies must be made up at your and my expense — by increased prices of goods in high demand.

As for state subsidies, ending them is long overdue. As world practices demonstrate, there is virtually no single sector today which cannot operate profitably. Conditions today are not what they were in the 20s and 30s, or in the period of postwar development. Only the old psychology remains, which we must rid ourselves of once and for all! This is exactly what the January 1987 Plenum of the CPSU Central Committee was stressing. There is evidence that agriculture, with active involvement with industry, can be efficient. Self-financing, new organisation of enterprises and production associations, the adoption of profit-and-loss accounting — all this creates an objective basis for profitable management of the economy, when it will no longer be necessary to 'extort' money from the population.

We are witnessing a time when democracy and *glasnost*, as the component parts of *perestroika*, are becoming the most decisive factors in increasing labour efficiency.

One of the key tasks is the selection, training and effective distribution of personnel. Responsible posts should be granted only to those who have earned them through experience, knowledge, dedication and honesty.

In the 70s we ignored man's perfectly normal ambition for material well-being, his desire to earn good pay for his labour, his desire for better material circumstances for his family. Somehow the idea was instilled in people that any one showing 'excessive' interest in the 'good things' of life was 'materialistic' and plagued with 'consumerism'.

However paradoxical, this propaganda was directed precisely against those people who were striving to create better material circumstances through their own labour, and encouraged those who established an 'underground economy' through which they channelled social funds for their own gains. This led to disillusion and skepticism, especially among young people. Many managers became cynical and engendered cynicism in their employees.

The new pricing mechanism should be based on three factors: labour productivity, balanced relation between cost price and selling price and comparison with the world market prices.

Komsomolskaya Pravda, 2 June 1987

STANDARD OF LIVING: CRITERIA AND PROBLEMS

Prof. NINA RIMASHEVSKAYA, Dr. Sc. (Econ.),
answers questions posed
by correspondent V. GOLOVACHEV

N. R.: If you ask a thousand people what 'standard of living' means to them, you'll get a thousand different answers. For one the criterion will be a car, for another — a dacha, for a third — food, for a fourth — housing and utilities, for a fifth — development of the services sector, for a sixth — all of the above combined, and so on. Is it possible to come up with some single indicator which would characterize the population's standard of living? In my opinion such an all-encompassing indicator is virtually impossible since the notion of 'standard of living', or more precisely 'well-being', embraces not only the growth of incomes and production of goods but also social, cultural and material demands as well. It includes all spheres: services, housing, education, medical care, cultural development, working conditions, moral values, and much more. In other words, the standard of living is a whole set of conditions.

V. G.: *You say that it is virtually impossible to make an exact measurement of the standard of living. But there are, after all, various approximate indicators. Which of these do you consider the most reliable?*

N. R.: The size of the per capita national income. This indicator is used by statisticians in all countries. But this is really a very approximate measure from many points of view. Firstly, how the national income is used is important, how much goes to consumption and how much to accumulation. Secondly, of considerable significance here is the price-setting system, the ratio between paid and unpaid services and goods, and so on. Another type of indicator, which in our opinion gives a more accurate picture of the standard of living, is the share of the consumption fund in the per capita national income. Is it clear what we're talking about? The consumption fund refers to what the population consumes bread, milk, carpets, cars, etc. If you divide this fund (in roubles) by the number of people in the country, you get the average sum per person. By looking at the annual increase in this sum one can estimate the increase in the standard of living. There is only one thing wrong with this. Such an indicator does not take into account the cost of many services. In health care, for example, it only takes into consideration expenditures for medication, equipment, hospital meals, and so on. While in fact a very substantial part of the cost of health care are the salaries of doctors and other personnel.

Therefore, I personally support the idea that in making calculations one should use the expanded consumption fund, which encompasses everything, including the full range of both material goods and services, such as medical services, education, child-care centres, tourism, etc.

V. G.: *It would be interesting to learn, with the help of this indicator, the dynamics of the standard of living in recent years.*

N. R.: We've calculated such data. First I'll give the absolute figures of expanded per capita consumption (in roubles) per month. In 1960 it was 46 roubles, in 1965—58 roub-

les. Continuing respectively for every next five-year period
it was 78, 99, 117, and 139 roubles (1985). And now let's
look at the growth of this indicator in terms of percentages.
In doing so, 1965 is compared to 1960, 1970 to 1965, and so
on. That is, the growth of expanded per capita consumption
is analyzed for each five-year period. And an interesting
fact is revealed: from 1960 to 1965, the growth rounded off
at 26 per cent. Continuing respectively, we end up with 34,
27, 18, and 19 per cent. That is to say, the rate at which the
standard of living grew slowed down noticeably in the years
characterised by stagnation in our society. In other words,
the standard of living did improve, but, shall we say, at
a slower pace. Overall, in the 70 years of Soviet power the
standard of living in our country has increased significantly.

V. G. *In one of your lectures you named yet another important indicator of the standard of living — the share of
foodstuffs in the structure of consumption.*

N. R. That's right. The lower the share of foodstuffs in relation to other goods in the overall structure of consumption, the higher the standard of living. This is explained by
the fact that once this most important need is efficiently satisfied, other needs become more significant and diverse.
This indicator is convenient in that it makes it possible, to
a certain extent, to compare the standard of living in different countries and 'rank' them accordingly. In the US, for
example, the share of foodstuffs in the structure of consumption is 22-23 per cent. In the Soviet Union in 1985 it
evened out at 39 per cent (without alcohol — about 26 per
cent).

Here, too, it is interesting to look at the dynamics. In
1960 the share of foodstuffs in the USSR was much greater — almost half of the overall volume of the structure of
consumption. In 1975 it was 44 per cent.

V. G. *Just the same, you believe that we are still noticeably
lagging behind certain developed countries in this sphere?*

N. R.: For the time being, yes. But everything depends on
how we go to work on the problem. After all, the standard
of living is not manna from heaven; it depends on the efficiency of our labour, on our ability to adopt effective methods of management. Let's compare, for example, labour
productivity in industry. In 1985 in our country it was 55

per cent of that in the United States. In agriculture the percentage was much lower. This has a significant effect on important components of the standard of living; I have in mind, above all, the goods and services. The fundamental restructuring of the economy will enable us to narrow this gap dramatically.

V. G. *What about the dynamics of labour productivity over the last few decades? In that period did the gap between our country and the US increase or diminish?*

N. R. It diminished. At first, rather quickly: in 1950, labour productivity in our country was less than 30 per cent of that in the US, by 1960 this figure had already reached 44 per cent, and in 1970 — almost 53 per cent. But then, in the years of stagnation, this indicator froze at 53 per cent.

In making this comparison, I would like to emphasize that indices which point out the still significant gap in labour productivity do not give a complete picture of the difference between the standard of living in the USSR and in the US. How national income is distributed among the population, as well as many other factors, also plays an important role here. Differentiation of incomes in our country and in the US has nothing in common. More than 30 million Americans live in poverty, while 0.008 per cent of the population has the combined wealth of half the residents of the US located in the lower part of the 'social pyramid'. This cannot be overlooked.

V. G. *You said that the share of foodstuffs in the structure of consumption enables us to a certain degree, albeit very approximately, to estimate the standard of living in different countries and 'rank' them accordingly. Which are the top three countries?*

N. R. Such a cut and dried categorisation cannot be made. However, according to statistical averages, it seems the first three would include Sweden, the US, and Switzerland.

V. G. *And with whom do we rank on this clearly conditional list?*

N. R. According to very rough estimates, behind England and France and on a level with Italy.

V. G. *In what sphere, would you say, do we lag most of all?*

N. R. In the service sector. Its share in the overall volume of consumption is extremely low — somewhere around 10 per cent in the last decade. Extremely low indeed. In a number of other countries this indicator is over 50 per cent. The tendency in the structure of consumption is changing in the direction of services — tourism, customer services, repair and maintenance, etc. As we mentioned earlier, the share of foodstuffs is diminishing and the share of services is growing.

V. G. *The standard of living is closely connected with price dynamics. Could you explain more about this dependency?*

N. R. Here again it is important to examine a complex of problems. Above all, we must analyze the increase in incomes, the amount of consumer benefits provided by social consumption funds, etc. Such an analysis shows that, all things considered, the standard of living in our country is steadily rising — sometimes faster, sometimes slower, but rising.

V. G. *But aren't prices changing too?*

N. R. Without a doubt. However, earnings and benefits received are increasing at a faster rate. Now let's look at why prices increase. First of all, the quality of products is improving. Therefore, it is only natural that prices should increase. Secondly, it sometimes happens that even when quality is not improved, prices still go up. This reflects failings in our price-setting system. The third factor is a shortage of goods. This leads to speculation, a 'black market', and so on. Finally, an increase in prices due to the decreasing availability of lower-priced goods. This can be blamed on the producers.

V. G. *In your opinion, what is the average annual rise in prices?*

N. R. If you take only the official price indices, the average increase is not very significant — less than half of one per cent a year. But what is really going on here? The official price of trousers, for example, has not gone up. However, you cannot find a cheap pair for sale anywhere. The factory has cut production of them. But there are expensive ones available. So, people buy the expensive ones — what else can they do! Thus, the average price of real purchases is growing.

Unfortunately, official statistics tell us nothing about the price dynamics of real purchases in relation to family budgets, the 'consumer's basket', etc. But, as you can see, if we take the dynamics of these prices they are growing faster.

V. G. *What is your view on the idea of price reform?*

N. R. That it is, beyond doubt, essential. But it must be carried out in such a way as to ensure that the average standard of living is not reduced. And this was declared, in no uncertain terms, both at the June 1987 Plenum of the CPSU Central Committee and in the speech given by Mikhail Gorbachev in Murmansk. How can this be accomplished? Various opinions will be expressed in the course of a broad, nationwide discussion. In my opinion, the simplest method would be to organise things in such a way as to stabilize the index of real purchases. We are not talking about establishing set prices, let's say on meat, at a maximum level — let there be both relatively cheap meat and comparatively expensive. The average price will grow, but in the process the cheap goods will still be available. This is one side of the issue. But in order to truly stabilize the index of real purchases, we must at the same time lower the prices of a number of essential items. Everything must be accounted for in order to ensure that the standard of living, especially among low-income families, pensioners and students, is not, of course, reduced.

Our studies have shown that for low-income families the average price of purchases, of meat and meat products for example, is higher than for high-income families. Here it is important where a person buys the meat. At factories, amalgamations and institutions a system of advance orders operates. But pensioners (they make up one-third of the low-income households) have no opportunity to place such orders and must often buy meat at cooperative stores or the market. Thus it turns out that the average price of such purchases is significantly higher for low-income families than it is for high-income families (income of 150 roubles or more per family member). The price reform should, in my opinion, do something to level out this social discrepancy as well.

V. G. *What influence do social consumption funds have on the standard of living?*

N. R. The amount of consumer benefits the population receives today from the social consumption funds makes up approximately 30 per cent of their total incomes. In the future this share will increase.

The social consumption funds perform two important socio-economic functions. One is the material support of those who are unable to work, in particular the elderly; the other is to ensure equal access for all sectors and groups of the population to health care, education, housing, child care, etc.

Without the social consumption funds it would be impossible to resolve effectively the above-mentioned issues. The disabled would become the dependents not of society as a whole but of the working people of particular families. In view of the existing differentiation of earnings and income, certain strata of relatively low-income families would not be able to meet many of life's basic needs.

A restructuring has begun in our country, radical changes being introduced in managing the national economy aimed at accelerating the country's socio-economic development. This makes it possible to substantially raise the people's standard of living.

I would like to emphasize once again that the raising of standard of living depends most directly on us, on the efficiency of our labour. In order to improve our lives we must work more productively, more diligently and at a level of higher quality, showing a special concern for economical utilisation of resources. In a word, we must each get involved and take a real interest in our work. This is the key to a further substantial increase in our standard of living.

Trud, 24 October 1987

The topic under discussion is the restructuring of the old bureaucratic mechanism for managing the economy. Recently various agricultural ministries with duplicate functions were closed and a new single organisation — the USSR State-Agro-Industrial Committee (Gosagroprom) — was created in their place. Staff reductions and even the complete elimination of ministerial bodies, is continuing.

For example, the RSFSR and all union and autonomous republics have ministries for community services. Mindful of the numerous complaints against the service industry, Soviet economists decided to examine the work of these ministries — not to see if their operation could be restructured and radi-

cally improved, but to ascertain if they were needed at all. After reviewing the problem from all sides the conclusion reached was that these ministries could be shut down without any detriment to community services.

In early 1988 a Scientific Council of the USSR Academy of Sciences held a conference to discuss the issue of 'The economic mechanism of the sphere of communal services at the modern stage of development'. Addressing his audience, the chairman of the conference began: 'There are ministers, deputy-ministers and officials of republican communal service ministries present in this auditorium. I want to tell you right now, comrades: we are proposing to close down those ministries...'

It isn't difficult to imagine the reaction in the auditorium to that opening nor to the further developments.

There was an interview with TATYANA KORYAGINA, D. Sc. (Econ), in Izvestia *on 28 January 1988, 'Why does a barber need a ministry?'.*

The bad situation with the republican ministries for communal services has become so evident today that it gives rise to another question: why were these ministries set up in the first place?

Other ministries, including the union ministries, present a more difficult problem: hundreds if not thousands of people work in each ministry. They do their jobs diligently, send out mountains of letters, telegrams, instructions, requests and other necessary and not so necessary papers. They demand the strict implementation of their orders, organise on-the-job verifications, and so on and so forth. The misfortune is that in the way ministries function today, not only does their 'bustling activity' not improve matters, it slows and halts them, even turning them back, since what we have is paper-pushing, i.e., bureaucratism in its pure form. Perestroika has made notable changes here. In the summer of 1987 the Ministry of Machine-Building for Heavy Industry and Ministry of Electric Power Production Machinery were abolished and replaced by a single Ministry of Heavy, Power Production and Transportation Machinery. The two ministries, which together provided 1702 jobs, were reduced to 1022 places. In other words, 680 persons became redundant, or, one out of every three employees. One of the two ministers retired, and the 14 deputies were pared down to 9. It was thought that *some of the people who were dismissed would transfer to the sphere of services where there is an acute shortage of qualified personnel. But not one employee of the two ministries sought a job in the service sphere; they all found work in other agencies.*

On 1 March 1988 the USSR Ministry of Machine-Building for Light and Food Industry and Household Applicances ceased to operate.

On the evening of 8 March 1988 Soviet radio and television announced that the Presidium of the Supreme Soviet of the USSR was streamlining two ministries and a state committee — the Ministry of Public Education of the USSR, the Ministry of Higher and Specialised Secondary Education, and the State Committee of the USSR for Vocational Training to create a single State Committee of the USSR for Public Education.

Reforms in the sphere of public education have been needed for some time. This topic has been discussed in hundreds of articles and interviews with those officials in the country responsible for national education. The question, 'On the course of perestroika *in secondary and higher schools and the Party's tasks for its implementation', was discussed on 17-18 February at the Plenary Meeting of the CPSU Central Committee.*

Most complaints were directed against the schools. It is no secret that many times, in the race to achieve quick results, innovations have been introduced to the detriment of long-range programmes. And society has paid dearly for this — suffice it to recall the difficulties with vocational training in recent years. What efforts were made to help adolescents, no matter how remote their homes, to discover their abilities? In the 1960s a group of distinguished Soviet scientists decided to seek out gifted schoolchildren and encourage their interest in the sciences. To this end, boarding schools were set up under the aegis of universities, as well as summer schools where children studied together with scientists, and educational Olympiads were held. Classes in mathematics, biology and chemistry were organised, and schools specialising in teaching foreign languages, physics and mathematics began to spring up everywhere. Later enthusiasm waned when these schools (especially the foreign language schools) began to enroll not so much gifted pupils as the children of influential parents. Gradually, many of these schools were closed down.

One of the few special schools set up in the sixties that remains is the Correspondence Physics and Mathematics School affiliated to Moscow State University. At present approximately 16,000 pupils from grades 8-10 study at this school, and there are 43 affiliates operating in conjunction with other universities around the country. IZRAIL GELFAND helped to found this school and is the permanent chairman of its scientific council. Academician Izrail Gelfand is a world renown mathematician. He is a member of the British Royal Society, the National Academy of Sciences of the USA, the French Academy of Sciences, the American Academy of Arts and Sciences, the Irish Academy of Sciences and has received honorary doctorates from the universities of Oxford, Paris, Harvard and others.

The following is an interview with IZRAIL GELFAND.

TALENT SHOULD NOT BE WASTED

Why are you so interested in schools, in the first-year students that attend your seminars?

Our pupils are our life. I learn as much from them as they do from me. Modern mathematics is in a state of flux with changes occurring practically every decade. Talented young students are able to switch over quickly to the new way of thinking and teach me. So age is no drawback if you continue to learn and relearn. Andrei Kolmogorov, the eminent mathematician, produced new concepts in the latter years of his life.

I think working together with talented young people provides a foundation for the development of science. Many of my students have gone into scientific world and are now continuing the work we began together 15-20 years ago, and are doing it much better than me. Meanwhile, I am studying new problems with new students.

I have seen students who look like secondary school pupils sitting alongside professors at your seminars. But they don't

*seem self-conscious when you ask them questions. Do you
teach them to be bold?*

I have fifteen new students in mathematics... I try to give
them specific examples which might lead to something really interesting. Someone might react in this way: first, I'll
really learn the concepts and then I'll start my work. In this
case he is doomed to do the same as everyone else.

*In a paper on the rules of the Moscow gymnasium, Lomo-
nosov wrote 'as soon as someone exhibits a special keenness
and aptitude for science, all means should be used to persuade
the parents of such children to have them educated in the
sciences'. What is the nature of this aptitude and when is it revealed?*

Mathematical aptitude develops most intensively between 17 and 20 years of age. But the inclination towards
math should be encouraged at about 14 or 15. In my opinion there is no need to start intensive training too early.
Sometimes a child will stop growing, perhaps because he is
being overworked. Up until the seventh grade I would prefer to teach pupils math games. And then, starting in the
7th or 8th grade, I would begin the real study. There are
certain particularities in the development of mathematical
aptitude that should not be ignored. Let me clarify this with
an example. A well-known ornithologist put some hatchlings in a cage enclosed with plexiglass: they could see
other birds of their species but they couldn't hear them. The
song of the 'parent' birds was taped and then cut to reflect
both proper and improper sequences of sounds. If the birds
listened to the natural order of the sounds, they quickly
learned the song and were not confused by its subsequent
alteration. If the improper sequence was played right from
the start, the birds took longer to learn it. Up to a certain
age, however, they could quickly learn the proper sequence
afterwards. Beyond that cut-off age, they were unable to
learn it. Comparisons are risky, of course. But man also has
abilities that should be developed at the appropriate time.
That is why scientists suggest that military service should be
postponed for mathematics students. It is also hardly likely
that working a few years before enrolling in an institute of
higher learning is beneficial. There is a vulnerable age when
mathematical talent is weak. It is in the interests of society
to listen to the advice of the experts. At a later age a tempo-

rary hiatus from science has no deleterious effect; mathematicians who returned from the front after the Second World War successfully continued their work.

The signs of talent are quickness to learn, inner inspiration, and a clear preference for a favourite subject. But talent can be seen only in classes that gradually become more profound and complex.

We are losing enormous potential due to drawbacks in education and the failure to encourage capable people. Only a country as rich in talent as ours is able to maintain an excellent school of math despite this wastefulness.

After our first sputnik was launched the Americans demanded that their schools place more emphasis on science and technology. In the 1970s funds for education were limited in the US, but in the early 1980s the question of reform to improve the quality of education was raised once again. It appears that this is a sign of the times.

Of course. Not long ago I read that taking into consideration the important role of math for the technological future of the nation (this was how it was stated), a three-year programme for restructuring and improving mathematical science and the teaching of math was being worked out up to the year 2000. The programme is to be financed by the governmental and private organisations. One of the measures mentioned is the search for talent.

Today it is very important to have a high level of thought and concentration of talent at the crux of science. The revolutionary discovery of superconductivity has opened up vast opportunities for technological progress. The power of computers surpasses our knowledge of how to use them. Of course, science will eventually uncover everything within the scope of human knowledge. But it is not a matter of indifference to humankind if this happens sooner or later.

A year and a half ago I spoke to an American scientist who had been asked to organise a new faculty in the Massachusetts Institute of Technology to study neurophysiological vision and motion and apply the research to develop qualitatively new robots. I asked the American scientist about his ideas for the educational programme, and he replied that he didn't really have any yet. He had spent six months looking for five talented people in America in order to begin the work. And how did Igor Kurchatov begin the atom project? He gathered together a group of the talented people he knew.

When you spoke at a session of the Academy of Sciences and compared mathematics with an iceberg — the tip of which is applied mathematics and the part under water, fundamental mathematics — you expressed concern that the underwater part, without which the iceberg would sink, was diminishing. You linked this with the breaking of traditions, which are easier to lose than revive. What traditions were you speaking of?

First of all, about scientific traditions. When gardeners are asked how they grow such wonderful grass, they say the answer is simple: mow it for three hundred years.

Why did such relatively small countries as Sweden and Holland have so many famous mathematicians whilst the development of mathematics in the USA remained low until some of the talented scientists of the European school moved there? At the root is mathematical tradition.

Applied mathematics has been moved ahead primarily by those scientists outside narrow specialities. And it is the tradition in our country to have a broad mathematics training programme for the young.

I think that if we make the right approach we can establish the best level of math development in the world without significant expenditures. How can we do this? I would say, by turning to normal human values. We have to a certain degree lost our love for capable schoolchildren. I can still remember the school study circles and education Olympiads held in the 1930s, when distinguished young mathematicians were actively involved with Moscow pupils. It appears that the idea of working with pupils has been rekindled, but it is by no means flourishing. And there has been a shift in values where other indicators have become more important than talent: seniority, scores, references. Academician Nikolai Bogolyubov and I went before the Moscow University authorities to speak in favour of a young man who had not been accepted in the mechanics and mathematics department even though he had made mathematical discoveries as a pupil in school. Unfortunately, his composi-

tion mark blocked his way. He did get into another institute, but not in Moscow. I still have hope that Moscow
University will develop an interest in him. Such naturally
gifted individuals are rare. Meanwhile, he comes to attend
my seminars, but I don't know how long he will continue to
do so. I could give many such examples. It's the same problem when we make recommendations for post-graduate
course: a candidate's social activities can sometimes out-
weigh his creative ability, which might even be weak.

*But it is said that talent always breaks through in the
end.*

The ability of talented people to break through is, in
my opinion, greatly exaggerated. Unfortunately there are
many people in science who are very energetic but not
terribly creative. Talented people find it more difficult
than others to adapt themselves to the bureaucratic
system. And since our educational system is still notably
bureaucratised, they are often considered unsuitable pupils, students and teachers. By encouraging talent, we equalise conditions for their advancement and the common
good.

*The various privileges given to those taking entrance exa-
minations in institutions of higher learning are an effort to
equalise the starting opportunities of young people. But how
many of those who entered institutions of higher learning
thanks to lower entrance requirements later dropped
out? The problem is to equalise the starting opportunities of
youth in a real, not a formal sense — in accordance with
knowledge, ability and industriousness. Our readers often
speak about this topic. Professor E. Kulkov of Leningrad writes:*
'Perestroika *in the schools should include the creation of
conditions more favourable to the development of talent. Today we need the skills of self-education. But the ideal school
in the year 2000 is for some reason being discussed as a school
without homework, and so without any responsibility of the
pupil for self-education. As teachers in higher schools, we are
alarmed by the support for such innovations in general education schools. What is your opinion?*

I became involved with a correspondence school precisely because it helps capable and industrious adolescents

to find themselves. Experience shows that our graduates are favourably distinguished from other young people in their ability to work independently, and this gives them a real advantage.

In preparing for this interview, I read a hundred and fifty letters from this year's graduates of the Correspondence Physics and Mathematics Higher School. The enthusiasm and industriousness of these young people is truly remarkable. Every tenth student graduated with a medal, which means he took all his subjects seriously. The majority of them also participated in Olympiads, and some even attended two correspondence schools: like Sergei Solovyov from the town of Kosino, who attended both this school and the Physics and Mathematics School affiliated with the Moscow Higher School of Technology.

Many graduates, along with their parents, acknowledge that they would not have been able to make it into the 'hard' higher schools if they had not studied at this school. Yet today they have enrolled in eighteen universities around the country, the physics and technology institutes, technological, medical and pedagogical institutes and military academies. Are you happy or sad about that?

I am happy. Each child is gifted in his own way. If you are a romantic, you can imagine the time when teachers will reveal their pupils' talent. We teach mathematics at this correspondence school because it develops thought. Anyone will benefit from its study. I think this is as much a part of human culture as art.

When pupils from ordinary schools begin to study at this correspondence school, they bring the problems we discuss into their class, and talk about them with other pupils and their teachers. It works like fermentation. And if a 'pupil collective' headed by a teacher is formed, the general level is raised.

This school reflects the consistent and selfless help rendered by the students of Moscow University and other institutes to secondary schools. By the way, only about two roubles per pupil are spent each year, and 22 methodologists occupy only one room at Moscow University. We have by no means fully appreciated the opportunities for correspondence teaching which supplements school curricula.

In the dispute about education in the schools, some believe pupils should spend more time in work and vocational training, and in productive labour. Others are worried that the level of education and culture of the children has noticeably fallen. What do you think should be stressed?

A child's first work is study. And what should be stressed is an honest attitude to that work. If a pupil receives a D and when he is sure to receive a C in the final analysis, he learns a lesson in immorality and cheating, in double standards. But such lessons can be learned both in apprentice shops and literature classes. It is not labour *per se* that educates, but the surroundings in which an attitude towards it is formed. Of course, physical labour is useful. But in speaking about prospects for education, it must be remembered that an increasingly larger share of mechanical work will be transferred to machines, robots and computers. And modern technology requires a high level of culture, intellect, knowledge and responsibility. Chernobyl has served as a warning to us.

In a speech dedicated to the 70th anniversary of the Great October Revolution, the increasing significance of intellectual labour, the interaction of science, technology and society, and the role of talent were underscored. And this is necessarily linked with the development of the education we are providing in secondary and higher schools. That our government is concerned about education shows that it is far-sighted. Will we be able to bring up an honest generation that will not rely on falsified reports and the purely formal fulfilment of obligations? Will we be able to develop this generation's abilities in such a way that the general level of culture will be raised when these young people begin their work careers? We must make our slogan, 'From each according to his ability', a reality.

Interview by I. PRELOVSKAYA

Izvestia, 3 December 1987

One of the largest social programmes adopted in the USSR is the housing programme. The aim of this programme is to

1/*

guarantee every Soviet family a separate flat or individual house by the year 2000.

In 1987 ten million more square metres of housing were made available than in 1986 — a total of 128 million square metres. Of this total 18 million square metres, or fourteen per cent, was accounted for by individual construction and seven per cent, even less, by the housing construction cooperatives.

At such a rate of housing construction the list of those wanting to buy their own houses could well stretch into the next ten years or so. Furthermore, housing construction differs in various parts of the country. The rural areas, particularly, give rise to criticism. It is here that glasnost *has a special role to play, with housing being distributed on a more just system. A case in point is Georgia, which has recently adopted a fairer system of allocation.*

The list of those awaiting housing in this southern republic stretches on for a quarter of a century — 110,000 families are in the queue. Whereas in 1986 alone 170,000 square metres of housing space had to be excluded from the programme at a stroke due to its poor quality. What had happened was that these semi-built or completely unbuilt houses were included on the lists as if they had in fact been built and were ready for living in. It became clear that downright deception had been practised. Many officials in the building industry were dismissed from their posts and those responsible were brought to trial. To avoid this from happening again it was decided in the republic to abandon the old system of measuring the amount of housing built by the number of square metres and to measure it instead by the number of flats. Henceforth the plan would be decided as to the location, the number and the type of flats built, and not their overall square metres. Sessions of the Presidium of the Georgian SSR Supreme Soviet, at which matters relating to housing construction were discussed or reports on the availability of new apartment blocks were heard, began to be broadcast on Georgian television. This meant that the people themselves could now exercise independent control over the housing programme, knowing where and what kind of apartment blocks were to be built, how the flats within them were going to be planned and which organisations would be involved with housing allocation...

One interesting development in the country's housing programme has been the formation of the Youth Housing Com-

plexes. Two billion roubles are earmarked for housing controlled by these organisations by the close of 1990. Members of these complexes are young workers, engineers, students and scientists who design the houses themselves and work during their time off at constructing the buildings which they will one day live in or use, like kindergartens, clubs, amenity centres, etc. The All-Union Coordination and Methodics Centre at the YCL Central Committee has contacts with 200 such Youth Housing Complexes all over the country including the Leningrad Youth Housing Complex Building Trust, which is the first of its kind in the system.

According to information published by the State Statistics Committee, there was as of 1 January 1988, 1,712.5 million square metres of housing space in the Soviet Union that belonged to private individuals — i.e., excluding state flats and housing belonging to the Housing Construction Cooperatives and the Youth Housing Complexes. This is forty per cent of the housing space in the country. At the same time the amount of individual housing construction has been reduced from one five-year plan to another five-year plan, both in the country as a whole and in the majority of union republics. According to figures the annual average housing space made available for individuals in the RSFSR between 1981 and 1985 was 77 per cent less than it had been between 1961 and 1965. In Byelorussia and Kazakhstan the figure was 71 per cent and in the Ukraine, Georgia, Armenia and Estonia 50 per cent less. The amount of individual housing construction increased only in Uzbekistan, Lithuania, Tajikistan and Turkmenia (by 30-50 per cent for the same period).

The CPSU Central Committee and the Council of Ministers of the USSR have passed a resolution On Measures to Accelerate the Development of Individual Housing Construction. This resolution shows a radical change of attitude towards individual housing construction. It provides for measures to satisfy in the shortest possible time the needs of those families who wish to build or reconstruct their houses. By the year 1995 a further 60 million square metres will be made available. It also contains measures to improve organisation and do away with pointless limitations that exist on the allotment of plots of land and on building, as well as on the setting up of associations of individual builders.

Here is the story of one such experience.

BUYING A HOUSE BY INSTALLMENT

By YURI LUSHIN

'Saturday's a good day for work,' said Yuri Trashkov, Chief Architect of the Ust-Kamenogorsk Lead and Zinc Combine, as he looked round the building site. 'But just see what it'll be like tomorrow.'

'But tomorrow's Sunday,' I said in amazement. 'It's a day off.'

'That's right,' he agreed, not noticing my surprise. 'It is a day off, but the best day to get a lot of work done.'

It wasn't long before I realised exactly what he was talking about, and then the building that was going on here on the left bank of the Irtysh under the auspices of the combine no longer simply amazed me, it made me very happy for the people who were working there. What they were doing was building a town for 14,000 inhabitants, which would be called Metallurg. But the interesting thing was that the builders were the very people who would one day live there and they were using their holidays and free time to do it. This is why they looked forward to their days off so that they could 'get a lot of work done'. Whole families would arrive and set off for their individual plots — a total of 670 individual houses will be built in the town as a whole.

'When people are working for themselves they work hard and don't think about how much time they're taking,' said Gennady Klyuev, Secretary of the combine's Party committee. 'Many even work at night. For decades the word "private owner" in our society has had a negative connotation, and yet private building can help solve one of the big state problems. So we do everything to help the private builders.'

'How did the idea come about?'

'You could say life itself prompted us. But in reality it was the hopelessness of our situation. The point is that there were more than three thousand people on the waiting list for housing at the combine and the list was growing. Building could simply not keep pace with demand. Our workers retire at an earlier age than workers in other industries, and the new workers who come to replace them as often as not have no roofs over their heads: they had to wait ten years or more. But when the combine went over to self-financing and was able to make free use of its profits, the idea for individual building was raised. Every year we allocate garden plots, so why not build a house on this land and thus satisfy those waiting in the queue? Why not build a whole township of such cottages, with the combine's help naturally?'

'What does it actually amount to?'

'Well, it provides the necessary documentation, the building equipment and building materials — bricks, wood, ferro-concrete, etc. The combine does all the work connected with providing amenities — the roads, water, lighting, sanitation and heating. It also builds the schools, kindergartens, shops, a polyclinic and a recreation area — all at its own expense.'

'Alright then. Suppose I decide to build a house, but I have no experience. How do I begin?'

'Probably by choosing a plan,' said Trashkov. 'And there are a number of alternatives. Our architectural department, which was formed specially with this in mind, has drawn up five types of house plans to suit various tastes. Do you want a two-storey house? No problem. Or you can have a bungalow. Both have large kitchens and a garage on the ground floor. They have a sauna, a workshop and a storage room for pickles and such. They all have garden plots. If you have no building skills, you can attend courses given by the combine.'

'So, suppose I learn to be a bricklayer, but I haven't got the money. What am I to do? How much, by the way, does your house cost?'

'The most expensive is about 30,000 roubles.'

'That's a bit steep. You might never finish building it.'

'But the metallurgists who work at the combine earn good money. Furthermore, every one who wants to build a house can receive an 80 per cent loan. In the case of 30,000-rouble house, this would be 24,000 roubles. Furthermore, the combine will pay up to 20 per cent of the loan for its shock workers, and the rest is paid over a period of fifteen years. A good worker can also get an interest-free loan twice: first, five years after moving into the new house for fifteen per cent of the outstanding loan; and second, ten years after moving in for thirty per cent of the outstanding

loan. Now add that up and tell me whether it's worth building or not.'

I did, and came to the rapid conclusion that I should immediately stake out a claim and start digging foundations.
But like other doubting Thomases, who were now probably
feeling very sorry, I was too late. All the plots were snapped
up straight away and all I could do was walk around the site
and see how the more resolute were getting on with their
building.

In some places they were only laying the foundations, but
in others they were already putting on the roofs. On one
plot there were so many people working that it was almost
impossible to pass. About thirty men and women were all
hard at it, sifting sand, making up the mortar, lifting up
hods full of bricks, laying the bricks to form a wall. Others
were pouring cement into moulds and one person was making tea — you can't work without a cup of tea! The children
were training the cat for the housewarming.

'Who's house is being built here?' I asked.

'The Koganbayevs' family trust,' came the joking reply.

A few minutes later the head of the 'trust', Chinghis Ko-
ganbayev, a young foundry worker, came up and explained
that they were building a two-storey house. He was being
helped by his mother and father, sisters, nephews, relatives
of his wife, Ziyash, who worked at the local hospital, her
friends and his friends and friends of their friends. And this
went on every day off.

'We began in spring,' said Chinghis, 'and we hope to
have our housewarming in November.'

On the neighbouring site two young lads were fitting raf-
ters over the second floor. A woman came out and said to
me:

'It's a good house, isn't it?' And without waiting for a reply, she added: 'It's my son-in-law, Valery Gamula, who's
building it. He's an electrician and my daughter's a teacher.
For seven years they went renting, and you try and find
a place that you can fit two children into. And here they've
got a whole house to themselves. I help them as much as
I can. I also used to work at the combine before I retired.
And now I'm here as foreman.'

Kalymkhan Nurakhmetov was also preparing to cover
his roof. The design called for a roof covered with slate.

'Slate?' said Kalymkhan, 'you can't get slate anywhere. I'm using metal drums. I'm not joking. At the combine they bring in chemicals in metal drums, which then get sent to the breaker's. But if you knock out the bottom and then cut them and straighten them, they are excellent roofing sheet. And all they cost is kopecks. I need three hundred for the roof on my house and it works out a third of the price of slate.'

The town of Metallurg is for the most part being built by young people, and everyone you speak to shows great seriousness about the way he approaches the job.

'Doesn't this surprise you?' I asked the director of the Ust-Kamenogorsk Lead and Zinc Combine, Akhat Kulenov.

'Oh, it pleases me,' he replied. 'It pleases me very much. These houses are not being built only for the present, not for the near future. They are to stand in the coming century too. And the children and grandchildren of the builders will live in them. And that means the future of the combine will be assured.'

The reader might get the impression that the young builders face no problems. If only that were the case. There are continual complaints about the lack of cement, bricks and other items. Some people even have to stop building because of this. But the combine managers do everything they can to solve the problems that crop up.

The enterprise took on to its balance sheets the half-damaged brick factory that stood in the village of Glubokoye. They repaired it and got it running. But state plan deliveries were immediately set, and a considerable part of the factory's output had to go aside. Was that just? Evidently, the district administration should have had all the brick sent for individual construction during the first three or four years. Ferroconcrete sections will also be made at the combine, but is there any guarantee that this will not be 'run over' by some administration plan? So far individual building is divided into several terms. This year seventy houses are planned to be ready and these are the ones that get priority for materials. But there is the danger that even these plans will not be fulfilled, because the subcontractors may not be able to lay the district heating system or sanitation before winter.

Following the example of the metallurgists many other enterprises in Ust-Kamenogorsk region are also beginning individual housing construction. Obviously, they are watching the experiment at Metallurg with the greatest of interest.

Several months later I returned to Metallurg. It was the thick of winter, and the building site was experiencing a fairly hard frost. There was not the same kind of building enthusiasm I had observed previously. In places the snow-drifts reached the roofs. But the town went on with its daily life, although not quite so actively as I had expected. So what had happened since my last visit? Had the dreams of the individual builders come true? The answer was both yes and no. Yes, because the subcontractors had managed to bring in the heating before winter and lay the sanitation and water supplies. Yes, because seventy houses were made ready according to plan... But no, because the sanitation system was not yet working and there was no cold water (although, I repeat, the pipes had all been laid). No once again, because of the seventy houses that were sufficiently ready to be lived in, only five or six were actually being lived in. In two or three others interior finishing was going on. The rest no doubt would stand there until summer, when building was easier. Here it is necessary to point out that some local papers rushed out with articles claiming that five thousand people had already moved into new homes in Metallurg. I don't know who stands to gain from this kind of exaggeration, and I certainly do not intend to go to the other extreme. What is necessary, is a sober, real-istic analysis of the situation. And such an analysis shows that even by this coming winter there can be no mass house-warmings, since the town still has no kindergarten, no shops and no transport facilities. This is all planned for the near future, and then... Still, I will risk ending on an optim-istic note, in which I was encouraged by my acquaintance with Pyotr Yekimov, a fitter. Sitting on a pile of floor-boards, which were to be used in one of his rooms, he said:

'This is my house, see? My own house. No, you don't see. You'll only see, if you've been on a list for a flat for sixteen years. And this is not a flat, it's a whole house. It's got a roof and it's warm and I built it with my own hands in the space of a few months. My mother didn't believe it was possible — I too at first wasn't sure I could do it. But now everyone believes it, because there's not just one house built, but seventy... And this belief of ours is the most important thing — it is our future. That's what I think anyway.'

And that's what many other people, very many others, think too.

Ogonyok, 26 March-2 April 1988

Vyacheslav Zaitsev has been called the Soviet Pierre Cardin.

In autumn 1987 a Zaitsev collection was shown in New York and San Francisco and subsequently in Paris. And everywhere it was given rave reviews.

How did this all begin? Two American women came to Moscow, they looked at Zaitsev's collection and went back having bought a dozen or so dresses for themselves. These ladies were Ms. T. Kerim, President of the Intertorg company, and Ms. S. Stafford, the company's chief clothes buyer. They only had to show off their new dresses at business meetings, at the theatres and in private houses in New York for the questions to begin: where did you get them from? how much did they cost? The success of Zaitsev's dresses was so striking that, being businesswomen, the two Americans decided to open a Zaitsev House in San Francisco.

But let us leave the two American businesswomen and recall an angry letter which was sent to Ogonyok *from a certain Mrs. R. Slizhikova from Alma-Ata, who did not care much for Zaitsev's success abroad. Mrs. Slizhikova was far more concerned with another question, and one cannot but agree with what she said on this score: which Soviet dress designer would design clothes that were both stylish and inexpensive?*

LYDIA ORLOVA, editor-in-chief of the Soviet fashion magazine Zhurnal mod, *answers this far from rhetorical question.*

FASHION: REALITY AND ILLUSIONS

In the evenings after work my friend, who was on a visit to Moscow as part of her job as chief designer at a large aircraft factory, would rush round the shops looking for things to buy for herself and her friends. She had a long list and the money kept in a separate envelope. She would get back late in the evening tired out, and then open up the parcels she had bought. That was the bit I was most afraid of, because I had to look at clothes that had been bought in a rush, that were unsuitable and sometimes even bought by mistake. But my friend was pleased, happy even, as she pulled out her latest acquisition and looked at me impatiently, asking what I thought of it. It was very rare that I was able to share her pleasure. Either the colour of the garment was totally unsuitable — making her already tired face more pale, or the style was wrong — emphasising her defects, or it was more suited to her daughter than herself.

But my friend, who was accustomed to counting every rouble, knew this only too well. And because she was always disappointed with the results of spending her hard-earned money on poor clothes, she tried for a while not to think about it so as not to upset herself.

Our women are clever and work hard, whether in the work place or in their homes bringing up children. They usually make time for everything except themselves. And this form of selfless devotion often rebounds back on them. They're blamed for not being feminine enough, for not being as attractive as they could be, for not being fashionably dressed in the style of the times.

But where, when and from whom can they learn this?

Not at school, where ideas of dress are reduced to the absurd and the school uniform is foisted upon them as the perfect ideal. What about the technical college or the institute? Here, true, women are free to wear what they like, but after the strictures of school there often come spasmodic attempts to find oneself, one's character and individuality. And these attempts are clumsy, blind at times, and more often than not result in the sort of ghastly effect that makes passers-by on the street stare in utter amazement.

Those who are at work and bear the burden of family responsibilities find themselves in an even worse situation — they have to think not only about their own, but about the family wardrobe, acquiring it not as they would like, but as the family budget allows. The thing that helps here is one's youth, which is attractive by itself.

By the time a person at last becomes qualified and is able to earn enough to buy what he wants, other problems arise, the most important of which is probably to know what is suitable, what is fashionable and how to dress well.

The problem would appear to be quite clear — we need fashionable clothes. The Soviet people deserve to be able to dress fashionably. Only we don't know which particular fashion to choose. Pierre Cardin, perhaps? Or maybe Yves St Laurent? Everyone liked his exhibition here, and we at least know something about him... What about Nina Ricci? She's also got some interesting fashions, and they're fairly stable. Perhaps we should follow Anne Burda? She takes everything she likes from others and produces a purely German style.

Let us remember some forgotten history — the history of ... the beard.

Under Peter the Great and later under Catherine the Great the old Russian way of dressing was changed to a more European style and at the same time men were deprived of the privilege of wearing a beard. Only the Cossacks remained true to the old traditions.

In 1814, at the close of the war with Napoleon, Russian troops entered Paris and the Europeans were full of admiration for the beards worn by the heroic Russian Cossacks. A beard *à la Russe* became the fashion. The French wrote enthusiastically that 'the beard is the natural adornment of the male... Only a beard can give that special significance to the male face'.

Following the style of 'advanced Europe' the Russian dandies began to wear beards too, not suspecting that their own beard had returned to them, albeit with a foreign patent.

Isn't the same thing about to happen again for the umpteenth time? In recent decades there has been increasing interest in the work of Soviet clothes designers and Soviet fashion shows abroad are invariably successful. The 'Russian style' has always been fashionable in the West and we see its influence in the work of many of the famous de-

signers in Paris. So why is it that in our own country anything you like becomes fashionable, except that which our
own people design and which is deeply rooted in our own
traditional national costume?

There are various opinions about this. Fashion, say
some, is international and we cannot exclude Western influence. Of course, we cannot exclude it, and why should we
want to? But we too are able to influence the West. It is
usual to blame our light industry for all the problems, and
that does indeed have its own difficulties. But even so, why
have we not got our own means of creating fashion, why
should we have to keep up with fashion, chase after it? Why
shouldn't we create it ourselves, deliberately and carefully?
Why shouldn't we have our own fashion business, or earn
money by selling fashions?...

Incidentally, we have long known how new fashion is
made. First comes the idea from the designer, and we have
got plenty of ideas. The trouble is our approach to these
ideas is recklessly generous — we make no secret of them
and more often than not it is not us, but more active and enterprising people who use them to create fashions. The first
obstacle to the creation of our own fashions is the fact that
our ideas are made readily available and left unprotected by
patents. So at the first stage, while the idea has not yet actually been turned into garments for the market, it should
be kept a closely guarded secret, a 'company secret' as Westerners in the fashion industry call it. So obviously this is
our first mistake, but it is not our main one.

The trial sales of a design or its possible appearance at
a fashion show indicates the likely success it will have. As
soon as this happens there should be a broad advertising
campaign to get it off the ground. It is here that the machinery breaks down. Why? Because our light industry does not
have at its disposal sufficient means of advertising to persuade buyers of a garment's aesthetic and practical qualities.

Throughout the world it is fashion magazines which provide this kind of publicity. They are published on high quality paper with excellent photographs and print so that the
new fashion can be shown to prospective customers in the
best possible way. But what happens in our country? Fashion magazines, particularly those with patterns, are no
more no less than deficit items, and you cannot subscribe to

them. The all-Union fashion magazine *Zhurnal mod* which began publication immediately after the end of the Second World War comes out only four times a year with a circulation of 600,000. Another fashion magazine, which is more of a practical guide to dressmaking and is called *Modeli sezona*, also has a circulation of only 600,000, but comes out only twice a year. Both publications are quite popular abroad, so only a part of even that small circulation is available for internal consumption. Furthermore, the quality of the printing is poor and only a few of the illustrations are in colour, and as everybody knows colour in fashion gives significant information.

How can we create new fashions without the necessary and very specific means of advertising them? Let's say a designer creates a new and very interesting fashion and offers it for sale. Will the market understand it? Will it risk ordering it? Experience shows that more often than not the Soviet internal market prefers to be cautious, quite reasonably fearing that the customer who knows nothing about this new fashion and has no information on it will not buy it. And so the designer's idea having no support dies with the one single model. You should see the fashionable fur-coats that were not bought at the wholesale market simply because they were too fashionable!

But no clothes by themselves, even the most fashionable and the most beautiful, have ever made people well dressed. Taste, culture, understanding and knowledge of the laws of dressmaking and, particularly, the creation of an image, an image which accords with the times — these are what are most important. And this has to be learned and taught to others.

Just recently there have been a number of articles in the press about the publication in our country of the West German fashion magazine *Burda*. It is a beautifully produced magazine, well printed, on good quality paper, and opinions have consequently been voiced to the effect that *Burda* will help to dress Soviet people well. I think that this is just one of the illusions that fashion gives birth to — the illusion that this problem can be solved easily and quickly. None of us, I think, will be buying our clothes from Pierre Cardin and Nina Ricci, although it would be very nice if we could. It is our light industry and that alone which will be clothing us. And that is the reality which we must take account of. And so we must begin without delay to get it working so that new fashions can be created. And then we can have plenty of good clothes with our own Soviet patents on them.

Pravda, 31 May 1987

The Soviet Health Service

In search of a heart

The Soviet health service is a major branch of the social benefits structure. Tens of thousands of hospitals, polyclinics, first aid and emergency centres and pediatric services have been set up in the USSR, as have hundreds of medical research and training institutions. There is a network of services to care for the mother and child, a hygiene and epidemiological service and also extensive provision of sanatoria and rest homes. Some 1,200,000 doctors and 3,300,000 medical workers are employed in the Soviet health service.

The achievements of the Soviet health service have won general recognition. The principles upon which it is based and its organisation of basic medical and hygiene services have been recommended by the World Health Organisation as a model.

However, close study has revealed that the years of stagnation which paralysed the country's economic, social, political and cultural life also had a negative effect on the health service. Callousness, indifference and red tape appear there, too. This explains why the health service is currently a focal point of attention throughout the mass media. Medical treatment in the USSR is free, yet some people are ready to part with a lot of money to help their nearest and dearest. Unfortunately, it is precisely this which has been shamelessly exploited by many, from nurses to prominent doctors. In certain cities and regions of the country there are unofficial 'fixed charges' which the population is expected to pay. In December 1987, Literaturnaya Gazeta *published a letter from Dr. A. Rezhabek, who wrote: 'A rouble for the woman who "takes care" of delivering gifts to patients. A rouble for the medical orderly — then she brings the bed pan. A rouble for the matron — and she will give you a hospital gown that fits. Another rouble — and slippers will be found; yet another — and your bed-clothes will be changed. Have a word with the nurse (though not all of them will agree) — and for around ten*

18–867

*roubles she will keep a "special" eye on your elderly rela-
tive... As for the doctors, here the charges vary. One may accept cognac, another money — one fifty roubles, another —
five hundred...' Recalling the visit made by Mother Theresa
to the USSR in 1987, Dr. Rezhubek suggested that this ab-
normal state of affairs in our hospitals might be remedied by
involving believers in the nursing of the sick, 'particularly as
they are motivated by ethical rather than material considerations'.*

*This suggestion appears rather tempting. Care for those in
need has been performed by the church for centuries. However, it is scarcely necessary to rely solely on the selfless aid
of believers in caring for the sick: the causes for this situation
in the health service are to be sought deeper. The Soviet press
has carried numerous articles revealing that bribery is used to
obtain places at medical colleges for poorly qualified, and
even wholly unqualified candidates with no talent for the medical profession. The possible consequences are illustrated in
a tragic letter from Olga Gerasimova (Trud, 30 October
1987):*

*'In June 1987 I arrived with my children in the town of Kok-
chetav to visit my grandparents. During the night of 23 June
I discovered that Tanechka had a temperature of 39.6 C, and
sent for the emergency doctor. After examining the child and
finding nothing wrong, Dr. Amrina advised me to send for the
local pediatrician. This I did the following morning. It was sev-
en o'clock in the evening when the pediatrician, Kulyash Ka-
bekovna Tleuova, arrived. My daughter had a fever all day,
but I had given her no medicine, expecting the doctor to arrive
at any moment. The doctor told me that Tanechka had tonsillitis, and gave me a prescription (erythromycin and aspirin).
She added: "If her temperature goes up, give her some ice-
cream", and left. That night Tanechka's temperature rose
still higher, and I sent for the emergency doctor again. This
time it was a Dr. Zapototsky. "The lungs are clean, there's
no tonsillitis," he said. He gave Tanechka an injection and
left. The high temperature continued all night and the whole
of the following day. At nine o'clock that evening I once again
telephoned the emergency service as Tanechka's condition
worsened. Her temperature rose to 39.9C. A Dr. Kulish
came, "It's a virus infection," he said calmly. "It'll pass in
two or three days." He gave her an injection and left. Ta-*

nechka was still not taken to hospital, although I had asked them to. The following day my daughter was very listless and weak, spent the whole day in bed and refused to eat anything. In the evening she started vomiting.

'There was nothing left to do except take her to hospital myself. I telephoned for a taxi and went to the casualty department of the regional children's hospital for infectious diseases. The medical staff could see that the child was tormented by nausea, but the doctor on duty, P. T. Chuyenko, was in no hurry to examine her. He was standing in the corridor, chatting merrily to some girls. Finally he came. He examined Tanechka, looked at her throat, shrugged his shoulders and told us to go home. The child, he said, probably had gastritis or food poisoning. I was to give her plenty of water to wash out her stomach...

'I left the hospital carrying Tanechka because she was too weak to walk. She was lying in my arms like a rag doll, and I had no idea what to do next or where to go — to the taxi, which was still waiting for us, or back to the hospital which had just shown us the door. I finally decided to go back. I asked them to take some tests. The doctor reluctantly told a nurse to take a blood test. We waited until the result came and were told that everything was normal, and were asked to go home.

'I blame myself for my lack of determination, my timidity. Only now I realise how I should have behaved. I should have shouted, demanded that they hospitalise the child and treat her. Perhaps that would have saved my daughter's life...

'We arrived home, and Tanechka's condition grew worse by the hour. She was vomiting, her temperature rose, and she breathed with difficulty. At two o'clock that night I sent for the emergency doctor once again, and immediately insisted that we be taken to the hospital. The same Dr. Chuyenko was on duty. He had been asleep, and it took him some time to come round. He kept asking the same question two or three times. He sat down to fill out the card, which took half an hour, and was in no hurry to do anything for my daughter. Tanechka was getting worse, and I asked him to hurry up and do something. All he replied was: "Oh, this mother is getting on my nerves!"

'Finally he ordered Tanechka to be put on a drip. I carried her into the treatment room, the light was switched on, and

I could see cockroaches scurrying across the walls and over the couches. Tanechka was put on a drip, but her condition did not improve. All night she was running a high temperature and kept vomiting. When Chuyenko came into the treatment room, I asked him what was the matter with my daughter. He only shrugged his shoulders and said: "I don't know." I then begged him to send for another doctor if he was unable to diagnose the trouble, but he refused. After that he left again — probably to sleep. I thought it would never be morning. The doctors arrived not at nine o'clock but at ten.

'By then Tanechka had lost consciousness. When she came round, we were sent for an X-ray. I carried her there as quickly as I could, and they took the X-ray. None of the doctors bothered to look at it. They did so only when I began to shout at them. Tanechka had bronchial purulent pneumonia.

'The doctor in charge of Tanechka's treatment, Dr. G. G. Akhmetova, prescribed four injections of penicillin a day — despite the serious danger the child was now in! It seemed to me that a massive dose of antibiotics was needed! I was alone almost round the clock in the ward with my daughter, and when she lost consciousness and began to have convulsions, I myself gave her oxygen, myself switched on the equipment. Dr. Akhmetova came only when I began running through the hospital shouting for help. Then she went home. Dr. Baitursynova remained on duty, but she was constantly in the casualty department, and when she did come into the ward, she did not even know which side of the oxygen bag was which. In other words, my daughter was simply left in the hands of fate. I asked the doctor several times if sepsis might be developing, and was told that a blood test for sepsis had been taken, and that the result would be ready in three days.

'I also asked Akhmetova to telephone somewhere else for consultation — to Alma Ata, for example. This is often done when the diagnosis is uncertain. However she answered very formally: "Such questions are decided at a higher level."

'They were unwilling to take my daughter to the intensive care ward. I myself asked the head doctor and doctors of the intensive care ward, but they refused on the ground that there were no free beds. Only when my daughter was already dying were we at last given permission. We were told: "Very well, take her up to the 5th floor." My husband and I carried our daughter and rushed her upstairs as she was unable to breathe

without oxygen, and was having convulsions every couple of minutes. The lifts in the hospital were out of order.

'28 June 1987, our little Tanechka died... She did not live to receive the results of her blood test. Yet after the post mortem the pathologist told us that he had discovered nothing apart from pneumonia and sepsis. He even expressed surprise that she had died.

'Such tragedy struck our daughter and us, we are the most unfortunate people in the world. It is unbearable to write about it, but in the name of our daughter, and for the sake of the health of other children, we think it is our duty to do so.

'One doctor was negligent, another was careless, a third took his time, and as a result a child died.'

Can the death of a child be in any way compensated for by the warnings issued by the Ministry of Health of the Kazakh SSR to the 'doctors' described in the letter? It also appears that the warnings were a mere formality!

This tragedy occurred at a time when broad public discussion was under way in the Soviet Union on the need for a reform of the health service. When discussing perestroika *in the health service we should never forget for a moment that no amount of organising will be of any use if we do not expell once and for all from the service those who are indifferent and morally bent.*

A major document entitled 'Main Trends in the Development of Health Care and the Reorganisation of the Health Service of the USSR up to the Year 2000' was issued by the Central Committee of the CPSU and the Council of Ministers of the USSR in November 1987. This document identifies the causes which led to the spread of red tape, corruption, callousness, indifference, bad manners, and irresponsible attitudes on the part of the health service personnel... Sluggish economic growth in the country and lack of proper attention to management led to a reduction in the health care share of the state budget. The current system of pay failed to stimulate a desire to improve the quality of work or to raise the level of knowledge and practical skills. The document also formulates clearly and precisely the aim of the present reorganisation and defines the role and importance of medical aid.

WHAT'S THE PROBLEM, DOCTOR?

ALEXEI MOSKVICHEV,
Deputy Minister of Health, replies.

*All of us, both patients and doctors, realise that our health
service is in need of perestroika. So, shall we begin by turning
to the main issue of the day. Our first question: how does the
Ministry of Health envisage the next steps?*

To put it briefly, we must change radically the entire system of organisation and managing the health service. We
must improve the material and technical facilities and resolve the problem of medical personnel. We need to increase medical research and rapidly introduce new advances.
As you can see, this in effect means total restructuring.

*Could you tell us in a few words what measures the Minis-
try of Health is taking now?*

Of course. We have begun to identify problems and are
drawing up plans for rapid modernisation. There is to be rig-
orous inspection of the service provided by polyclinics,
hospitals and health centres — from now on their work will
be assessed solely according to results, i. e., the state of health
of the population. New criteria are being established which are
to replace the notoriously meaningless statistics — the 'bed
per day' and 'number of patients' attending the polyclinic.
The aim is to raise the quality of the entire medical service.

*This also includes, of course, diagnosis and preventive
treatment?*

Yes, that is one of our priority tasks...

*How will it be tackled? Presumably industry will need to
develop new diagnostic equipment which meets most modern
requirements?*

No, I wouldn't say so. Although industry should, indeed,
cease producing outdated equipment. Two Leningrad factories, for example, produce endoscopes, yet we still have to
purchase endoscopes from abroad as ours do not come up
to the required standards. Even then, the imported endo-
scope is designed to carry out three thousand tests and we
carry out five thousand. Ours withstands a maximum of
150 tests! In cash terms it means that each test costs 200
roubles! Therefore, we need to assess our capabilities and
make effective use of everything we possess. This means

collecting all the diagnostic equipment at present scattered around various medical institutions and concentrating it in one medical centre. In this way we can obtain a patient's diagnosis without sending him or her to several places.

Is this already happening?

Yes. Prototypes are already working in Minsk, Tashkent and Yerevan. Armenia is planning to create two more diagnostic centres in the near future. In the course of the current five-year plan, a network of 25 modern diagnostic centres will be set up around the country and the centralisation of diagnostic services will become law.

If you think I am dwelling on this aspect too much then it is because we also need to develop new attitudes on the part of the doctor, particularly the heads of polyclinics or hospitals. At present, every head of a major hospital, and particularly of a medical research centre, tries in all possible ways to acquire the latest medical equipment. Every day we receive dozens of requests from heads of regional Party organs and local Soviets for help in obtaining imported equipment. Clearly this is not the right approach. On the other hand, we cannot remove existing equipment from any medical institution, even if it is under-used.

What measures will be taken to improve hospital treatment?

One method is to classify hospitals. This means the creation of hospitals for intensive therapy (hospitals offering emergency treatment), convalescence hospitals and day clinics.

What exactly is a 'day clinic'?

The patient comes every morning at eight o'clock for treatment. In the evening he or she returns home. While he or she is at the centre, all meals are provided. Such centres could treat patients with ulcer complaints who do not require surgery but who need physiotherapy, drug therapy, etc. Many skin complaints could also be handled successfully at such day clinics. Why remove the individual from home? Such day clinics would make it possible to reduce medical personnel significantly. In addition we must bear in mind that we are not as yet able to provide in our hospitals conditions at least as good as those at home. The patient is used to living in his own flat with every modern convenience, and then he finds himself in a ward with one bathroom down the corridor. This does not assist rapid recovery.

And are there any such day clinics?

Yes, in Odessa, Krivoi Rog and Leningrad. They are attached to the polyclinics which slightly distorts the whole idea. We plan to turn over some of the existing hospitals for this purpose...

Which problem in the health service concerns the Ministry of Health officials most? Medical personnel, scientific research, management?

Today our country is well down the league in terms of expenditure per capita on the health service. The total budget is 19 billion roubles and includes sports. Of this, 80 per cent goes on hospital service. We are particularly concerned about expenditure on medicines. It is impossible to treat a patient for one rouble a day. Present medicines are undoubtedly better, but they cost a great deal more!

Might it not be possible to raise some contributions from the work place?

It is not only possible but inevitable. However here, as is often the case in a new situation not yet provided for by legislation, much depends on the manager of the enterprise, on his understanding of the importance of such assistance. We have factories with fairly good medical services, they have their own hospitals, convalescence homes with swimming pools and modern physiotherapy and sports equipment. This trend has increased over recent years. However, it is still not widespread. Every enterprise should have its own prophylactic service.

Let's go a step further: why not let the enterprise pay for the hospital treatment of its employees? This would benefit everyone, the patient, the enterprise and the medical institution...?

I think experience will provide the answer. We are considering a major experiment in Leningrad, Kuibyshev and Kemerovo Regions which involves such financial arrangements. But some things could be done immediately. Factories could finance the construction and maintenance of buildings, the purchase of medical equipment, offer additional financial stimulus to hospitals which provide modern medical treatment for their employees. It is particularly important, in our opinion, that they should help in purchasing medical equipment.

The health service requires additional resources. This explains the revival of the idea of organising a 'Health Fund', which would encourage voluntary contributions from enterprises, organisations and private individuals. I believe the right thing to do would be to centralise a part of the Fund (less than half) via the Ministry of Health, and the rest would be allocated to regions.

You said that four fifths of the entire health care budget was spent on financing hospitals. Is it true that only a small part of this sum is spent on treating the patient himself?

Yes, the average cost of one hospital bed is about eleven roubles a day. This figure includes food and staff salaries, which together account for approximately 56 per cent of the total expenditure. The rest goes on maintenance, sanitation, heating, etc. All these expenses are, of course, strictly controlled.

And medical equipment?

Some of it is prohibitively expensive, not just expensive. Our factories are willing to manufacture equipment immediately if it costs 200-300 thousand roubles. The apparatus used to measure arterial blood pressure cost originally 7 roubles 30 kopecks. Then there appeared new apparatus costing 30 roubles. The newest standard apparatus costs 40 roubles and is constantly breaking down!

Our conversation has taken a decidedly technical turn, but I would like to talk about the professional attitude of doctors, about the quality of medical training...

It is still not satisfactory: of the 350 thousand doctors who were called recently for in-service attestations, 30 thousand passed conditionally. One thousand doctors have been refused to continue practice. How did such a state of affairs arise? The training provided by our medical institutes is divorced from practical needs and overloaded with unnecessary studies. Training in medical institutes should be more individualised, and organised so that the student spends more time working with patients. The period of practical post-graduate training should be extended as doctor's competence depends both on his maturity and on his practical experience.

And if a student proves to be very 'average' — who needs an 'average' doctor? Either a doctor is a good doctor, or else no doctor at all! You cannot but agree with that.

Clearly, if a student is not satisfactory, then he or she should qualify as a medical assistant, and not a doctor... By the way, I should mention that we are now examining the question of doctors who have violated the oath. We believe it is essential to pass a law which would make it possible to annul their doctor's license.

The medical training of doctors should equip them to work independently. At the same time, the role of the general practitioner should be enhanced, and his work should enjoy greater prestige. With time we shall be able to take into consideration individual demands of the local population...

But might this not mean that the doctor who has, say, ten patients today will have twenty tomorrow?

I do not believe we face this danger. As I said earlier, the new plan is designed to improve the quality of work in health service institutions and to assess success by the improved health of the population. What is the general practitioner's responsibility? The number of visits? Of course not. He or she is responsible for the health of the 1,700 people on the register, and who are placing their trust in his or her medical knowledge and ability.

One thing I cannot understand is why, if someone has gone down with flu, is given three days' sick leave. Going out again may make the patient worse...

We share your view. Few years ago, doctors in one of the regions were given the right to issue sick leave for up to five days, with a possible extension to eight days. This had no negative effect on absenteeism. Beginning from July, we are starting to experiment — with certification up to ten days. If this proves a success, the practice will be extended.

Are you worried that some people will not want to work in the new way and will be satisfied with chasing statistics?

Yes, I am. But the work needs to be done and it must answer today's needs.

Interview by Maria SMIRNOVA and
Alexander YEVSEYEV

Nedelya, No. 25, 1987

In the USSR, 8.5 million people suffer from kidney stones. Around 200,000 are treated every year, many by surgery.

Complications may lead to the loss of a kidney. Hospital treatment is very long, on average 33 days and then it continues in out-patient clinics.

Medical specialists have been looking for a method of non-surgical treatment for a long time. ALEXANDER GUSKOV *has developed a radically new method of treating kidney stones. So radical, that the response of the medical profession has been sceptical.*

Dr. Guskov and his two assistants, Dr. Kremer and Dr. Medvedev spoke to Nedelya.

STONES IN DR. GUSKOV'S PATH

A new cure has been discovered, but is not being used. A patient writes:

'Twenty years ago I discovered I had kidney trouble when I had my first attack and ended up in hospital. Pain has driven me almost mad. Then, in 1986, I was sent to hospital. The doctors took an X-ray and suggested an immediate operation. I did not fancy an operation and tried to argue, but to no avail. They were ready to operate. Then a friend of mine brought me a short article about a Moscow doctor who is removing stones using ordinary sound. When you're in pain you'll try anything. This is how I got on to Dr. Guskov.

'When he had looked at my X-rays, Dr. Guskov said: "A difficult case, right at the limits of our abilities, but we'll try." I began sound therapy treatment at the end of October. I noticed the pains were disappearing. The treatment lasted ten days. Then Dr. Guskov announced that the stone will come out before the New Year. And, would you believe it, on 31 December the stone did come out. I didn't feel a thing, I turned it round in my fingers and still didn't believe it.'

After reading this story, we naturally wanted to ask Dr. Guskov about his method. First we wanted to know about traditional methods of treatment.

A. G. The majority of stones are formed in the kidneys, and while they stay there, the person knows nothing about them. One fine day, however, a stone breaks loose, and lodges in the narrow kidney duct. That is when severe pain begins, accompanied by shivering and a raised temperature. The kidney is unaware that the exit is blocked, and continues to work as usual. The pressure inside the kidney increases to such a degree that the tissue is unable to bear the strain and surgery has to be performed. However, this happens only rarely. In the majority of cases the kidney adapts, it slowly ceases to function and is no longer able to force the stone out. This is also bad, and here again, surgery is the solution.

And you got the idea of a cure without a scalpel and without pain?

A. G. Not straightaway. To begin with, we tried electrical impulses. This method, however, had its disadvantages: the treatment was painful and involved the use of electrical instruments. We could not think of an alternative for electrical stimulation, but continued our research. It was at this point that we noticed a connection: as soon as an impulse of a specific frequency, 2.5 kilohertz, was applied to the kidney, it produced an amazing result. This frequency seemed to possess some kind of mysterious power and the kidney began to function.

But where does sound come into this?

A. G. Well, 2.5 kilohertz is the frequency of ordinary, audible sound. So we thought we should use it. Electrical stimulation gave us the idea of sound stimulation: instead of electrical impulses, mechanical impulses were transmitted at this particular frequency. Sound signal passes easily through tissue, and thus a kidney can be stimulated externally, without introducing electrodes. It seemed a strange idea, but nonetheless I was confident it would work. What I now needed was the apparatus. Fortunately, by this time we already had close contacts with the All-Union Medical Equipment Research Institute and knew people there. V. Mikhailov and A. Vasilyev, were especially helpful. We explained the situation to them: in essence, we required an ordinary loudspeaker which emitted sound at the required frequency. They made one out of an old loudspeaker. We tried out the first sound stimulator on ourselves. We 'sounded' everything we could — back, stomach, legs, arms. When the apparatus was applied to the body, we could feel the muscles tensing. This meant that the kidney should have been receiving it, too.

Why do the kidneys and other tissues respond to sound?
A. G. I asked this myself. I read through a great deal of literature, in particular reports of hygiene specialists and bio-acousticians. I saw the light, so to speak, when I came across the works of Academician D. Nasonov published between 1940s and 1970s. They were investigating the effect of sound on various animal tissues (kidneys, muscles, etc.). In their material I found a reference to the same 'mysterious' frequency of 2-3 kilohertz. The explanation seemed to lie not in the nature of the kidney itself, but in some law common to all cells in the organism. Something within the cells responds to this sound! Very probably the sound sets up a resonance for the moment, there is no other explanation. Thanks to this resonance, the signal is intensified, and the kidney literally hears the command — 'Function!' Of course, here we mean that many processes within the cell — membrane, energy, regeneration, etc. — begin to function.

What is the advantage of sound stimulation?
A. G. The kidney begins to function again as normally as possible. This means that the risk of acute inflammation is sharply reduced. At the same time it stops those processes which lead to the destruction of kidney tissue. The kidney is able to expel the stone. Now that the organ is functioning normally, kidney pains also cease, and the general condition of the patient improves. Our patients are usually treated in out-patient clinics and do not have to take time off work. We even recommend active life as positively beneficial. Of course, some patients are treated in hospitals. We treated our first patient 7 years ago. Since then, sound stimulation has helped almost 400 patients. Return for a second course of treatment has been extremely rare. What is more, the number of kidney operations has been halved: now, out of one hundred patients, only around 15 undergo surgery.

Yet, nonetheless, operations are performed. Your method is not a universal panacea?
A. G. Of course not. Nor could there be one. If the stone is too large, or has a jagged surface, it has to be removed surgically. In critical situations, when the functioning of the kidney is seriously impaired, it is impossible to restore it to normal. There are also other complications.

Judging by what your patients say, Dr. Guskov, the method

*of treatment couldn't be simpler. It would not take long to
learn? Will our industry manufacture suitable apparatus?*
A. G. The design for INTRAFON-1 — as we named our instrument — has been available for some time and is currently produced on an experimental basis. The instrument
is not expensive to manufacture, and is therefore within the
means of any polyclinic, hospital or sanatorium. However,
before proceeding with production, we need to assess the
demand for it. The plant asked the USSR Ministry of
Health how many would be required annually. The reply
was: 'None. There are no orders.'

*Perhaps your colleagues had not heard of the new treat-
ment.*
A. G. We began to publish articles in 1983, especially in the
journal *Urology and Nephrology*, with Professor V. Ryabin-
sky. But there was no response. We spoke at meetings of the
Moscow Society of Urologists and at various conferences
but all we encountered was disbelief.

But why?
A. G. The very word 'sound' provokes suspicion. Many
doctors believe in the usefulness of vibration and ultra-
sound, but not ordinary sound! Then, for about one hundred years there prevailed a view that to restore a kidney to
functioning when a stone is blocking the urinary duct is impossible. No one seems to discard these generally held
views. Some specialists have been infuriated by the suggestion that stones can be expelled painlessly.

Did none of the urologists wish to try out your method?
A. G. There was interest expressed by Doctor F. Zatiura,
a Czech specialist and assistant to the chief urologist of
Czechoslovakia, Professor J. Kuchera. In August 1986 he
came to visit us in our laboratory with representatives from
Tesla*, and we began to work on the design of a Soviet-
Czechoslovak kidney sound stimulator. Then, from the beginning of 1987 things began to move. After a few reports in
the press, patients learned about sound therapy and began
to request it from their doctors. Our colleagues began to visit
us to learn more about our method. At last we won supporters. The opponents of this method — those who reject

---

* Tesla, a Czechoslovak firm specialising in electrical and audio instruments.— *Ed.*

sound therapy out of hand, not even taking the trouble to examine it, do not flinch from calling us charlatans! Yet one only has to acquaint oneself with the research material and, most importantly, with the patients we have treated successfully. Naturally, if methods of stimulation are to be widely used in urology, then we need to have better means for diagnosing the kidneys' damage. Polyclinics are poorly equipped with diagnostic equipment, and introducing this method of treatment in hospitals would not be cost-efficient. There is, however, a solution. Diagnostic centres, which are being introduced currently in major cities, would be ideal for our treatment. We have another instrument — INTRATON-1 — for the electrical stimulation of urological organs. This is also having hard times — the idea of stimulation is somehow not attractive for many urologists. There is another aspect. We are generally sceptical of our own research, yet very quick to spend foreign currency on expensive imported equipment. Yet our patent office is packed with inventions and discoveries which are not given a chance. It may even be that in a few years we will be obliged to purchase from abroad sound stimulators similar to our INTRAFON-1. An irony, if there ever was one.

Interview by YELENA KOLESNIKOVA

Nedelya, No. 29, 1987

There is another medical specialist attracting great attention — NIKOLAI KASSYAN *from the small Ukrainian town Kobelyaki.*
Anyone who has suffered pain in the small of the back will know what torture it can be. And what about those who have suffered from osteochondrosis for years. Many are turning to Dr. Kassyan. 'This year I will be thirty-eight, I have suffered from osteochondrosis for about twenty years. After a while I began to have several attacks a year. I have tried every possible kind of treatment. I am very worried as I am the only 'adult' man in the family and am unable to do anything. Could I please come to you for treatment?...' Another letter: 'I am still quite young and have two children. Three years ago

I twisted my neck. When I woke up one morning I turned my head sharply and something cracked in my neck. Since then I have been in continual pain and cannot lift my head...' And another: 'I suffer from osteochondrosis. I spend up to three months a year on the sick list. I can assure you, I do not want to be an invalid at the age of forty...' Etc., etc.

A reporter from Ogonyok *was sent to Kobelyaki and began his article with a description of the following scene: 'I notice that I am not the only person walking the street at night (Doctor Kassyan holds his surgery at night, during the day he works as the head of the Psychiatry Department of the Leshchinsk Hospital. He sleeps four hours a day — Ed.). Someone is limping down the street with the help of a walking stick. I can see two more in the distance, helping each other along. I set off at a brisk pace, passing first one group, then another. The first group is carrying children; the second group consists of a woman and several teenage girls. We all turn down a side street, at the bottom of which a street-lamp is burning. Cars are parked almost the whole way along both sides of this narrow street. There are many people. Some recognise me as a reporter and beg me not to take up his time. His seconds are precious...'*

Let us interrupt the reporter at this point. Was it an exaggeration that he spoke of seconds? All those who saw the television programme 'Good Evening, Moscow' in October 1987, in which Doctor Kassyan appeared, will remember what happened: an osteochondrosis sufferer had been brought to the studio, unexpectedly for Kassyan. There, before an audience of millions of television viewers, the doctor was 'put to the test'. Kassyan asked the patient to strip to the waist; he felt the patient's lumbar region, suddenly seized the patient from behind, pressed him up against himself, shook him, then laid him down on a couch and delivered two sharp blows to the small of his back. Then he calmly asked him: 'Get up...' The expression on the patient's face was of astonishment. With a confused smile on his face, still not understanding anything of what had happened, but already feeling better he asked: 'Is that all?' 'That's all, you're cured,' replied the doctor. The entire treatment had taken precisely 13 seconds...

QUEUING UP FOR DR. KASSYAN

By V. BELITSKY

On the second floor of a hotel in Moscow, the corridor was packed with a large crowd. 'Where are you going?' some of them shouted at me. 'We've been standing here all night!' 'We won't let him through.' Others simply asked: 'Come on, get to the back of the queue!' Others shouted furiously. I realised that I would probably not be able to keep my appointment with Dr. Kassyan, who had come to Moscow for two days only.

Early in the morning, people knocked on his door:

'Are you up yet?' In the afternoon, having escaped from his patients for a few minutes break he was tracked down by others:

'Doctor, will you be much longer?'

Dr. Kassyan from Kobelyaki is a well-known specialist in therapy through manual manipulations. However great his fund of energy, he was unable to continue seeing people. Priority was given to children and invalids. Then he took refuge in one of the hotel's offices. Dr. Kassyan uses a traditional method practiced by his father and grandfather before him. In the course of two or three minutes he literally shakes up the patient, and in the majority of cases instantly relieves the pain. The day before a doctor had brought a patient on crutches. He was bent with pain. A few minutes later he left the hotel room, still a little unsteady on his feet, unable to believe that he was walking unaided on his own two legs, carrying crutches under his arms... Nothing short of a miracle! News travel fast when people are in pain and relief becomes a possibility.

In April 1987 the USSR Ministry of Health gave help to develop manual manipulation therapy. Nikolai Andreyevich told me that more than 90,000 people have already been put on the waiting list for an appointment. If urgent cases are given priorities, as they are, Dr. Kassyan is fully booked till 1993!

The Ukrainian Deputy Minister of Health has visited Kobelyaki. He approved plans for building a hospital with 100 beds and a rehabilitation centre. Will this be enough? Of course not.

Whilst the impatient crowd in Moscow was trying to break into Kassyan's room at the hotel, by chance the Academic Council was meeting at the Ministry of Health. Here everything was very orderly: a report, second report, speeches, questions. One professor declared that this was in any case not a matter for the Academic Council, but for medical practitioners. Another objected that it was precisely a matter for the Academic Council, since what was being done by Kassyan and other similar practitioners required more research. They discussed whether someone should be sent to Sweden where this method was practiced, but came to the conclusion that the special tables used there would cost about half a million roubles in foreign currency, and perhaps an ordinary couch would do. A few jokes were thrown around on this subject. There then followed a not very long discussion on the main point in the report: 700 doctors had taken a course in manual manipulation therapy but no one knew where they were practicing. Finally, no one had noticed that Kassyan was not at the meeting — though, in fact, no one had thought of inviting him. I realise, of course, that this issue is far more complex. However, one cannot but conclude that, at least for the moment, the discrepancy between word and deed is rather too great.

...What a pity that the Academic Council was not meeting at the hotel. I am certain that a talk with those standing in the queue would have taught them a great deal!

Trud, 3 October 1987

Another interesting development is taking place in the treatment of sepsis. In 1985 Izvestia *published an article on a new method of purifying infected blood with the help of — pig spleen. It was being tested during transplant operations. Not surprisingly, after the article appeared, a wave of requests for help arrived in the laboratory of Professor ANATOLII TSYPIN, one of the inventors of the new method... Sadly, the majority of requests had to be refused: some because the method was still in its infancy and had been tried only in the most acute cases of sepsis, others because this innovation had never been tried on children... Moreover, with*

*all the will in the world one intensive care unit in one hospital
cannot provide help for everyone.*

*Then came the news that the clinical tests had been complet-
ed. In the meantime the new method was introduced in
a number of cities (Leningrad, Kiev, Kharkov, Tbilisi, Ros-
tov-on-Don, Donetsk, Sverdlovsk, Kirov, Alma Ata, Sebasto-
pol). As we can see, Moscow is no longer the sole centre for
treating critical cases. Hundreds of lives have been saved, including those of children.*

TWO YEARS ON

By L. IVCHENKO

'We were afraid,' explains Anatolii Borisovich, 'that a pig
spleen is larger than the spleen of an adult, and therefore, of
course, considerably larger than that of a child. This means
there is danger of some blood loss after passing through this
living filter. Practical experience has shown that a part is indeed retained. But the part is so small that it can be disregard-
ed. The loss is easily made up by a small dose of transfu-
sion.'

Everything began, as always, with a hopeless case. There
are occasions when doctors try every conceivable method in
order to save a life. One might say that the doctors in Kurgan were clutching at straw in an attempt to save the life of
twelve-year old Czech schoolboy Tomash Fondish.

Tomash was very ill indeed. In Kurgan, where the boy had
come to be treated by Professor G. Ilizarov, he developed
severe blood poisoning which affected the lungs, liver, kidneys and heart... Every possible type of medicine was tried,
but the child's condition was deteriorating. It was then that
the doctor in charge of Tomash in the intensive care unit,
A. Borisenko, decided to try one last resort—Professor
Tsypin's method. An urgent request was sent to the Institute of Transplantology by the Czechoslovak Embassy. Dr.
Tsypin and his assistant Dr. A. Makarov put their apparatus in ambulance aircraft and went. Then other cases followed, other patients. But this was the first flight in an aircraft ambulance and the first child patient.

Things did not go without hitches. Kurgan airport was not receiving due to bad weather. The plane landed in Chelyabinsk but there was a car waiting. Half way along the road another car met them, and the doctors were taken to the Kurgan children's hospital. The spleen was ready. The entire procedure of perfusion, as this method is called, took 40 minutes. They pumped the child's infected blood through the fresh, living spleen, an organ designed by nature to counteract infectious microbes and toxins. The natural filter dealt with the infection and simultaneously stimulated the defence mechanisms of an organism exhausted by its battle against infection. It has been established that the live donor spleen sheds biologically active substances into the blood of the patient.

'Was this done under an anesthetic?'

'No need. The procedure is virtually painless. In the case of a serious condition, medicines and solutions are usually administered intravenously, and it is relatively easy to insert additional tubes. As a rule we prescribe some kind of tranquilliser in order to relieve tension. However, Tomash coped marvellously, chatted with us during the treatment. He speaks Russian very well!'

By the following day Tomash's condition had already improved noticeably. Two days later the doctors thought it necessary to repeat the procedure in order to be certain of full effect, since the septic infection had seriously affected so many organs. The doctors from Moscow spent a week in Kurgan and then left, confident that the danger was already past. The parents, needless to say, were overjoyed. Three weeks later the boy had recovered satisfactorily.

Tsypin and Makarov had left, but were soon flying out again, this time to Sverdlovsk. Specialists in Sverdlovsk, having heard that the Moscow team was in the neighbouring city of Kurgan, had arrived there to study the new method. They then asked for help in treating a patient who was critically ill.

'We had already done all we could,' recalled Dr. Zlokazov, 'but without success, and the patient's condition had become critical. It was only after he had been connected up to the live donor spleen twice that he began to recover... This method has been used in two other hospitals in the treatment of critical cases where all other methods had failed. It saved quite a number of patients who were on the brink of death through various severe infections. Results like these are encouraging, so we are waiting impatiently for methodological recommendations enabling wider use of this method.' Having helped the Sverdlovsk doctors to save one dying patient, Tsypin and Makarov also treated three others, one of whom was a young girl who had suffered a serious septic infection through having squeezed a boil on her face...

I asked Dr. Tsypin if there had been cases where their method had failed.

'We have had cases of every kind. However, as a rule we have been successful, and our intervention has helped to save lives,' replied Anatolii Borisovich. 'We have not, of course, always been able to respond to every appeal for help. That is why we attach importance to training specialists in a number of cities, and prepare methodological recommendations. When these are published, the new method will become more widespread.

The specialists who have discovered the method of haemosorption do not see it as the answer to everything. It should be used alongside other tried methods of intensive therapy. However, it must be noted that where pig's spleen was used as a filter, the number of deaths was halved.

Specialists from the FRG, the USA, Canada and Spain have indicated interest in this method. It is already practiced in some other socialist countries. Professor Tsypin's laboratory is conducting experiments on animals to see if this method can be used in treating other illnesses.

Izvestia, 7 October 1987

Human Rights

What is meant by human rights whenever the Soviet Union is under discussion in the West is only one component of the concept — freedom to leave the USSR, or even more specifically, the freedom of Jewish emigration from the Soviet Union under any pretext, such as the reunification of families, freedom of movement or simply the person's desire to live wherever it suits him best.

However, there is nothing more incorrect, nothing which distorts more the real state of affairs than reducing the whole spectrum of human rights to a person's right to leave his homeland. The numerous dramas that at times end in tragedy stem from the inability to see that the issue of human rights does not consist solely of the right of Soviet citizens to leave the USSR.

The broader scope of our understanding of the problem could be seen from the previous sections in this volume. Here, we shall concentrate on the issues that could be of use in explaining the Soviet view of the human rights issue in all its complexity.

Perestroika *begins with the individual — this has almost become a cliché in the Soviet press. This idea is so obvious that hardly any comment is required. Still, we should try to bring its essence into sharper focus.*

It is true that perestroika *begins with the individual, for the simple reason that man, in Marx's phrase, as the sum total of social relations (and the essence of each person is revealed precisely in this totality) has always been and will always remain the main asset, the object and subject of history, the means, aim and, in the final analysis, purpose of history. Let us recall another of his famous definitions: communism is 'the complete return of man to himself as a* social *(i.e., human) being.' Marx's use of the word 'human' to make his point clearer is most significant. It reveals the main difference between the Marxist view of the nature of the new social system and that held by all other ideologies which do not recognise communism as the highest and most humane form of social organisation.*

Let us, however, return to Marx: 'This communism, as fully developed naturalism, equals humanism, and as fully developed humanism equals naturalism; it is the genuine *resolution of the conflict between man and nature and between man and man — the true resolution of the strife between existence and essence, between objectification and self-confirmation, between freedom and necessity, between the individual and the species. Communism is the riddle of history solved, and it knows itself to be this solution.'*

These words, which for the first time in the history of philosophy set forth the human *nature of communism, were written by Marx at age 26 in 1844. In fact, Marx was to spend the rest of his life elaborating and scientifically substantiating this essentially simple thought: 'Communism as the* positive *transcendence of* private property *as* human self-estrangement, *and therefore as the real* appropriation *of the* human essence by and for man; communism *therefore as the complete return of man to himself as a* social *(i.e., human) being — a return accomplished consciously and embracing the entire wealth of previous development.'*

There is nothing to be added to or subtracted from this formula. It expresses Marx's idea in such a complete and clear-cut form that any commentary, to say nothing of interpretation, will inevitably distort the presentation.

As if foreseeing that these words would be taken repeatedly out of context, repeatedly stripped of their true meaning — the true, human essence of communism — the 25-year-old Engels wrote one year later, in 1845: 'What is involved is to create for all people *such a condition that everyone can freely develop his human nature and live in a human relationship with his neighbours, and has no need to fear any violent shattering of his condition... Far from wishing to destroy real human life with all its requirements and needs, we wish on the contrary really to bring it into being.'*

What Marx formulated with chiselled precision as a law of social development, Engels brought down to earth in concrete, tangible form. Indeed, doesn't the 'appropriation *of the* human *essence by and for man' imply the right to 'freely develop his human nature'? And what else could 'fully developed humanism equals naturalism' point to but the desire to create* for all people *'real human life with all its requirements and needs'? In other words, to create a* life *worthy of* man, *and* man *worthy of this* new, human life.

They say that all brilliant ideas are simple. Yet nowhere can we find, throughout the history of human cognition, a simplicity to match Marx's and Engels' brilliant discovery of the nature and principles of communism.

The simplicity of truly brilliant ideas also consists in their universality. History moves in capricious and meandering ways; there are times, stretching into the decades, when the concerns of the immediate present take priority. In solving these issues, people tend to lose sight of essential, long-term goals. The consequences of this short-sightedness are only too well known, viz., *the bitter lessons of Soviet history. Nevertheless, at the turning points of history — and today's* perestroika *in the Soviet Union is nothing if not a turning point — the brilliant simplicity of these laws of social development 'suddenly' reveals its strikingly specific applicability.*

Indeed, isn't the programme for the renewal of life suggested by Marx and Engels applicable today? Consider 'embracing the entire wealth of previous development'. What else could Marx and Engels have had in mind but the wealth of material and spiritual culture accumulated to date — the human experience, a healthy morality, and the achievements of industry and science. And doesn't 'the complete return of man to himself as a social *(i.e., human) being' indicate a restructuring of society such as to replace inert, politically indifferent people (I want to go where life is better and easier), who work like automata, with free and equal people enjoying the unlimited opportunity to develop their potential and interests, to satisfy every one of their own — and hence equal for all — material and spiritual needs?*

By 'equal for all' we mean the equal opportunity *to develop all the talents that socialist society guarantees* each and every one *of its citizens, and not the notorious 'levelling off' which cost our society so dearly. 'Levelling off' was rejected by Marx and Engels as the pipedream of universal happiness (see Marx's* Critique of the Gotha Programme*). For Marx and Engels the* sine qua non *for the construction of com-*

munism was the comprehensive development of the productive forces. This postulate is more than relevant today. Because without the comprehensive development of the productive forces (and here we have yet another argument against 'levelling off') 'privation, want *is merely made general, and with* want *the struggle for necessities would begin again, and all the old filthy business would necessarily be restored'.*

It goes without saying that abject privation *is out of the question in the socialist society of today. But doesn't the limited variety, and occasionally the complete absence (oh those damned shortages!) of various essentials — be it consumer goods or foodstuffs — resurrect 'the old filthy business' that so disgusted Marx and Engels? To cite but one example of this 'filthy business' which became public knowledge thanks to* glasnost *in the Soviet Union: in 1945, at the end of the Great Patriotic War, which consumed more than 20 million people in its flames, to say nothing of the material losses incurred, the Soviet state had to support 365,000 orphans; today there are over one million (!) children in orphanages throughout the Soviet Union, and what is more, most of their parents are still alive. Can there be any business more filthy than this? It becomes even more appalling when we consider that each of these children has a mother, father, grandparents and other relatives, close or distant as the case may be.*

We realise that this filthy business cannot be ascribed solely to the 'struggle for necessities' (suffice it to compare the living standards endured by Soviet citizens in 1945, when there was a real shortage of real necessities, *and the living standards and social security of today). Nonetheless, we should not reject out of hand the 'struggle for necessities' (even considering that times have changed so that the category of 'necessities' has expanded beyond all recognition to include the luxury items of yesteryear). Perhaps it does indeed have something to do with the 'filthy business' cited above.*

In general, when discussing the 'struggle for necessities', or in a broader sense, the struggle to satisfy human needs which resurrects 'all the old filthy business', we must bear in mind the sum total of the highly complex, negative economic, social, political, ethical, psychological and other phenomena captured today in the single word stagnation. Glasnost *stimulated the thorough-going analysis of this negative phenome-*

non in the Soviet press. Economists, philosophers, historians, jurists, people of all ages and walks of life openly express their often differing points of view — and this is good. Good for the single reason that this free exchange of opinion contributes to a better understanding of the deep-rooted processes in social existence, to the search for the best ways to promote perestroika.

As we see, it is unwise, if not to say simply unforgivable, to reduce the issue of human rights to the right of Soviet citizens to leave the USSR freely. Dozens, hundreds and even thousands may leave. Let them leave. The procedure for obtaining an exit visa is becoming more and more streamlined. What about the millions of Soviet citizens who haven't the slightest desire to emigrate to another country? Don't these millions enjoy the right to live the kind of life Marx and Engels envisaged? They certainly do. And that is why today, more than ever, the issue of rights in the Soviet Union (which is understood in a far broader sense than in the West) has acquired a special significance. For, as has been justly said, perestroika begins with the individual. *We should like to add that it begins in the name of man, for the sake of creating the most* humane *society on Earth.*

Not a single rouble sent to the account of the Soviet Children's Fund is spent to maintain the staff of its Board (the personnel's salaries are paid from the funds raised by publishing the monthly Semya *(Family) and carrying out other forms of creative work). As of early October 1987, 125 million roubles had been deposited in account No. 707. For whom is this money intended?*

The Presidium of the Board came to the unanimous conclusions that the funds should be first of all allocated to children's homes. Today, the country has 420 of them. The 35,200 children kept there are under three years of age. They are divided into groups of 15 to 17. Reducing the number of children in the groups to between seven and ten will make it possible to improve their physical and mental well-being and create for them a home-like environment. The funds channeled to children's homes will also make it possible to hire 1,777 more tutors whose total salaries will amount to 2.95 million roubles a year. The state could not allocate such funds until 1990. With this in mind, the Presidium of the Board decided to use, without waiting for 1990, its funds to improve the physical and mental health of children in children's homes.

It is gratifying to note that people from many countries support the movement to protect the rights of orphans launched in the USSR. Here is the list of donations that had been sent to account No. 707 by foreign citizens by 7 November 1987:

Austrian schillings 96,720
US dollars 1,776
French francs 10,150
Swiss francs 1,000
Deutsche marks (FRG) 10,055
Deutsche marks (GDR) 605
Spanish pesetas 5,000
Polish zlotys 7,600

THE SOVIET CHILDREN'S FUND

An interview with ALBERT LIKHANOV

Two years ago a CPSU resolution on orphanages was adopted. Little has changed since then, don't you think?

The 1985 resolution concerning orphanages focused mainly on the problem of facilities and supplies. Before the resolution a teenager in an orphanage had three pairs of socks, whereas after it he had seven; before he had one coat, now he has two; before he would wear his pants for five years, now he wears them for a shorter period. The personnel of the orphanages had their wages considerably increased.

But... the basic problem remains the same. The resolution was taken but not implemented in spirit. It contained phrases about the need to pay more attention to the life of teenagers and children in children's homes and orphanages, but nothing really important has yet happened. Many responsible bodies continue to disregard children's homes and after the resolution only a few people began to pay some attention to orphanages. The old system continued to operate. On receiving the resolution many high-up leaders sent it down to subordinate bodies, say, to the regional department of state education. The latter's boss then sent it down to his subordinates. And so on and so forth in familiar descending circles.

I am sure now that the Soviet Children's Fund, a national voluntary organisation, called upon to carry on the Leninist traditions of care and concern for children, has been firmly established, and that those at the highest level will ensure the 'decisive turn of the Party, trade union and Komsomol organisations, of Soviet and economic bodies, the work collectives of head and patronage enterprises, and of the broad public to the urgent problems related to the upbringing and education of children and teenagers', narrow and formal approaches must be ruled out.

What is most outrageous about orphanages and children's homes is the gap between our socialist principles and ideals and their realisation as applied to children's institutions. What sort of social justice is it when most of the children kept in the orphanages after they finish the eighth grade are shoved into vocational schools, when only fifty orphans from all over Russia were able to go to college in 1987? According to the material that I have about the Irkutsk orphanage, the kids there were not only beaten, mocked and abused, but the orphanage director, following the Party's resolution on strengthening the material base of orphanages, bought ... lots of crystal and china sets for herself.

Orphanages, boarding schools and children's homes have for a long time been a closed system. It should be opened and made accountable to society. Currently the People's Control Committee is carrying out a random check of orphanages. The data so far collected and published by the magazine *Kommunist* shows that only one-fifth of the one hundred and fifty orphanages have been recognised as adequate. One-fifth! All the rest are in bad shape, and this means various abuses being committed by staff, including theft. There are certainly decent people, there is Antonina Khlebushkina in Tashkent, there is Alexander Katolikov in Syktyvkar who has acted as father for many children. But side by side with them are many people who abuse the advantages of their posts and capitalise on children's defencelessness. An atmosphere of teachers' lawlessness reigns in many orphanages. This is a system where the most defenceless suffer from the pressure of adult injustice.

You have not said anything about the causes of the tragedy which befalls the children in such institutions. Present-day orphans more often than not have parents. Would you excuse me Comrade Chairman if I asked you: when did you last visit an orphanage or children's home?

Last time? Yesterday. I visit them regularly for that matter. Everything about them is painful, that goes even for the good ones. What strikes you most is not their poverty or everyday difficulties, but the psychological situation. Children there are largely deprived of hope because they have lost all faith in adults. You were right in saying that almost all of them have parents. But most of the parents have abandoned them, are serving time in prison or have become alcoholics.

Children there live as all children do without thinking of their lot every minute. Each of them is absorbed in something. But just recall the televised round table discussion attended by Alexander Katolikov, director of Syktyvkar Orphanage No. 1. Have you watched it?

Everything seems to be going well there and I have a profound respect for this remarkable person whose entire life is without exaggeration a feat of heroism. I feel, however, that Katolikov did not say everything. Remember what he said about the thousands of letters children from his orphanage sent out, searching for a relative, a support in life, a connection with the outside world. Isn't that shocking? In other words, no matter how well-fed, clothed, and shod they are, no matter how deeply engaged they are in the education process, this is not all they need. Much about their mentality, world-view and state of mind is unresolved. They send letters to nowhere. Does this mean that they will get answers from nowhere? From no one? It is hard for them to escape their loneliness. It is still harder for them when they leave orphanage. The friendlier the children are in the orphanage, the harder it is for them to leave their 'home' and to go to live in the hostel of a vocational school or a factory where loneliness hits them all the more bitterly. Thus the axiom of Khlebushkina, Katolikov and other orphanage principals is creating an oasis of virtue, as it were. But if we talk about the system as a whole, we must recognise that hundreds of children come to orphanages and leave them feeling that there is no justice in the world. This feeling is instilled in them since their childhood. Can a decent human tolerate this? This is something that has always enraged me. There is a curious social phenomenon in this country — we hate unpleasant stories. A person might notice something that pains him and understands that he ought to interfere, but for all that, he does practically nothing. That is to say he is compassionate or sympathetic, he sheds a tear and then he wipes it away and resumes his journey. He doesn't want to return to the bitterness and misfortunes of these children. It is more than once that I heard decent people saying, 'What is going on there is horrible. I was there once and I will never go back again. It rends my heart.' What happens is a sort of egotistic alienation of part of society from these children and their problems.

And in general, what is happening to children in our society? We once hypnotised ourselves with assertions that children were our only privileged class. This self-hypnosis has lead to increasing child mortality. During 1986 alone 140,000 infants under 12 months died. How much do we know about child oncology or child cardio-pathology? Or about juvenile delinquency?

Don't you think that these 'child issues' largely mirror all those painful problems that face our society and are now being talked about in public? Don't you think that in fact they reflect the painful processes in our social and moral life?

Yes. I do believe that the disaster is rooted in the state of our society over the last decades. In a word, there was one state of affairs and in deed, another.

Today we are facing the task of instilling in people's consciousness the importance of child-related issues. We should raise our voices in defence of children, we should help them... We will regain our health as children become healthier.

Furthermore, consider statistics, true and false. In this country a million children are deprived of parental care. Only 300,000 of them are cared for in orphanages, boarding schools and children's homes. The remaining 700,000 are placed under the care of a guardian or trustee. But no one knows anything about the quality of trusteeship and guardianship. Are there any objective indications by which we can judge them? How many such children are there in a district, region or republic? Where exactly are they now and what is their condition? How do their guardians treat them? Inspectors from the departments of public education are supposed to 'keep an eye' on such children. That is exactly what they do and nothing more. The quality of their supervision and the analysis of the situation these children find themselves in are not worth talking about. I feel that it is a task of the Children's Fund to exercise constant control over all the orphanages and all the children placed under guardianship. The Fund will inevitably come into conflict with various departments of the Ministry of Education. But that is exactly what the country needs today. We should stand up and fight for these children.

This is evidently not the only task the Soviet Children's Fund is called upon to undertake. During your television appearance you said that the Fund was not simply a savings bank. What other tasks should the Fund address?

To assist invalid children, among other things. Is our society fully aware of them? No. It knows little. War invalids are passing away. Their place is taken by children born invalids. What do we know about this problem? I have been to many boarding schools for invalid children. They are the responsibility of the Ministry of Social Security and not the Ministry of Education. What can I tell you? I believe a revolution is needed there too. People should be responsible for children even before they are born. Aren't children of alcoholics a serious problem? Go to any children's home and see for yourself. A horrible sight.

Child health care, child rest and recreation industry... Here, in our Children's Fund, many enormous moral and social problems will be addressed. The Fund ought to assist in resolving them. What about the family? What is happening to it? There can be no doubt that the foundation of the family should be strengthened. But in what way? This is a question to be considered by a public organisation.

The Fund will be there, the Fund will publish its own weekly *Semya* (Family). Plans have been made to set up in Moscow a Childhood Research Institute under the USSR Academy of Pedagogical Sciences. The institute will deal with the whole spectrum of problems related to the children in this country. It will undertake accurate research, careful study of the issue of childhood. In fact, we don't know much about it, we lack statistics in many areas. What we know is that annually, a total of 700,000 children are left in single-parent homes. Their ages vary from 12 months to 18 years. While in China, for instance, the divorce rate is far below one per cent. Plus, there is practically no alcoholism... We often look to the developed countries to find out how things are there. There, too, serious work is being done to strengthen the family.

There are certainly things we can boast about. We have a beautiful children's theatre, a puppet theatre, but this is only an oasis in a desert. There are many unhappy children in two-parent homes. There are many families where children have both parents and yet are terribly neglected. But no one is permitted to take them away from their father and mother. Although these children grow like weeds, sleep on straw, if you will, and don't know what it means to have clean bed clothes and a bath. This is no exaggeration, this is the bitter truth.

I believe we need a social institution which will be empowered to tackle problems of vital importance to children. We should rely on kindness and kind people, not on figureheads. Even the Fund's personnel should deal with the problems directly, being good organisers, capable of inspiring others... If what we create is a bureaucratic structure where no one is willing to move a finger, our cause will perish. We are in search of good people. We have found many of them. But the search will continue. We need people of all professions, of all walks of life. In fact, we are creating a new public, popular organisation, an organisation of adults for children. We have never had one of this kind.

I hope that the Children's Fund will enable many people to fulfil themselves. I have many letters from such people, from ones who are willing to work. There are letters from engineers, for instance. Let me cite one. 'I am 40 and my husband 48. We have plenty of free time and would like to use our abilities for something else besides our work. We have decided to re-educate ourselves in an entirely new field.'

This confirms the idea I have had for a long time. There are many people born in the 1930s and 1940s who feel their lives are not complete. At the same time, we were brought up to strive to serve society. Children are something one can easily devote oneself to. Their gratitude is always rewarding even though not expressed in words. I am pleased to read in many letters that people would be happy to work in children's homes.

We have not discussed children's health and the question of coordinating activity of councils of trustees and the legal aspect of the activities of the Children's Fund. Meanwhile, control over the observance of the legislation related to the protection of children's rights and interests is highly important.

The Children's Fund is to initiate and stimulate the improvement of legislation in the interests of the child. We have problems in connection with notarial issues and inheritance rights. It would be good to have a law providing for the mutual responsibility of parents and children. While a child is small the person who has given birth to him is responsible for him in many respects. But when the parents grow old, their children should act responsibly towards them. Moreover, we should adopt a declaration of children's rights, a document of moral and political significance which will guarantee children's rights and society's responsibility for them.

The Children's Fund should have a powerful legal department to provide judicial protection to children. We need experienced lawyers to conduct affairs concerning the protection of children. They should be honest and humane.

Let me cite an example. There was a case in Leningrad when a mother died and her daughter was taken to an orphanage. The mother and daughter had lived in a large communal apartment. What did the neighbours do? One might think that they occupied the dead woman's room at least for a time. But no. They rented the room out and the rent received was put in a savings account in the name of the daughter. When the girl returned from the orphanage, she got her room back plus the money in the savings account.

You can imagine that quite different examples could also be cited. There are many cases of children taken to orphanages and their rooms or apartments being misappropriated by 'kind' neighbours or relatives. A boy may return from the army to find he has no home. So here are the two possible approaches to children. I am committed to the humane approach.

Society, including the Party, must create conditions to improve our moral standards. We should become more humane, always remembering that we are humans. I believe that the Children's Fund will enable many of us to prove our worth in the most sensitive and the most pure area — the concern for children. Although we can create many other institutions where people can find worthwhile things to do. This is a big country and there are many things to do.

Finally, could you tell our readers the account number of the Soviet Children's Fund.

Gladly. *Account No. 707.* Soviet citizens working abroad or foreigners may contribute foreign currency. Vneshtorgbank (Bank for Foreign Trade) has opened a special *account No. 7070.*

Interview by Tatiana PORETSKAYA

The early 1970s and the late 1980s saw a number of sensational trials for what was described as 'economic crimes'. These 'crimes' were committed by people who held managerial posts in the economy. Shackled in their work by innumerable instructions, they were compelled to violate these in the interests of the common, not their own, good. One of those sentenced to a long term was IVAN KHUDENKO, director of the successful Akchi state farm in Kazakhstan. He did not live to see his case reviewed and died in a corrective labour camp.

Human rights were violated not only because of the strict adherence to innumerable and often absurd instructions, but also because of the ambitions of the higher-up management and personal enmity between people of various levels of importance in the structure. Not infrequently this was behind the institution of legal proceedings. An outrageous case is cited below.

THE CASE OF VITALY SURGUTSKY

By IGOR ABAKUMOV and FYODOR DYOMIN

On the morning of 18 November 1983 he was summoned to the district Party committee to sign some important papers. He was surprised: didn't they know that he was on holiday? An hour later he came into the office where the members of the bureau sat. A minute later he understood everything — his personal case was to be heard. He listened to all the accusations and as calmly as possible explained that the 'facts' were either distorted or falsified. He begged to sort them out, but no one listened to him. A vote was taken and the bureau members went to the conference hall where the participants in the plenary meeting were already waiting for them. The procedure repeated itself.

This was how the 48-year-old Vitaly Surgutsky, director of a well-known state farm near Moscow, was expelled from the Party and sacked from his office within an hour. Why? Neither he, nor his colleagues ever learnt the answer. Some said that he had stolen 130,000 roubles, others that he was about to run away to Canada. Whatever the real reason, he was imprisoned for 2 years.

They say there's no smoke without fire, but this was not the case here. No one now can erase from his life the 20 months Surgutsky spent in solitary confinement.

We have known him for a long time. He came to the Moscow Region from the Krasnoyarsk Territory in February 1976. There is always a shortage of good directors and he was willingly accepted. An agronomist, a graduate of the Academy of Social Sciences of the CPSU Central Committee, a Candidate of Sciences, with a background as collective farm chairman, district executive committee chairman, district Party committee secretary — is there a better biography? He was asked to take over the Tuchkovsky state farm in the Ruza District.

The farm was in a deplorable state — lacking personnel, fodder, facilities. Cows with calfs could only stand if they were pulled up by ropes. Surgutsky agreed to take up the job. He sent trucks to the Ukraine and Smolensk to fetch straw. He himself spent days at the wheel in search of seeds, fuel, and spare parts.

For a start he tightened discipline. The sowing campaign was carried out on time. He made cuts in the managerial personnel so as to pay more money to the mechanics for whom the state farm had a far greater need. In the autumn, the farm had fully supplied itself with the required amount of fodder. Small wonder — everyone could now understand the terms of payment. Since then the farm never bought fodder, but, on the contrary, sold excess fodder to its neighbours. This was the new style of work — economic levers replaced administrative commands.

In three years' time the farm's name was a regular feature in the newspapers as it was now the only state farm in the district to have a stable profit. Roads were built, its workers lived in apartment houses with modern conveniences; the farm had potato and grain storages, a garage, a calf house, etc. From the outside, it seemed a fairy tale come true: *veni, vidi, vici.*

In the spring of 1983, the Timiryazev Academy set up a post on the Tuchkovsky state farm to study the effect of erosion-proof tillage. In the summer, there came a request from Moscow to consider the possibility of sending Surgutsky to Canada as a member of a Soviet delegation to study the Canadian experience of soil protection against erosion.

In November he was summoned to the district Party committee.

People tend to hope for the best. Surgutsky, too, hoped that in a week or two the bad dream would pass. He hoped that the regional Party committee would clear the matter up. But the people there gave him a cold reception. Those very people who just the day before had cited his state farm as a model one and beamed whenever they met him, now looked at him curiously as if they knew something about him he himself did not.

The long nine months without work followed — no one would hire him. He was homeless, too: the apartment he had lived in went with the job and he lost this together with his office. He had no money. When he was sacked, he was not paid the balance of his salary. He filed several complaints asking that justice be done or that he be told the reasons why he had been expelled. If only he could know the price he would have to pay for these complaints!

The former Ruza District prosecutor V. Dmitryakov recalls:

'I was summoned by the first secretary of the district Party committee Veretennikov and ordered to have Surgutsky arrested. I refused. I didn't have any grounds to do that. He called me in several more times and became more and more annoyed. He would suggest the places to conduct the search. What were the motives? Surgutsky had written to higher bodies, so they now had to substantiate his expulsion from both the Party and his office. They started checking the materials gathered by the Party commission of the district committee but failed to find anything. Veretennikov was beside himself with anger. He would call my superior at the office and some other places. He would tell me that the regional Party committee knew that Surgutsky was a criminal and that I did wrong to be so slow in arresting him. I was repeatedly requested to account for myself and was finally given a Party reprimand... At last the legal action was instituted by the regional procurator's office.'

It was hard to establish when exactly the clouds started gathering above Surgutsky's head.

The reader will remember in what state the district had been before Surgutsky, a total stranger, came. It took him a short time to make the farm a working success. He was constantly praised at conferences, interviewed by reporters, consulted by scientists and invited to appear on television. Could the local people who had been there before him and had their own plans for the future tolerate all that? The story was not a new one — the 'cataract' could only be treated in one of the two ways: either they had to improve themselves or they had to stop him. The latter was not hard to do, the more so as Surgutsky with his hot temper was easy prey. He was a difficult and tough man. He would cook his own chickens for the tractor drivers and, at the same time, could pretend not to notice the outstretched hand of a district leader who had failed to keep his word.

In his second year on the farm he had a clash with the secretary of the farm's Party committee who got so carried away with investigating 'signals' that almost the entire collective became involved in the process. When it came to investigating the rumour about the love affair between the driver and the milkmaid, Surgutsky flew into a rage and told the man publicly what he thought of him. The district leadership tried to reconcile them, but the secretary would not give up his position as a fighter 'for the purity of the Party ranks'. In order to cover up the scandal, he was transferred ... to the district Party committee and put in charge of a department. His name was Veretennikov, the very same man.

In September 1983 Veretennikov was elected first secretary of the district Party committee. As soon as Surgutsky went on holiday, the chairperson of the Party commission Bebneva was told to start a dossier on him. In November the director was summoned to the Party bureau. None of the bureau members with whom we met had studied the materials in advance. Veretennikov had counted on the surprise factor. Several staff of the Party committee had been told to stand guard at the doors so that they could stop Surgutsky in case he sensed the danger and decided to leave.

What was in the dossier? One of the files read: 'In defiance of established rules, Comrade Surgutsky's garden house has three stories.' Isn't this impressive? Yes, if you have not seen it for yourself. We have. It is an ordinary house. It has one storey, an attic, and a basement, all according to the blueprint.

It was not until nine months later that the regional Party committee gave orders to let Surgutsky have a job. This was how the former state farm director, a Candidate of Sciences, became manager of a state farm department in the Mozhaisk district. In February 1985 there came a knock at the door: 'I am from the prosecutor's office. Please come along with me.' There was a militia car waiting outside. He got in not knowing that he would never come back. In the evening the door of his solitary confinement cell clanged shut behind him.

He was to spend 20 months there. He was to mark his fiftieth birthday there. The report that his mother could not withstand the news of his arrest reached him only after a long delay.

His head swam with the accusations with which he was confronted: 'The embezzlement of 2,523 roubles, a 20,000 rouble bribe, an attempt at taking a bribe of 30,000 roubles.'

At first he would laugh, appeal to the logic of the investigator from the regional prosecutor's office, Kucherinov, then fly into a rage, then ridicule the stupidity of accusations, then realise that all that was in earnest. He had to fight. He started to make notes, from memory, of the interrogations, analysing every detail of the accusations, studying the terminology and perusing the legal code... He realised that Kucherinov did not dispose of a single fact and that during the trial the whole structure of his accusations will collapse. Provided the trial was going to be objective. Provided... With every interrogation his belief in objectivity waned. Although Kucherinov represented justice, he failed to see the obvious.

Violations of the law... He heard many farm directors and chairmen saying frankly that if one observed all the conflicting instructions, one would never be able to produce a ton of meat or lay a kilometre of asphalt road. One would learn the taste of misfortune being caught between the concern for the harvest and people's needs on the one hand, and the barrage of orders and instructions on the other. On top of all that there is the inviolability of the authorities. The chances to survive are slim. There are many of those who ruined themselves because for the sake of common cause they overrode someone's orders. Many were caught for the slightest misdemeanour simply to remove them from someone's path, to hinder or muzzle them. Why should our economic managers be doomed to such a fate? Why should people who see to it that you and I are fed properly constantly have to defend and justify themselves? Throughout the country there are not more than 50,000 farm directors and chairmen, 0.01 per cent of the nation's population. Most of them are the best people to be had in this area, selected for their jobs by life itself. They should be cherished as the apple of one's eye. However, they were removed with a shocking alacrity, under the motto 'there are no irreplaceable people'. More often than not, they were honest, capable and talented people who are especially needed today when one bright head is valued far more than hundreds of talkers and when everyone understands that nothing can be expected from an economy that works like a turnstile.

Days and months flew by. He became a veteran in his prison cell; people came and went, spring gave way to summer, he moved from the upper bunk to the lower and it seemed that there would be no end to the torture. Surgutsky was hungry for news from the outside — what was happening outside was long awaited and amazing, the country was swept by change. He was happy when in the speeches or articles by his colleagues he found confirmation of his ideas. He was excited when he read about the cases of justice restored because it concerned him too. The only question to which he could not find an answer was whether the change would reach his prison or not.

Surgutsky wrote about 100 appeals asking for a different investigator, a second inquiry and the inclusion of new factual material in his case. They were all refused. He complained that he could not read the badly copied documents of his case. Kucherinov denied his request for better copies.

The time of the trial came. The public prosecutor A. Koshkaryova ended her speech with the words: 'Sentenced to ten years hard labour with all property confiscated.'

On 6 November 1986, the Moscow Regional Court chaired by R. V. Nazarov announced the verdict: 'Acquitted due to the absence of a criminal act ..., of a *corpus delicti*. To be released from custody in court.'

That was all. Not guilty. Acquittal is followed, as is known, by the restoration of one's rights and compensation for the damage done. However the procurator has the right to protest if he does not agree with the verdict. Such a protest was presented in this case to the Supreme Court of the RSFSR. On the day of the session, however, the protest was revoked by the republican procurator's office. On 19 February 1987 the not-guilty verdict was legally affirmed. Surgutsky was again told: 'Not guilty!'

But the matter did not end here. To this day the question of compensation is under legal debate. We won't go into the details. We can only say one thing: a person acquitted more than six months ago has still not had his rights reinstated.

And here we are again in Ruza. Changes are going on here too. Veretennikov is no longer on the district committee. He was removed for 'behaviour not befitting a Party member'. This unpleasant case was widely talked about. But it remains on the conscience of those who at one time declared him the 'model official'.

The day the Supreme Court of the RSFSR convened another director of the state farm was brought in because the former one resigned as soon as he heard of Surgutsky's acquittal.

The Timiryazev Academy post is no longer there. Under Veretennikov the experiments with erosion-proof tillage were declared charlatanism.

The state farm buys fodder from its neighbours again.

Last winter the rest of the straw procured under Surgutsky was used up. The farm now ranks among the non-profitable ones and has to be subsidised by the state. Housing construction has ceased and experienced personnel are leaving the farm.

When we called on people on the regional Party committee they found an excuse to avoid meeting us. As for Surgutsky, they said, well, he was an experienced director but his temper ... and, in general, let the court and the procurator's office sort things out for themselves... Besides, they said, he is not a Party member. The matter is a complicated one and it needs to be studied with care.

The whole story has continued for three and a half years. For three and a half years an experienced manager has been put out to pasture, and the farm he made a working success is on the decline. Does this benefit anyone at all?

Another question arises. We can assume that Surgutsky had made enemies on the farm and among the district and regional authorities. That happens. But why did the protective mechanisms of the Law and the norms of our democracy fail to operate?

Izvestia, 24 July 1987

Many readers are concerned about the fate of VITALY SURGUTSKY. *The editors of* Izvestia *have received 540 letters all containing the same question: how is Surgutsky?*

In October 1987 Izvestia *returned to the story of Surgutsky. It has turned out that not only individual readers are concerned about his fate, but also whole institutions. Thus, Surgutsky was invited to visit the All-Union Research Institute of Agricultural Biology. After a week he became its deputy director. This was completely unexpected by both himself and the director. How did this happen? The director, Member of the Academy of Agricultural Sciences,* GEORGI MUROMTSEV, *gives the following explanation:*

'Science has become an autonomous operation, by this I mean that an experienced agricultural scientist, well-versed in legal matters, ought to establish connections with industry. After having met and spoken with Vitaly Surgutsky, a decision was reached. Acting in the way a contemporary manager must, he quickly adjusted to his new role. Moreover, he is

a real warrior, unbending under any circumstances. This is a quality so needed today.'

On 1 October 1987 yet another event occurred: Surgutsky received monetary compensation for the years of his 'forced absence'. By the order of the Regional Court of Moscow, he was paid 22,359 roubles and one kopeck. I. Borokhova, branch manager of the State Bank of the USSR, commented: 'In 23 years of work, I do not remember an instance when a rehabilitated person was paid such a sum. I think this is a just decision, definitely a sign of the times.'

Surgutsky then donated 300 roubles for erecting a monument to the soldier hero of ALEXANDER TVARDOVSKY'S *'Vassily Terkin.'*

'This soldier taught me determination. Unfortunately I am unable to donate more at this time. I have a lot of accumulated debts. Friends have supported me when I was unemployed. As far as the money is concerned, it does not give me much pleasure. After all this is neither a case of wages nor is it an award; a moral damage is not measured out in roubles.'

This is true. For three years the good name of Surgutsky was publicly dragged through the mud. And those who either willingly or unwillingly encouraged this did not even attempt to apologize. This does not even include the punishment of those officials who profited from this story. They, by the way, did not suffer in the least from all the consequences of their mistakes (or designs?) for which the government assumed responsibility.

No matter how great the compensation for the 'forced absence', it will never surpass the moral damage inflicted on a person by illegitimate actions. This is obvious! Soviet people need the guarantee that the law and only the law will stand guard over their rights written in the Constitution. They need a guarantee against any violation of the law, no matter who the violator, a guarantee fraught with serious consequences not for those whose rights have been violated, but for those who have violated these rights.

Perestroika *in the Soviet judicial system is aimed at the creation of these guarantees. The following is an interview with* VLADIMIR TEREBILOV, *Chairman of the Supreme Court of the USSR.*

THE LAW AND ONLY THE LAW

Could you say a few words about the foundation upon which the Soviet judicial system is built?

The foundation of the system was set by Lenin. In early December 1917 the Decree on Court was signed, abolishing the old tsarist judicial system.

It took the enormous talent of Lenin and the vast knowledge and enthusiasm of his associates to create a truly people's court based on the genuine democratic principles of justice, in the interests of the newly created state of the working people. There are more than 13,000 judges in the Soviet Union. In the last elections more than 850,000 People's Assessors were elected.

In regard to Soviet courts we cannot, of course, forget the grim thirties and forties. The numerous violations of the law which took place at that time were not, however, the result of our socialist system as is asserted by our ideological opponents. They were the result of deviations from socialism and of a blatant disregard for the law on the part of some officials, made possible by the atmosphere of the personality cult.

The Communist Party gave this a principled evaluation. Great pains have been taken to rehabilitate arbitrarily repressed people. This work is still going on. In 1984-87 alone the Supreme Court of the USSR reconsidered cases and rehabilitated more than 240 people who were groundlessly condemned in the thirties and forties.

What must we now do in order to keep from repeating the mistakes of the past?

It is absolutely necessary to change radically the work of the courts. The change is suggested by the lessons of the past, which we have previously discussed, and the state of affairs today when we still encounter many violations of legality by law-enforcement bodies and serious juridical errors. Some courts are still bent on passing guilty verdicts and mechanically repeat the conclusions of preliminary investigation. But *perestroika* is gaining momentum. Perhaps not as obviously and as quickly as we would like. This is testified in part by a certain decline in the crime rate and in the number of prison sentences in cases where those guilty can be punished by other means. The courts have begun to

approach seriously the evaluation of the preliminary investigation. For example, in the first six months of 1987 the
number of cases returned for further investigation or dropped on rehabilitation grounds, as well as the number of
non-guilty verdicts, was considerably greater than during
any six-month period in the past years. Proposals on restructuring the investigative machinery, the Bar, etc. are being drawn up.

However, we need further judicial reform, a reform
which would involve a change in the work of not only the
court but also of all other law-enforcement bodies responsible for the administration of the law.

What, in your opinion, should this reform involve?

We need more *glasnost* concerning court statistics. Information should be provided to the public every year and in
greater detail than at present. This should be the responsibility of the USSR Ministry of Justice whose business it is,
among other things, to compile statistics. *Glasnost* can also
be promoted by launching a judicial newspaper.

It would also be advisable to heighten the role of the general public in the work of the courts. It would also be useful to determine the volume and character of work to be
carried out by the investigative bodies which prepare the
'groundwork' for the trial. They should be made more independent and responsible, while the supervision of the legiti-
macy of the investigator's actions by the prosecution should
actually involve supervision and not patronage. We should
provide for more effective guarantees for the accused's right
to defence. This can be achieved, above all, through restructuring the way in which the Soviet Bar operates and revising
criminal law, the law of criminal procedure, labour law, etc.
so that they fully correspond to the new context in which
our society and democracy is developing.

In my view we should revise, once again, the system
whereby judges are elected so as to improve the personnel
standards.

Corrective labour institutions, too, are in need of change.
What should lie at the core of the judicial reform is the
guaranteed independence of judges.

*This is quite a programme... I would like to clarify a few
points. You are talking about the independence of the courts.
Their independence is guaranteed by law, isn't it? Neverthe-*

less, we often hear about judges delivering a sentence under pressure from officials. How can we stop such practices?

You are right, there are instances of meddling in judicial affairs on the part of government officials, managerial and Party bodies. Unfortunately, not all judges have enough civic courage to oppose overt or covert pressure, requests and instructions, or manipulated public opinion. This means we need additional guarantees to prevent outside influence on judicial decisions. What could help, for example, is passing special legislation on the culpability of those who meddle in the activity of the court or show disrespect for it, including responsibility for failure to appear in court.

You are talking about the need to heighten the role of defence in the judicial process. This is being broadly discussed today. There are many different opinions. We would like to hear your point of view.

The opinions are diverse, indeed. I feel that with the purpose of creating additional guarantees for people under investigation, it would be just and reasonable to amend the existing law and allow the lawyer to become involved in the case not after the preliminary investigation has been completed, and not following the institution of proceedings, but after the accusation has been brought against the person.

I feel it necessary to restrict the grounds on which the accused can be taken into custody before trial. This severe measure is often applied arbitrarily. Confinement before trial should be restricted to extreme cases. We feel it would be reasonable to make the law more precise and to reserve the prosecutor's right to prolong the term of confinement before trial to not more than six months. The term could only be prolonged beyond that period by the Supreme Court of a Union Republic or the Supreme Court of the USSR.

It would be advisable to revise the system and the manner of reimbursement for the lawyers. The Bar should be staffed by only highly-qualified lawyers. Much should be done in order to improve standards.

Many letters to Pravda *raise the question of enhancing the role of the general public in the judicial system...*

I support that. I believe that in order to further the democratisation of the Soviet judicial system and to develop socialist self-government accordingly, it would be expedient to increase the number of people's assessors involved in the examination of the more complicated cases. This proposal does not imply a lack of trust in judges: it would simply be a measure guaranteeing a more careful investigation of such cases.

In my opinion, it would be advisable to replace the public defence lawyer and the public prosecutor participating in the trial by one person, namely, a representative of the public who would present to the court his opinion of the verdict, appropriate punishment and measures to prevent violation of the law.

It would be advisable to increase the role and widen the jurisdiction of comrades' courts, administrative commissions and commissions for the affairs of minors. We need to be more bold in attracting the general public into educational and supervisory work in prisons and similar institutions, and encourage people to assist the officers of the law in getting compensation for damages caused by the crime.

Sometimes the courts, acting under the thumb of those who issue orders and instructions, convict persons who show initiative and enterprise, which, incidentally, matches the spirit of the times. Why does this happen?

Indeed, many of the instructions and orders, especially those issued by administrative bodies, have become outdated and should be changed. We should either revise or replace them promptly. This is an immediate task for ministries, departments and production associations. As far as the courts are concerned, they should proceed, in investigating each concrete case, from the understanding that if an order or instruction is not consonant with the law, it should not be followed.

Let me illustrate my point. A collective farm chairman in Kazakhstan, intent on getting the farm over a bad patch, decided to pay bonuses to the best workers so as to give them more incentive. His decision, announced at a general meeting of the collective farmers, was approved by consensus. Nevertheless, the chairman was held criminally responsible for 'the embezzlement of particularly large sums of money'.

This year, the plenary session of the Supreme Court of the USSR gave a thorough consideration to this case. It revoked the previously adopted decision, and the case against the chairman was dropped due to the absence of *corpus delicti* in his action. By adopting this decision, the plenary session of the Supreme Court of the USSR sought to prompt the courts to take a new, correct approach to the estimation of the legal force of orders and instructions. They can only have legal force if formulated in accordance with the law.

What proposals concerning the Supreme Court itself can be made in connection with perestroika?

I think that the Supreme Court of the USSR should not simply repeat (albeit at a new level) what has been done by a people's, regional, territorial court or the Supreme Court of a Union Republic. Its mandate should transcend the limits of the judicial rights of other courts, permitting the solution of fundamental questions of judicial practice.

Although the 'separation-of-power' theory is unacceptable for us, granting the Supreme Court of the USSR certain rights in constitutional supervision would be timely and beneficial. For instance, at present the prosecutor has the right to appeal against any unlawful decision or ordinance issued by an administrative body or an official. If they disagree with the prosecutor's protest, the problem is solved not through resort to the law, but with the help of Party and other bodies.

In my opinion, we should see to it that prosecutors' protests against the unlawfulness of standard acts should be submitted to the court. The right to turn to court with a request to declare normative acts, rules, decrees, instructions, etc. to be contrary to the Fundamental Law should be granted, for instance, to the All-Union Central Trade Union Council and to some republican bodies.

If while examining a case the Supreme Court or any other court finds that the given ordinance or other legally binding act has been issued by a ministry or department contrary to the law and that the citizen under trial has been called to account for breaking it, the court should exercise the right to declare the act contradicting the law and thus null and void.

It would be advisable to improve the nomination and discussion procedure for candidates for the post of judge in the USSR Supreme Court. This stage in their election should be made more open and public with new legislation being passed to define who is entitled to take part in this process and how they should act. Law relating to the USSR Supreme Court is in need of other amendments, too.

Interview by G. OVCHARENKO and A. CHERNYAK
Pravda, 5 December 1987

Between 2 January and 13 March 1938 the Military Collegium of the USSR Supreme Court under the chairmanship of V. V. Ulrikh, with Andrei Y. Vyshinsky as public prosecutor, heard the criminal case against members of the so-called Right-Trotskyite block, who were charged with conspiring to abolish the social and state system of the USSR, restore capitalism and reinstate the power of the bourgeoisie. According to the prosecution, they conspired to attain these goals through espionage, subversion, sabotage and terrorist acts intended to undermine the economic and military power of the Soviet Union. They were also charged with the murders of Sergei M. Kirov, Vyacheslav R. Menzhinsky, Alexei M. Gorky and with conspiring to murder Vladimir Lenin.
   Among the defendants were:
   Nikolai I. Bukharin — joined the revolutionary movement in 1905, took part in the revolution of 1905-1907 ... member of the Russian Social-Democratic Labour Party from 1906 ... arrested several times by the tsarist authorities ... sent into exile in the Far North, from where he escaped abroad ... during the October Revolution took part in the armed uprising in Moscow ... from December 1917 was editor of the newspaper Pravda, *and later of* Izvestia *... elected as an alternate member of the Political Bureau, and then as a full member ... was a member of the USSR Academy of Sciences;*

   Alexei I. Rykov — the son of a peasant, joined the RSDLP in 1899 ... arrested by the tsarist police nine times for revolutionary activities ... after the October Revolution became People's Commissar for Internal Affairs and later, Chairman of the All-Russia Council of the National Economy, Deputy Chairman, and then Chairman of the USSR Council of People's Commissars and the RSFSR Council of People's Commissars ... served as People's Commissar for Communications from 1931 to 1936 ... in 1923 elected a member of the Political Bureau, on which he served until 1930;

Arkady P. Rozengolts — joined the RSDLP in 1905 ... took part in the October Revolution and Civil War ... member of the Revolutionary Military Council of the Russian Republic ... supported Trotsky in the 1920s but later broke with him ... before his arrest was head of a department of the People's Commissariat for Foreign Trade;

Mikhail A. Chernov — member of the Menshevik Party from 1916 ... joined the Bolsheviks in 1920 ... was People's Commissar for Trade in the Ukraine and a member of the collegium of the USSR People's Commissariat for Trade ... from 1934 was USSR People's Commissar for Agriculture;

Christian G. Rakovsky — born in Bulgaria ... an activist in various Social-Democratic organisations from 1889 ... at international congresses headed delegations of Social-Democrats from Bulgaria and Romania ... joined the Communist Party in 1918 ... served as Chairman of the Ukrainian Council of People's Commissars ... was Soviet envoy to England and France;

Pavel P. Bulanov — member of the Communist Party from 1918 ... served with the People's Commissariat for Internal Affairs ... from 1929 performed the duties of Secretary of the Commissariat.

Also among the defendants were two doctors: Lev G. Levin, D. Sc. (Medicine), a consultant at the Kremlin clinic, and Ignaty N. Kazakov of no party affiliation, the administrative and research director of the State Research Institute of Metabolism and Endocrine Disorders.

Other defendants were: V. A. Maksimov-Dikovsky, who was head of the Central Accounting Department of the People's Commissariat for Railways at the time of his arrest, and P. P. Kryuchkov, Director of the Gorky Museum; I. A. Zelensky — Chairman of the Centrosoyuz; V. I. Ivanov — USSR People's Commissar for the Timber Industry; P. T. Zubarev — USSR Deputy People's Commissar for Agriculture; G. F. Grinko — USSR People's Commissar for Finance; F. Khodzhayev — Chairman of the Uzbek Council of People's Commissars; S. A. Bessonov — counsellor at the USSR Embassy in Germany; D. D. Pletnev — Professor at

*the Institute of Functional Diagnostics; N. N. Krestinsky—
USSR First Deputy People's Commissar for Foreign Affairs; A. Ikramov—First Secretary of the Central Committee of the Communist Party of Uzbekistan; V. F. Sharangovich—First Secretary of the Central Committee of the
Communist Party of Byelorussia; and G. G. Yagoda, the
former People's Commissar for Internal Affairs.*

*V. V. Ulrikh, the Chairman of the Military Collegium,
pronounced sentence on 13 March 1938. Of the 21 defendants on trial, 18 were found guilty of treason for their involvement in espionage, sabotage, subversion and terrorism and
condemned to death with confiscation of property; the remaining three were sentenced to long terms of imprisonment.*

*Fifty years later, on 4 February 1988, a plenary session of
the USSR Supreme Court chaired by Vladimir Terebilov,
voted unanimously to repeal the sentences and drop criminal
proceedings in the absence of a* corpus delicti *against Bukharin, Rykov, Rakovsky, Rozengolts, Chernov, Bulanov, Levin,
Kazakov, Maksimov-Dikovsky and Kryuchkov. The convictions of 10 other defendants in the 1938 trial—Zelensky,
Ivanov, Zubarev, Grinko, Khodzhayev, Bessonov, Pletnev,
Krestinsky, Ikramov and Sharangovich—had been reversed
earlier, and all had been rehabilitated. The USSR Procurator's Office did not lodge a protest against the conviction of
Yagoda.*

JUSTICE AND US

Lessons of the 1930s

By Professor ALEXANDER YAKOVLEV
D. Sc. (Law), USSR State Prize winner

Before me lies the court report of this trial issued in 1938.
It includes the indictments by the public prosecutor Vyshinsky, the testimony of witnesses and defendants, speeches by
the defence counsel and the defendants' last pleas.

Reading this document, one is overcome by a strange,
uncomfortable feeling. The participants in the trial were,
without exception, unanimous. Even the defendants willingly accused themselves of the gravest of crimes, each one

incriminating himself and confessing. No one challenged the prosecutor or the witnesses. No one even attempted to refute the fatal evidence, but only contributed additional details to it. What is remarkable about the trial is that the public prosecutor Vyshinsky was in total control. Vyshinsky needed only to expose and brand the accused, and the others would follow suit. The judges were silent. The defence counsel did nothing more than plead for leniency in sentencing. There was no discussion, no cross-examination of the evidence, no expert opinions. Indeed, they were hardly needed, as the defendants themselves described in detail what sort of villains they were.

The impression left is of a well rehearsed performance.

The defendants in the Moscow show trials were accused of unprecedented crimes: conspiring to cede the Ukraine to Nazi Germany and the Far East to Japan; causing natural disasters, cattle plague, crop failures, accidents, as well as bad planning, financial errors and other misfortunes during those troubled times. They were accused of sabotaging crop rotation; causing an outbreak of the plague among pigs and anaemia among horses, of intentionally delaying the completion of a flax mill; of destroying meadows; of attempting to ruin the alfalfa crop. One of the doctors was accused of killing a patient by leaving him asleep on a garden bench on a hot April midday. Other defendants were accused of poisoning an official by spraying his office with a solution of mercury and acid. The defendants pleaded guilty to all these crimes.

How could such a thing happen?

All revolutions had one thing in common: they broke with the past for the sake of a better future. The world was divided into poles of good and evil. In a revolutionary struggle, suffering and violence were justified in the name of future happiness. Concepts and ideas became black or white, true or false, and people were willing to sacrifice their lives for the sake of a revolutionary ideal. Once the old system had been smashed and the previous government toppled, it was time to build, establish and create. The role Lenin played in the country's transition to peaceful development is well known. In terms of criminal justice, this meant abandoning 'red terror' and open suppression of the class enemy in favour of law and order.

After Lenin's death, political slogans and inflammatory epithets were used for selfish ends in the struggle for personal power. The abuse of political power during the time of Stalin's personality cult was reflected in the criminal justice system, too.

People were manipulated and led to believe that some imminent danger threatened what the revolution had achieved. This menace was embodied in the formula 'enemies of the people'. Even dedicated service to the October Revolution was seen as the enemy's way of camouflaging his real activities. The enemy was all-powerful and all-embracing ('hornets' nests of enemies').

Since the goal was allegedly to rout the forces of evil, the means for doing so were unimportant and the need for evidence was often ignored as being a remnant of 'rotten bourgeois liberalism'. Illegal methods of interrogation became the rule.

Those who were slow to incriminate the accused were themselves accused of being 'aiders and abettors of the enemies of the people'. 'Enemies of the people' became non-people, doomed together with their relatives, friends and even acquaintances. Those who did not plead guilty were considered dangerous because they 'did not disarm themselves'. Those who confessed were required to reveal their accomplices. The numbers of accused grew quickly. The punitive system itself bred 'enemies' and their existence justified the system's expansion.

The lawlessness of the 1930s was backed up by the introduction of brutal and inhumane criminal legislation.

A law was adopted in 1932 under which embezzlement of state, cooperative or collective-farm property was considered a capital offence. Provided there were mitigating circumstances, the death sentence could be reduced to ten years' imprisonment. This law was amended in 1935 to include anyone over the age of 12. In 1937 the prison sentence for embezzlement was increased to 25 years. According to eyewitnesses, criminal repression was characterised by drives to increase the numbers of repressed, mass trials and convictions of collective-farm and industrial workers and legal action or punishment meted out for trivial offences.

Today we are learning political, moral and legal lessons from the past.

The most important of these political lessons is the Communist Party's democratisation drive and its efforts to create a legal state that will be able to withstand infringements of civil rights and freedoms, arbitrariness and lawlessness. We still have much to do in this area, but the process has at least begun. The Political Bureau commission's review of the purges in the 1930s, 1940s and early 1950s, together with the recent decision by the Plenary Session of the USSR Supreme Court to rehabilitate the victims of the Moscow show trial of 1938, are by no means the only indications of this. The concept of an interconnected, interdependent and, in many respects, integral world, that has emerged in the spirit of the new way of thinking, is also of major importance, as are the practical steps taken by Soviet diplomacy to establish friendly relations with the outside world and reduce mutual hostility and suspicion to a minimum.

The moral lesson is that no aim, however lofty, no idea or principle should be used to justify unscrupulousness, or serve as a cover for cruelty, baseness or lies, because it is impossible to achieve honest ends by dishonest means. There is another lesson: everything secret becomes public knowledge sooner or later. The use of unjust means in those years betrayed the ideals of socialism and sacrificed a great goal to a lust for personal power.

We are all learning legal lessons, too.

An indication of criminal justice's social maturity is the recognition of certain principles whose renunciation made possible the deplorable situation in those years: the innocent were punished, while their accusers flourished, and the organs of justice became an instrument of arbitrary rule.

Experience shows that the true aim of criminal law is to maintain an appropriate level of social justice. For this the law must contain a minimum of grave deeds and determine punishment in strict proportion to the seriousness of the crime and recognise punishment as being the last resort in such matters. After all, punishment is a source of suffering, it is an evil, albeit a necessary one. We cannot do without punishment, but its indiscriminate or excessive application can only break down the public's sense of law and order, breed cynicism and destroy the integrity of socialist society. One may fear an unjust law, but one will never respect it.

The result will be only greater psychological cruelty and callousness in the public consciousness.

The development of criminal law, in all its forms, is characterised by three main features: the evolution from punishment imposed upon first suspicion to punishment only once guilt has been clearly proved; from proof of guilt based on forced confessions from the defendant to legally obtained objective evidence; and the independence of judge from prosecutor; the enjoyment of equal rights by prosecutor, defendant and counsel for the defence; the decisive role of the court.

Anything unproven simply does not exist in judicial thinking. Justice can only be where such judicial thinking triumphs in court, and where an arduous search for objective, material and documentary evidence is the main concern of the investigation. What cannot be tolerated is a situation where all power is vested in the investigator, the judge is passive, and the defence counsel unseen and powerless.

Equally unsatisfactory is a system whereby three people — a judge and two lay assessors — decide a defendant's fate. Votes by two of the three are sufficient to sentence a person to death. At the end of the 19th century in Russia a majority vote of a twelve-man jury was required to impose the death sentence; in the case of a hung jury the defendant was declared innocent.

Criminal justice has had an unusual history. By its very nature, it is supposed to deal with criminals, that is to say, not with the majority of citizens but with a criminal minority. But it is specifically here in its relationship to this minority that the nature of society is exposed in all its nakedness. A society's criminal justice system reflects its level of civilisation, its recognition of the rights and legitimate interests of the individual, and its respect for the dignity of the individual. If everything is in order in this area of society, then, more likely than not, everything is in order in other areas as well and vice versa. Our own bitter experience shows that if we encounter lawlessness and arbitrariness in the criminal justice system, then all of society is in danger, irrespective of innocence or guilt (more than that, sometimes honest and naive people are more vulnerable than cunning and cynical ones). So, let's be vigilant, let's see to it that the rights of the individual in the criminal justice system are guaranteed! Alexander Herzen wrote: 'Of course, sometimes a criminal hides behind these strictly observed and zealously defended rights. Let him hide. Far better that a crafty thief should go unpunished than every honest man tremble in his room like a thief.'

The monstrous villainy during the trials of 'the enemies of the people' should not be called a distortion of justice, a vice of the judicial system. This is not justice at all, it is injustice. Lessons must be and are already being learned from the past by all of us together and individually, for today the future is in our own hands.

Moscow News, 14 February 1988

Culture:
PERESTROIKA Unleashed

Theatre, art, cinema,
music, television

Perestroika *released a veritable firework show of remarkable literary works, some of which the Soviet people had already heard about, others of which they knew nothing, despite the fact that they were written ten to sixty years ago: 'Heart of a Dog' by* Mikhail Bulgakov, *'The Foundation Pit' by* Andrei Platonov, *'Requiem' by* Anna Akhmatova, *'The Right of Memory' by* Alexander Tvardovsky *and 'Doctor Zhivago' by* Boris Pasternak. *Also published were novels and novellas by* Vassily Grossman, Alexander Bek, Daniil Granin, Vladimir Dudintsev, Anatoly Rybakov *and other writers. And although literary criticism is not particularly sparing of writers, taking it to task for mistakes it made in the distant and recent past, the reading public has nevertheless seen that writers, more than anyone else, have prepared public for* perestroika.

It is no secret that magazine articles, particularly those by economists and historians, are read avidly in the Soviet Union today. Periodicals featuring writings by Abel Aganbegian, Lev Abalkin, Tatyana Zaslavskaya, Nikolai Shmelyov, Gavriil Popov, Yuri Afanasyev *and others are snatched up and read voraciously. Nevertheless, it is also no secret — and enough time has elapsed since April 1985 to confirm this — that not one book written by an economist or historian in the last few decades has become a bestseller.*

In this respect it is writers — new ones as well as those no longer with us — who have shown themselves to be ahead of their time and of urgent relevance in today's world. It is difficult to single out one name which could be considered the literary groundbreaker of perestroika, *someone who anticipated it and did everything to make it happen. Each of the authors mentioned above, as well as others whose works have been published in recent years —* Chinghis Aitmatov, Viktor Astafyev, Vassily Belov, Vassil Bykov, Andrei Voznesensky, Valentin Rasputin — *to name but a few — have in some way contributed to the awakening of social consciousness, without which* perestroika *would not have been possible.*

And yet if we are to judge by public opinion polls, the most popular novel of 1987 was clearly Anatoly Rybakov's Children of the Arbat. *It would be untrue to say* Children of the Arbat *met with unanimous praise among readers (this is only natural, the same could be said about Valentin Pikul's* The Favourite, *which was the most popular novel of 1986).*

Regardless of what one may think of Children of the Arbat, *the fact remains: no other work of fiction published in 1987 had such an enormous impact. Therefore we are opening our section on culture in the USSR with an interview with* ANATOLY RYBAKOV.

EDUCATING THROUGH THE TRUTH

Q. Anatoly Naumovich, since the publication of your novel numerous Western correspondents have come to see you. What are they interested in first of all?
A. I was visited by twelve television companies, three of which were American. Today, the whole world is interested in knowing what's going on in our country, whether it is serious and how long it will last.

I spoke with US Secretary of State George Shultz. He is a diplomat and expresses himself judiciously. He asked me what *glasnost* was. I grasped the implication of his words and replied: your revolution took place in 1776, you declared independence and passed the Bill of Rights. You claimed to be the freest country in the world! Under your influence the French Revolution was carried out... But it wasn't until 1865 — ninety years later — that Blacks were freed in your country.

How does one reconcile slavery with freedom of the individual? Revolutions are not linear processes. There are good things and bad things to be said for every country. Things to be proud of, things to be ashamed of. Our country is no exception. A frank attitude must be taken to our history. It should be spoken of openly with the people. This is *glasnost*.

Q. *Are there limits to* glasnost?
A. Truth is the only limit! What other limit could there be?
Q. *Anatoly Naumovich, your earlier works are considered classics of children's literature. How do you regard them today?*
A. I regard them with great affection. My works for children include *The Dagger, The Bronze Bird, The Shot*. They reflect my childhood in the twenties. Incidentally, in *The Shot*, in the last part of the trilogy, there is a Sasha Pankratov. I want to emphasise the continuity...

I'm particularly fond of *The Dagger* because it's the first book I wrote. I put all my hopes of becoming a writer into that book. It was written and published when I was thirty-seven years old. You see how late I began to write.
Q. *That is normal nowadays. First book at forty...*
A. Pushkin died when he was thirty-seven... My situation before the war was very complicated — the novel tells about it. Then the war. When it ended in 1945 I was in Berlin. I was a front-line officer. It was after the war that I decided to write *The Dagger*... Why do I think a lot of these books? Not only because they're interesting, because they're gripping. But because they're moral, just like my trilogy about Krosh. They are essentially about morality... I don't know how to express this. Critics do a better job of that...

My characters are moral, Krosh may be slightly puerile, but he reveals an inborn morality. The characters in *The Dagger* are of another generation, they are children of the revolution who were unselfish, devoted to the idea, possibly somewhat intolerant, but honest.

They loathed careerists and consumerists. They embodied the traits of the revolution.
Q. *Anatoly Naumovich, let me ask you two rather unusual questions. What has hindered you most in life and what has helped you most?*
A. In life? (*pause*). This requires some clever, aphoristic reply... I was my greatest hindrance. And help (*laugh*).
Q. *Would you please talk about your childhood, about your school chums? Who were your teachers?*
A. My childhood was spent in Moscow, in the Arbat. From the first through to fifth grade I went to school on Krivoarbatsky Lane. My father was a prominent engineer. The Arbat was a quarter inhabited by educated people and

even the school I attended was under the auspices of the Central Committee for the Improvement of the Daily Lives of Scholars (TsEKUBU). I began going to school in 1919. The country lived on politics. We were highly impressionable children and everything that happened around us happened before our very eyes.

Moscow was in ruins, factories did not operate... What do I remember? I remember standing in a queue at a bakery and on my palm was written 'No. 221'. They were distributing rations, two ounces of bread a day... I went to a good school. An old-type grammar school. It was run by the Khvostovs, a family of progressive educators. Lunacharsky retained headmistress Khvostova after the Revolution. I was a Young Pioneer. My sister and I joined a Young Pioneer group at the Sverdlov factory. Back then pioneer organisations were formed at factories rather than at schools. It was probably a better way...

Q. *What did pioneers of those days do?*

A. Basically we worked with street urchins. In 1921 famine hit the Volga region and homeless children streamed into Moscow. We gathered them, pulled them out of the gutter, out of the world of delinquency and drew them into socially useful work. It was not easy, being children and all... We participated in all actions: preparing for holiday celebrations, fund-raising for building a navy and air force... Back then we went around with collection pots shouting: 'Help us create a mighty Soviet fleet!' We'd go right up to someone on the street and say: 'Please, sir, our fleet needs money!' And the person would drop a coin in the pot...

After finishing a seven-year school I transferred to another school which was very interesting. It was called MOPSHKa and we, its pupils, were called 'mops'. MOPSHKa was an abbreviation of Moscow Experimental Model Communal School of the People's Commissariat of Education. It was created as a boarding-school for Komsomol members returning from the front, 15-16 year-olds, soldiers and commanders of the Red Army. Semi-literates, you see... There they lived and learned the three R's. There were some fine teachers at MOPSHKa. Peryshkin taught us physics, math was taught by Berezovskaya, who also wrote a textbook. The best teachers you could have... Pestrak was our principal. He was shot before a firing squad in 1937. A remarkable, outstanding educator of that time.

It was a very socially conscious school, our lives there were thoroughly defined by Komsomol ideals. And since MOPSHKa had a top-notch teaching staff, it drew children of Kremlin officials, many children whose parents were People's Commissars. But we didn't accept everyone into the Komsomol. No doubt it was marked by a certain puritanism. This is unavoidable. But good traits predominated: you couldn't lie, you had always to tell the truth regardless of whose interests it affected. The greatest insult was to be called a 'careerist'. 'He's a careerist!' Such a person was given a wide berth...

Q. *Tell me, over how long a period of time did the country's moral climate change?*

A. I think it started at the end of the twenties with the consolidation of Stalin, his administrative machinery, his single-minded views... After all, NEP did not mean just private enterprise. Lenin saw NEP as a wide-ranging policy of building socialism via economic means. Stalin, however, believed he could build socialism using administrative methods, coercion. To do this he created a bureaucratic machine which under his leadership reconstructed the country. This was augmented by his vanity, mistrust, cult of personality and lawlessness. Lenin did his utmost to keep Stalin away from power. If Lenin had lived another half a year everything would have been different. He could have removed Stalin from the leadership of the party apparatus and our country would have developed along Leninist lines.

Q. *What in your opinion were the results of this policy? Are traces of the cult still noticeable in our social consciousness?*

A. The results of all this were one-sided development of our economy, imbalances which still can be felt today, and millions of victims. And the most frightening thing of all was a change in the psychological climate of society, in the consciousness of people who began to live in fear, as one man thought for them, made decisions for them. They did not have the right to make their own decisions. Everything was done 'at the initiative of Comrade Stalin'. Everything! Even knitting a pair of mittens was done 'at the initiative of Comrade Stalin'.

Today, in an age of rapid scientific and technological advances, when each person must make his own decisions quickly without awaiting orders 'from above', when there is an urgent need for independent thinking and bold action, this frightening state of mind that resulted from the cult of personality is slowing down our society. We have to change the psychological climate. That is why we began with culture, literature, cinema, the mass media. They determine the moral atmosphere in our country. Economic results will not be long in coming.

Q. *Anatoly Naumovich, there have always been deep-thinking and honest people in our society. How could they reconcile themselves with what was going on, how could they let it happen?*

A. What can a person do to counter an avalanche of mass disinformation? Besides that, Stalin began to make use of repression toward the end of the thirties. Fear set in. That did it, people already began to keep quiet. It happened very quickly. But what is interesting is that when the war began people again changed, faced with peril, faced with death. Yes, they freed themselves from oppression, from denunciation, suspicion, mistrust: the war brought out the genuinely human elements in people, they had not been quashed. Nothing human can be quashed for ever. That should always be borne in mind.

Q. *Those are sad things you're saying... Do you have any letters with you from people responding to your novel* Children of the Arbat? *What kind of reactions did you get from readers, old as well as young?*

A. I'll quote you two letters which I think are interesting. Here's the first one: 'It is well known that V. I. Lenin complained about the sluggishness and scant literacy of the peasants with whom we build socialism. Do you think that in the thirties the leadership of the party and country had an easy time solving the problems of socialist construction as regards advancing the human factor?... Were there really needless victims?...' That letter was signed: Cand. Sc. (History), associate professor, author of a book and chapters in *History of the CPSU* and *History of the Second World War*, author of dozens of articles, journalist, and so on and so forth. Here is a scholar for you who believes that the peasants of our country were so ignorant that millions had to be destroyed for their own good! And this person writes the *History of the CPSU*, historical works, mind you, which are meant to edify our youth. How can a normal person say: 'How is it going to be possible without victims?' Then you do the tree-felling yourself!...

And another letter from an electrician: 'Dear Sir, I've been reading the novel *Children of the Arbat* for five days now. I cannot explain the state I find myself in. It cannot be expressed by words. It is a triumph of Leninist ideas. Only a year ago I could not hope for such things...' A long letter, a wonderful letter. Someone who understands fully...

One reaction from a history scholar, a monster who dares to speak of the necessity of victims, and another reaction from a young person.

Q. *I'd like to ask you one last question related to Stalin. It's a question many people have requested me to ask. What do you think about the film* Repentance?

A. I like it, it's positive like any progressive work of art... It's well done. It's another matter altogether that allegory is alien to my style of writing. I write simply. Writing abstrusely takes no effort...

Q. *It's probably difficult for a writer to do either.*

A. It's definitely difficult to write simply. Failing which the reader has to solve enigmas, and I don't like enigmas, I don't like riddles... *Heavy Sand* is written very simply...

Q. *Where did you get the idea for* Heavy Sand?

A. I wanted to write about love. I had a friend. He worked at a motor transport depot in Ryazan before the war. He told me this story. His father came here from Switzerland with his grandfather. One day while strolling through Simferopol his father saw a young girl... Crimean Jewish women are very beautiful... He was the son of a well-known Zurich professor, she — a cobbler's daughter. She did not want to live in Switzerland. They returned to Simferopol, had children. He was arrested and later released...

After the war I met up with my friend and he told me that his parents had been shot by the Germans. I was struck by this fidelity, this love: all for her he left his country, gave up his career and perished with her in a ditch along the road to Sudak. I wanted to write a short novella about love. I went to Simferopol and saw that the whole atmosphere was alien to me. So I decided to shift the action to the town where my grandfather lived. He was an indomitable old man. He lived in a small town in the Ukraine and during the Moscow famine of '21, '22 and '23 my mother and I went there to live. My aunt was still alive then, and even though she was eighty years old she was still of lucid mind. She told me stories about the family. Later, when I tried to imagine the couple there, the novel was born.

Q. *Anatoly Naumovich,* Heavy Sand *brought you world renown. Did you take advantage of the success of this book to try to publish the first part of* Children of the Arbat? *After all, the first part was written back in the 60s...*

A. I did in fact write the first part of *Children of the Arbat* twenty years ago. And Tvardovsky did everything he could to get it published in *Novy Mir*. But it didn't work out. I finished the second part in 1978. When *Heavy Sand* came out I said to myself, 'Aha, now I'll get somewhere!' And look what happened. They still wouldn't publish it! Then I wrote the third part. Foreign publishers offered to publish it abroad. I declined. *The Times*, the *Herald Tribune*, the biggest papers in the world printed my reply in bold letters: 'This novel is needed by my people, my country, and above all must be published at home.' My time has come. I regard it a writer's duty to write for one's people and stand by one's people, in bad times as well as good times. I had faith that *Children of the Arbat* would be published sooner or later, maybe only posthumously.

Q. *What lies at the source of your faith?*

A. We must move forward. We are a great power and we must keep step with the times. There is something called the instinct of national self-preservation, it's more powerful than any circumstances. In order for us to move forward, to keep up with progress, we must think, create and act freely. And in order to do this we need *glasnost*. *Glasnost* means first and foremost the chance to speak the truth. Not everyone, of course, likes the truth. Remember the letter that I read to you...

Q. *The history scholar's? Well, he certainly speaks with a sense of conviction... And yet the words of the young electrician are more convincing. Wouldn't you say so?*

A. Herzen would have called our conversation a 'rhyme of generations'. The children of the Arbat have grown up, grown old. 'Live by the truth,' they tell their grandchildren, hoping they'll be understood. And their grandchildren should understand.

Interview by ALEXEI ZAITSEV

Smena, January 1988

THOUGHT-CONSCIENCE

By ANDREI VOZNESENSKY

It is chilling to recall the words spoken by the great Enrico Fermi after the atomic bomb was tested in Alamogordo: 'Don't bother me with your pangs of conscience. This is above all great physics!'

Our only hope for salvation today resides in an attitude which I would sum up as 'thought-conscience'.

When the rain and the rivers, which should cleanse and purify, are now contaminated by pollution as an outcome of industrial development — made possible only by man's thought — it seems to me that the time-honoured dictum 'act according to your conscience' should be changed to 'think according to your conscience'.

Go to the market. You won't find a cauliflower or a melon that has not been treated with pesticides. The poor market women innocently become complicit. 'Educated' to feed their chickens hormones and antibiotics, is it not ignorance and immorality not totally unlike that of the miscreants at Chernobyl?

It is too late to advocate a return to patriarchal pastoral existence. Today the race for new knowledge is blinded by an ignorance of consequences, thus becoming immoral. The world can be saved only by a science that is imbued with thought-conscience.

It has become fashionable to question and even discredit the achievements of scientific progress. But even during the times which we now call the period of stagnation there existed oases of conscience, for example in our Academy of Sciences. Certain steadfast academicians could not be broken by brute pressure from above. Their personal reservations could be likened to the 'secret freedom' that Blok admired in Pushkin. They would not be forced against their conscience.

Take P. D. Baranovsky who refused to sign the death sentence for St. Basil's cathedral and was banished.

Certainly, we have no need to delve back in history to Galileo and St. Sebastian... The population shudders when reading today about the blighted life of a scientific genius who was imprisoned for 'trotskyism and monarchism'. *Glasnost* is not simply dispersing clouds, it is purifying. I quote lines from an earlier poem of mine: 'And Vavilov, villainously hunted, planted a seed of conscience in the country.' I can see in my mind's eye the statue not yet erected to him, standing with unbowed head next to Pushkin and Timiryazev. It would be timely to erect such a monument — and not only to him. People are now looking to the image of this scientist as the embodiment of conscience. They know instinctively salvation can be a practical possibility only if science is conjoined with morality. In this context it is clear that a scientist's denunciation by his colleagues is doubly despicable.

And what can be said about the academician who almost destroyed Lake Baikal?

Today our writers and our honest scientists are fighting to prevent changing the course of rivers and similarly to prevent tampering with the true course of morality.

Baikal, Borodino Field, the Mikhailovskoye oaks, the dark waters of the Kolyma — these are not simply beautiful scenery, they embody the soul of the people.

Buinitskoye Field lies six kilometres from Mogilev. At his request, the ashes of Konstantin Simonov were spread over that field. On the 12 and 13 of July 1941 it was the site of a fierce battle, one in which the poet took part. People lay flowers at the memorial and newly-weds visit the spot. From all over the country people come to pay homage to the memory of the poet. But this year the All-Union Simonov Readings were not held in November as planned. A grey-haired writer and friend of the poet was near to tears when he reported that the Moscow writers' request to hold the readings at Buinitskoye Field had not been approved by local authorities...

It is obvious that the people of Byelorussia are not to blame for this; the Byelorussians have great respect for the memory of the poet. I have spent much time in Byelorussia where the long-suffering, vast landscape has whispered poems to me. I have been enchanted with the Byelorussian speech rhythms in the verse of Rygor Borodulin. It was the Byelorussians who aided me during my hard times. Honour and internationalism are in their blood; it is folk conscience that cries out in the books of Vassil Bykov and Ales Adamovich, and in the works of Maxim Tank, Svetlana Aleksievich, N. Gilevich, G. Buravkin, V. Neklyaev... Then why should the questioning puzzled eyes of the poet seem to gaze at us from Buinitskoye Field?

Last summer I happened to be in a plane with one of our Air Force Marshals. Once off the ground we began to converse. The marshal took out a notebook into which he had copied figures from an article about Fyodor Raskolnikov: '3 out of 5 marshals, 10 out of 10 army commanders of the second rank, 50 out of 57 corps commanders, 154 out of 186 division commanders'... The Army has much to hold against Stalin.

It is altogether impermissible to corrode thought with lies.

Unfortunately, we have lost a great deal in rushing to follow an almighty plan, in tolerating the reign of blind faith, dark forces and witch hunts. The number arrested during Stalin's tyranny equates the number of denunciations. Denunciations were made out of envy and from base instinct; because someone wanted a small room in a communal apartment; because someone wanted to get even; because of a woman. We studied textbooks of falsified history from which the names of Blyukher and Tukhachevsky were erased. I feel shame for this because I, too, as a youngster believed the slanders against these honourable people!

In 1987 a textbook entitled 'Soviet Rus' was published. The book does not even contain the names of former heads of state, such dissimilar leaders as Stalin, Khrushchev and Brezhnev. Why? How can the causes of today's extraordinary events be understood? Was it pure accident that in this textbook all party congresses except the 20th and 22nd were mentioned?

And should we blame the writer who just recently expressed indignation at the appearance of 'heaps' of newly-declared geniuses — Pasternak, Mandelshtam, and so on.

He never encountered their names at school. *Other* 'geniuses' were in his textbooks. And how was he to know that Mayakovsky called Pasternak a genius?

After fostering mediocrity, chopping off the arms and legs of the tortured body of our literature and robbing our youth of it, the authors of one-sided, mendacious textbooks which have defamed Bulgakov and Akhmatova for years are now coming before the people. Yet instead of acknowledging the damage they have done they display haughtiness and arrogance.

The Russian intelligentsia has never shaken hands with the Black Hundred.

I have myself long been accustomed to criticism. Take for example any autumn issue of certain magazines, which a poetess of my acquaintance calls 'Voznesensky journals', so often do they call attention to my humble name. 'Accept praise and slander calmly' said Pushkin. What dismays me is that they are trying to turn our literature, the conscience of the nation, into a shower of verbal abuse. Do our times merit such a low level of polemic? Truth can best be established creatively, in verse or prose.

I want our literary criticism to be revitalised with young blood. Unfortunately the talented critic Vladimir Novikov, sensitive and subtle in his response to poetry and the author of more than one hundred books and articles, has for years been rejected by the Writers' Union admission committee.

Even the dead are not left to rest in peace. Vysotsky, our rough grain conscience, lives on if only because he still provokes and enrages the enemies of truth. The forces of reaction howl when they hear his songs. Even now his detractors shriek about him in articles, and his grave is periodically ravaged. Recently some young sailors put their jackets on his grave as a gesture to their favourite poet; even these spontaneous tributes were surreptitiously removed!

On 24 January the Soviet Culture Fund organised a fund-raising event in Luzhniki for the Vysotsky Museum. The poet's friends and fellow theatrical people formed the organising committee. It was important that the poet should not be smoothed over and turned into a 'golden boy'. But even here we encountered ugliness masquerading as morality. The 'financial guards' would not permit passing round a list for donations during the event. Apparently they considered the poet's fans to be potential criminals because they suggested that receipts be given for every five-rouble donation and they required a militiaman to be stationed by the safe. How can people who do not believe in the integrity of others teach us morality?

In November I was invited to read my poetry at the Likhachev Car Plant. Most of the audience came from the plant's technical college, where they attend classes after a hard day's work. These were not the 'prols' enshrined in dogma. They were educated, passionate truth-seekers, highly knowledgeable about contemporary music and literature. A smelter with a 12-year work record spoke profoundly about complex prose. Seven written questions concerned the works of Pasternak, suggestions included the publication of the letters of Alexandra Kollontai and the memoirs of N. Mandelshtam. It was a thinking audience.

Not so long ago I asked Academician Andrei Sakharov what he thought science needed most of all; he answered: 'liberation and trust'. Unfortunately, science is too often considered in a utilitarian way. Galileo did not produce immediate benefits. The empty shelves in our food stores are to a great degree the result of the Lysenko debacle, which promised immediate results. True, Nabokov and Platonov are being published, but what about Freud? L. Badalyan, an academician of the Academy of Medical Sciences, rightly complains that psychoanalysis is completely divorced from clinical practice in our country. When the human brain becomes something that can be controlled by medical science morality in science is especially important.

I recently received a letter from some young Siberians brimming over with enthusiasm for the idea of erecting a monument in Krasnoyarsk to Count N. P. Rezanov, the intrepid adventurer who dreamed of building a bridge between America and Russia and the hero of the rock opera *Juno and Avos*. When asked to design the memorial I suggested a kind of music box with the figures of the romantic Count and Conchita, his young lover from San Francisco.

In the evening the melancholy melody of a love song would be heard in the snow-covered square. Young couples passing by, the city's residents and guests would listen...

Mrs Rockefeller, the wealthy American, was in spiritual

harmony with this scenario when, on discovering during her visit to Novgorod that the priceless 15th century icons she owned were from St. Sophia's Cathedral, returned them to Russia forthwith.

In December 1987 the leaders of the two world superpowers met in Washington to try to mitigate the lethal power, the fruit of a science subjugated to the God of War, Mars. It is an immoral peace when neighbours hold a pistol to each other's temple.

I recall a conversation I had with the American President while sitting on the antique, high-back chairs in the Oval Office of the White House. The portico of the famous building on the green lawn was on fire in the same year — 1812 — as the buildings of the Arbat in Moscow. I began to talk about Tolstoy, Dostoyevsky and Chekhov. A few minutes later, apropos of nothing, the President told me he was against nuclear war and the arms race...

The agreement was signed. Next a fifty per cent reduction is envisaged, then the complete elimination of the nuclear deterrent, and then the remaining weapons... Humanity will triumph over the narrow class approach. If this happens it will be the culmination of the greatest revolution in the history of the world, the liberation of science from the military yoke. Intellect, thus liberated, could rescue exhausted mankind from the perils of today and the future. Science would become humanist, fulfilling the dream of utopians and poets like Rousseau, Rezanov, Khlebnikov, Blake and the Beatles. My dream is of a human society that is free, open and boundless — like thought.

Impossible? Tertullian's dictum was affirmed centuries later by Niels Bohr: 'It is certain because it is impossible.'

Rather than serve the God of Mars we should fly to the planet Mars together.

Is humankind morally ready for this?

Izvestia, 5 December 1987

'WE MUST NOT STOP MID-WAY!'

An interview with VASSIL BUKOV conducted
by N. MATUKOVSKY

V. B. The most remarkable thing today is that there seems
to be an overall understanding of the necessity for *perestroika*, especially for developing a new consciousness,
democracy and *glasnost*. We have dared to look our past,
present and future squarely in the eye.

N. M. *But there are people who are saying and writing:
there's no need to dig into the past; it wasn't at all like some
literary figures would have us believe now; why all this revision? What do you say to these people who are so defensive
about the past?*

V. B. At all times there have been people quite satisfied with
their lives, their legal and social position, and with the authorities in power, so they never wanted to change anything. Even today they are prepared to do everything possible
to preserve the order they love so much, to defend it morally and try to base their position on 'objective necessity'.
For example they would like to see the authority of their
idol, Stalin, left intact, believing that the destruction of the
idol will jeopardize their position. For them the truth could
entail great loss. They care little about the fate of the new
generation which has witnessed the exposure of humiliating
lies. Yet the fate of socialism is in the hands of this generation.

People dispute the significance of Stalin; they compare
the myth with the reality. It is true that we built socialism
and won the war when Stalin was General Secretary —
there was no one else at that time, no one to whom he could
be compared. But that is just one aspect of the problem. We
now have enough facts to enable us to judge his leadership
from a distance, from a historical point of view. And we realize how reprehensible his methods were and what tremendous losses were caused by his total lack of trust of anyone, his desire to try to solve single-handed all the country's
problems, even in those spheres where he had no experience. We may recall the episode recounted by former People's Commissar B. L. Vannikov about the PPSh sub-
machine gun cartridge drum. Ignoring the opinion of the

experts, Stalin took a liking to the cartridge drum of the Suomi, a Finnish machine gun. He ordered their production to replace the cartridge-trays. This decision was paid for with the lives of countless numbers of soldiers throughout the war. Stalin made fatal decisions in science and culture as well. How can we refuse to examine these things in detail? Of course we could postpone the decision until the next generation, as was done in the 1960s. But the next generation will hardly be grateful to us for that. A disease that festers inside is fraught with unpredictable consequences.

N. M. Today we know the names of some of the former 'nameless' individuals who aided the personality cult. It's good that they have been named, but what next?

V. B. If we are serious about following a policy of *glasnost* and democratisation, on which I personally am in no doubt, then we must not stop mid-way. If we do, the revolution will lose its momentum. Khrushchev struck a great blow when he revealed the crimes of Stalin and his minions. But he stopped mid-way. That was one of his greatest mistakes.

Today times have changed. There are a number of people who are nostalgic about Stalin, although they criticize him at the same time. And they do this in all sincerity; though he more or less provided for their old age, they blame him for their moral uneasiness. Others have been successful in reviving phenomena that have long lay dormant. For example, Lysenko's son claims that Vavilov denounced himself, and that the Lysenko school of science long ago proved its advantage over Vavilov's genetics.

Strangely enough, the revivers are increasing in numbers. Three months ago the newspaper *Sovetskaya Byelorussia* published a thought-provoking argument: former informers and falsifiers should not be held accountable because they were loyal to Stalin and sincerely had no idea they were destroying innocent people. A month later a different author, in the same paper, went even further and seriously tried to substantiate the 'guilt' of S. Nekrashevich, a well-known Byelorussian scientist and academician repressed in 1937 and completely rehabilitated in 1955. It causes one to think: this newspaper accuses anew an individual who was rehabilitated long ago at the decision of the USSR Supreme Court in the absence of a crime (*corpus delicti*). What is this? Political naiveté or an attempt to give an old car a new

engine? In my opinion the reason lies in our irrational tolerance of the consequences of that evil cult and its atmosphere of repression. Some people view this tolerance as
weakness and consider it a sin not to take advantage of it. If
we do not protect society from them, there will be no guarantee against their perfidious attacks.

N. M. *Since we seem to have unintentionally moved to a discussion of the past, let me touch upon another painful topic.
The 10-12th century Church of the Annunciation in Vitebsk,
where, according to legend, Alexander Nevsky was wed, was
torn down; the Church of the Transfiguration, Peter the
Great's cottage, and the building that housed the first Byelorussian theatre were destroyed in Minsk...*

V. B. If there was no concern for people, there certainly was
no concern for their heritage. The fact is that bureaucracy
and culture are incompatible. Bureaucracy needs power,
not culture. If it is still tolerated, it is only as a part of
a 'consumer service/culture' entity, where culture might be
altogether absent. Have you noticed that currently many
people do not seek real culture but even make a proud show
of the lack of it! This leads to the spread of supposedly
harmless swearing, which is common not only among the
masses, but also at every bureaucratic level. And together
with this, we see an almost obsessive passion for neat col-
lars, nicely furnished studies, Japanese electronic equipment, scientific titles...

Byelorussia's material culture has always had its share of
suffering: each European war was devastating. Nonetheless, some things remained, some pitiful little reminders of
past centuries. But the comrade bureaucrats have gradually
made their way to them. They took no chances and struck
at the very root in Minsk, Vitebsk, Polotsk and Grodno.
Pretending to wage a struggle against the 'infamous past'
and the 'opiate of the people', they destroyed the centuries-
old history of a nation.

And did anyone receive a reprimand for this barbaric
act? I haven't heard about it. Explosions were being heard
all across the Republic. And where demolition wasn't possible due to insufficient equipment, a more primitive, but no
less effective method was used: an agile steeple-jack would
climb to the top of a cathedral and open a part of the roof.
The snow, rain and wind finished the job. Did this happen

so long ago? And aren't similar things going on today? Why did they have to put a metro station next to the very walls of a 17th-century cathedral? Couldn't they have built it a few hundred metres further away? Cracks have already begun to appear in the walls of the Cathedral, and the trains haven't even started running yet. What will happen when they do? But then, as always, the guilty will not be found. I'm afraid no one will even look for them.

N. M. *Vassil Vladimirovich, a writer, one who even writes about the distant past, cannot but also think about the future. Essentially, everything he does is for the future. It's good that certain important and essential works previously unpublished are now being made available. But with respect to the so-called contemporary theme, what literary heroes should appear in new books?*

V. B. That's not an easy question... During its seventy years Soviet literature has had its share of different, often mutually contradicting, sometimes even flagrantly speculative opinions. A host of general concepts were invented. At times the Union of Writers felt such an urgent need to create a hero for mass emulation that an emergency forum was promptly called and the appropriate tasks were set for the writers. Each period, each leader made a deliberate effort to achieve a flattering reflection in the arts. Each stagnant five-year period tried to achieve immortality in literary works. All branches of industry were striving for eternity. Literature did its best, but no matter how hard it tried, it was still reproached for lagging behind the tumultuous events of life.

As a result literature was on the verge of losing literary criteria. This insipid and sentimental hack work did not correspond to anything. The works that could have served as standards were not published and wound up either in locked cupboards in editors' offices or in the desk drawers of the authors. With painstaking effort entire groups of editors, publishers and critics persisted in this work. Many of those who have today so jubilantly given writers the 'green light' were among these groups. They have already been restructured...

N. M. *I'd like to know your personal opinion about* perestroika. *What do you think is not going as well as it should? What should be restructured first of all?*

V. B. Everything must be restructured. That is evident to all. We have reached a point where all spheres of life require radical restructuring. The most important thing, the priority as I see it, is the restructuring, and in some ways the abrupt change, in our consciousness. But this is also the most difficult. Of course, we would like everything to be accomplished as quickly as possible, but the process we have begun will be an extremely long one. It cannot be hurried or squeezed into a few years. The modern self-consciousness of society has been formed by decades of powerful social influences. Will it be possible to overcome this legacy in a couple of years? In other social and political conditions and at another time, I would perhaps say it would take several generations to accomplish radical change. But today I will say something else: we cannot prolong *perestroika* over a long period of time. The historical opportunity before us must be utilised with maximum speed. What are we to do? How are we to do it? We must break through the 'I can't' mentality. The important thing is not to stop. Even the briefest let-up could lead to a reversal. And that would be catastrophic for all our hopes and plans.

N. M. *How do you see* perestroika *in literature?*

V. B. Personally I see it in the new, truly profound way literature must delve into life, into all its aspects and history. For decades literature was content with graceful stylistic passages and banalities. Countless likable, philosophical-minded and progressive protagonists, production workers and managers at all levels, filled the pages of our novels, choruses sang the praises of factory accomplishments, and we examined exciting tempests in crystal glasses. And how just and satisfying to everyone were our endings!

Yet this was a time of economic stagnation, legally sanctioned deception and ecological disaster. How was it possible to corrupt entire regions, how did our legal bodies become morally degraded? Did literature look the other way? Were all writers wearing blindfolds? The writers saw everything. But their response was not enough to influence their literature.

Fortunately, contemporary journalism was the first to join the cleansing struggle. We writers should also take advantage of the new opportunities.

N. M. *Do you not think, Vassil Vladimirovich, that many wri-*

*ters of late are paying too much attention to their own inter-
personal relations? All this about dachas, apartments, and
large editions?*
V. B. No, I don't think so. As we know, there are no vac-
uums in life. Social relations do not tolerate ambiguity in
interpersonal relations. The recent commotion among
those who serve the muses is nothing more than a reaction
after years of silence in which there arose so many problems
and certain figures were seen to be distinguished. They were
distinguished, but no one dared to express their true attitude toward them — they were too high-ranking, and their
sponsors would not allow any criticism. Spurious 'authorities' thrived, and the number of false figures grew. They included the quiet and the complacent as well as the aggressive and hostile.

It has long been observed that people love writers 'already gone'. Just look at Yesenin, Bulgakov, Pasternak,
Tsvetaeva, Gumilev, Akhmatova and many of the master
artists of our national culture. But the time comes when
millions will remember nothing about the works of the recent favourites of the authorities, the popular authors 'always on call'. Clearly, this must be a manifestation of the
eternal wisdom and higher justice of life and literature.
*N. M. Vassil Vladimirovich, I am purposefully not going to
ask about your new work...*
V. B. I myself don't like to talk about something that isn't
ready.

Izvestia, 9 March 1988

ACCORDING TO CONSCIENCE
An interview with VALENTIN RASPUTIN conducted
by ELVINA SHUGAYEVA

*E. Sh. Judging from your books and articles, you believe that
man's conscience is the primary mover of man's actions and
behaviour. This is what you are telling us; and we read and
see that the only true path to take is the one the individual's
conscience chooses — this is what we should all do. But once
we close the book we discover that this is not always what
happens in reality. If a person of conscience were to ask you:*

what should I do now in these difficult, crucial times; how can I live according to my conscience?... How would you answer?

V. R. How to live and act according to one's conscience? First, morally and spiritually, we should be correctly oriented, in other words, we should know the coordinates along which life should move. This is because there have been many instances where moral concepts have been altered or substituted by something else. And this did not begin yesterday or in the thirties. It started much earlier, probably one hundred years or more ago. And while there might have been certain instances where social morality was improved, much was lost later.

A great crowd of people attended Dostoyevsky's funeral. Twenty-five years later, only nine people gathered at the great writer's grave. This was how much the attitude had changed to this ruler of men's minds, as Dostoyevsky was then called, to a man who was revered and who, in fact, was a ruler of minds. The minds had changed, and different rulers had appeared. The attitude to Dostoyevsky had been radically altered.

In just the same way, by the beginning of the century or, at the very latest, the start of the First World War, the concepts of morality, spirituality and conscience began to lose their former contours and actual meaning, becoming more and more sentimental, faded artifacts in the trunks of our grandmothers. In another ten or fifteen years it even became awkward to remember their existence. New needs overshadowed them and turned them into the ideology of an outdated regime. It seems that conscientiousness held out longer than the rest, but then it, too, was made into an instrument of obedience. Morality was replaced by the observance of written laws, and political expediency took the place of spirituality. Life became oriented toward the extraneous, while the inner world was censured.

E. Sh. But the guidelines are, after all, well-known and eternal. Everyone has an idea about a system of values. And moral guidelines are being determined quite frankly by the public today. So what is the problem here?

V. R. The discussion should now be about truth. There can be no improvement of the individual conscience until the social conscience demonstrates its adherence to truth.

Shukshin said that morality was truth. This is true. But

morality is not just truth alone, although this is where it begins and on what it stands. It is easier to speak the truth today. But we are very tentative about it, starting from a certain point in time, from the period of stagnation. Yet it was silence that made this stagnation possible. That is why we are concerned today that not everything is being said. This means that there is a place to retreat. Having led his troops out to Kulikovo Field, Dmitri Donskoi ordered his men to remove the bridges — it was to be either victory or death. There was no place to retreat. Our society is now facing the same moment of decision. Silence, like cancer, can lead to new lies, and we are not morally healthy enough to overcome new lies.

Everyone today is aware of the exceptional danger posed by the uncontrolled actions of the Ministry of Land Improvement to nature, the economy and morale. The public has long requested that control bodies undertake a fundamental revision of its role. What are those tens of billions of roubles spent on, what is being done to the land they work on, and what is the economic result from the expenditure of these funds? But, just as before, few listen to the voice of the public. With great effort — and thanks to a government resolution — we were able to temporarily halt the project to divert northern and Siberian rivers. And so? The projects were halted, but what good is that if there is no change in financing, if the guilty are not punished and if Minister of Land Improvement N. Vasilyev receives a high state award. This causes consternation and is seen as support for the 'diverters'.

One can't help but think what might seem to be an absurd idea, but one that is not entirely groundless: will the funds that will be released from the dismantling of intermediate-and shorter-range missiles be used for other arms and increase the power of the Ministries of Land Improvement, Energy, Timber and Paper-making, and other ministries and departments whose swaggering behaviour in their own country is reminiscent of colonial policy?

Increasing the power of, say, the Ministry of Land Improvement, and continuing to condone a cost-intensive economy can only do harm to the state.

E. Sh. *I would not be surprised, Valentin Grigoryevich, nor, no doubt, would you be, if someone would now comment:*

*there's Rasputin talking about Lake Baikal again, about the
diversion of rivers... And in truth, much has already been written about these topics, so much that the public might be under
the illusion that it is enough, that both problems have already
been solved...*

V. R. Concern about nature will never disappear, or will
disappear only together with nature. The Lake Baikal problem was not solved with the adoption of the government resolution. There have been resolutions passed before, and
had they done even half what they were supposed to, the
fate of Lake Baikal would be different. But the ministries
were able to alter the provisions with other resolutions or,
not even bothering to do that, simply ignored them. Again
this is a question of conscience, of its expression in work
and public life.

It must be acknowledged that there has never been
a more decisive resolution passed specifically for the purpose of preserving Lake Baikal than the April 1987 document. But it, too, is annoyingly inconsistent. In particular
I am speaking about the clause which calls for building an
industrial waste removal system at the Baikal Cellulose
Plant. Of course, Baikal doesn't want those industrial
wastes, but a pipeline is not going to save the lake. This is
an ineffective half-measure. They agreed to 'A' but didn't
have the gumption to agree to 'B'.

*E. Sh. The stratification of society is a phenomenon of the
period of stagnation, and it has warped the spiritual quality of
life. Bureaucratic distortions and all kinds of abuse have so
twisted our lives that it sometimes seems impossible to put
things straight. Do you see any changes in this situation?*

V. R. There have been changes. If we take the vertical aspect of stratification, the bureaucracy and the people, the bureaucracy feels rather uncomfortable at the moment, or
rather *did* feel uncomfortable. It seems to me it has mus-
tered its strength as of late. Impunity, on the one hand, and
the solidarity of the apparatus against the practical implementation of the new way of thinking, on the other, have
restored its feeling of durability. It is beginning to grow accustomed to the commotion, and has even taken on the role
of creating the commotion itself.

But the most disturbing stratification is in the horizontal
aspect. Today it is hard to speak of the people as being

a whole, united by a common goal. The major goals are lost in words and cluttered by those of secondary significance. As never before we are showing ourselves to be a people eager to demonstrate its differences: in age, nationality, culture, taste and profession. The people was always united and inspired by concern for the land as birthplace, a provider, as something eternal. When this concern weakened it was inevitable that the ties among the people would weaken as well. And as long as the people continue to forget and try to filch from their Motherland, we can expect no improvement in the future. The restructuring of the consciousness must begin with this ABC principle, the one on which everything rests, starting with the first perceptions of a baby and ending with the integrity of state figures.

E. Sh. *Many people are alarmed by the inroads made by mass culture and the depreciation of moral values. But what can be used to counter this decline? Prohibitions, we know, are not the best method. But what strong, effective countermeasures are there?*

V. R.—One's own, national culture and all the variegation, all the richness of the cultures of other nations. In the world as a whole nations at all periods of time have created great art that is sufficient to regenerate and satisfy any spirit. All that is necessary is to introduce a child to it at an early age, to teach it to perceive the beauty of sounds and words.

Mass culture is a psychosis of consumption; it is a sign of either spiritual emptiness or disorder. An individual who has grown into a personality does not succumb to this psychosis. The herd instinct is for the weak, those who copy what others do.

I don't believe that a young person who knows Glinka, Moussorgsky, Pushkin, Dostoyevsky and Tolstoy would become a mindless rock fan. In a word, the hearts that are not taken by us will momentarily be taken by our enemy. Yet our schools today, with their formalism and dogmatism, are only capable of turning pupils away from the classics and from beauty. And then there is the television with its new youth programming: rock, rock and more rock!

E. Sh. *Valentin Grigoryevich, do you have a clear plan of action against the encroachment of mass culture and those attitudes toward it that you do not agree with?*

V. R. Everywhere in the world today people are seeking their roots. We are the most forgetful nation, though we too are beginning slowly to regain our memory. We are collecting and performing folk art, with great difficulty we have recalled our traditions in folk crafts. We have made the decision to publish important works on our history, the works of Solovyev, Karamzin and Klyuchevsky, and have begun to observe the momentous dates in our country's history. But we are doing this slowly, half-heartedly, keeping an eye out for whoever likes different songs or doesn't care for our history. The Society for the Protection of Historical and Cultural Monuments was organised in Russia, but disregard for its work and its recommendations placed it in an impotent and humiliating position. As a result, monuments continue to be torn down. Whether in Moscow or in Irkutsk, if an apartment house for the *élite* is to be built, no one is concerned with the preservation zones or with historical inviolability.

The question of the people's daily cultural concern and behaviour is an important one. This culture is not of a high level. Unconcern, rudeness, vanity—never before have these existed in such magnitude. The way in which we make use of the freedom and *glasnost* we now have reflects the low level of cultural behaviour and consciousness. We are ready to make anarchy out of our freedom, to introduce foreign influence and denounce patriotic activities with our *glasnost*. Thousands of unofficial unions—this is a helter-skelter of ideas, tastes and morals, a cavorting around with programmes and actions, an unwillingness to rely on the people's experience. I by no means object to unofficial organisations. I even pin my hopes on the monument protection and ecological movements. But what is alarming is that most of these unions are far removed from the problems and needs of the people and country. They are busy with egotistical interests and parasites of democracy.

But there are so many problems. The bad thing is not that there are so many but how we intend to solve them. Either by using borrowed programmes or with our own reasoned solutions.

E. Sh. *Society, of course, has a great influence on us. It shapes and educates us. There is no way to escape this. But how important is self-education in the formation of a personality?*

V. R. Self-education is probably the most important thing. It is the origin of independent views, individuality and civil orientation, and all the more important since public education is so bad. In a word, put your hope in it [public education] but don't spare your own efforts. You can achieve success only by knowing and being capable of more than it gives. In order to counter anti-culture in today's situation you must have an idea where it comes from, who organises it and what are its goals. To fight the 'reversers' we need to know their secret sources. You won't read this in the newspaper; a person comes to know this by himself.

Every society protects itself with the help of its value judgements. This is as it should be, but an individual should not accept them blindly. If he understands their significance, he will stand up for them with more determination. I will conclude by saying that we have a great need right now for the active individual. But he must have vision, be able to discern right from wrong, and be correctly oriented. Then it will be possible to live according to one's conscience.

Literaturnaya Gazeta, 1 January 1988

ART AND TRADITION

By ILYA GLAZUNOV
People's Artist of the USSR

For an artist *perestroika* means, above all, the opportunity to express one's position—honestly, daringly, objectively. I recall Chaadayev's comment that even the most talented individual could not be an artist if he had no insight into the secret of his times. But what exactly is this secret? I think more than anything else it is the perceivance of what is good and what is evil.

My approach is reflected in my work. For thirty years I have endeavoured to express truth, and to heighten the self-awareness of the people. My ideal was to achieve a high level of realism; I have no liking for the creation of abstract forms or for photographic naturalism.

I have been asked many times about *perestroika* in the
fine arts: everyone is anxious for change here as well. Questions vary. I do not think *perestroika* implies a kind of lic-
ence to 'revel in democracy'; it is not a freedom 'from' but
an enabling freedom 'for' deepening through art our knowledge of our motherland Russia and its people.

The period of stagnation caused great harm. Today we
experience the effects of the erosion of fundamental principles in our art, the absence of an abiding awareness of the
struggle between good and evil and, not least, an inability
to see art as a mode of thinking in images.

Where can we point to artistic discoveries that match our
momentous times? Why are there so few profoundly innovative works? Why, in exhibitions from the Kuznetsky
Bridge to the Krymski Bridge, are there so few outstanding
works that attempt to comprehend the history and fate of
our people?

Why is there an alarming trend to return to the twenties,
to become infatuated with avant-gardism and abstract self-
expression that has little or nothing to do with reality? Can
a shop-bought mirror with the inscription 'Portrait of
a Contemporary' really be called innovation in art? And
what about the blank canvas with the inscription— 'I was
in a bad mood and couldn't do anything'? These 'works'
truly unmask these painters and reveal their failure in art.
By the way, the two 'works' were actually hung at a recent
exhibition.

As I see it an artist who did not have professional training will almost certainly be a dilettante, and a dilettante will
usually be a 'modernist' hiding behind a guise of various
'isms'. Having lost contact with the real world, he has no
objectives, no idea or orientation, but will nevertheless
claim to be a painter of modern '*élitist*' art. There are those
young people who must flaunt innovation at all cost, rushing after fad and fashion, seizing on a pseudo-discovery,
masquerading behind stale formal experiment. In trying to
reflect truth the dilettante goes in for photograpic naturalism, now known as hyper-realism. Abstract art can lead to
naiveté. But do we have any interest in a naive conversation
partner? The essence of art is to be found in the answer to
the question—what and how?

The revival of the avant-garde movement will lead to

a dead-end. Seventy years after, the avant-garde has become the rear-garde. It is part of history. Repin's student, Isaak Brodsky, exerted enormous effort in his time in order to reaffirm the principles of the Russian school of realism. At the present time the key necessity is to preserve tradition. We must cherish and nurture the school of Soviet art which, together with the great European schools, has given us wonderful artists, diverse in their outlook and their creative endeavours. In my opinion only through the path of tradition can we pursue a fruitful creative search that will produce works to match the spirit of modern times.

It is of course a good thing that the doors of galleries, exhibition halls and even parks and streets are open for all to exhibit their works. What has happened, however, is that some putative 'innovators', complaining about recent restrictions and prohibitions and dressed in the aura of past persecution, stand before the public like emperors without clothes. The works of these 'geniuses' have the stigma of cheap imitation, artificiality and pretentiousness. They turn their back on Russian and European traditions in art. And yet their works are being praised.

Critics and the press are greatly influential in moulding public response to particular works. Without question, a most important aspect of critical appraisal and analysis is to retain a sense of good-will, and to avoid the temptation to work out a grudge. Just recently the ambitious aims of one group (or one clan) of artists were allegedly the justification for treating another group with partiality. We must not equate the partisan fight for group interest with genuine competitiveness or with free creative competition. Group interests pose a mortal danger to our culture. In art circles they obstruct and frustrate tolerance and respect for the non-conformity and individuality of the artist and the talented people who may perhaps in some ways be misguided, but nonetheless are sincere and honest in holding the views they do. Life's experience has an immense diversity. The wider the discussion and controversy, the greater the concern to solve the problems of our society, the more virile our art will become.

We could usefully recall the long forgotten first congress of Russian artists held in 1914. We mention only two of the artists, Repin and Kandinsky, who addressed the meeting with fundamentally opposing views on art. The congress was distinguished by the seriousness of the response to questions posed, the earnest controversy and the deep concern for art in Russia.

In contrast how awful it is that some of our critics are still unable to break away from their old habits and continue to apply outmoded appraisals and judgements that reek of moth-balls. Either they are sticking labels on artists right and left or they are dubiously crowning this or that artist with a laurel wreath.

I am certain that *élitish* art cannot be justified. Nor can 'art for the masses'. Genuine art is comprehensible to everyone. For whom, for example, did Surikov, Ivanov, Vrubel, Fedotov and Nesterov paint—for an *élite*, for the rabble, or for the people at large?

I am concerned for the future of our young artists and at the same time the fate of the Soviet school of art. It is impossible to extend the frontiers of art and at the same time build on a rich tradition without a high level of professionalism based on a national school. Only by means of such a school can tradition be continued and the future of Soviet and Russian art be safeguarded. What a genius Surikov was when he declared that because he loved and admired the composition and style of the old masters so strongly he saw it everywhere in life.

Tradition is at the root. A campaign against tradition is a campaign against culture. I believe that today we are cheating young artists—and also our future—when we neglect to generate in our schools an appreciation of national consciousness in the highest meaning of the term. The implications inherent in the attitude of students emerge clearly enough when Litvinsky and myself take the master portrait class. When we speak about the mastery of technique, the style of the great schools and tradition in art the students introduce polemic and controversy centred around homespun avant-gardism and leftist trends. In effect this breaks continuity in tradition, substituting for it a discourse on how each new generation in art discovers its own laws, applicable only to itself. I am convinced that such 'personal' laws never have had and never will have any validity whatever.

The sign of the times, the evidence of change, must be

that artists who take a firm stand for realism in art have the opportunity to use the press, television and media generally to contest the views of those who advocate 'anything goes' in art. Only creative competition, open discussion of works with wide sections of society, only genuine *glasnost* concerning the evaluation of art can ensure progress and aid our creative endeavours.

There is great concern today at the closure for a prolonged period of the Tretyakov Gallery, the Russian and Historical Museums, and the Manezh. Is it feasible to contemplate the abrupt suspension of the music of Mozart or Rachmaninov? But that is comparable with what has happened in the art world: today there is virtually no way to view the immortal works of Ivanov, Repin, Rokotov, Rublev or Surikov. Why? What can be done? An entire generation is being deprived of the opportunity to know this great art merely because various cultural and construction agencies are unable to agree on how to build new galleries and museums sooner. Is it so impossible to find a place for the temporary exposition of world-famous treasures that belong to all humanity?

And there is another problem: the severe shortage of specialists. We need a whole school of restorers. Can the dozen or so specialists being trained today accomplish very much at all? Insufficient money is being spent, and more than a few architectural masterpieces — our heritage, our pride — are falling into ruin. Fortunately the Party and the state are making a great effort in conservation. For example the restoration from the ashes and ruin of destruction by war of Pavlovsk, Gatchina, Pushkin, and of Leningrad itself.

Our capital is another matter. In the past few decades Moscow, as we know, has lost many renowned architectural monuments. Leafing through monographs and books on Russian history and reading the memoirs and eye-witness accounts of foreigners, we realise what riches we have lost. It intensifies our conviction that we must preserve what remains of our inheritance.

It is sad to note that publicity to preserve our historical and cultural legacy is on a rather low level today. The All-Russian Society for the Preservation of Historical and Cultural Monuments, of which I am one of the founders, is

working sluggishly, with little initiative and with little or no
involvement of the youth. It was good that the recent congresses of the Union of Architects and the Union of Russian Artists, at which I was a guest, raised urgent problems
concerning the preservation of historical and cultural monuments. And it was very good that the Politbureau of the
Central Committee of the CPSU discussed and approved
the resolution passed by the Council of Ministers of the
USSR, 'On the all-round reconstruction in the historic centre of Moscow in the period up to 2000'. The reconstruction
and restoration of historical and cultural monuments and
the enlargement of museums and exhibition halls are key issues for us.

In conclusion I would like to refute both here and abroad
the rumours circulating that I am the founder and leader of
the Pamyat Society. For example the French journalist
France Nuvel, among others, wrote on these lines. I am surprised that the French journalist did not find the time to
come to talk to me. He would have learned that I am and
always have been a Russian, a Soviet citizen, a patriot and
internationalist. I have no connection with Pamyat.

A number of good people — patriots of their country and
loyal to the Soviet people — belong to Pamyat. Unfortunately, sometimes adventurists and chauvinists find advantage in attaching themselves to such healthy elements. Internationalism is a bouquet of national cultures. I am for patriotism and genuine efforts to preserve the peoples' legacy,
for disinterested work for the good of our multinational
Fatherland. We must affirm what is positive.

I believe in *perestroika*, in the bright future of our great
people.

Pravda, 27 September 1987

*The past year or so has been a difficult one in the Soviet thea-
tre. Companies have been torn by internal disputes and squab-
bles. The experiment in self-management which began in
1987 in more than 80 theatres has not yet produced the new
plays hoped for, in tune with* perestroika *and* glasnost. *But
new studio-theatres and theatre-workshops have appeared in
Moscow, Leningrad, and other cities, and some amateur com-*

panies have turned professional. Summing up the first year of the experiment, VASSILY ZAKHAROV, *the USSR Minister of Culture, said in* Izvestia*(25 January 1988): 'It is still very difficult for many theatres. It is no accident that roubles and profits have taken first place during the experiment. The children's repertoire was cut for the sake of profit; the drive to get extra funds at any price led to theatres' refusing commercially unprofitable tours and travelling shows, especially in country areas. There is a real danger of the commercialisation of dramatic art.'*

A leading figure in the fight to revitalise Soviet theatre is the actor MIKHAIL ULYANOV, *a member of the Central Auditing Committee of the CPSU. Ulyanov himself has felt many of the troubles that have beset Soviet theatre and cinema. His work in a series of TV films scripted by Mikhail Shatrov lay on the shelf for 17 years before being televised. Many people think his portrayal of Lenin the best in Soviet cinema. In the Vakhtangov Theatre, where he has worked for years, he was involved in a fierce battle that ended in the autumn of 1987 with the transfer of the chief producer, Eugene Simonov, to the newly founded Friendship Theatre, and Ulyanov's election to the post of art director. The first play under the new directorship was Shatrov's* The Brest Peace, *which had its first night (attended by Mr. Gorbachev) on the eve of the Washington summit.*

The founding of the Union of Russian Theatrical Workers, in place of the old Russian Theatrical Society, was a major event for perestroika *in the Soviet theatre. The election of pugnacious, hard-hitting Mikhail Ulyanov as President of the new Union augured well for its future. But the road to* perestroika *and self-government in the theatre has been a hard one, as Ulyanov describes in this article from* Sovetskaya Kultura.

The Hard Road to Self-Government

Our Union of Russian Theatrical Workers has been in existence for a year. How much heat was generated in the effort to establish it! How much temperament was displayed publicly at the inaugural congress! What hopes theatre people put in their Union! Yet, already, other voices are being heard: was it worth making such a song-and-dance about it? The position of actors has not improved. There's been no appearance of new masterpieces. Generalities have not been translated into concrete action.

What can I say to that? A great deal. The theatre experiment is going ahead, and the Union is taking a direct, active part in it. A new system of theatrical training, worked out by masters of theatre themselves, has been proposed and adopted. The practice of holding theatre festivals has been decisively altered; they are ceasing to be showpieces and thematic, and are becoming business-like, working reviews of achievements.

But there is truth in the bitter words addressed to us. Of course we are a long time getting started; it sometimes seems to us that what we are accustomed to is more comfortable and (the main thing) calmer and quieter than the new, which calls for effort and nerves. The traditional Russian habit of carrying out radical reforms without changing anything if possible still immobilises many. Of course, we need to begin *perestroika* with ourselves, but that is excruciatingly difficult. We've lived through hard times, and they have left their mark on our careers.

Many of us have been gagged, deprived of the right to say what bothered us most. We were prevented from publishing, from engaging in our chosen work, in fact our creative life was not only inhibited, but damaged.

We could be bribed by trifling prizes, and petty and major privileges. And we kept quiet and became tame and obedient.

But we couldn't be deceived. Our nature is such that we feel the falsity of fancy, high-sounding words, or affected, mild ones, resounding promises, and simulated cheerfulness. We understand everything; but it's another matter what we do about it. That is a matter of conscience.

But those who have taken the idea of *perestroika* to heart as the only possible future, have ceased to be afraid. And when, today, after a spell of tense, official silence, we again hear familiar, ever more confident voices saying 'Don't you dare!', 'It's not your business!', 'We'll manage without you!', we are no longer terrified. A start has been made; things have been set in motion, and that movement, I would like to hope, is irreversible.

Russian theatre is racked with conflicts. The troupe is fighting the producer; the producer cannot find a common language with the manager; the leaders of a theatre find themselves in conflict with the culture department; the culture department 'dares' to disagree with the workers of the Party regional committee. The conflicts are very diverse, but there's nothing to be frightened about in them. The unresolved problems, dissatisfactions, frustrated ambitions, and unexpressed truth — all that, stifled for years, has burst out into the open. And it's a good thing it has. The appearance of well-being and complacency has given way to a look of anxiety. But the theatres are continuing to put on plays, and the actors play roles. Sooner or later a calm understanding that *glasnost* is an inevitable, necessary condition of democracy (which we have still only begun to learn) will come to replace appearance. The conflicts continue, but there is something common to all of them, for all their differences. Competence is fighting incompetence, and is not always winning.

Militant incompetence at various levels — that is what the Union has been up against from the very first days of its existence. The Union is not fighting for power, as it seems to some, but for the simple, obvious truth that *all affairs must be carried on by a competent person, a specialist, a professional.* But what has become obvious in politics, in the economy, in medicine, and industry has to be demonstrated and proved in the theatre. And this is not always the case.

A regular session of the Union secretariat was held recently, at which it seemed we would be considering a routine matter of the work of several of our not especially distinguished branches, and the theatrical situation in their areas. I must admit that the secretaries, who have seen much, were thrown into utter confusion. What a tangle of seemingly insoluble problems which hadn't been tackled for years. What routine and what ignorance! Above all the *incompetence* of those responsible for taking the decisions, and who received salaries far higher than the actors.

They may all be incompetent — the actors, producers, and critics. For decades the question of the reform of theatrical training was not tackled; the standard of teachers declined; so-called colleges were arbitrarily set up in the provinces and were of a far lower standard than the secondary theatrical schools. And the theatrical school turned out a legion of grey actors without a hint of individuality or talent, dozens of producers who lacked talent and detested actors, and a host of critics who did not know how to watch a play and write about it. Ruined careers, lost generations. But it is even more terrible when the incompetents are people with the strange, mysterious label 'listed'.*

A managing-director who is a specialist in theatrical affairs is a rarity, although professional theatre administrators are trained in Moscow and Leningrad. I don't want to repeat truths that have become banal, but more and more facts are coming to light which show that the profession of theatre director has become a 'listed' job, an appointment by local cultural authorities that they often use to 'kick upstairs' favoured people who have made a mess of other jobs.

For decades theatrical opinion has been persistently asking that *the art director should be the sole head of a theatre*. He may be a producer, an actor, a playwright, a critic, or a manager, if these are people who have a deep understanding of the creative problems of the theatre. But administrative workers are evidently easier to order around than artists; so that a decision obvious to everyone is clouded over by cunning excuses, and lost in the deepest recesses of offices. Conflicts continue in the theatres; 'listed' managers decide the repertoire, sign the distribution of parts, head the arts councils; and more and more often one hears the very complex artistic process labelled 'theatrical industry', and a production 'the end product'. It's a disgrace!

The Party has put a task of historical significance on the agenda, namely to transfer some of the functions of state administration to public, social self-government. The creative unions, which are actively accepting and supporting *perestroika*, are one of the structures of this self-government.

Russian theatrical workers, who are far from languishing in idleness, are ready to take on additional commitments. But the local cultural authorities are not ready for such reorganisation. And it is most alarming and disturbing that

---

* Ulyanov used the Russian word *nomenklatura* here, a jargon term which means, among its many nuances in the Soviet Union, the list of top officials appointed from above.— *Tr.*

people who ought to be carrying out the ideas of *pere-stroika*, i.e. local Party and Soviet leaders, are defending wrong methods of secret, administrative, command decisions. We often hear locally that (they say) these are your, Moscow's affair; we have already endured a great deal and we're enduring this. But *perestroika* is gathering force, and its wheel may yet run over such feeble bosses. This is what they fear, which is why they are putting up such a resistance.

The view of theatrical public opinion is being ignored when basic matters of theatrical business, including questions of personnel, are decided. There is practically no *glasnost* when the candidates for such important posts as producers and even managers are being discussed.

How are we going to get ahead with the work? How are we going to look our fellows in the profession in the eye? Dozens of theatres where conflicts are raging are expecting help from the Union. Words won't put out this fire. You can't hide it away in a pocket as these officials, at any rate, would like. There is a view that the Union was given power but doesn't know what to do with it. But the Union has no real chance to tackle the problems arising, in spite of the provisions of its rules. It has only the strength of words, only reliance on public opinion. But just try to convince those who are oblivious to any opinion except that of their superiors and their own.

Sometimes one wants to chuck the whole thing; for there's still the work one loves — the theatre and acting. One only has not so much energy. You're rehearsing a very complicated part in a fine play; you are working with an interesting producer — and you can't concentrate. Your thoughts return again to the conflict in Novgorod, to the situation in Kuibyshev. You remember people's faces, and their eyes, and their hopes. No, you have to grit your teeth and beat your head again and again against the stone wall of the established stereotypes, inertness, stagnation, and official incompetence. If we abandon the struggle, give up, we'll never be able to look our colleagues in the eye. Not in life, not on the stage, not from the screen.

Total indifference to the careers of creative workers is the other side of incompetent leadership. Talented producers and interesting actors are leaving the theatre, quitting because they've lost hope of receiving understanding and support. And they hear, as they leave: 'Never mind. We'll find someone else.' At a session of the Union secretariat, the chief producer of the Chechen Theatre, Soltsaev, told us how the republican officials light-heartedly dismissed the theatre's leading actor, Davletmirzaev — sacked him without even finding time for a talk. If the head of the department of the Party regional committee concerned, Saikhanov, had been seriously interested in art, and had remembered Lenin's words about a respectful, caring attitude to talent, he would not have spoken his high-handed, bureaucratic words to the secretariat — 'No one's irreplaceable'.

There *are* irreplaceable people in art, Comrade Saikhanov, and always will be! No one today can replace Efros, or Papanov, or Mironov.* There are others, but there will never be ones like them.

The Union will continue the work begun, defending the right of the theatrical community to decide its own fate. That is what it was founded for. That is the task the Party has set it. The fight against incompetence is a hard one, but we have no other way. We have to reach the necessary understanding with all competent people in the Party, local Soviet, and government bodies, and we will. And we shall get it accepted that only professional, competent people can work in the theatre. We know that the other creative unions, who have also decided to carry out *perestroika* in deeds rather than words, are also meeting similar problems.

But we also need state, government support. It is necessary for the rights granted to the creative unions by their new statutes and rules to be given the force of law. Surely it's time to draft and pass a special resolution on the rights and competence of a creative union.

The people in the Russian theatre are modest and appreciative. They will respond to consideration and care with maximum results in creative work. They have not been spoiled by too much care. It is important that words spoken from rostrums are not isolated and divorced from concrete affairs; for calm, confidence, and a feeling of social justice and responsibility to be inherent qualities in every theatre

---

*   They all died in the year before this article was written.— *Tr*.

worker. Then we shan't have to blush when we hear bitter words in the secretariat of the Union that there is tendency to play at democracy in the theatre, instead of implementing democracy, to play at *perestroika* instead of reconstructing.

Sovetskaya Kultura, 24 October 1987

ROBERT STURUA: THE TOPICAL AND THE ETERNAL IN THE ART OF STAGE DIRECTING

By KONSTANTIN RUDNITSKY

It is hard to imagine the destructive power of a ball of lightning, when it melts through a window pane and floats slowly into a room. Robert Sturua is the same. When you talk to him, and he answers your questions phlegmatically and lazily, it would be impossible to imagine what kind of energy was inside him. His round face is good-natured. His speech is evasive and sly, his voice soft. Laconic phrases, unpretentious humour. Not a trace of self-importance or putting on airs. He would never say 'my creative work', 'my concept', 'my quest'... His vocabulary is down-to-earth and businesslike: 'our work', 'what we're trying to rehearse here', 'well, it hasn't come out quite as I wanted it to'... It is usually thought that a theatre director and head of a celebrated drama company should be strong-willed, tough and powerful. Perhaps, he is like that deep down inside, but in conversation he appears to be the opposite: a gentle man full of endearing charm, kindness and sensitivity. His talent comes out in his irrepressible tendency to play, to constantly fantasise and improvise, and in his sudden, unpredictable and often paradoxical reactions. Only occasionally, behind his round glasses, do his dark eyes flash with devilish fire to remind you of his hidden temperament. Then you begin to understand why Robert Sturua's premieres are like fireworks calling forth awe and debate — first in Tbilisi, then in Moscow, and later in London, Mexico City, Krasnoyarsk and Riga.

An almost forgotten play, *Kwarkware Tutaberi*, written

in the late 1920s by Polikarp Kakabadze, was revived by Robert Sturua in 1974, during a period of complacency and bragging, when systematic and not altogether unsuccessful attempts were being made to brush up the image of Stalin that had been seriously damaged by the 20th CPSU Congress. Sturua's production of *Kwarkware* was a series of tragi-farcical variations on the theme of inhuman and ruthless tyranny. In one of these variations, the grotesque image of the 'leader of nations' was presented to a stunned audience. The actor Ramaz Chkhikvadze came on the stage, his face white with heavy makeup like a marble mask. He was barefoot. He acted out now a ceremonial portrait, now a caricature, all the ups and downs of an imaginary deity. This barefoot maniac in a tight-fitting soldier's tunic walked slowly along the footlights, grinding out his words with an important air, and sometimes looking suspiciously at his stooges, numb with fear. It was supposed to be some sort of meeting. But the discussion was being interrupted increasingly by uneasy and menacing silences. And then, finally, the dictator fixed his icy gaze on one of his associates and gave an abrupt bark of a laugh. The person on whom his eyes fell rose meekly, without so much as an attempt to defend or justify himself. The dictator's escorts rose up behind him like shadows and led him away, his life over. The meeting continued...

Stalin was not named and the play ran unhindered — it was even shown on tour in Moscow in 1976 — but everyone recognised the 'leader of nations' for who he was. Some grumbled, others rejoiced. Sturua was uncompromisingly against the attempted revival of the Stalin cult.

A deep antipathy to totalitarianism is as characteristic a feature of his art as his implicit belief in the ultimate triumph of democracy and in the creative power of the masses he has always dreamed of freeing. It is this belief that sets the merry-go-round of Bertolt Brecht's *The Caucasian Chalk Circle* in motion. The carnival atmosphere unleashed by Giya Kancheli's music raises Simon the soldier (played by Kakhi Kavsadze) and Grushe the kitchen-maid (Iza Gogishvili) into spokesmen for the Georgian people. Sturua, however, does not believe that everything Georgian is poetic and beautiful by definition.

The moment I touched on this topic in our conversation,

his face clouded over. 'Flattery is a lie, and the vilest kind at that,' he said gloomily. 'Lisping and cringing to one's own nation betray a mercenary heart. Flattery is profitable. Flatterers are welcomed at every table, then set against those who are unable to lie. When Giya Danelia'a film *Don't Grieve!* was released in Tbilisi, there were people who said Danelia "did not love his countrymen", that he was not a Georgian. Otar Ioseliani's film *The Fall* was hidden from the public for years on the pretext that it insulted national dignity. What kind of dignity is it that shuns the truth? There's no such thing as a man or nation without sin. I am equally sickened by sugary Russia-style soap operas and pompous attempts to glorify the Georgian past. Herzen was right when he said that patriotic zeal of that kind is not far removed from hating your neighbour.

'Antagonism in international relations begins precisely here — with flattery, conceit and indiscriminate approval of everything "ours". In Fellini's films, love for Italy and Italians is present with bitter irony and mockery. He looks fearlessly at his people's past and present. Genius is a free agent, it does not fear frankness. I remember reading somewhere that Shukshin had learned things from Fellini. Good for him. I'm trying to learn, too.'

It was not perhaps the right moment to mention Stanislavsky. Robert raised his arms in mock despair and said jovially: 'I give up. Unconditional surrender. Of course, there's no denying he's a genius and a teacher, but let's not start idolising, please. Sometimes I think idolatry is our biggest problem. If we idolise Stanislavsky, we forget Meyerhold and Brecht. If we idolise Lenin, he stops being the vital, thinking and innovative person he was and becomes a sort of oracle knowing all the answers beforehand.'

The freedom with which Robert Sturua treated the Lenin theme in Mikhail Shatrov's *Blue Horses on Red Grass* confused the bureaucrats so much that the play which opened the Rustaveli Theatre's 1980 Moscow tour was performed only once and then crossed off the programme. Audiences were tactfully informed that the play had been replaced because one of the actors had fallen ill.

Since the USSR Ministry of Culture stubbornly insisted on gala productions to mark various jubilees, the Rustaveli Theatre's wilful repertoire was often out of step. Gala productions are alien to Sturua. For the 40th anniversary of the victory over fascism in 1985, he staged *Doomsday*, a play based on the memoirs of the prominent Germanic philologist, Mikhail Kveselava, who was present at the Nuremberg trials. At the centre of the play was the far-cically exaggerated figure of Hitler, played by Chkhik-vadze. During the *Doomsday* dress rehearsal I sat next to a woman from the USSR Ministry of Culture. She was in agony. The mischievous style of directing made her panic. 'It's too much for me,' she whispered worriedly, in the naive hope that I might talk Sturua into bridling his fantasy. It would have been as easy as trying to talk a volcano into not erupting and upsetting the local population.

Sturua has a closely-knit team of actors around him who are quick to understand his meaning. When he saunters noiselessly to the stage and climbs up, the actors watch him attentively, following his every movement and word. Often, however, it is guesswork or natural feeling on the part of the actor which adds a certain nuance to the production, that the director had not foreseen. Sturua loves those moments. He works in close partnership with the composer Giya Kancheli. After an opening night, Robert usually says, 'Giya suggested this... Giya found that...', to which Giya Kancheli smiles in assent, saying: 'Yes, Robert told me he needed some choral singing here, a passionate tango there, plus a bit of good ragtime some place else. He always knows what he's after.' 'More or less,' Robert corrects him, 'but Giya gives me the kind of music that clarifies what is unclear and simplifies what is complicated.'

Much of their joint work depends on improvisation, on 'trial and error'. That is why the end result, however apparently unambiguous, always has an element of mystery about it, a quality which defies words.

'If I could explain everything, you would be bored,' Robert says with a smile. 'And so would I...'

Just over three years ago, shortly before her death, the veteran Georgian actress Veriko Andzhaparidze went to see Giya Kancheli's opera, *Music for the Living*, produced by Robert Sturua at the Paliashvili Opera Theatre in Tbilisi. Both the director and composer, as well as the conductor Djansug Kakhidze, were convinced that the complex and unusual production would not be to the taste of their honoured guest. But Veriko was moved to tears and talked about the production's magical mistakes which defied explanation but were what made art into art.

In *Music for the Living*, performed in five languages (Sumerian, English, Italian, French, and Georgian), menacing images of evil and aggression were opposed by a chorus of clear children's voices sadly but fearlessly counterposing the gloomy grinding of the grandiose machinery of our nuclear age.

Turning to Shakespeare's *Richard III* and *King Lear*, Sturua wanted to emphasise these classics' topicality, to reveal their relevance to modern audiences. When reproached with having 'distorted' the author's concept, Sturua stubbornly quoted Brecht: 'Theatre serves society, not the author.'

The stage designers he works with do not try to reproduce heavy-weight, historical settings for his productions. He has no use for vaulted ceilings, fireplaces, armour or halberds. Sturua's Richard wears an SS trench coat, Cordelia — pedal-pushers and a black blouse. Shakespeare's characters carry tennis rackets or umbrellas. Often costumes parody military outfits — uniforms, gold and silver braid, epaulettes, and so on. War is a theme in many of Sturua's productions. He never misses a chance to express his deep aversion for the very idea of militarism.

As a stage director, Sturua has an instinctive, almost physiological aversion to conventional and hackneyed forms. While rehearsing Mikhail Shatrov's *The Brest Peace* at the Vakhtangov Theatre in Moscow, he got the glum and dispirited company buzzing with activity. Mikhail Ulyanov said that such rehearsals were bliss for actors. 'Even if it's a complete flop in the end, it will have been worth it. We're realised ourselves as artists, we've experienced that wonderful feel of risk. Sturua involved us all in a project we had not dared to dream of before.'

The Brest Peace has not flopped. On the contrary, the play has been running for three months to a full house, the cast's enthusiasm flowing out over the footlights to embrace the audience.

In April 1987 in Tbilisi, after the dress rehearsal of *King Lear*, Robert Sturua told me of his plans to produce Chekhov's *The Cherry Orchard*. In his usual laconic manner he hinted vaguely at how he planned to produce the play. But then it happened that Shatrov, Sturua and I turned up in New York together as part of a Soviet theatre delegation. Shatrov had the page-proof of his new play, *On... On... and On...!* with him. Sturua read it and immediately wanted to produce it. He looked at me apologetically and said: 'What do you say to my postponing Chekhov? Perhaps Ranevskaya will forgive a short delay? Shatrov's play has got Lenin, Bukharin, Trotsky, and Stalin again, and I've an idea already how it could be done. I just can't get away from politics. It's almost a kind of narrow-mindedness, isn't it?'

As I was finishing this article, Robert Sturua turned up suddenly in Moscow and rang me. 'Well, is it to be Shatrov or Chekhov?' I asked. He answered firmly, 'Chekhov first.' To be honest, I don't think it really matters which play comes first and which second. The art of stage directing lies in the border land between past and future. I do not presume to foretell the surprises and magical mistakes his coming production may hold in store for his audience.

Moscow News, 14 February 1988

A TIME LIKE NO OTHER

Film star LYUDMILA GURCHENKO talks

THE ACTOR'S PARADOX

The acting profession is the most responsive of all professions to innovation, change and ideas, yet paradoxically it is precisely among us professional film actors that there are no ideas, where we think 'it'd be better not to change anything at all'. Not even the brightest of people have been able to think up an idea which would provide a film actor with work. Not every film actor can or must work in the theatre or in variety. He does not need a powerful voice, strong features or height, as in the theatre. What shows on film is something else, something inexplicable, which the actor does not possess in real life. It is a mystery, a special something the star possesses.

With rare exception, a young actor finishing drama

school very soon becomes a nobody with a diploma. He has a profession, but no work. So that the film actor won't grumble, so that everything remains calm in the kingdom, he is given money for doing nothing and left to his own devices. This long period of unemployment has such a damaging psychological effect that he ends up losing faith in himself, in people, in promises, in resolutions and slogans.

But life must go on! Against his will the actor is obliged to undergo certain transformations, to adopt patient, enigmatic silence — the 'golden mean' — respected by all and sundry; to learn to walk with a smile down the road he is told to, or to polish his actor's temperament through trade union or Party work.

But aren't an interest in life, vitality and inner happiness components of good health? And who exudes these? The actor. Paradoxically again. I know from my own experience that each new role seems to be the last, that tomorrow is enveloped in mist and darkness. That's why I've never taken part in discussions on the so-called 'actor's problem', which were constantly flaring up, then subsiding, leaving questions unanswered.

Off we go to the film festival, camouflaging the 'problem' with a pretty frock and a fixed smile. This time it promises to be something different. How many famous and prestigious people have come to it! An actor is chairman of the jury, which has never happened before. There were none of our fifty Soviet film stars on the presidium — only our cinema-goers know them, and at an international film review, they want to see foreign film stars, first and foremost. It's understandable. Thanks for sparing us the awkwardness. As always, of course, we have 24 new stars, while the poor French make do with the same old Delon, Belmondo and Girardot... An experimental PROK club was started up in the evenings and all the guests I had the chance to speak to welcomed the idea.

'Are there times when you don't get any parts?'
'If I'm not interested in a part, I don't take it.'
'What do you do then?'
'I play in shows or on the stage or rest at my villa, while my producer looks for a script and a director.'

Abroad, I've learned to field such questions deftly, without even lying... But my very first interview!

'How's life...?'

'Fine, thanks.'

'No, I mean tell us about how and where you live.'

I found such a direct question tactless at the time. We don't ask foreign actors those sort of questions. 'I've got two lovely...'

'Villas?'

'Yes ... they're ... very unusual...'

'How much do you earn?'

'As much as I need to live comfortably.'

'What do you mean by "comfortably"?'

'I mean the way I live.'

'Is there censorship here?'

'We always have a film editor.'

36, KROPOTKINSKAYA CAFÉ

This is all a preliminary to a phone-call I had during the festival.

'Robert Wise, the US film director and President of the Oscar Film Academy, and his wife would like to meet you. They'd like to ask you out for dinner or tea.'

'But they're guests here. We should invite them.'

'Well, go ahead, if ...'

'Where can I take them? Oh, I know. Let's make it tea.'

'Hold on a moment... OK, your place tomorrow at 4 p. m.'

The next day at four o'clock sharp a dark-haired woman with her husband, the famous Robert Wise, turned up at my door. Wise's *West Side Story* was an international success, and was released here too ten years later. Robert Wise is an elegant, elderly gentleman with kind blue eyes. It was his wife's first visit to a Soviet actress's flat, but Robert Wise had been in Moscow before with his film in the early 1970s. We had a wonderful time. We sang, listened to music and the food was, in their words, 'delicious'. Even the interpreter said that time had flown by imperceptibly. My guests knew only three words in Russian, *khorosho* (good), *glasnost* and *talon* (coupon).

As soon as the word *talon* was mentioned — everyone at the festival had been given coupons for food — a shadow flitted across their faces.

'And now we'd like to invite you for dinner tomorrow. Where do you suggest?'

Where indeed? Before, I'd have suggested the Aragvi Restaurant. But, unfortunately, or maybe, fortunately, my husband and I had been to the Aragvi the week before — to liven up our usual plain diet with something spicy. There was a new sign outside — First Class Restaurant — but inside the walls were just the same. The same old naive drawings of planes, wineskins, sheep, beautiful girls and Young Pioneers. The same old bracket lamps shining warmly. Only don't eat anything! The very sight of the waiter turns your stomach. It certainly doesn't make you believe in radical changes — every restaurant with a glorious past has its traditions, but to get stale bread, or underdone suluguni - cheese in the Aragvi... There was no point in complaining. We went out silently onto Gorky Street. What changes?

The next day the interpreter phoned and said that if we had no objections, we could meet at the 36, Kropotkinskaya Café at 8 p. m.

At the 36, Kropotkinskaya Café, a tall, pleasant-looking man met us and led us through into a room decorated in soft browns. A trio was playing quietly. A young girl, without any of the usual attributes of a waitress, even without a notepad, came over immediately. She said that she was delighted to meet an actress she had seen at the cinema, whispered slyly that the kitchen staff would try to produce something extra special, and then brought a salad that she called *Station for Two*, after the film. It was all very original and nice. Later on she addressed the guests in perfect English. It was their turn to be surprised. And we were too. We had never yet been addressed in Russian in any restaurant anywhere in the world. But then, things are just beginning to take off.

What had begun yesterday at tea, now continued today at dinner. The musicians played everything, from the most typically Russian to the most typically American. Robert Wise, for whom music is something natural, commented on the musicians' performance and his wife sang along with them, urging me to follow suit.

'We've got several thousand unemployed actors. It's very hard to make a living, there's so much competition. Actors work as drivers and waiters to earn money to go on dance and drama courses. There's a lot of competition, but we value talent highly. It's good if you get paid here when you're not working — we don't have anything like that.'

We had signed the Visitors' Book and were about to leave, when a young man at the table next to ours stood up, sat down at the piano and played a popular melody from *West Side Story*. He had probably heard Robert Wise's name mentioned. The US director and his wife looked at each other in confusion and smiled. Anyone who works in the creative arts will understand this smile and happiness, all those people who have created something during their life and seen it taken up by everyone. It was the finishing touch, and when, as we said our goodbyes, Robert Wise added: 'We'll never forget this day', I believed him.

ON THE LOOK-OUT FOR TALENT

...Maybe, there's no need to take on 15 people for a drama course? Only two or three of them, at the most, end up acting in films. Maybe, we should only take on three or four, but ones who can do everything, and make sure teachers are with them from morning till night, living their lives with them, sharpening and polishing up their talent? When we watch figure skating, we know exactly who are Chaikovskaya's or Tarasova's pupils. They are an 'individual' product. I mentioned this idea five years ago at the Fourth Congress of USSR Film Makers and haven't been on the platform since.

Today, with *glasnost*, we can say things openly, we can be what we are and say what we think. I've nothing to lose. Everything I've done in my life, I've done myself and at the expense of my own health. When I went into hospital after the film *Applause* and had an opportunity to look back over the last ten years of my insane life, I realised I had neither money nor good health.

Talent provides the state with roubles and foreign currency, yet there is no one person interested enough in it to protect and support it. If talent makes its own way independently and starts to produce profit — all well and good. But if suddenly the situation changes, then talent has to fight tooth and nail, and it's not been trained to do so. Once you stop making profit — goodbye, there are plenty more where you came from. But is there such a thing as superfluous talent? They kill it, then next thing it's 'we're on the look-out for talent'.

A film actor is not a free agent. His master is talent — enterprising, creative, businesslike and daring. It tortures and torments a person, as a role does an actor. This rare talent has led some of us far away from our country and landed others in dock. Now we are beginning to feel the lack of such agile capable people. But it is not possible to be a director, an administrator or an actor's agent for 100 roubles a month. 'Why isn't it possible? I get 100 roubles a month too. Why's he better than me? We're all equal.' No. If you are talented, daring and creative you have no right to be equal to every one else. If it weren't for you, a creative and daring person, we'd be standing still. *Perestroika* hasn't taken shape from nothing, it has come about through our suffering, so that we can move forward. It's come a bit late, but better late than never!

A while ago I was at a press conference in France answering questions. I felt that I had a clear, bright head and a calm and kindly face.

'Do you have censorship?'

'Everything that was prohibited earlier has now been released.'

'Would you like to live better?'

'Of course. Everybody in the USSR wants to.'

Moscow News, 6 September 1987

On the eve of the 70th anniversary of the October Socialist Revolution, the CPSU Central Committee and the USSR Council of Ministers made public a resolution awarding the 1987 USSR State Prize to VLADIMIR VYSOTSKY, *actor of the Theatre in Taganka, author and performer of songs.*

For over 20 years millions have been listening to his songs spellbound. The man who wrote them has at last won official recognition. It has come seven and a half years after his death.

We publish the Russian original and an English translation

*of Vladimir Vysotsky's song 'These I've Not Loved', which he
wrote in 1969.*

Я не люблю фатального исхода,
От жизни никогда пе устаю.
Я не люблю любое время года,
Когда веселых песен не пою.

Я не люблю холодного цинизма,
В восторженность не верю, и еще —
Когда чужой мои читает письма,
Заглядывая мне через плечо.

Я не люблю, когда — наполовину
Или когда прервали разговор.
Я не люблю, когда стреляют в спину,
Я также против выстрелов в упор.

Я ненавижу сплетни в виде версий,
Червей сомненья, почестей иглу,
Или — когда все время против шерсти,
Или — когда железом по стеклу.

Я не люблю уверенности сытой —
Уж лучше пусть откажут тормоза.
Досадно мне, что слово «честь» забыто
И что в чести наветы за глаза.

Когда я вижу сломанные крылья —
Нет жалости во мне, и неспроста:
Я не люблю насилье и бессилье, —
Вот только жаль распятого Христа.

Я не люблю себя, когда я трушу,
Досадно мне, когда невинных бьют.
Я не люблю, когда мне лезут в душу,
Тем более — когда в нее плюют.

Я не люблю манежи и арены:
На них мильон меняют по рублю, —
Пусть впереди большие перемены —
Я это никогда не полюблю!

THESE I'VE NOT LOVED

I would not like my ending to be fatal,
My zest for living life will never wane.
For me all seasons of the year are hateful,
Unless with joyful songs I entertain.

No love I feel for cynicism's coldness,
No trust in folk with over-gushing ways —
Or those who like to read across my shoulder
My private letters with intruding gaze.

For doing things by halves I have no liking
And cut-off conversations charm me not,
I like it not when at one's back they're sniping,
And equally I hate the point-blank shot.

I simply loathe the gossips' speculations,
The crawling doubts, the spurns that honours hedge,
To be rubbed the wrong way is devastating,
Like steel on glass it sets the teeth on edge.

All supine, smug self-satisfaction shames me
I much prefer to go to the extremes.
That 'honour' is a term forgotten pains me,
That talk behind one's back is now esteemed.

And when I witness wings crushed to perdition,
I feel no pity — here's the reason why:
I don't like force or mealy-mouthed submission, —
I save my pity for Christ crucified.

When courage fails I scorn my lack of merit,
At persecuted innocence I smart.
I'm vexed when folk pry into my private spirit
And mock the feelings closest to my heart.

I don't like circus rings, I loathe arenas:
With grand ideas diminished by the droves, —
Whatever be the future changes' meaning
This is a thing I'll never learn to love.

1969
Translated by Jessie Davies

UNSUITABLE THOUGHTS FOR A JUBILEE

By NATALIA KRYMOVA

I'm afraid my remarks may strike a discordant note amid all the activities, publications and reminiscences marking the 50th birthday of the late Vladimir Vysotsky (25 January 1988). But let us imagine for a moment that he is still among us. What kind of birthday celebrations would there be? Of course, there would be a large and happy circle of friends around him. Doubtless, many people who knew about his birthday would have sent greetings. But would he have been nominated for the State Prize by Soviet film makers? Would our publishers be fighting for larger printruns of his books? And how many of these books would have come out over the last seven years? Would there have been the constant flow of requests from newspapers and magazines for 'something not yet published'?

I don't think so. 'I can't say much for the living, but we take good care of the dead.' This is an uncompromising opinion — just like everything Vysotsky said or sang. The meaning of this bitter (and perhaps eternal) truth is valid not only for the time in which he lived.

It has become commonplace to say that he sang and wrote about the things we discuss openly today. This is partly true. First of all, a lot of people still understand his art only superficially. Secondly, is *glasnost* today really a door thrown open to every powerful and socially motivated talent? Vysotsky's talent, voice and inner independence were literally a thorn in the flesh of those who denied freedom of poetic self-expression, who feared for their official position and privileges, etc. This is common knowledge now, too. But listen to what the poet Yevgeny Yevtushenko — not an official — wrote recently: 'In my opinion, Vladimir Vysotsky was neither a great poet, nor a singer of genius, nor a composer. Yet, thanks to his strong and inimitable character, all the various parts of his life came together to form a major poetic figure.' According to Yevtushenko, in a period of 'poetlessness', Vysotsky, thanks to his character, if only partially, 'filled that vacuum with his songs'. Well, everyone is entitled to his opinion, and I don't feel like arguing with a living poet about the stature or nature of a dead one. I'm sorry, however, that Yevtushenko chose in this way to publicise a hastily written play about Vysotsky, which is, to put it mildly, of doubtful literary merit. It proves that even in the age of *glasnost*, criteria may be distorted, Vysotsky's name may be used to disguise hackwork and opportunism, and the editors of the influential journal in which the play was printed will see nothing unnatural in it. In short, Vysotsky might have found today's life easier, but only relatively so.

As for his writer-colleagues' psychology, one can certainly understand them. Every poet needs to be appreciated. If appreciation could be measured and the amount bestowed by people on Vysotsky divided equally among all other poets, then everyone would be satisfied. But there seems to have been some misunderstanding: some writers get their books published, large printruns, collected works and the like, but all the nation's love and gratitude goes to Vysotsky, who was not even a 'great' poet, but just an 'inimitable character'.

Vysotsky's jubilee is being celebrated in the age of *glasnost*. But we should not forget that we all used to live in a different age which can hardly be erased immediately from our memories. Like it or not, human psychology cannot be changed radically overnight. Here, for example, is the verbatim report of a recent talk of mine with an editor. He glanced at my manuscript, entitled 'He Who Did Not Fire' and said: 'No, this'll never get through. There's no point in even discussing it further. You don't know how things work up there.' He pointed to the ceiling. I said: 'Why won't it get through? It's already been published!' I named the journal. He replied: 'Has it really? Well, that changes things completely...'

What is this? Just the same old official, editorial psychology, perhaps no longer openly censorial, but still not in the slightest independent, because independence is unprofitable and inconvenient.

Vysotsky's poetry showed us an unpredictable and indomitable energy of mind, soul, will and voice. Later, when that living phenomenon became a 'literary legacy', our attitude towards the poet acquired a new quality. Attempts were made to hush up his influence, while others opposed this. As a result of general changes, Vysotsky was granted 'official recognition'. It was, in fact, historical recognition, the recognition of Vysotsky being of historic significance. At the same time, of course, there appeared the danger of commercialisation, of empty words, clichés, a museum atmosphere, 'prestigious' memorial gatherings — in short, everything that was so emphatically against Vysotsky's character.

A more serious change in our attitude to his art has to do with the deep and significant relationship between the past and the present. Vysotsky did not live to see the changes taking place in our society, but they have become a watershed in the posthumous fate of his art and the stimulus for a fresh look at what he did.

The term 'the years of stagnation' is often used too lightly, as if implying that everything bad — stagnation, lawlessness and silence — is in the past, and justice now reigns supreme. I don't know about anyone else, but I personally feel uneasy about such verbal recklessness. A difficult process involving millions of human lives and destinies is reduced to a simplistic catch-phrase. If we look more closely at yesterday's and today's realities, all apparent simplicity vanishes, and life becomes dramatic and paradoxical. Looking at Vysotsky from a historical perspective, it is paradoxical that for over 20 years Vysotsky spoke and sang at the top of his voice, breaking the silence, breaking barriers, attacking apathy. And this was during the so-called 'years of stagnation', silence and inhibitions. This art was truly democratic, both in form and content, and never sought to fit anyone else's conception of what it should be. It simply was. Vysotsky professed nothing less than democracy and *glasnost*, not knowing these were later to become state policy. What is remarkable is that the general public responded so strongly to this poet, well before the critics, or today's intellectuals or politicians.

What conclusion can we draw from this story? To my mind, it is simply this: One may judge Vysotsky's poetry as one pleases, one may find fault or merit in it, but one will never find falsehood there. He never lied one iota. When truth is out of favour, the instinct of self-preservation prompts humans (and poets) to keep silent or reconcile themselves to evil. In Vysotsky's songs, the moral reference points were so clearly marked as to deprive him of poetic 'complexity' or 'mysteriousness' which are traditionally characteristic features of the poetic élite.

'How few are we, the elect...' Pushkin's Mozart says to Salieri. Vysotsky was one of these few elect, a position guaranteed by his absolute truthfulness.

It would be wrong to think that in the so-called 'silent' years people did not talk to each other at home or on the street. Those who worked by the sweat of their brow in order to live, feed their families and raise their children, were not irrevocably silenced. They retained their sound judgement and always found ways to express it and Vysotsky's sensitive ear was attuned to these popular sentiments. He had an ear for how they read between the lines of official reports, freed their own minds and speech of all bombast and never lost hope of living just lives where high words and deeds went hand in hand. In his art Vysotsky, though he was an actor, always relied on what 'is', rather than what 'seems' — I mean the latent, the not immediately apparent, self-sufficient life of the masses.

In this way Vysotsky introduced a whole host of characters into literature and song that had never been given a hearing before. Hence his fantastically rich vocabulary, his mastery of colloquial Russian. That may have been uncouth, but at least was untouched by greater evils. Hence his fearlessness in exposing the tragedy of past history and present-day life. It was his duty as a poet to walk side by side with the people and record all their experiences. Hence his particular brand of humour, provoking thought rather than hollow laughter. It is a very popular, Russian kind of humour, used to protect the humanity in human beings. Hence, finally, his musicality and predilection for song as a form traditionally used in Russia to express everything from suffering to joy, from laughter to tears. In this sense, Vysotsky simply revived a tradition dating back time immemorial.

Today, some of the things of which he spoke have become a thing of the past. Vysotsky has been awarded posthumously the USSR State Prize. His birthday celebration is to be held in one of the capital's largest concert halls. It will be a charity concert in memory of someone who never tired of doing good for others. Some people will be upset at not getting tickets, but for selfish reasons — it always looks good to be seen with the famous.

What if a familiar figure in a sweater with a guitar slung across his shoulder suddenly appeared in the middle of this smart crowd, walked quietly over to the microphone and began to sing? He would sing about all of us, about the years and events that have gone by without him. He would help us understand how various people think about *perestroika* and all our current worries and concerns. We would learn how drivers, writers, ministers and soldiers think about it all; who is 'for', who is 'against' and why; who's still clinging to his office chair and doesn't give a damn about the rest. It would suddenly become clear that demagogy and hypocrisy are still alive and well, but that, hopefully, common sense, honesty and order will someday prevail.

It was good that Vysotsky lived amongst us. It is something we can be proud of. But, oh, how we miss him today.

Moscow News, 17 January 1988

The USSR Central TV Studios recently showed the film Risk *directed by Dmitry Barshchevsky with script by Natalia Violina. The 90-minute film was watched by some 200 million people according to preliminary estimates.*

The film analyses the critical moments in history — the period of the Cold War, the Cuban crisis of 1962 and others — when the alternative of war or peace faced humanity particularly acutely. The film takes a fresh look at the development of missiles and the way this altered political relations. The film is about our planet, about all of us, who are responsible for the preservation of peace on earth.

We asked Academician ANDREI SAKHAROV, for whom this documentary film is largely biographical, to share his impressions of it with us.

ANDREI SAKHAROV: 'IT IS ABSOLUTELY IMPERATIVE TO SPEAK THE TRUTH'

Impressions of the film *Risk*

I take the film's main idea to be that speaking the truth is a risk, but absolutely imperative.

The film lifts the veil of secrecy covering many tragic episodes in our history. Of course, it's not the whole truth yet, the film is reticent about some things and, in my opinion, too traditional and unobjective in its assessment of certain historical events. Nonetheless I am grateful to the film makers for having said a lot of things and taking a risk for the sake of a difficult truth.

Over the last few days I've already heard that many viewers were shaken by the story of Sergei Korolyov's arrest and imprisonment, which is told in the film with a blacked-out screen. What's clear is that this was not just the personal fate of one outstanding man, but the fate of many other people too and one of the reasons why our country found itself in such a tragic situation in 1941. Of course, there were other very important reasons too, but they do not fall within the subject matter of the film. The film shows us Stalin not as a demigod, but as a man with many weaknesses and shortcomings. The whole terrible truth about Stalin and his era has not yet been told, but this was not the task of this film. At the same time we see Korolyov's entry in his diary on the day of Stalin's funeral. The entry is full of deep grief and confusion. I remember that at the time I expressed almost the same feelings in a letter to my wife. Afterwards I was ashamed of this. If I try to analyse myself, I think that Stalin's name was above all associated with everything we held to be most important.

That part of the film devoted to Julius and Ethel Rosenberg is very disturbing. They were executed in the USA on charges of passing secrets about the A-bomb to the USSR. However, if we're going to speak about this, then we shouldn't keep quiet about the fact that the Rosenbergs' execution was US counterintelligence's revenge for the Klaus Fuchs affair. Both during and after the war he had been passing on important atomic secrets to the USSR on ideological grounds. He was exposed only after he left the

USA. If we do not mention this then the truth is incomplete.

I think it's a good thing to see a return to an objective assessment of Nikita Khrushchev's role. The attitude to him even today amongst broad sections of the population is quite unfair, in my opinion. Khrushchev was a world figure. The film shows him speaking at a UN session, where he called for universal disarmament, for peace without weapons — something we're aspiring to today. One of the steps he took was to considerably reduce the army and armaments in the USSR.

There are some striking frames in the film. One of these is the face of a boy, the son of one of the missile specialists captured and shot by the SS before the arrival of the Americans. It symbolises, as it were, the horror and senselessness of war and fascism.

Another frame shows us Hiroshima, destroyed by the American bombing. A group of Soviet military advisers have come over. Their faces are concerned, they are still motivated by the psychology of war. But this is already the beginning of a new epoch and of new tragic problems facing all humanity.

The Caribbean crisis is one of the film's central episodes. However, it does not mention the fact that it all started with the installation of our missiles in Cuba. These were exceptionally dramatic events. In the form of documentary, the film shows us the world at that time on the brink of thermonuclear catastrophe. It is terrifying to watch. Kennedy's and Khrushchev's actions show them to have been outstanding statesmen. That time the catastrophe was avoided. An agreement was reached on the direct 'hot line' and through diplomatic channels on the withdrawal of our missiles from Cuba, on US guarantees not to invade Cuba and to remove their missiles from Turkey and Italy. But even if we have the most outstanding statesmen in power, this cannot be a reliable guarantee of peace if there is no *glasnost*, no openness of society, no democracy. This is the lesson of the Caribbean crisis and of the film.

The film gives us an acute sense of our personal responsibility for peace and this is more important than whether we take the film to be optimistic or pessimistic. The most terrible thing is half-truth or silence, which is the same as lying.

I was very impressed by the opening and concluding frames of the film where Mikhail Gorbachev gives his first comments on the results of the Reykjavik meeting. We all saw the live transmission at the time from the Icelandic capital, but a cinema screen brings out the emotional impact. We understand it not only on a factual, but on a psychological level too. We understand the enormous weight of responsibility and realisation of the historic role that lies on Gorbachev's shoulders and those of his comrades-in-arms. But this is our responsibility too.

Moscow News, 8 November 1987

Joint International Ventures

Options still available

When discussing the USSR's foreign trade one cannot simply blame the economic stagnation of the last decades. An in-depth analysis of our difficulties is called for. How to surmount them? This question has been addressed to the USSR Academy of Sciences' Institute of Economics of the World Socialist System.

VLADIMIR SHASTITKO, *Assistant Director of the Institute, D. Sc. (Econ.),* VYACHESLAV DASHICHEV, *Department Head, D. Sc. (Hist.), and* VALERY KARA-VAYEV, *Senior Research Fellow, D. Sc. (Econ.), are interviewed by* A. CHEREPANOV.

WHAT IS SLOWING US DOWN?

International Economic Ties:
Reality and Perspectives

We have gathered in order to discuss a very important problem that affects the restructuring of our economic system and the way it works. Let's start by discussing its fundamental characteristics.

V. Dashichev. Before me is the *Trade and Development Report* published by the UN in 1987. Let's take a look at the graph which shows the USSR's sales figures of high technology to developed capitalist countries. In 1985 it represented only 0.23 per cent of our sales to the West, compared to 13.2 per cent of developing countries' trade with the West.

V. Shastitko. These and many other figures clearly show

the specifics of our international trade. It hasn't changed in years. This trend was set before the war when only four export items comprised 70 per cent of our trade turnover — timber, wheat, oil and coal. It is essentially the same now, although it's true, we've taken wheat off the list and added several different types of raw materials. But just as before they form the basis of our export economy, comprising about 60 per cent of our total exports. Raw energy makes up over 80 per cent of our exports to developed capitalist states. We've turned into a one export nation. This is really a paradoxical situation! On the international market our country with its advanced science and powerful industries is the bargain basement for raw materials for developed countries.

And so our 'one export economy' began to slow us down...
V. S. What do you mean 'began'? It was always so. It is just that now its consequences affect the economy even greater.
V. D. For the majority of raw materials, we have already lost the opportunity of expanding our raw material exports. The increase in oil output as compared to the last five year plan is miserly. We're standing still in our output of coal. It's the same thing with iron and manganese ores. Our timber industry is developing erratically — first a small increase, then a drop in production.
V. S. Perhaps the only area where there is an increase is gas. However, alongside our inability to effect a quantitative growth in these export items, their price on the international market has fallen off sharply in the last few years. Even the small increase in oil prices as a result of the problems in the Middle East and the Persian Gulf will not cover our losses in hard currency.

These losses necessitate limiting or even discontinuing some Soviet foreign trade operations, affecting the import not only of consumer goods, but also of machinery and various equipment, and could eventually have a negative impact on the modernisation of the whole machine-building complex.
V. Karavayev. We have lost about six billion roubles in the last 18 months as a result of the drop in export prices for raw materials. If our former annual earnings for exports to the West were around 20 billion roubles, then now they have fallen to 13 billion.

Soviet Scene 1988

This is just the end result. What caused this to happen?
V.S. The underlying cause of this situation is the generally unsatisfactory condition of the economy, governed for too many years by incorrect conceptions about the international trade and its place in the national economy. That is, export used to be considered only a means to eliminate the imbalances that constantly arose in the internal market.
V.K. Everyone has an interest in imports. From the majority of economic managers all you ever hear is 'give, give, give'. Our imports are scattered across thousands of enterprises instead of being concentrated in those areas that determine scientific and technological progress. We have bought billions of dollars worth of equipment abroad, but the old economic mechanism has not encouraged the industries and enterprises to use them efficiently. Much needed new technology has been ruined simply because it was left to rot outdoors. The scope of these losses is even greater if one also considers the long-term losses due to the fact that the expensive new equipment stood idle and was becoming outdated. And exports? These have been and remain a burden for most of our enterprises because it is possible to sell only products of the highest quality on the world market. Our consumers are quite a different matter. They'll buy anything because they can't find it anywhere else. It's absurd. There are some managers in the economy who consider export plans ... a punishment, because of all the effort involved.
V.D. This has all led to our not being able to get a strong foothold on the international market in spite of our efforts, particularly as regards production machinery. Here are a few characteristic examples.

The West German company *Uni Ost* was selling our tractors for us but we delivered them in such a condition that the firm had to build their own repair workshops to finish the job off properly. This resulted in their losing up to 200 man-hours per tractor. Once they had evened out their sales, the contract was cancelled, although our exports to them were due to be increased by 150 per cent.

Likewise, a small West German company, *Slavia Tours*, organised steamship tours for West Germans to the Soviet Union. From 1979 to 1984 profit of 18 million deutsche mark was made from our cooperation with this company. Then at some point we broke the contract simply through ignorance of a number of West German laws and the company bore the losses. We refused to make reparations and broke off relations with it. *Slavia Tours* went bust. How can we consider ourselves good business partners if we conduct business in such a fashion?

V. S. One of the main reasons that is slowing down our export is the quality of our goods. Only 40 per cent of our total production of machinery is up to international standards.

V. D. Allow me to point out one important fact. We spend the majority of our income in hard currency from exports on purchasing food products abroad. So agriculture too is holding back our foreign trade. Purchases of grain alone in the West amount to between 30-40 million tons a year, and this in spite of the fact that about 700 billion roubles have been invested in agriculture over the last 20 years.

This situation is not new and has existed for a long time.
V. S. Our large income from the export of raw materials in the seventies created the illusion of 'super-efficiency' in our international trade. Colossal figures lulled us into a false sense of security. We thought we would always be able to export oil. However it did not turn out that way—the volume of our foreign trade turnover is already falling off. In my opinion this clearly demonstrates the effect of the period of stagnation. We did not look ahead, but allowed our short-term successes to blind us to what was happening on the foreign market. For example, the drop in price for raw materials caught us completely by surprise.

In principle the source of these problems lies in the prewar years, from which we've inherited our frequent relapses into isolation. In 1939 our international trade turnover was only 270 million roubles, conditioned by the political situation at that time, when hostility forced us out of the foreign market. This economic isolation cost our economy dear.

V. D. Look at the economic structure of the United States today. It is similar to ours; there is a similar high degree of self-sufficiency, but foreign trade in the USA has always been more important than here. Only about 8 per cent of the Soviet Union's gross national income is from foreign trade as compared to approximately 15 in the USA.

As you can see, we are far from receiving the benefits

from the international division of labour. Attempts to isolate ourselves from the world were justified by notions of economic invulnerability. But there are a whole number of branches of industry where there is no need to fear dependence. Is the import of refrigerators and vacuum cleaners really so dangerous?

V. S. If you talk to any of our managers not involved in foreign trade they'll tell you that dependence on foreign trade is bad.

That is to say that we have inculcated into them for years the idea of economic isolation?

V. S. Yes, they are not inclined to establish foreign ties and therefore do not understand that the net result of utilising the international division of labour is an increase in production efficiency. We could produce something inexpensively here, sell it at a high price abroad and in return buy products that are not profitable to produce at home. Ricardo formulated the law of relative costs, which no one has abolished, since it is based on objective reality. It doesn't make sense for us not to observe it.

V. D. The level of economic and technical development of any country, and especially any world industrial power, has depended on, and continues to depend on, its involvement in the international division of labour. Whether this is fair or not is another question. Not participating in the international division of labour means condemning ourselves to economic and technical backwardness. The growth of world interdependence is a particularly topical subject for discussion today.

But the Council for Mutual Economic Assistance has existed for almost forty years, and functions as an international division of labour within the framework of the Warsaw Treaty countries.

V. D. We have achieved a lot during these years; particularly striking has been our ability to coordinate the economic plans of the various member-countries and realise a number of large economic projects together. This is something we can be proud of. However, our forms and methods of interaction within the CMEA framework now need to be fundamentally updated, since they no longer correspond to our new demands.

V. S. CMEA is now confronted with serious problems.

Everything that we discussed above is more or less characteristic for all of the participants in CMEA. We need to change over from institutional to economic methods of management. Up until now, integration within CMEA has existed at the top, or on a 'macro-level'. Plans would be agreed at that level and instructions passed down. Enterprises were merely the instruments through which these were fulfilled — there was no communication from bottom to top.

V. D. What are the results of such administrative integration? Cooperative production within CMEA at present is only a small part of its total trade turnover. That includes the exchange of machinery. This is in spite of the fact that on the world market there is an increasing tendency towards joint ventures and more specialised production. In the EEC such joint ventures represent appoximately 40 per cent of production. This is achieved first and foremost by direct contact between enterprises leading to an increase in trade turnover, the perfection of international economic structures, and, finally, to increased efficiency in home production. The type of integrated cooperation we have in CMEA is not capable of directly affecting the economy of the various socialist member-countries on a micro-economic level, i.e. the labour force involved directly in production, agriculture, science and service industries.

V. S. The urgent need for fundamental changes is obvious. A summit conference in 1984 and a meeting in Moscow in 1986 discussed the situation within CMEA. It was recognised that our Achilles' heel was our scientific and technological backwardness. We cannot yet close the gap between ourselves and the West in a number of areas, and in some, such as electronics and the synthesis of new materials, this gap is widening.

As you know, in 1985 the Comprehensive Programme of Scientific and Technological Progress was adopted. The programme was well thought through, but it came up against our main problem of imperfections in our economic system both on a national level as well as on the level of CMEA.

What makes the programme unworkable and how can we change the situation?

V. S. At the meeting in November 1986 in Moscow particular attention was paid to the perfection of CMEA's economic system. At the 43rd session of CMEA in October 1987 this became a central issue. Our new system for the country's economic management will doubtless have an impact on our cooperation with CMEA too. It is already beginning to do so, as we are creating the legal, organisational and economic prerequisites for enterprises to take part in foreign trade and be on an equal footing in this with various central organs and ministries.

V. K. We are creating the prerequisites for changing over from a macro- to a micro-level of cooperative activity, to direct cooperation between primary links in the economic chain, which will be vitally interested in pursuing this.

V. S. This idea is the basis of the reforms within CMEA. How the reforms will turn out is difficult to say at the moment, because not every country has the same approach. Each has its own specific interests, though we are all agreed on the necessity of direct contacts, joint enterprises, cooperation and specialisation. In short, on the necessity of real economic integration amongst the socialist countries. This is not something that can be achieved in one day, there is a lot of work ahead of us that cannot be completed simply by issuing orders.

Let's take a brief look at how our foreign economic relations are to be improved in the future.

V. S. In August 1986 a number of corresponding resolutions were adopted concerning the fundamental restructuring of our foreign trade. Over the year since then 21 ministries and 70 enterprises have been given the right to trade directly on the foreign market. However, like any other reform, it has encountered its fair share of difficulties. Cost accounting is slowly being realised, not always along original lines, and economic control levers on enterprises' and associations' foreign trade are being introduced. We haven't got a unified exchange rate. We've had to renounce the numerous accepted currency coefficients due to their economic incompatibility. We haven't got a customs tariff. There are many things we haven't got and which we must create urgently.

Ministries which have been given foreign trade departments are keeping up successfully with import plans, which cannot be said for exports. They haven't the right people, having recruited their own inexperienced staff instead of taking on competent ones from the Ministry of Foreign Trade.

But what is most important is the lack of initiative and inertia at all levels. It is essential that every one of our economic managers understands the importance of foreign economic relations. This is *perestroika's* main problem in this area.

It is also necessary to regulate the system of management at the centre. The State Foreign Economic Commission has still not got a clear idea of its role, while the Ministry of Foreign Trade no longer has one. Yet how long this period of transition will take depends to a large degree on these departments. We can not allow it to drag on ... time waits for no one.

Izvestia, 9 October 1987

The causes for the slow development of the Soviet Union's foreign economic relations are manifold and have accumulated over several decades. Perestroika and new approaches are urgently called for here, but it would be a lie to say that only objective circumstances are at fault. Bureaucracy, excessive self-assuredness and often the irresponsibility of specific people on whom the development of international economic contacts depends, play an extremely negative role in this respect. As evidence, let us take a look at a letter from Manuel Arse published in Izvestia *on 30 March, 1988 in the column 'Letters not for Publication'.*

'I am the General Director of the Eastern Department of the Spanish company, Inargos, which produces biological fertilizers and medical preparations from pure synthesised amino acids. These products not only improve the yields and quality of agricultural produce and livestock but are also biodegradable. This is a new and very alluring field and our technology is the subject of interest in many countries.

'We have conducted business with the Soviet Union for more than two years already and until recently had had every reason to be satisfied with our business partners. Izvestia *wrote about our joint venture in its 197th edition in 1987 and helped us in many ways, which is why I am writing to you now when we have reached a deadlock in our affairs.*

'When we began to sell our product to the Soviet Union we

found out that there was no specific state organ set up to handle this type of import. When concrete decisions had to be made it was not clear to whom we should refer and a great deal of time was lost going from one organisation to another in search of a business partner. At last with the help of the State Committee for Science and Technology, we made contact with Agricultural Academy, the Institute of Tea, Tea Production and Sub-Tropical Cultures, the Institute of Plant Biochemistry in Tbilisi, the Institute of Medical and Biological Problems attached to the USSR Ministry of Health, a number of other medical institutes, and finally with the Pharmacology Committee which was very interested in our offer. In Estonia we signed a document to set up a joint enterprise for the production of bio-fertilizers.

'*In Uzbekistan there was also great interest in our product and it was decided to test them to increase cotton harvests. However, in order to conduct the experiment they needed permission. We had come full circle. Just as two years ago, the necessary documentation was in the hands of Gosagroprom which sent it to the State Commission on Chemical Pesticides and Weedkillers. But our biological fertilizers and livestock biostimulators are not chemical-based. But worst was yet to come... In February this year we had a meeting with A. F. Kosenko, Chairman of this Commission, together with members of the State Committee for Science and Technology, and representatives from Uzbekistan.*

'*Our conversation with Kosenko was a parody of a business meeting. First of all he announced arrogantly that he was a very busy person and had no time to spare. That he had been informed of the details in his car and considered it pointless to try to make profit out of it and to continue discussions. After this I lost all interest in the conversation, and feeling insulted, told him I would refer the matter to his superiors. To this he replied that I could refer it wherever I liked, and adding that our 'pesticides' needed registering, left the room.*

'*I have to say that I'm following the progress of* perestroika *in your country with great admiration and interest, and conduct business with you not only because I want to make money, but also because I love your country. Business is not my only tie with you. I am well acquainted with the Soviet people and wish them every success in the difficult process of reconstruction. But how can I negotiate with a business part-*

*ner who doesn't know the difference between pesticides and
biological fertilizers?*

*'But even if our product and technology do give good re-
sults after experiments in your country, to introduce them we
will have to have this same Kosenko's permission, which
means that all our efforts turn out to have been in vain. I ask
you, is this the way to conduct business? I'm writing to you in
the hope that you can help me. Perhaps Kosenko is nonetheless answerable to someone?'*

*Unfortunately, foreign businessmen all too often come into
contact with people like Kosenko whose incompetence and arrogance can only harm business relations. This is why our
Western partners are so notoriously cautious about entering
into joint ventures with the USSR. Some are ready to do so
today; some are not sure, while others play a waiting game. In
this respect, we should like to draw our readers' attention to
the opinions of three representatives of West German firms.*

IS IT DIFFICULT TO DO BUSINESS
WITH THE RUSSIANS?

The Opinions of West German Industrialists
on Joint Enterprises and Other Topics

Interview by S. GUK and B. LYSENKO

Salamander, Inc.—'We Are Ready.'

Our first speaker is Franz Josef Dazert, president of the
internationally known company, Salamander, Inc., who is
setting up a joint enterprise in Leningrad for the production
of fashion shoes. He was recently in Moscow to sign a second contract to set up a similar factory in Vitebsk.

'We expect the multi-stage production cycle to be ready
in 3 years, turning out four to five million pairs of shoes
a year. The necessary equipment, both Western and Soviet,
has been decided on jointly.

'What we produce will be chiefly for sale within the Soviet Union. However, it will be necessary to examine the
balance of currency against profits and expenditure and it

will be expedient therefore to buy certain items and chemicals, for example, in the West. We will have two balances — one in roubles, the other in hard currency.'

We asked Mr Dazert who would buy our shoes if the Western market was already saturated, to which he replied that they would not be using our foreign trade organisations but selling them themselves through their own trade network. This was not the main problem.

'The major criterion will be that of quality. The final result will depend directly on this. If the quality is high, we can be assured of our profits. Your country is in the process of *perestroika* and any new organisation must establish itself firmly within the framework of your system. Of course there are problems, difficulties and friction. We ought to have been able to purchase the necessary equipment more quickly, but with your system of shared responsibilities the decision-making process is unduly prolonged. However, I don't wish to overdramatise the situation. Let me repeat — quality is the decisive factor.'

Mr Dazert explained that quality is not controlled so much as created. Every different type of leather has its own peculiarities, and attention must be paid to this from the very beginning, when the hide is being removed. Quality control begins here. There should be spot checks at every stage (cutting, sewing, gluing) in the production process. Only then can we talk about final quality control of the finished product. Defects need to be discovered at the earliest possible stage so as not to jeopardize the whole process.

'Therefore,' he continued, 'we attach great importance to this spot checking. It's the only way to assure success both with your customers and our own. Claims on defective goods must be kept to a minimum. We intend sending over our specialists and advisors to your enterprises to teach your staff not only to make quick decisions, but also to be able to introduce exact and efficient correction into production. People like that don't grow on trees — they have to be trained.'

Daimler-Benz — 'The Beginning Is Making Deals'

Professor Werner Niefer (PhD) is the vice-president of the firm Daimler-Benz which has recently merged with two

other commercial giants Dornier and Motoren- und Turbi-
nenunion (MTU). He is also chairman of the Foreign Trade
Assistance Foundation in Baden-Vurtemberg and the control department of MTU. In addition to these activities, he
is head of Fraunhofer, a conglomerate of various institutes
involved in research technology. Professor Niefer often tra-
vels to Moscow and was last here to conduct negotiations
with the USSR Ministry of the Automobile Industry. He
declined to discuss the details of these negotiations but indicated that possible collaboration lay in the field of light vehicles, technology, supply of materials, welding and car-
body paint work.

He considers the current situation to be excellent for joint
ventures, although Daimler-Benz has not yet made
a breakthrough. What is the reason for this? 'Well, both
sides have their reasons,' he says cautiously. 'We need to
weigh up everything carefully, meet and discuss things
again.'

Is it difficult to do business with Russians?

'Let's say it's not easy. In Moscow I've noticed that
everyone's only interested in joint ventures, they don't want
to hear about anything else, but there are other forms of
collaboration. During negotiations our Soviet partners always exclusively want to sign deals on joint enterprises.
I understand the fact you have foreign trade balance deficit
and want to remedy the situation through joint enterprises,
but this may mean missing out on other profitable business
deals.'

W. Niefer recalls how fifteen years ago he was conducting negotiations with the Chinese. They asked him to build
a factory that would produce 100,000 trucks a year, they
would deliver these back to him so that he could sell them
and cover his expenses. Unfortunately, this same type of
reasoning is beginning to appear here.

'You must abandon the illusion that someone is going to
build a factory for you and then sell the finished product on
your behalf when we can produce it ourselves. What we
need is agreements on supply of goods. We have immense
'know-how' market in Baden-Vurtemberg. We can help get
rid of the weak spots in your production and technology,
but you must be ready to put cash down immediately before
we start talking about joint ventures. Here is a good exam-

ple of what I am referring to: a colleague visited one of your factories, where they were missing one piece of machinery for the complete production cycle. This item costs 4,000 DM. It would take you a long time to make it yourself. That's the sort of case where you have to put your hand in your pocket without questions. Gorbachev is correct, you need to modernise, but joint enterprises are not the only answer. You must be able to clearly define what your most urgent needs are and find suppliers to fill the gap. After that, joint enterprises can be the next step.'

Dr Niefer once again interrupted the conversation to say that Soviet foreign trade organisations were letting slip chances of earning foreign currency through their own sluggishness. During one of his visits to Moscow he had agreed to sell Soviet folk handicraft in the FRG. His wife had come to Moscow three times, the affair had dragged on for 5 years and nothing came of it eventually. She said, 'I don't understand it. Everywhere I went they said everything was fine, but when I asked about the selection and terms — no answer.' She prepared to put down cash but everywhere the reply was the same — not now, come back in three years' time.

'We are ready to collaborate but not if it means Mercedes Benz building a factory for you and then having to sell your products as well. For example, you sell lorries in Europe. If you were then to buy Mercedes engines from us, these could then be serviced at our stations. Those are the kind of business deals we're prepared to offer in the first instance.'

The 'Stihl'—Yes, But Not Straightaway

Hans-Peter Stihl is the president of a company producing power saws, with branches in the United States, Australia and Switzerland. He will take on this position after Otto Wolff von Amerongen retire as president of the Association of Chambers of Industry and Commerce of the FRG.

'We got the impression after discussions in Moscow that the Soviet leadership is interested in close collaboration with the FRG and I must add that this interest is mutual.'

Is it difficult to do business with Russians? It takes

a great deal of time for mutual trust to be won, but on the other hand, once Soviet organisations do trust you, then they are willing to enter into a very open cooperative relationship. We asked Mr Stihl how he would do business in our place.

'I am not familiar enough with Soviet industry to be able to give you advise, but I believe the question of economic calculations and defining the cost of the final product is very important. You're still not very advanced in this respect, in my opinion. In your place, I'd start by purchasing components for the production of equipment you urgently require. You can buy the components, assemble them yourselves and then go over to your own production of these, until you start producing all the equipment on your own. This refers to all branches of industry. We do the same whenever we begin to collaborate with another firm. There is no other way. This is the general tendency in industrial development.

'The problem is that when Soviet companies set up joint enterprises they want to start exporting their products immediately on markets that we already control. We don't particularly like setting up an enterprise in the USSR that's going to compete with us. The solution is to agree beforehand on where the products will be exported.'

*   *   *

These are the opinions of three 'captains of West German industry'. Of course we are not asking anyone to take their views at face value since they have their own business interests at heart and not ours, but the point of view of the West German business world deserves businesslike discussion.

Izvestia, 20 February 1988

A one-of-a-kind aluminium fluoride plant recently completed in Achinsk, Eastern Siberia, was built with the help of French technicians. An identical plant with half the capacity was built in France by Aluminium Pechiney.

CONFLICTS ALSO
BOOST COOPERATION

At the Soviet-French Construction Project in Achinsk
By BORIS IVANOV

The Achinsk plant has already reached the planned output. Nowever, the quality still falls short of the terms of the contract: first grade has not been given to the whole of output, as the French side guaranteed, but to just one-third of it.

'This often compels us,' says *Anatoly Zaruba*, the plant's chief engineer, 'to make claims on our colleagues. For instance, the firm guaranteed the faultless operation of the ventilating turbines of reactive gases for two years. But we have already replaced them on two occasions. We regret to say that four out of five graphite pumps for hydrofluoric acid wear out. French contract supervisors still cannot say why this is happening. Well-founded claims can be levelled at us as well. They primarily concern two aspects: Soviet personnel at the plant have not yet attained the necessary skills, and stable supplies of essential raw materials have not been properly organised. I think that the conflict situation that has arisen is, though undesirable, fully understandable because what is in question is the implementation of a joint large-scale and technologically original project. It is gratifying that the rather sharp production discussions have not spoiled our good relations with French colleagues.'

This appraisal is shared by *Raymond Minaux*, the chief engineer of the Achinsk project, who arrived in September 1987 at the head of a group of experts from Aluminium Pechiney.

'I am happy to be able to say only good words. Before our arrival we were concerned about the plant's performance. The information we received by telex in France was terse, of course. M Robin (director of the French mission) informed us only of the difficulties that cropped up, but did not indicate what worked well. We saw this only on coming to Achinsk. Of course, there were difficulties that are commonplace in starting up and adjustment, and I myself, my

colleague-experts, the French contract supervisors and Soviet specialists took steps to quickly solve the problems.

'On the other hand, we stated that our contract supervisors were happy both at the plant and outside it. We knew
this from reports, but now we saw it with our own eyes. We
saw well-appointed flats, rooms and furniture. We saw the
shop where the French can buy everything they need. This
is particularly important in winter. After all, my compat-
riots are not used to frosts. Two paces away from the apartment house there is a restaurant where they serve delicious
meals. We saw with our own eyes that the Soviet side had
done a lot to make the French working in Achinsk feel at
home.

'Mention should be made of two other things. About the
beauty of the local natural environment and about the good
relations between the specialists of France and the USSR.

'We are close to completing the contract. Guaranteed
technical indicators will be received very soon. Our contract
supervisors will return home. They have told me that they
will be sorry to leave Achinsk. They have spent a very interesting period of their life here. Some of them didn't know
anything about the Soviet Union before, but now they are
positive about the living conditions here. Even if sharp differences do occur from time to time, their sole purpose is to
optimise the work of the plant. One would feel bored without difficulties. We are very happy both professionally and
from the personal point of view.

'I am sure that industrial cooperation between our countries will expand. Some time in the future the construction
of an aluminium plant is possible.'

Moscow News, 18 October 1987

The Soviet booster rocket Vostok *lifted an Indian-made
IRS-1A satellite into orbit, completing the first commercially-
based launch in the Soviet Union of a foreign artificial Earth
satellite.*

SATELLITE ORBITED UNDER CONTRACT

By SERGEI LESKOV

The record of Soviet-Indian cooperation in space research goes back many years. Among its landmarks are the flight of the mixed crew comprising Yuri Malyshev, Gennady Strekalov and Rakesh Sharma, and the three successful launchings from Kapustin Yar cosmodrome in the USSR between 1975 and 1981 of the Aryabhata, Bhaskara-1 and Bhaskara-2 satellites, which carried out a vast programme of astrophysical and ecological observations. In the opinion of Professor Rao, director of the Indian Space Research Organisation, the assessment of natural resources from space is particularly important to his country. For instance, the practical use of making a snow map of the Himalayas can be illustrated by the fact that flooding causes the country 200-million-dollars' damage a year. Consequently, there is an acute need for environmental monitoring from space.

The new satellite, which is of exclusively Indian manufacture, is intended for the study of the Earth's natural resources. The IRS-1A is equipped with the latest optical scanning system, and its three still cameras, sensitive to both visible and near-IR light, can survey up to 150 km at a time.

Professor Rao says that the satellite, which is to remain in orbit for three years, will photograph the territories of a number of developing Asian and African countries. Experts from 18 countries have been trained to decipher information coming from space. Professor Rao stressed that problems of vital importance to the entire region include finding subterranean water sources, holding back the desert, and preserving tropical forests.

The Soviet side will see the satellite through the initial 90 days from the Medvezhyi Ozyora tracking station near Moscow. After post-launching problems, if any, have been dealt with, control will be taken over by the Indian mission control centre in Bangalore, the scientific capital of India. Incoming data will be processed by the centre in Hyderabad. The satellite works to a tight schedule. The camera lenses focussed on the Earth within 24 hours of liftoff, in the satellite's eleventh loop, after the solar-cell panels had opened out and the satellite had steadied itself. The project is being carried out under a contract signed by the Soviet foreign trade organisation Licenzintorg and the Indian Space Research Organisation. The USSR Glavkosmos central administration of space technology, development and use for national economy and science offers any country the chance to have its satellites launched from Soviet cosmodromes. The Soviet launch vehicle *Vostok* has an excellent performance record; 89 of the 90 launches to-date have been successful.

New Times, 25 March 1988

Pepsico Incorporated of the United States and Glavobshchepit of the Moscow Soviet have agreed to bring Pizza Hut to Moscow.

GOOD FOOD SERVED FAST

By V. TOLSTOV

Carl Neegle, the head of Pepsico's East European sales, and Andrew Rafalat, the head of Pizza Hut's technical service talked to me about their plans.

'We are intending to start small,' said Neegle. 'We're opening two restaurants. One will accept foreign currency, and the other, roubles. Before expanding we have to see if the American system of public catering suits the Soviet consumer.'

'Are you worried the venture could fail?'

'We are hoping for success, but any commercial enterprise involves some risk. This is normal. A businessman must evaluate the risk and cope with risk situations. I have the impression that Soviet business people do not quite have this ability, and fear taking the responsibility for making a risky decision, even when the chances of success are not bad.

'Pepsico is not aiming for instant profit. We do not want to make money, take it and run. We have big plans; they are connected with long-term and mutually beneficial cooperation. We have developed good cooperative efforts with Gosagroprom. Our specialists have jointly developed drinks made out of fruit juices which are abundant in the Soviet Union as a result of changes in your wine industry. Now we are approaching the final stage of creating a joint enterprise — a plant producing fruit juice concentrates for non-alcoholic beverages.'

'You talked about having big plans. If it's not a secret, what are they?'

'The company is making an offer to Gosagroprom to expand its network of bottling plants. We're suggesting a double increase in the bottling of Pepsi Cola. In exchange we will sell champagne and various kinds of vodka in the United States, and we will provide the equipment to produce soft drinks.

'We are trying to make our ties mutually beneficial; therefore we are not only selling, but buying from the Soviet Union. The company values this cooperation. The Soviet Union is a reliable and honest partner, perhaps like no one else in the world.'

What will the Soviet-American version of Pizza Hut be like? Andrew Rafalat said the restaurant will have a nice interior, good furnishings, good quality food and excellent service. The main dish will be different varieties of pizza. The restaurant will also offer salads, desserts and soft drinks. The American and European Pizza Huts also serve beer and natural wines. Usually about one-fifth of the pizzas are sold to take out.

Like Pepsi Cola, which has the same standard quality no matter where it is produced in the world, Pizza Hut pizzas should not deviate from the usual recipe. That is why the pizzas made in Moscow should not be any different from those in London or Glasgow. This requires high quality flour, pepperoni, mozarella cheese, ham, tomato paste or fresh tomatoes of a specific quality.

At first the necessary ingredients will mainly be bought from foreign suppliers. Some of the foreign currency earned will be used for this purpose. But Pepsico suggests developing the production of these ingredients in Soviet enterprises. In the future these products can not only be supplied to Pizza Hut restaurants, but also offered on the international market. According to Andrew Rafalat, the flour produced at plant No. 3 in Moscow can be used already, but the production of pepperoni, tomato paste, cheese and ham still has to be developed to meet Pizza Hut's standards.

Pepsico suggests using the first joint ventures to train personnel who could in the future apply their experience in other fast food establishments.

Negotiations between Pepsico Incorporated and Glavobshchepit are advancing towards a mutually profitable goal — the creation of a network of joint Soviet-American enterprises.

Izvestia, 28 February 1988

The World Scene

"A new way of thinking".
Any progress to report?

In 1987 TV viewers around the world had a chance to see Amerika, *a 14-part serial made by ABC. Many will have seen this production dealing with an imaginary Soviet occupation of the United States, and so there is no need to dwell on its contents. It is interesting to note, however, that an opinion poll taken among US viewers in February 1987, coinciding with the serial's appearance on American TV screens, showed that 70 per cent of those surveyed considered their country's occupation by the Soviet Union to be a real possibility.*

In autumn 1987 a project called International Peace Barometer *was set up on the initiative of the Sociological Research Institute of the USSR Academy of Sciences with a view to investigating public opinion in East and West on issues relating to war, peace and new political thinking. The project represents a joint effort with sociologists in other socialist countries, as well as France, Japan and Finland. Identical polls have been carried out in the Soviet Union and the United States with the assistance of the Gallup organisation. Asked whether the Soviet Union posed a threat to the United States, only 12 per cent of Americans replied in the negative.*

So what's the matter? Why is it that even among teenagers, who usually take a more optimistic view of life, only 29 per cent of American boys and girls believed in the possibility of friendship and cooperation between the Soviet Union and the United States, while 72 per cent of Soviet youngsters considered it quite a feasible proposition?

This must be the result of a mistrust which has been built up over many years. Yet there is even widespread ignorance in the United States of the changes taking place in the Soviet Union today. KRIS KRISTOFFERSON who played a leading part in Amerika *admitted in an interview he gave* Izvestia: *'Unfortunately, my knowledge of your country is restricted to information from Dostoyevsky's novels and the US press. I have only a vague knowledge of Soviet history. I can cite no Soviet author, composer or movie figure. True, I've managed somehow to see a film made by Eizenstein and not long ago I saw a recent film "Moscow Doesn't Believe in Tears" which was shown on our screens.'*

We have an enormous job on our hands if we wish to win the world's trust. There has to be a fundamental re-think in attitudes and a few myths will need to be demolished.

A significant start has been made...

In March the Soviet Defence Minister DMITRY YAZOV met US Secretary of Defence Frank Carlucci in Bern, Switzerland.

Maj. Gen. GELIY BATENIN relates the highlights of the meeting.

THE FIRST EVER IN POST-WAR YEARS

The Bern meeting of the Soviet and US defence ministers is certainly an outstanding event in the dialogue on security, disarmament and the stabilisation of bilateral relations that has recently been promoted between the two countries in various forms.

For the first time in post-war history the Soviet and American leaders responsible for the defence and security of their countries have sat face to face at the negotiating table. They discussed military aspects of the key political issues involved in removing the threat of war, especially nuclear war.

Such a talk would have been inconceivable two years ago. A solid political foundation for the Bern meeting was laid by the Geneva, Reykjavik and Washington summits, and the concrete results of these high-level talks: the INF Treaty, the fundamental decisions on strategic offensive weapons and compliance with the ABM Treaty, and the

*   *Izvestia*, 18 February 1987.

preparations for talks on conventional arms in Europe, ending nuclear tests, and the prohibition and destruction of chemical weapons.

This range of problems, which faces not just the Soviet Union and the United States but the whole of the world community, is linked in one way or another with the military doctrines of states, and the ideological basis of military policy that underlies the present structures of armed forces and the directions of their further growth.

In this sense, military doctrine could either give birth to another nuclear monster in, say, the form of a directed-energy weapon, or lead to the elaboration of non-nuclear, non-offensive defence strategies, that is, strategies most suitable to the comprehensive security system.

Therefore, it is no accident that the *character of the Soviet and US military doctrines was a major item on the agenda at the Bern talks*. Interesting and useful though it was, the talk on this subject did not lead immediately to any mutual recommendations on changes to be made in military doctrines so that they do not increase military confrontation but, on the contrary, ensure greater predictability and stability in the military equilibrium between the Soviet Union and the United States. Time, and permanently operating, broadening meetings between military experts on both sides are necessary for this purpose.

The Bern meeting of the Soviet and US defence ministers has brought such a mechanism into action. A programme worked out there envisages the profound analysis and mutual discussion and solution of military-political and military-technical issues connected with disarmament and security. Further steps are planned for the immediate future.

First, to hold consultations for a deeper understanding of the content and direction of the Soviet and US military doctrines, and to consider the possibility of *exchanging data on the armed forces of the United States and the Soviet Union* and, after consultations with their allies, *on the armed forces of NATO and the Warsaw Treaty*. Such an exchange of data would also help start talks on the reduction of armed forces and conventional arms in Europe on the basis of the mandate that is now being elaborated at the Vienna follow-up meeting to the Helsinki conference.

Second, it is planned to study ways of monitoring sea-launched nuclear cruise missiles, and consider proposals to hold an early joint experiment to detect the presence of nuclear weapons on board ships. If the effectiveness of such control were proven, it would help establish whether the number of sea-launched cruise missiles carried by the navies of the two countries is within the limits on their strategic arsenals, which are now being defined at the nuclear and space arms talks in Geneva.

Third, to carry on the policy of improving mutual understanding and strengthening confidence in the military field by expanding contacts and ties between the armed forces of the Soviet Union and the United States. The defence ministers have instructed the chiefs of staff of the armed forces of their countries, Marshal Sergei Akhromeyev and Admiral William Crowe, to work out programmes in this field.

Fourth, to draw up principles and institute an appropriate forum for bilateral consultations on the military activity of the Soviet Union and the United States with a view to preventing incidents between their armed forces. In other words, efforts should be made to avoid violations of the Soviet-American agreements on the prevention of incidents on the open sea and in the air space over it (1972) and on military communication missions (1947).

The Soviet-American dialogue in the military sphere has thus reached a new level. It should play an important role in constructive cooperation for the sake of universal security. Soviet-American relations in the military field can and should develop, through dialogue, from confrontation to constructive cooperation.

New Times, 25 March 1988

IF WAR BREAKS OUT THERE'LL BE NO ONE LEFT TO PROVE THEIR POINT

VALENTIN FALIN, chairman of the Board
of Novosti Press Agency (APN),
and ALEXANDER BOVIN, *Izvestia* political analyst,
discuss ways towards general survival

Valentin Falin. Public opinion abroad is gradually coming to recognise that the Soviet Union's priority is peace and that it stands for excluding war from international relations as a practicable and achievable political goal. Some sceptics, however, will note that it has not always been the case. For decades the USSR regarded military confrontation between capitalism and socialism as inevitable due to the very nature of imperialism. When did Soviet doctrine change and will it not change again if the East gains military superiority over the West?

Although some people may find it unexpected, the answer to this question is that the decisions of the 27th CPSU Congress are consistent with Lenin's Decree on Peace. Even under changed historical conditions and on a different material foundation, our attitude to war remains, of course, unchanged: war goes against a nation's best interests and is an unsuitable tool for realising national policy. The party has always stood firm on this point.

Alexander Bovin. When we were trying to prevent war in the 1920s and 1930s we were thinking only in terms of a respite, a spell of peace. Theory and practical policies were based on the assumption that war would break out sooner or later.

Our approach today is radically different. We see efforts to prevent world war as efforts to achieve lasting peace, rather than as efforts to increase the space between two wars.

The difference is qualitative. It is brought about rather by objective reality, than by 'tactics'.

V. F. In the 1930s, the USSR put forward the concept of 'indivisible security'. Sadly, it did not meet with the understanding and support of other powers. Today we recognise that the world is an interdependent entity. Security must be universal and as far as the USSR and USA are concerned, mutual. The problem of security has become principally a political one and its solution by military means is increasingly inappropriate.

If the idea of integrity were accepted as the basis for decision-making among nations, then existing military mechanisms, at least in their present form, would be superfluous.

A. B. There is another thing that was particular about our views in the 1930s. We believed that while imperialism existed, war was inevitable. Now we proceed from the basis that since the historical and social environment has changed, then the 'nature' of imperialism must necessarily respond to this environment. It is therefore realistic, even if imperialism still exists, to sever the links between cause and effect, between the *possibility of war* and *its being unleashed*. In fact, our entire concept of a non-nuclear, non-violent world proceeds from the possibility of preserving peace with imperialism still in existence in the world.

V. F. Imperialism as a system is no stranger to the instinct of self-preservation. It was able at times to pick the lesser of two evils. For the West today war is the incomparably greater evil. Hence the political alternative to the military solution of all international conflicts.

A. B. I think there are two 'instincts' at work here. Firstly, there is the instinct of social self-preservation, which prevents the possibility of war between imperialist countries. Imperialist differences are not allowed to come to the surface and turn into military conflicts in the face of world socialism. Secondly, there is the instinct of physical self-preservation, which radically reduces the chance of its starting a deliberate nuclear war against socialism, because the first to start such a war would be the second to die.

This leads us on to another question: would the elimination of nuclear weapons mean a return to a situation where the possibility of war between capitalism and socialism would reappear?

V. F. In abstract, theoretical terms it cannot be excluded that someone, under certain circumstances, might risk a military venture. But the possibility of this is insignificant within the framework of an interdependent world and the closer nations draw together, politically and otherwise, the less likely it is to happen.

A. B. The possibility of world catastrophe or holocaust

has made universal survival into a key issue. It is a question of paramount importance to humanity today. We even place it above class interests, a change in our position that I would call epoch-making.

V. F. Lenin identified himself with ideas, interests and categories common to all humanity. It was Lenin who said that there might arise a situation where class interests would have to be sacrificed in the name of broader interests. Our ideological opponents prefer to ignore Lenin's fundamental thoughts and instead they counter these with polemical words and assessments of his made in the heat of fierce controversy.

A. B. Lenin's writings do not require updating. Neither is there any need to 'sanctify' each new turn of events or new understanding of these events with a phrase or formula of Lenin's. In following Lenin's path we should rely first and foremost on our own experience, on our own power of intellect. The new way of thinking advocated by the party is *creative* thinking.

Creativity, the enrichment and modification of theory are inseparable from debate and discussion. In the present situation, will peaceful coexistence remain a form of class struggle on the world scene? Some people think not, believing that universal human interests take precedence. I consider this conclusion rather hasty.

Universal human interests do exist, but alongside these there still continue to exist class interests, social antagonisms and the struggle between the two systems. In this context, I believe, peaceful coexistence remains a form of class struggle on the world scene, but an exclusively peaceful form which benefits universal human interests.

The nature of this class struggle is changing because neither capitalism nor socialism can envisage their interests being realised with the aid of war.

V. F. My understanding of peaceful coexistence is slightly different. It is true that the renunciation of war does not eliminate class antagonisms, ideological struggle, or smooth out social differences. There is no doubt that these contradictions and incongruities should be manifested in non-military ways, but I think that coexistence is primarily about finding common ground. Peaceful coexistence has become an indispensable condition for the existence of the human race and without it no-one will be left to prove their point. If we are consistent in our desire to free a state's policies from ideological distortion, then there is even more reason for ridding peaceful coexistence — as a means of communication between states rather than between classes or world outlooks — of everything not directly relevant to ensuring civilisation's survival.

A. B. I think it's practically impossible to free peaceful coexistence from class and social interests, or from the influence of world outlooks. It's impossible to understand correctly a state's policies when viewed outside the class context.

V. F. Experience shows that ordinary people and politicians often distort or even falsify the meanings of certain concepts and terms. Take, for example, pacifism, a term coined long before the socialist revolution. Pacifism was, at one time, a form of struggle by certain social groups against growing militarism. Later it deteriorated into passive protest and non-resistance to the evil of war, making no distinction between just or unjust wars. Today the idea of a non-violent world free from the obscenity of militarism creates new possibilities for pacifist circles.

A. B. Today we too have become pacifists as far as nuclear war is concerned, that is to say, we are absolutely and unconditionally against nuclear war. A just nuclear war is impossible because justice is only for the living.

Would a third world war stimulate social progress? Of course not. Mao Zedong once maintained the opposite, but, apart from him, no-one else has pursued this line. What we have here is a new theoretical proposition that violence cannot be abstractly considered the midwife of history, for violence could now end history altogether.

V. F. Some US statesmen say that in a nuclear war probably 'only' 95 per cent of the population would die, including themselves in the five per cent of survivors.

A. B. There can be no winners in a nuclear war. Both Ronald Reagan and Mikhail Gorbachev have said so. It has been said for nearly 20 years. But look what happens in practice. Nuclear weapons are constantly being modernised and their precision and reliability increased. What is the point when a nuclear conflict will end in death anyway? The only logic in it is if one has a limited nuclear war in mind, if one thinks its escalation can be controlled. This is what the Americans believe. We say that control is impossible, because any 'limited' war would end in world war. Or that's what we say in principle. But in reality we sometimes act as if war can be controlled.

V. F. If that is what is happening, then it is because of the inertia to which we have been captives for so long. The Soviet Union was obliged for decades to try and catch up with the Americans until parity was achieved not in theory but in practice.

A. B. We should abandon the race for symmetry. It is unnecessary. Sufficiency does not require symmetry.

V. F. But Washington has a logic of its own. It sees the arms race as a way of waging war to deplete other countries because the US relies on a broader economic base. Hence the policy of strength in peacetime.

A. B. Some other questions also need to be seen in a new light. Today the most important way to defend our country and show our patriotism is to do everything possible to prevent nuclear war. Protecting our country from nuclear war is the highest manifestation of patriotism today.

V. F. Defence of one's country and internationalist duty are organic to patriotism. But do they provide an exhaustive description of patriotism?

Take Lenin's slogan 'Stick bayonets in the ground'. Or his advocacy of the defeat of tsarism in World War I. Was that a patriotic position? Take the Bolsheviks' decision to disband the army right after the revolution. Was that a patriotic decision or not? Hence, a socio-political concept cannot exist outside of time and space.

However, while the danger of war is there, defence of our country will naturally be at the forefront. Only disarmament will rid us of this task. If we believe it is possible, we must learn to make out the shape of the world by the early 21st century. What will this world without nuclear weapons be like? What will happen if the Warsaw Treaty Organisation's proposal to deny states the material possibility of waging offensive wars is realised? The road to a non-violent world will be a long one, but humanity must begin preparing its consciousness for it now.

A. B. Isn't it a bit early? There is the opposing side, too, and its views of today and the future do not coincide with ours on all issues, to put it mildly.

V. F. Our foreign policy is prompted not so much by necessity as by conviction. This sets it apart from that of the other side. We do not consider the alternatives of a bit more force here, a little less force there, but force nonetheless. The CPSU and the Soviet state have firmly opted for a policy of common sense. Common sense demands that conditions be created where the use of force is impossible, both in theory and practice. The Delhi Declaration by Mikhail Gorbachev and Rajiv Gandhi has advanced the concept of a non-violent world, i. e., it has developed an idea, which would have been proclaimed heretical by a dogmatic Marxist only yesterday. But we have had to pay too high a price for our state's 70 years of experience to afford the luxury of a continued flirtation with dogmatism.

What is the main significance of the October Revolution for civilisation as a whole? Firstly, it has provided a conceptually new social alternative, proving that it is possible to build a world without exploitation, without national oppression, a world of equal nations, a world where all processes are democratically controlled. Secondly, the October Revolution produced the idea of a world without wars, a world without violence.

Both these merits are of equal importance. With time the second one has gained even greater importance as peace has become a condition of preserving life on earth.

A. B. This country came into being with the doctrine of peaceful coexistence. We wanted to ensure that the principle of peaceful coexistence regulated relations between states of differing socio-economic systems. But we have achieved more than this. The principle of peaceful coexistence has become universal and is now being increasingly applied in relations between states irrespective of their socio-economic systems. This is the tremendous contribution we have made to world development, to making relations between states civilised. This is to socialism's credit, to the 1917 Russian Revolution's credit.

Moscow News, 8 November 1987

Hunger remains one of the world's most serious problems despite the fact that for years some of the world's leading scientists have turned their attention to it.

The mind refuses to believe that every minute 24 people in the world die of hunger. Hunger is more than just a problem of the developing world. It concerns us all.

A. IVANKO discusses this question with ANATOLY GROMYKO, Director of the USSR Academy of Sciences' Africa Institute, and with businessman G. STARR, and professor BERNARD LEAVEY, who initiated 'Project Hunger'.

HUNGER CANNOT BE TOLERATED

GROMYKO: Hunger is an acute global problem reaching catastrophic proportions. Over a billion people, or one-fifth of the world population, go hungry. From 13 to 18 million people die of hunger each year, or 24 people, including 18 children, each minute. Human life, especially that of children, is fragile. In the worst years, an estimated 15 mln children die of hunger. The problem of hunger is especially acute in Asia, Africa and Latin America. A vast zone of hunger stretches both to the north and south of the equator.

STARR: If a bomb equal in size to the one dropped on Hiroshima were dropped on the planet every three days, the number of victims would be equal to the number of persons now dying of hunger. The bombing of Hiroshima changed history. Yet, to our shame, our attitude toward hunger, a chronic phenomenon of our time, is much more subdued. Among the causes of hunger are inflated military budgets, scanty allocations for social needs, a demographic explosion, economic backwardness and environmental imbalances. There is not one clear concept, not one general philosophy or system capable of doing away with hunger. Yet the existing food reserves are enough to feed the current world population 1.5 times.

IVANKO: What can be done to change the situation?

GROMYKO: It is entirely possible to stamp out hunger. All countries should cling together to tackle it. Politicians and businessmen should do their utmost to eliminate military and political confrontations and establish multilateral cooperation between all countries, the USSR and the United States included. This idea is a part of the Soviet proposals for step-by-step disarmament and for the elimination of nuclear weapons. By scrapping lethal weapons, mankind will increase its chances for combating hunger and for improving the economic situation of many poor countries. A hunger-free world cannot be attained without resolute efforts for radical disarmament. Poor countries cannot feed themselves and fight backwardness as long as military confrontation and local conflicts continue to rage. Confrontation and conflicts can result only in tens of millions of more deaths from starvation.

STARR: We lack the political will to do away with hunger. During World War II we succeeded in defeating Nazi Germany. The USSR and the United States were then allies. People are aware that today we have a unique opportunity to eliminate hunger. It is our intention to draw the attention of the American public to the possibility of a Soviet-American agreement to solve this problem. Mankind faces a common enemy — hunger. This should be enough to push all our differences to the background. The USSR and the United States possess vast potentials. But the political differences between them render it impossible to eliminate hunger.

IVANKO: Could you be more specific as to what the Soviet and the US governments could do to combat hunger?

STARR: Picture a conference hall in Geneva with a large table in the middle. Two men — the Soviet and American leaders — are sitting at the table, giving a two-minute press conference announcing that the Soviet Union and the United States have just agreed to a joint project to eliminate hunger before the end of the century. Imagine another press conference held a half year later, at another location, with African statesmen joining the Soviet and American leaders. They announce jointly that efforts have been launched in an African country to stamp out hunger within five years through a development programme. It is high time we undertook concrete actions. And for this we need the right political atmosphere.

IVANKO: Is it feasible that an agreement could be reached at a government level?

STARR: I think it is. Besides, it is simpler to settle disarmament questions within the framework of a food programme. Why hold one's partner at gunpoint?

GROMYKO: Agreement is not only possible, but essential. There is no alternative. Starvation must no longer threaten the Third World. All governments must pool their efforts to eliminate it.

IVANKO: Yes, but ideological disputes are inevitable in deciding which country is to be helped first.

STARR: They are, but they have to be dealt with.

LEAVEY: Take the campaign to fight smallpox. A vaccine was discovered in the late 18th century, but it was not until the mid-1960s that the United States, the Soviet Union and other countries who supported the WHO campaign launched a drive against smallpox. It took us a decade to bring the disease under control throughout the world. Once governments agree to tackle a global problem, ways can be found to do so. Where there's political will there's a way.

GROMYKO: Both Americans and Soviets look forward to the meeting between Mikhail Gorbachev and Ronald Reagan. Both sides wish the summit every success. It should give an impetus to the resolution of major global problems. The political climate that will emerge after the summit should help to fight hunger, a goal that requires no less persistence than disarmament.

IVANKO: What can the academic community do to help?

LEAVEY: We must step up Soviet-American cooperation to fight hunger and search for new ways to do so.

GROMYKO: Efforts must be raised to a higher, more sophisticated level. That's up to Soviet and American scholars and their colleagues in other countries, the developing world included. They must look for ways to update international relations in keeping with new political thinking, which promises us a world free of wars and hunger. That noble goal must bring the international academic community to work out effective, scientifically sound recommendations for political leaders. The world academic community is in need of major changes. Palliatives and lofty-sounding slogans will not help the world eliminate hunger. We need concrete efforts on a large scale.

Izvestia, 18 August 1987

'THIS IS TRULY UNFORGETTABLE'

On May 29, 1988, on a clear, balmy day in Moscow, Air Force One carrying President Ronald Reagan touched down at Vnukovo-2 airport, commencing the President's first visit to Moscow and his fourth meeting with Soviet leader Mikhail S. Gorbachev. And although no important arms reduction agreement was signed during the five-day visit, as was in December 1987 in Washington, the many hours the two leaders spent together, Ronald Reagan's encounters with Muscovites, Nancy Reagan's trip to Leningrad, the frank discussions on Red Square, the Arbat district, the House of Writers, Moscow State University and at Spaso House, the American ambassador's residence — allow us to say that as a result the Soviet and American people have begun to trust each other and understand each other more.

Before departing from Moscow Ronald Reagan made the following statement:

'I'm full of gratitude to Muscovites for the kind attention and cordiality which were shown to me and my wife throughout our stay in the Soviet Union. Much has been written about Moscow hospitality, and even more has been said, but at least once you've just got to feel it for yourself. When meeting with people on Moscow's streets and squares, although such occasions were few, I saw friendly, open faces, and felt all the time the sincere warmth with which Muscovites welcomed their American guests. I kept wanting to answer in kind, to express some words of heartfelt gratitude. But they were swallowed up by the thunderous applause and squalls of greetings. This is truly unforgettable.

'Naturally, I'd seen pictures of the Kremlin and old Moscow before. I must admit, however, that I never imagined that it was so beautiful. I was amazed by the perfection of the Kremlin — the whole ensemble and each of its ancient buildings. While still on the way to Moscow, I thought it might be nice to take a stroll around Red Square. I did it. And my guide, if I can call him that, for this amazing stroll, was Mr. Gorbachev. Together we went out onto Red Square, and went around stopping to talk with the numerous visitors to the capital's most picturesque place.

I also saw the endless line of people at the Lenin Mausoleum.

'And one last thing which I already mentioned. In fact I was even quoted, but maybe not always clearly understood. I would simply like to express my most profound respect for Soviet women, whose wisdom, industry, and fortitude are the foundation of Soviet society in which they play an outstanding role.

'Good-bye, Moscow and Muscovites!'

Moscow News, 12 July 1988

How the others see us

Regrets? Skepticism? Hope?

IAN ELLIOT:
SEVENTY YEARS
IS A COUNTRY'S YOUTH

An interview with a leading British Sovietologist
who is a professor at the Royal Institute
of International Affairs and the author
of a number of books on Soviet foreign policy

Q. *How does Mr Elliot see* perestroika *developing in the Soviet Union?*
A. This is the most interesting period for the last twenty years. A serious and far-reaching reconstruction is taking place in all areas of Soviet life. And in a very positive direction, which many people here in the West did not expect. As for people like myself, who have devoted their whole lives to studying the Soviet Union, we look upon *perestroika* as something that is essential. And we take great satisfaction from the changes that are taking place in your country.
Q. *What do you think about the* perestroika *of the Soviet media?*
A. In the last couple of years the Soviet media have become simply unrecognisable. Before that, you see, for us who work every day with the Soviet press it was not in the least bit difficult to tell in advance what your papers would say on any given theme or on any given event. This has now become impossible. Reading the Soviet press today is tremendously interesting. There is a feeling of honesty about what is being written which, I fear, did not exist before.
Seventy years is the lifespan of a man, but in the life of a state it is a very short period. And your country, really, is a very young one.
Q. *Sovietologists today show a very definite bias in their discussions on the development of Soviet society during the twenties and thirties. They claim that the panacea for all our economic difficulties during that period was the purchase of technology from the West. But in fact at the time the main*

obstacle to the development of mutually beneficial trade was not a lack of resources in the USSR for acquiring imports, although there were probably some difficulties in this matter, but the hostile attitude of the bourgeois governments. It is sufficient to recall in this connection a cynical headline in The Times *in the twenties, which stated 'Bolshevism Should Be Healed with Bullets', and this paper at the time was the mouthpiece of British ruling circles.*

A. One must agree. During the Civil War, Britain, the United States, France, Italy and Germany all took part in the military intervention in Soviet Russia. This alone confirmed the fears of the Bolsheviks that the West was hostile. And in the Far East the country was attacked by Japan. But as time went on the situation changed. The United States was the last of the Western countries to recognise the Soviet Union, which it did in 1933. But a number of capitalist entrepreneurs were ready to trade with Soviet Russia immediately after the Revolution. Take Armand Hammer, the President of Occidental Petroleum, for example. And since the Western countries were never monolithic, in all probability there were opportunities for better trade.

Q. No one is disputing that such trade was possible. The question is on what scale. It must be remembered that even after they had concluded diplomatic relations with the Soviet Union, the United States, Britain, France and a number of other countries still remained hostile. This can be seen in the series of plots that were uncovered to overthrow Soviet power. But there are examples of such attitudes that are more recent. Just recall the position of Britain, France and other European countries on the eve of the Second World War. Look at the Munich deal. And the 'phoney war' which Britain and France waged against fascist Germany. Who was that war being waged against? We in the Soviet Union are quite convinced — and there are numerous historical documents to confirm our conclusion — that the main aim of London and Paris at the time was to provoke a clash between the USSR and Germany, and not to take up arms against fascism.

A. You mentioned Munich... Historians in the West sometimes sharply criticise the British government of the time for making a pact with Hitler. On the other hand, Hitler represented a serious threat to Britain, and we had to do something. Now, of course, it is easy to criticise and judge those who were ready to sign a treaty with Hitler. But the pacifist movement in Britain at the time, which was huge and which had begun after the First World War, applauded the agreement. And the policy of the British government of 'peace at any price' was widely supported.

At the same time, however, there were many politicians who were opposed to appeasing Hitler and these were forced into retirement. One such was the future Prime Minister, Winston Churchill. He was a firm opponent of Munich. Furthermore, the Soviet Union at the time was not Britain's 'natural ally'—many British companies had lost enormous capital investments as a result of the Revolution in 1917 and this affected all subsequent governments in their relations with the Soviet Union. Therefore you are right when you say that there were political forces in Britain who wanted a conflict between the Soviet Union and Germany. It was thought that such a development would be the easiest solution to the problems facing Britain. But, of course, I can understand that this policy would be considered by the Soviet Union as political treachery committed without consideration of the real situation. And don't forget that it was typical of British governments to want to stand aside from European conflicts.

Q. *Excuse me, but this latter statement does not accord with historical fact. You yourself recall the Civil War when a British expeditionary force was sent to Russia. Britain was actually behind bourgeois Poland when it attacked Soviet Russia. The White Poles invaded the Ukraine and took Kiev, and King George V sent a telegram of congratulations to Pilsudski. Then there was the Soviet-Finnish War. It is now no secret that London and Paris were preparing to send troops into that military conflict, and yet the curious thing is that at the time both Britain and France were already at war with Germany, but showed no desire whatsoever to move from passive contemplation of the aggressor to taking specific action against him. And then you may recall the campaign of anti-Soviet hysteria in 1939 over the Soviet border along the Curzon Line. And yet it was Britain itself that in the early twenties suggested this border after the Soviet-Polish conflict. But this did not stop voices being raised in London for war to be declared against the Soviet Union. So what is this policy of British non-intervention in European affairs?*

A. As for the Curzon Line affair, this did in fact take place as you said. But at the time Britain looked upon the policy of the Soviet Union as a deal with Germany to share Poland. Now many historians in the West admit that the territory which lay within the new borders should not be regarded as Polish. Historically it belonged to the Ukraine and Byelorussia. But at the time these actions were seen through the prism of the secret protocol with Hitler. The Soviet Union's move into the Baltic states and its territorial claims on Finland were also regarded as aggression. In fact, little Finland was in a state of armed conflict with its huge neighbour. And this is how many saw the events of those years. For this reason there were a large number of volunteers both in Britain and France who were ready to go and fight for Finland. Later, of course, when we became allies with the Soviet Union, these accusations of aggression were replaced by the warmest feelings towards the Soviet Union and the Soviet people.

Q. Why was the Western press so hostile to the Soviet Union on the eve of the war?

A. I would find it difficult to speak about the Western press in general, but as for the British press, attitudes varied. *The Manchester Guardian*, for example, took a position that was directly opposed to, say, *The Times*. I have to admit — with regret, since I worked on that newspaper for several years — that *The Times* during the late thirties was quite clearly pro-Hitler, and this of course today looks terrible. It is shameful to remember how that paper wrote about the Nazis in the thirties. But this was a reflection of the views of the establishment which looked upon Hitler as a buffer against communism. During the war this attitude changed. So everything changes, even press priorities.

Q. Do you think that the media in the West in general and in Great Britain in particular have changed their attitude to the Soviet Union since the beginning of perestroika?

A. There can be no question at all that it has. Today the Soviet Union is looked upon in the West as a dynamic society that is faced with a number of problems which it speaks about boldly in a bid to find a solution to them. Besides, attitudes to your country have been very much influenced by the popularity of your leader, his style of leadership and his desire to complete *perestroika* and bring about radical changes in international relations.

Soviet society has become more understandable now. A country which talks openly about its difficulties, miscalculations and mistakes cannot present a threat to other states — and there are very many people in the West who believe this. Take this simple example: previously in the Soviet press and in statements made by officials prostitution was claimed to be a product of the capitalist system, a characteristic feature of the capitalist way of life which did not exist in the Soviet Union. And so we Westerners would make snide remarks like: 'So who are these girls who get into the Moscow hotels where English visitors are staying? Foreign imports?' But today in the Soviet Union prostitution, drug addiction and the means to deal with these social evils are being openly discussed. What has been the reaction in the West? More or less the following: yes, there is indeed a problem of drug addiction in the USSR, but it is on nothing like the scale that it exists in the West. So from the idea that used to be current that we had nothing to learn from the Russians we have moved towards a new understanding of the Soviet Union. We've both got our problems and we've both got our achievements, so why not learn from each other?

Q. *What feeling do you have towards a country that in seven decades has moved from a backwater to a superpower?*

A. In the seventy years of Soviet rule the peoples of your country have suffered foreign military intervention during the Civil War and the Second World War which did uncountable damage and cost millions and millions of lives. Yet despite all that the Soviet Union has developed successfully. It is sufficient to look at a statistical map of the world economy to see the role the Soviet Union plays in the modern world. And no sober-minded person could deny these achievements. The guarantee of success of *perestroika* is the policy of *glasnost*, which allows all members of society the opportunity for showing initiative. There is no doubt about Soviet economic success. But what appears more attractive for me is the great social experiment which for seventy years has been running in your country. When I was still a student and had just begun studying the Russian language and Soviet history, I came to the conclusion that your society had one important distinguishing feature — its humanity and concern for people.

From my trips to the Soviet Union I have come away with the firm conviction that the Russians and all the other peoples of your country are very kind and friendly. I wish them all good luck.

Interview by Yu. SAGAIDAK

Komsomolskaya Pravda, 8 September 1987

CRITICAL MASS FOR SECURITY

Scientist's responsibility for his discovery

PEIERLS' lecture, which sparked quite a few heated debates, mirrored the complexity of the present situation in which the world has found itself since 1940 when Professor Rudolf Peierls of the University of Birmingham calculated for the first time the critical mass of uranium-235 necessary for the development of an A-bomb. The Bomb that split human history into 'Before' and 'After'.

Admittedly, I was brought to the Display Centre of the Space Research Institute not by a desire to hear once again about the mind-wrenching realities of the nuclear race. I was interested in something different. Claude Eatherly, the pilot who dropped That Bomb, went crazy. His brain could not handle what he did. And they, those who directly fabricated it, what happened to the souls of these people at that time, in 1945?

Robert Oppenheimer once said: 'Physicists knew their sin'. Rudy Peierls was one of them. Those who knew. What does he think now?

'Yes, we were well aware of the consequences,' he says. 'Already at that time, in March 1940, when Otto Frisch and I calculated that a mere kilo of uranium was needed for a nuclear blast (instead of several tons, as it was presumed by most scientists who worked on this project), we understood that the main secret of the atom bomb was out — that it *could* be made. We also came to understand that it would possess incredible devastating force and told our government that it was inadmissible to use a weapon which would kill such large numbers of any civilian population. This is why the atom bomb could not be included in Britain's arsenals. Our calculation became known in the United States, and Frisch and I were invited there to take part in the Manhattan Project, in which Oppenheimer, Szilard, Fermi, Teller and other prominent physicists had already been involved. At first we worked in New York where a factory for isotope separation was being built, then we moved to Los Alamos where work started directly on the Bomb.'

'You considered it an unacceptable weapon for Britain, but quite permissible for the USA? Already visualizing its monstrous effect, you nevertheless began working on it and now say that you don't regret this. How did you manage, after Hiroshima, to come to terms with yourself?'

'Understand: a war was on. Work in the same direction was also carried out in German laboratories. And if *their* quests were crowned with success? Besides this, there is also the mentality of a scientist. If it is already clear that a problem is soluble, it means that its further development is *inevitable*. How can one keep aloof in this case? Yes, we were aware that this weapon would bring about mass losses among the civilian population. But first, at that time in Los Alamos, it seemed to us that our job was science, whereas it was up to brass hats and policy-makers to pass the decision. The important thing was to explain the consequences to them. In this we relied on our committee, which included Oppenheimer, Fermi and Lawrence. And wrongfully so. They did not raise particular objections to its use. But there is also another aspect of the matter — Rotterdam, Coventry, Hamburg, Dresden — no fewer people were killed there during the bombing raids than in the bombing of Hiroshima. Who knows, were it not for these precedents, Truman might possibly not make up his mind to do that either. As a matter of fact, even today I cannot understand why it was not enough to show the Japanese the first testings of the bomb on 16 July. Possibly the USA apprehended that the experiment would fail, whereas it had only two or three bombs in reserve. At that time it planned to occupy Japan and was afraid of sustaining heavy losses.'

'Don't you think that Hiroshima was needed to show everyone, and the USSR in particular, who would really rule the world in the postwar period?'

'No, I don't think so.'

'And what did you know about the work of Soviet scientists on similar weapons?'

'Practically nothing.'

'In 1950, Klaus Fuchs was arrested in Britain. He was accused of transferring the secrets of the Manhattan Project to the potential enemy. Did you know him?'

'Yes, he was my staffer. It was I that, on coming to know his works, enlisted him in research already in Britain. He was undoubtedly a talented scientist. I, it is true, didn't know that he was a Communist. When the leakage of information from Los Alamos surfaced already after the war, suspicion fell on myself and Fuchs. But obviously I was put through a thorough check.'

'Now it is already known that Fuchs was motivated by ideological considerations, by the profound conviction that in the fight against a common enemy one side should not have any secrets from the other. But was the information passed by him really important? After all, if this were so, the atom bomb would have been created in the USSR not in 1949, but earlier. Doesn't it mean that Soviet scientists were advancing along their own path?'

'Fuchs' contribution could hardly be substantial. I once asked Academician Artsimovich how much time Fuchs had saved for you. He said not more than a year. In the work of such magnitude this is no time. So that you are probably right. Such are the dialectics of science: if a problem is soluble in principle, it will be solved sooner or later. It's a different matter, of course, that at that time we did not imagine that such an arms race would start as a result of our work.'

'There were some who imagined. Remember Niels Bohr, for instance. His conversation with Churchill. The scientist believed that trust and cooperation were indispensable between our countries in this question.'

'Yes, exactly at that time (in the spring of 1944) he received an invitation from Kapitsa to come to Moscow and he wanted to take the mission of telling the Russians *about the very fact* of work on the Bomb. But a horrible misunderstanding occurred. Bohr, as we know, expressed his thoughts in a very complicated and lengthy way. Moreover, he spoke softly and quite inaudibly. And the only thing that Churchill understood from that inarticulate mumbling was

that the famous physicist wanted to give the secret of the
atom bomb to the Russians. He was horrified. At that time
Bohr hardly evaded imprisonment. But life has shown how
right the scientist was when he saw in the still unborn nuclear weapons the reason of the future division of the world
and a threat to the whole of civilization."

'Enrico Fermi's wife recalls that after August 1945 every-
body in Los Alamos felt guilty. In general this feeling was
then experienced by all nuclear scientists, even those who had
nothing to do with Manhattan. It was then that the question
of scientists' responsibility for the results of their work for the
first time became the most dramatic moral problem of all sci-
ence — it became its exposed nerve.

'Many scientists, yourself included, realized their moral
duty in the global anti-nuclear movement. It is common know-
ledge, also, that your movement has already done much on
this path. But there is also the following. When they say how
many scientists are in one way or another linked to the mili-
tary-industrial complex, the impression is that official science
is merely the tip of the iceberg, the main bulk of which is hid-
den from public opinion. In the eyes of ordinary people this
looks like roughly the following: scientists make discoveries,
the military turn them into weapons, politicians try to come to
an agreement not to use them, and in the meantime scientists
make fresh discoveries. An oppressive fatal chain... Do you
believe in the possibility of interrupting it?'

'Yes, of course. But not at its first link. I have already
said: there is a dialectic in the development of science. It is
meaningless to prevent scientists from making discoveries.
What is needed is to persuade the military and politicians
not to turn the achievements of science into weapons. And
here, I believe, a very big part can be played by the world
scientific community. It is scientists that can explain the potential danger of one or other discovery and bring it to the
knowledge of public opinion.'

'And how in this connection do you visualize the participa-
tion of scientists in the SDI programme?'

'In the discussion after my lecture at the Institute of
Space Research, Academician Sakharov wittily remarked
that, whereas the main secret of the atom bomb was that it
could be made, the open secret of SDI is that it cannot be
made. Both in the USA and in Britain there are scientists

who have refused to do research in the framework of this
programme and those who continue it. For instance, at one
of our universities a group of experts work on the development of an optical computer. In principle it can be used in
SDI. But this is an exceedingly interesting problem in itself
and, inasmuch as it is being financed, scientists will try to
satisfy their scientific interest without bothering too much
about what is going to happen in future.'

*'As I see it, there is some moral defect here. Don't you find
that nuclear weapons have greatly altered human morality?'*

'Simply, fear has taken deep root in people. In this sense
you are right.'

*'Now, for the first time in nuclear history this fear will di-
minish by exactly two classes of missiles. Real chances have
appeared for the establishment of a climate of trust between
the USSR and the USA. The trust that is needed for the complete renunciation of nuclear weapons. But the following
I find strange: you, a veteran of Pugwash, working for the elimination of nuclear weapons, questioned in your lecture the
possibility of bringing this about in the foreseeable future ow-
ing to the lack of effective means of control. But doesn't the
agreement reached, and the subsequent 50 per cent reduction
of strategic arms proposed by the Soviet Union imply the
elaboration of the necessary means of control?'*

'There is hope for confidence. But the situation should not
be overestimated. For the time being the combination here
is as follows: the less confidence there is the stricter must be
the control. The way to absolute confidence, under which
nuclear disarmament is only possible, is longer than it can
be expected today.'

*'And, saying this, you take a rather critical attitude to the
principle of the sides' equal security. But what other principle
can serve as the criterion in political discussions on arms reduction?'*

'But, no, I think that this principle is very good. Simply,
I believe, it does not mean an equal quantity of yields on
one or other type of weapons. After all, speaking seriously,
who believes today in the possibility of fighting a war with
nuclear weapons? To deliver the first strike and not to receive a crushing retaliatory blow? It means that the sole
purpose of nuclear weapons is the "balance of terror", or
deterrence. How much do you need for this as a minimum?

It's hard to say. But not 25,000 warheads on each side, as is the case today! We in the Pugwash movement have arrived at the conclusion that 1,000 is enough.'

  '*What do you think it is that people miss most of all today?*'
  'We have already spoken about this: confidence.'

Interview by VLADIMIR KYUCHARYANTS

Moscow News, 20 December 1987

During the visit of the British Prime Minister, Mrs Marga-ret Thatcher, to the USSR in March 1987, the British-Soviet Chamber of Commerce opened its office in Moscow. What is the purpose of this organisation and what is it doing today?

These questions are answered by the chief of the bureau PYOTR BIRYUKOV *and the Commercial Counsellor of the British Embassy,* ROBERT CHASE.

THE COMMERCIAL SIDE

'The BSCC, a joint British-Soviet Chamber of Commerce, was set up seventy years ago by business circles in both countries in order to promote trade relations between the USSR and Great Britain,' said Pyotr Biryukov. 'Today the organisation has a membership of more than 500 British companies and some sixty Soviet foreign-trade associations and other organisations like the USSR Chamber of Commerce and Industry, the Bank for Foreign Economic Affairs of the USSR, and Intourist. This year many of those Soviet enterprises that have been given foreign trading rights have expressed a desire to become members of the BSCC. The number of British companies that are members of the Chamber is also growing.

'Our task, as we see it, is to help expand and enlarge British-Soviet trade, and to this end the Chamber provides information and publicity. It publishes a journal and a quarterly information bulletin, it circulates information on Soviet organisations with foreign trade rights and on Soviet exports, it gives help in holding exhibitions, symposiums and seminars and examines the possibilities for setting up joint ventures.'

'I should like to recall,' said Robert Chase, continuing the conversation, 'that during Mrs Thatcher's visit mutual interest was reaffirmed in increasing the growth of bilateral trade by 40-50 per cent, as had been stated in the talks between Mrs Thatcher and Mr Gorbachev in London in December 1984. By 1990 it is intended that trade between our two countries should reach the sum of 2.5 billion roubles. In recent years both sides have tried hard to re-establish the former importance of our trade relations which date back to the signing of the first official agreement by Elizabeth I and Ivan the Terrible in the 16th century.'

'In what areas are the most successful trade developments to be seen?'

'A major £260 million contract has been signed for the building of an automated control systems plant in Yerevan with GEC and Simon-Carves. Another important contract was signed with John Brown for the building of a polypropylene plant in Budennovsk. Overall, our trade increased by 19 per cent last year.

'There are also at present some twenty British companies holding talks with Soviet organisations on the formation of joint ventures, and this is an important new development in our cooperation. These talks are currently covering such varied fields as agribusiness, machine building, the chemical, oil and gas industries, medicine, biotechnology and so on.'

In conclusion Counsellor Robert Chase said: 'British industry and British firms would like to make their contribution to the process of *perestroika* which is now taking place in the Soviet Union by helping to modernise Soviet industry and sell Soviet goods to third markets, and by providing information and knowledge in such areas as finance, banking and management.'

Interview by V. MIKHEYEV

Izvestia, 5 April 1988

Anthony Burgess occupies an important place in contemporary English literature. A fine stylist (Burgess's second profession is as a composer), he has never confined himself to a brittle shell of self-sufficing aestheticism but has always been obsessed by the moral problems of his age and his so-

ciety. 'Obsession' is, indeed, the title of Gore Vidal's review of
the first part of Burgess's autobiography which recently appeared in the weekly New York Review of Books. Vidal
writes of his friend: 'Now, in the sad—the vain, I fear—
hope that once we've known the trouble he's seen we will forgive him his unfashionable originality and prodigiousness, he
makes confession not to merciful god but to merciless us.'

The novel A Clockwork Orange, which Stanley Kubrick
made into a film in 1971, has brought Anthony Burgess
worldwide fame. It is hard, if not impossible, to retell its
story. It is about a gloomy anti-utopia and its heroes—
youths who enjoy total impunity. By way of an experiment
Alex, who is also the narrator, undergoes a kind of reflex therapy which totally rids him of all his aggressive instincts.
Turned, as a result, into a pathetic, spineless creature and certainly not a person of exemplary moral standards, as the scientists had presupposed, Alex proves incapable of adapting to
the cruel world which has given birth to him.

Burgess has written twenty-eight novels in all, not counting
his books of social and political articles, literary criticism,
children's stories, poems, a large number of magazine articles
(one of the latest about the moral aspects of the AIDS epi-
demic), plays, cinema and television scripts, translations and
opera librettos. The writer is still in excellent shape and sticks
by his principles. One may not agree with him but one cannot
help but admire his refined, passionate, and bizarre manner of
writing.

Anthony Burgess has turned out to be a prophet of many of
the negative phenomena in the life of the West and, first and
foremost, of Western young people. This is why the editorial
office of Literaturnaya Gazeta sent him some questions
which he kindly wrote replies to.

ANTHONY BURGESS:
'...SUBSTITUTING FEAR FOR MORALITY'

L. G. In your novel Clockwork Orange you defined many
of the problems which the West had to cope with ten or fifteen
years later, in particular, the rapid increase in juvenile

crime.What was the world described in the novel for you: pure fantasy or a prediction?

A. B. Clockwork Orange, or Mechanical China Apple, appeared in 1962. It was meant to be prophetic rather than a mere fantasy. I had been in Leningrad the previous year and noted that you had your problems with youth as we had. It was discovering this that impelled a kind of dialect which is a mixture of Anglo-American and Russian. I called it nadsat.* There were no punks then, but there were the equivalent of your stilyagi. What worried me was the prospect of the state's using Pavlovian ** conditioning to burn out the aggression in postwar youth. This has not yet happened, but it may. The forecast of unsafe streets and juvenile criminality has come true, but it is as old as Shakespeare's time, when apprentices behaved atrociously in London and were sometimes hanged without trial. There is always a destructive tendency in youth, the result of their having energy but not any capacity to use it in acts of creation. I feel unhappy about the fulfilment of my prophecy, but I object to being blamed for youthful violence. It is true that Stanley Kubrick's film has been influential in promoting bad behaviour among the young, but I did not make the film.

L. G. What is the main difference between your generation and today's adolescents?

A. B. When I was a teenager or nadsat back in the 1930s there was little juvenile violence because youth had not become a terrain separate from maturity. One hoped to grow quickly out of youth and become adult. The war helped. My generation fought our own Great Patriotic War from 1939 to 1945 and this siphoned off our aggressive instincts. Since the war youth has been frustrated — no war to fight, the prospect of nuclear disaster — and has also become a prey to capitalistic exploitation in the field of music, dress, manners. This is happening in Russia too — pop music, drugs, the feeling of being spatially distinct from the older generation. It is not a political phenomenon and the state can do little about it.

*   Nadsat — the Russian suffix which corresponds with 'teen'.— Ed.
*   Burgess is referring to Pavlov's teaching on conditional reflexes, which the fanatical methods of the experimenters in Clockwork Orange are based on.

L. G. *What do you think about young people's moral values, principles and ideals today — are they still the same as yours were?*

A. B. Our Western young have nothing to believe in except the ability to prolong the present — which means ignoring the past and the future — chiefly through the use of drugs. They have no moral standards. Sex is freely available, though possibly AIDS is beginning to act as a deterrent (not a moral one, of course). It is probably true of all of us that we are substituting fear (super-Chernobyls, atomic war, the death of the planet) for morality. Christianity is proving reactionary and dangerous. I cling to remnants of my familial Catholicism and have certain basic standards which have turned me into a kind of anarchist with a powerful belief in the importance of free will. I do not trust the state, nor do the young. They're probably right. The state is no repository of moral values. There's no such thing as an individual ethical system, but all of us cling to the Judaeo-Christian remnants, as did my grandfather's old friend Karl Marx. Human life ought to be sacred, and we all believe that, even the young.

L. G. *What, in your opinion, are the most important problems of your young people?*

A. B. Young Britons see no future in a country with millions of unemployed. The problem is education — education for leisure, with a concentration on literature and the arts. They are not receiving this. They make do with poor substitutes — videocassettes and pop music. They will not talk to us old. Their 'culture' is self-contained. They desperately need teachers they can trust. They don't have them.

L. G. *If a young person wanting to commit suicide phones you, what will you say to him?*

A. B. I've received such calls. Suicide attempts are screams for attention. Words of concern, love, calm words about us all having to cope with the human condition sometimes help. But finally free will exists. We must all do what we consider it right to do. I find that my suicidal tendencies come in old age.

L. G. *And, lastly, what is your attitude to violence on the screen? You see, a film directed against violence shows scenes*

*of violence itself and thus objectively aids its propaganda.
How do you personally solve this contradiction?*

A. B. There's too much screen violence, but there was always too much violence in literature — from Shakespeare to Dostoyevsky. It seems that sex and violence are the major artistic themes and always have been. I object to the violence in so many films because it is motiveless, gratuitous (this is not true of 'Hamlet' or 'King Lear'). But a narrative — film or story — without motivated violence is unthinkable. Even democracies start by being violent. Aggression, as the Russian Revolution showed, is sometimes necessary to clear old ground for new building. Aggression for its own sake — the French *acte gratuit* — is senseless.

Literaturnaya Gazeta, 26 August 1987

VANESSA REDGRAVE:
A MONOLOGUE ABOUT
WHAT MATTERS MOST

When I started work on the part of Isadora Duncan and began collecting material, I acquired for the first time some basic knowledge of the October Revolution. Of course, I read Duncan's book *My Life*, and a number of works about her relationship with Yesenin. In her autobiography she wrote, in particular, about her arrival in Russia: 'Yes, I am coming here, to a new world, and I am leaving behind the old world.'

And this amazed me.

I felt that as a ballerina she was capable of bringing about revolutionary changes in the world of dance. In the book *My Life* the illustrious ballerina writes about how she arrived in St Petersburg in 1905 — the day after the soldiers had fired on the workers coming into Palace Square with a petition for the tsar. Isadora's train arrived at midnight, and by chance she spotted a funeral procession of workers carrying the coffins of their comrades who had been killed the day before. In her autobiography she writes about the tremendous shock she got seeing this scene. She told herself that from that moment on the meaning of her activity as an actress had changed for her. Everything she had at that time, her life and her dancing, she decided to dedicate to the workers and the oppressed.

Of course, this woman's ideas were imbued with the kind of conviction only formed in special personal ordeals, which often make a person bitter; but what attracted me was this woman's capacity for compassion.

When the actress came to Russia after the Revolution, she noticed that there had begun to appear people who were seeking privileges. She saw the bureaucracy which had arisen outside and inside the Party. She was extremely worried by this. She spoke with Lunacharsky and asked him why such things were happening. Lunacharsky did not take her fears seriously and made a joke of the whole thing. This amazed me as well.

When Isadora went to the United States with Yesenin, she wanted with the help of her art to tell the American public about the October Revolution, about her support for Russia, about the liberated people, about how, in her opinion, the events in Russia should facilitate the liberation of oppressed peoples the world over.

And she spoke of all this by means of her dancing and during public performance as well. She was, of course, victimized. And in Boston and Philadelphia the press tore her to shreds. Her art was revolutionary, and she was essentially a revolutionary herself, already in the ideological sense.

Of course, I did not understand much but working on Isadora's character, following the paths of her searchings, I became more and more inspired by the ideas of the Revolution.

That is possibly why I think the revolutionary resolutions passed at the 27th Congress of the CPSU, at the most recent plenums of the Party's Central Committee, and also at the congresses of writers and film-makers are extremely important. Workers electing the heads of enterprises, self-financing, and also the organisation of a system whereby ruling bodies would be answerable to the rank-and-file, and would not ignore them as had previously happened — all these are great initiatives.

I am often asked why I take events in Russia so much to heart. I answer — for two reasons.

My father (he died in 1985) belonged to a generation

which struggled for socialism and was faithful to its principles. In the late '20s and early '30s father, like many other
English actors, writers and artists, focussed his attention on
the Soviet Union. He assumed that the international crisis
and, in particular, the crisis in Britain could only be solved
by socialism.

However, the questions which troubled him then were
brushed aside by the leaders of the British Communist
Party. Father was poked fun at but he went on dashing
about in search of answers and very soon found himself in
a blind alley. As he wrote in his recently published autobiography, he saw nobody in the Britain of that day who
could have led the people who were disillusioned by the
existing system; in a word, he retreated.

However, if someone had explained to him then that the
main enemy of the workers of capitalist countries was to be
found inside these states and not outside, and if they had
done so in a calm and restrained manner, he could have escaped that terrible inner crisis which engulfed him more and
more.

In other words, I get agitated when I think about the
USSR, not only because I have read many books about the
history of your country and I am theoretically well-
prepared, but also because my father changed radically towards the end of his life. He, of course, was still a brilliant
artist but he grew progressively sadder and quieter...

It always used to surprise me that whenever I tried to talk
to my father about socialism in the USSR and discuss with
him my political views on the revolutionary process and my
political activities, he would fall silent, and more than once
I saw tears in his eyes. This was long before he fell ill but
even then he could not force himself to talk to me, and I felt
that I was possibly upsetting him. But I could not understand why!

And only during the last three years of his life could we
freely discuss many of the things that had been inwardly
tormenting him. By that time he had written a book and
was feeling quite well for the first time.

When I travel back in my thoughts to that far-off period
of history, the '30s, I think that the lessons of that time are
extremely important for the success of *perestroika* in the
USSR today.

I keep a close watch on the Soviet press. A few weeks ago in one of your publications I read an article saying that if the bureaucracy, all the conservative forces holding back society, weren't exposed, *perestroika* might be substantially delayed. And so it is vitally important not only for the Soviet Union but also for the working class all over the world that the resolutions already passed by the Soviet Government and Party, resolutions of tremendous, to my mind, creative force, are fully implemented. I know that the working class is the only revolutionary class which proved capable of accomplishing the October Revolution under the Bolsheviks' leadership.

The working class has not lost its inner essence to this day.

I, true, was born into the family of a professional person and not of a worker, but professional people's interests are inseparable from those of the proletariat, and I, as a member of my trade union, am speaking namely from these standpoints. Incidentally, I am by no means the only person in Britain who has such an, I would say, ardent attitude to *perestroika* in the USSR.

What makes me look towards the countries of socialism with such hope? What has formed my world outlook as a whole? Now I shall try to answer these questions very specifically.

My political views were formed many years ago under the influence of the ideas of Lenin and other theoreticians of the Russian Revolution. I came to Leninism myself.

I joined the anti-war movement in my youth. It was a critical moment of history — the time of the Caribbean crisis. And from the anti-war movement I moved on to political work. Even now I often ask myself questions. And I suffer torments searching for the answers. You see, in my young days I came to feel responsible for the fate of the world and at that time I also thought I should put all my energies into finding a real political way of averting a nuclear war.

Gradually I realised that the anti-war movement could not give the answers to all the questions plaguing me, and my political path turned towards my brother who was a member of the Socialist Workers' Party. I discovered that my answers could be analysed; my brother gave me books in which I could find a link between the October Revolution and the world situation. I realised that the Russian revolution had been forced to defend itself from enemies. However, it was also then that I found out in detail about Stalin. Not as a personality but as a phenomenon, about his true roots. And about the roots of bureaucracy. For the first time I saw the whole picture and not just fragments of it. For the first time I saw history not as a confrontation between Good and Bad people, but as an infinite vista from the past into the future. That was when I really came to Lenin, to his theoretical heritage. I came knowingly.

Today Lenin's teaching is not losing its topicality in politics, or ideology, or even economics.

Britain (and the United States) are presently undergoing a very serious economic and political recession. The major American banks no longer have sufficient funds to act as creditors if some crisis were to occur.

Imperialism fifty years ago had access to creditors of such a kind, or knew how to find them. Here is an example. After the Wall Street Crash in 1929 the American and English banks shifted the after-effects, the brunt of the financial crisis, to the German banks. And this in many ways helped the turn of German capital towards fascism, the breaking up of the trade unions, the suppression of every kind of opposition, the striving for 100 per cent profits and the creation of slave labour without which it was impossible to get such fabulous profits. It was the economic situation, in my opinion, that lay behind the formation of concentration camps in Germany.

Now the position is such that there are no creditors, and America has changed from the biggest lender into the world's No. I debtor. This, what's more, is common knowledge. The banks of America and England are now waging a fierce financial war against the Japanese. And this war is getting daily more acute. The leading capitalist countries of the West and Japan are attempting to shift their economic burden to the developing countries whose standard of living is falling sharply as a result. And there is no end to these processes. What's more, they are now fraught with the threat of a future disaster.

Everywhere and nearly always an economic crisis brings in its wake a political one. In Britain it is manifest in the un-

precedented number of unemployed people and in the way
the trade unions' legal rights are being eroded. A six-month
professional training scheme has supposedly been created
for young people but this is essentially a gimmick. In such
a manner young people not only do not acquire essential
work skills but also merely sell their labour for next to
nothing, for far less than the rates won by the trade unions.

British young people are highly dissatisfied with their lot.
The town authorities hardly do anything for them. Schools
are having their subsidies taken away, and there are not
even enough textbooks, writing paper, and sports equipment. In a word, not enough of all the things young people
cannot exist normally without.

What's more, the professional training scheme is riddled
with racism: whereas, say, young white people are accepted,
someone of Asian or Latin American origin may be refused. And if they are accepted, they're made 'whipping boys'.
After a short time they're only too pleased to give up their
'training'. And also all young people (both white and black)
are extremely worried about the threat of nuclear war.

...But for all that I shall now go back to the problem of
perestroika in the USSR. In this connection two instants
seem to me most significant. Firstly, much has already been
done to open the way towards the truth and to record true
history. In the form of articles or even novels. Like *The
Children of the Arbat* (I haven't read the book itself but I've
seen reviews of it in *Ogonyok*). Or plays by Shatrov and
Vassiliev (I saw his *Tomorrow Was War* in March).

Writers, playwrights, journalists, actors and film directors are reconstructing true history — this is very important
for *perestroika*. As Shatrov wrote: the real truth is essential
if *perestroika* is to be irreversible.

What's more, and this, to my mind, is the second important instant, maximum efforts must be made to ensure that
all the resolutions already passed are fully implemented.

I am greatly impressed by everything that Mikhail Gorbachev is saying and doing. I absolutely agree with him
when he asserts that the country has exceptional need of
a real breakthrough on the theoretical front, grounded on
a strict analysis of all the realities of social life, and on a
scientific basing of the aims and prospects of forward movement. After all, it is hard to imagine successful forward

movement using a method of trial and error. Society would
pay dearly for this. The art of political leadership is not to
keep silence and amass contradictions but to solve them in
good time. I am not quoting word for word but giving,
I think, a faithful rendering of the General Secretary's idea.
He believes in *perestroika*, and his conviction is being transmitted to other people. But, of course, good faith alone isn't
enough. And it would be very sad if people only said, 'Yes,
I believe in it, I'll support it!' and then did nothing else but
wait. However, the international situation, objective factors
existing in the world now (but not in the '30s), all facilitate
perestroika.

I am deeply convinced that *perestroika* in the USSR must
mark the start of *perestroika* in the ideas of people the
world over. This must be helped along by the intelligentsia
of the countries of the West and East. In other words, the
task of *perestroika* is facing not only the great Soviet people
who have put up with such a struggle and made such sacri-
fices. The world does not have the right to forget that the
Nazis suffered a devastating defeat at the hands mainly of
Soviet people, albeit weakened by the loss of their most talented army chiefs in 1937.

Sometimes I am asked if there are enemies to *perestroika*
in England. I consider that every decent, honest, thinking
person, whatever his profession,will hope *perestroika* is successful, regardless of what he knows or doesn't know about
the Soviet Union, or about the processes taking place
there.

At the same time I should like to mention that the Socialists or those who call themselves by this name are incor-
rectly depicting the essence of *perestroika*, and falsifying it.
This is a move to the right, they say, this isn't socialism, it's
a stunt.

The capitalist press is printing claims of a similar type but
the source of this lie is easy to detect. No honest person, be
he an actor, scientist, office employee or worker, regards
perestroika with prejudice. Most people do not believe in
the bourgeois definition of *perestroika* as a stunt. And it is
not so much the overt enemies of *perestroika* who are dangerous as the ones who claim it isn't socialism. These forces,
incidentally, have a definite influence on Britain's trade unions as well. They are blinded by dogmatism and their habit

of thinking in a formal manner, and, what's more, they are defending their privileges.

And there is another factor. In England bourgeois ideology has a vast impact on the working masses. Unfortunately, images fed by events of the past have become deeply ingrained in English people's minds, and the events taking place today do not give them a sense of anything changing, and if they do give them a sense of something, a mechanism of 'selective impressions' is triggered off. Many English people are, however, eager to read your journals and newspapers. People want to know what is really going on in the USSR. So, your press is creating beneficial conditions for the destruction of former stereotypes. We are all delighted by *glasnost*, by the sweep of criticism and self-criticism in the Soviet press. This cannot fail to make a positive impression on the peoples of the West.

The policy of *perestroika* has a huge number of sincere supporters in Europe and America. The Soviet Union is not isolated now on the international front as it was in the '20s, '30s and '40s. The planet's progressive forces and the working class must unite in the struggle for true democracy.

Yes, we set great hopes on *perestroika* in the USSR. Today many people's thoughts are again focussed on the Soviet Union because of the unprecedented economic and political crisis in the West. The attention of very many people of the arts, workers, young people, trade union members is now keenly fixed on your country for they want to find an alternative.

Ogonyok, September 1987

Complete List
of Articles

NAME INDEX

QUIET FLOWS THE DON

Mikhail Sholokhov
First unabridged translation of the modern Soviet literature classic
Translated by Robert Daglish

'...Daglish, always scholarly in his approach, not only consulted all available variants and notes, but spent three days in Vyoshenskoe as Sholokhov's guest. The resulting translation, based on the 1928 and 1939 editions, was checked against the master copy provided by the author. Daglish loved and savoured the Cossaks' salty talk.

This is to be felt in the translation, as are the smells, sights and sounds of the Don. As the only unabridged and approved version, it is a contribution to knowledge as well as art.

(Avril Pyman, The Independent)

ISBN 0569 08956 5 Hardback 2 Volume Set £12.95

RUSSIAN ARCHITECTURE OF THE SOVIET PERIOD

A. Ikonnikov

Professor Ikonnikov's seminal work traces major changes in Russian architecture from the turn of the century's romanticism to the explosion of new forms appearing in the early Soviet period. Reference to plans different from a list of completed structures is especially valuable, as are the plans for an integrated urban development. Emphasis on solving the housing problem of the population is a key note, especially when dealing with the period from 1935 to 1939. Professor Ikonnikov takes the reader a step further from the habitually scornful approach to the massive edifices of this period.

The book closes with a section devoted to architecture of the last few decades, beginning with the rebuilding of cities destroyed in World War II. City planning of recent years – and up to the year 2000 – is examined, including the reconstruction of Moscow, Leningrad and other cities. The development of mass-scale residential housing and the conflict between standardisation and individuality is examined with flare and with insight into the need for a major re-assessment of the citizens' needs. After all, it is the architectural and building term *perestroika* which characterises the new and exciting developments in the Soviet Union today.

ISBN 0569 08953 0 Hardback £9.95